European Sourcebook of Crime and Criminal Justice Statistics - 2003

212

European Sourcebook of Crime and Criminal Justice Statistics - 2003

Second edition

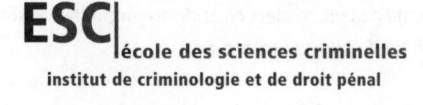

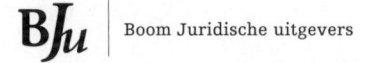

Home Office

ESC | école des sciences criminelles
institut de criminologie et de droit pénal

BJu | Boom Juridische uitgevers

Justitie

Wetenschappelijk Onderzoek- en Documentatiecentrum

Onderzoek en beleid

De reeks Onderzoek en beleid omvat de rapporten van door het WODC van het Ministerie van Justitie verricht onderzoek.
Opname in de reeks betekent niet dat de inhoud van de rapporten het standpunt van de Minister van Justitie weergeeft.

Copies of this report can be ordered at the distribution centre of Boom Juridische uitgevers:
Boom distributiecentrum, Meppel the Netherlands
Phone   +31 (522) 23 75 55
Fax   +31 (522) 25 38 64
E-mail   bdc@bdc.boom.nl

Voor ambtenaren van het Ministerie van Justitie is een beperkt aantal gratis exemplaren beschikbaar.
Deze kunnen worden besteld bij:
Bibliotheek WODC, kamer KO 14
Postbus 20301, 2500 EH Den Haag
Deze gratis levering geldt echter slechts zolang de voorraad strekt.

De integrale tekst van de WODC-rapporten is gratis te downloaden van www.wodc.nl.
Op www.wodc.nl is ook nadere informatie te vinden over andere WODC-publicaties.

© 2003 WODC

Alle rechten voorbehouden. Niets uit deze uitgave mag worden verveelvoudigd, opgeslagen in een geautomatiseerd gegevensbestand, of openbaar gemaakt,
in enige vorm of op enige wijze, hetzij elektronisch, mechanisch, door foto-
kopieën, opnamen of op enige andere manier, zonder voorafgaande schriftelijke toestemming van de uitgever.

Voorzover het maken van kopieën uit deze uitgave is toegestaan op grond van artikel 16B Auteurswet 1912 jo. het Besluit van 20 juni 1974, Stb. 351, zoals
gewijzigd bij Besluit van 23 augustus 1985, Stb. 471, en artikel 17 Auteurswet 1912, dient men de daarvoor wettelijk verschuldigde vergoedingen te voldoen aan de Stichting Reprorecht (Postbus 882, 1180 AW Amstelveen). Voor het overnemen van een gedeelte(n) uit deze uitgave in bloemlezingen, readers en andere compilatiewerken (art. 16 Auteurswet 1912) dient men zich tot de uitgever te wenden.

No part of this book may be reproduced in any form, by print, photoprint, microfilm or any other means without written permission from the publisher.

ISBN 90-5454-408-2

The European Sourcebook of Crime and Criminal Justice Statistics – 2003 (second edition) was prepared under the auspices of the Council of Europe by a group of experts including:

Martin Killias (chair)
Gordon Barclay
Paul Smit (website)
Marcelo Fernando Aebi (tables and database)
Cynthia Tavares (secretariat)
Bruno Aubusson de Cavarlay
Jörg-Martin Jehle
Hanns von Hofer
Beata Gruszczyñska
Vasilika Hysi
Kauko Aromaa

The second edition is an update of the first edition (published by the Council of Europe in 1999) and covers the years 1995-2000.

List of participating countries and national correspondents:

Vasilika Hysi (Albania)
Anna Margaryan (Armenia)
Arno Pilgram (Austria)
Charlotte Vanneste (Belgium)
Nikolena Tsenkova (Bulgaria)
Ksenija Turkovic (Croatia)
Androula Boularan (Cyprus)
Simona Diblikova (Czech Republic)
Flemming Balvig, Suzanne Clausen (Denmark)
Andri Ahven (Estonia)
Kauko Aromaa (Finland)
Bruno Aubusson de Cavarlay (France)
Georgi Glonti (Georgia)
Jörg-Martin Jehle (Germany)
Calliope Spinellis (Greece)
Imre Kertesz (Hungary)
Noel Sullivan, Noel Carolan (Ireland)
Umberto Gatti (Italy)
Andrejs Vilks, Kristine Kipena (Latvia)
Algimantas Čepas, Darius Valatkevičius (Lithuania)
No national correspondent (Luxembourg)
Joseph A. Filletti, Stefano Filletti (Malta)
Cornelia Vicleanschi (Moldova)
Paul Smit (the Netherlands)
Vibeke Sky (Norway)
Beata Gruszczyñska (Poland)
Maria João Morgado Costa (Portugal)
Nicoleta Iliescu, Adina Vlasceanu, Alina Dorabant (Romania)
Alexander Salagaev, Alexander Shashkin (Russian Federation)
Eugen Placintar (Slovakia)
Marko Bošnjak (Slovenia)
Marcelo F. Aebi (Spain)
Hanns von Hofer (Sweden)
Martin Killias (Switzerland)
Yusuf Ziya Özcan (Turkey)
Anatoliy Zakalyuk (Ukraine)
Gordon Barclay (UK: England & Wales)
Michael Willis (UK: Northern Ireland)
Katy Barratt (UK: Scotland)

Preface

In 1993, the Council of Europe charged a Committee of Experts[1] with the preparation of a feasibility study concerning collection of crime and criminal justice data for Europe. There were reservations regarding the comparability of legal systems, offence definitions and data collection procedures between different countries but it was recognised that, despite similar problems (such as offence definitions and data collection procedures which may vary between U.S. States as they do between European countries), the American *Sourcebook of Criminal Justice Statistics* provides information on all the U.S. States.

The members of the Council of Europe's experts' committee decided to carry out a feasibility study by collecting data on offences and offenders recorded by the police, prosecutions, convictions and corrections through members of that Committee who had access to the data in 10 particular countries.[2] The report was received favourably and in 1995, the Council of Europe decided to enlarge the Committee in order to include other parts of Europe.[3] The first official edition of the *European Sourcebook of Crime and Criminal Justice Statistics* was published by the Council of Europe in 1999. It covered 36 countries and was reliant upon national correspondents in each country.

After the first edition, the Council of Europe was no longer able to sustain the costs of the project. The UK Home Office, the Dutch Ministry of Justice Research and Documentation Centre (WODC) and the Swiss Department of Foreign Affairs (through the University of Lausanne) appreciated the value of having such a network of national correspondents and were reluctant to lose it. Consequently, they agreed to share the financial and other resource implications in order to produce a second edition. A smaller Committee of Experts[4] reviewed the first edition in an attempt to improve the comparability of the figures wherever feasible. In particular, changes were made to the prosecutions chapter after a study of the prosecutorial systems throughout Europe. Data on offences recorded by the police is now available for countries (particularly in Central and Eastern Europe) for which no such data were included in the first edition because of concerns about their reliability.[5] In addition, there is now extensive data on correctional statistics and on the use of "alternative sanctions" throughout Europe.

---

1   Members were: Gordon Barclay and Chris Lewis (United Kingdom), Hanns von Hofer (Sweden), Jörg-Martin Jehle (Germany), Imre Kertesz (Hungary), Martin Killias (Switzerland, Chair), Max Kommer (the Netherlands), Wolfgang Rau (Council of Europe, secretary), Pierre Tournier (France).
2   France, Germany, Hungary, Ireland, Italy, the Netherlands, Norway, Sweden, Switzerland, United Kingdom
3   New members were (in addition to the members of the original group): Marcelo F. Aebi (secretary, Switzerland/Spain), Andri Ahven (Estonia), Bruno Aubusson de Cavarlay (France, replacing Pierre Tournier in 1998), Uberto Gatti (Italy), Zdenek Karabec (Czech Republic), Vlado Kambovski (Macedonia), Alberto Laguia Arrazola (Spain), Calliope Spinnellis (Greece), Paul Smit (the Netherlands, replacing Max Kommer in 1997).
4   See the list of members on p. 5.
5   In several countries, police figures are extremely low compared to what is known from (often local) crime victimisation surveys and reporting rates. The Committee felt that the gap between real and "expected" rates of offences recorded by the police is of interest, since it may depend on police practice in some countries.

The Committee wishes to thank all those who, in whatever capacity, have worked on the second edition. First of all, our thanks go to the national correspondents,[6] to the secretary, Cynthia Tavares (Home Office), to the data administrator, Marcelo F. Aebi (and his team at the University of Seville, Spain) and to the website[7] manager Paul Smit (WODC). We hope that this new edition will continue to promote comparative research throughout Europe and make European experiences and data available across the world.

Martin Killias, Chair

---

[6] Listed on p. 6.
[7] www.europeansourcebook.org

Contents

General introduction: The European Sourcebook Project		**11**
1	**Police statistics**	**21**
1.1	General comments	21
1.2	Tables	33
1.3	Technical information	74
1.4	Sources	84
2	**Prosecution statistics**	**87**
2.1	General comments	87
2.2	Tables	93
2.3	Technical information	106
2.4	Sources	116
3	**Conviction statistics**	**119**
3.1	General comments	119
3.2	Tables	125
3.3	Technical information	184
3.4	Sources	189
4	**Correctional statistics**	**191**
4.1	General comments	191
4.2	Tables	196
4.3	Sources	232
5	**Survey data**	**235**
5.1	General comments	235
5.2	Tables	238
5.3	Technical information	243
5.4	Sources	249
Appendix I	**Offence definitions**	**251**
Appendix II	**Population figures**	**267**

General introduction:
The European Sourcebook Project

Background

1. The assessment of trends in crime and criminal justice has been a permanent concern of the Council of Europe. Periodic events, such as criminological and penological conferences and colloquia and, in particular, the quinquennial Conferences on Crime Policy have been set up to keep those trends under permanent review and to provide those responsible for tackling crime and running criminal justice institutions with appropriate up to date information.

2. Due to ongoing developments in Greater Europe and the ensuing enlargement of the membership of the Council of Europe, the necessity for such periodic assessment and comparison in the above mentioned areas had become even more apparent.

3. Against this background, the European Committee on Crime Problems (CDPC) created (in 1993) a Group of Specialists on *"Trends in crime and criminal justice: statistics and other quantitative data on crime and criminal justice system"* (PC-S-ST). The Group was composed of experts from France, Germany, Hungary, the Netherlands, Sweden, Switzerland and the United Kingdom.[1]

4. During a relatively short period of time, a great number of theoretical and technical issues were addressed. These issues included data comparison, offences to be considered and their definitions, appropriate table formats, statistical routines including counting rules in the various countries, interpretation of the available data, infrastructure needed for a full implementation of the European Sourcebook Project etc.

5. In 1995, the Group presented the European Sourcebook of Crime and Criminal Justice Statistics: Draft model (Strasbourg: Council of Europe, 1995, 194 pp.) to the CDPC. The Draft model presented crime and criminal justice data for the year 1990 for twelve European countries. Extensive technical comments were added to the tables in order to document the numerous methodological problems that are involved in international data collections. It was stated that: "Having found a practical and satisfactory way of handling the difficult problem of varying offence definitions and counting rules, the Group reached the conclusion that a European Sourcebook on crime and criminal justice statistics was indeed feasible." (op. cit., p. 190).

---

[1] The members of the Group were: Martin Killias (Switzerland), Chairman of the Group, Gordon Barclay (United Kingdom), Hanns von Hofer (Sweden), Imre Kertesz (Hungary), Max Kommer (the Netherlands), Jörg-Martin Jehle (Germany), Chris Lewis (United Kingdom), Pierre Tournier (France). HEUNI was represented as an Observer (Kristiina Kangaspunta). Secretary to the Group: Wolfgang Rau, Directorate of Legal Affairs, Council of Europe.

6. Thus, at its 45th plenary session in June 1996, the CDPC entrusted the Group of Specialists with the preparation of a compendium of crime and criminal justice data for the whole of Europe. The final document should represent an enlarged version of the already existing Model European Sourcebook covering, if possible, the total membership of the Council of Europe and presenting crime and criminal justice data for the years 1990 to 1996. Additional specialists in the collection of statistical data resulted in the enlargement of the Group and members were given responsibilities as "regional co-ordinators".[2]

7. In its work, the Group took account of the periodic surveys carried out by the UN and INTERPOL. These surveys relied on the provision of data by national sources asked to follow standard definitions. This approach contrasted with the Group's adopted methodology, where a co-ordinated network of national correspondents provided data from current statistical sources within each country. This data was then supplemented by the collection of information on statistical and legal definitions. The Group, which included several members involved in recent UN surveys, felt that this approach would allow more comprehensive and accurate data to be produced.

8. The system of national correspondents required that each country should have one person responsible for the collection and initial checking of the data. Each correspondent would be an expert in crime and criminal justice statistics and act as a helpline. They would also be entrusted with checking their country's reply to ensure good quality data.

9. The list of national correspondents was endorsed by the CDPC. The national correspondents had full responsibility for the accuracy of the data provided by their respective countries. A group of three or four national correspondents were "coached" by each member of the Enlarged Group in their capacity as "regional co-ordinators".

10. The revised formal questionnaire was finalised in the summer of 1997, in both official languages of the Council of Europe. Completed questionnaires were received from 36 countries (including England & Wales, Scotland and Northern Ireland).

11. The data was checked and corrected during the second half of 1997 and the first half of 1998. The data collected was put into a database that was set up by the *Institut de criminologie et de droit pénal* (ICDP) of Lausanne University

---

[2] The new members of the Enlarged Group of Specialists were: Marcelo F. Aebi (Switzerland), Andri Ahven (Estonia), Uberto Gatti (Italy), Zdenek Karabec (Czech Republic), Vlado Kambovski (The Former Yugoslav Republic of Macedonia), Alberto Laguia Arrazola (Spain) and Calliope Spinellis (Greece). Paul Smit (the Netherlands) and Bruno Aubusson de Cavarlay (France) joined the Group in December 1997 and April 1998 respectively.

during the summer and autumn of 1998.[3] The data in paper format was then returned to the regional co-ordinators for checking in co-operation with the national correspondents (for further details please refer to the section on *Validation*). The report was drafted during spring 1999.

12. After the publication of the first edition in 1999, the Council of Europe was, unfortunately, no longer able to support the project financially. In 2000, in order to maintain continuity in a data collection effort (which was seen as important) and especially to avoid dismantling the network of correspondents (from 40 countries), the UK Home Office, the Swiss Foreign Ministry (through the University of Lausanne School of Criminal Sciences) and the Dutch Ministry of Justice agreed to continue supporting the project until publication of the second (i.e. the present) edition.

13. The three new funding agencies commissioned a small group of experts with the task of updating the European Sourcebook of Crime and Criminal Justice Statistics.[4] As one of its first tasks, the group revisited the list of national correspondents in an attempt to cover all Member States and to revise the questionnaire. A large number of national correspondents met to discuss the progress on the work during the European Society of Criminology Conferences in 2001 (in Lausanne, Switzerland) and 2002 (in Toledo, Spain). The United Kingdom, the Netherlands, Switzerland and Finland provided financial assistance to enable many correspondents from Eastern Europe to attend both the European Society of Criminology Conference and the European Sourcebook meeting in 2002.

14. In the space of five meetings, the experts group devoted considerable attention to reviewing data received from the countries. With the co-operation of the correspondents, errors in the tables published in the 1999 edition were identified (see comments in individual chapters). This seems to have considerably improved the validity of the data for comparative purposes. This conclusion is supported by a tentative study comparing police data from the European Sourcebook with international crime victimisation (ICVS) and Interpol data for 1999 for twelve Western European countries.[5]

15. Students at the University of Sevilla (Spain) have entered the data provided by the national correspondents into the database, under the direction of Marcelo Aebi and with funds from the Swiss Ministry of Foreign Affairs.

---

3   The database was developed by Marcelo F. Aebi, who produced the tables presented in the European Sourcebook. They were devised in Excel and SPSS for Macintosh.

4   The members of the new group of experts were: Martin Killias (Switzerland, chair), Gordon Barclay (United Kingdom), Paul Smit (the Netherlands, website administrator), Hanns von Hofer (Sweden), Jörg-Martin Jehle (Germany), Bruno Aubusson de Cavarlay (France), Beata Gruszczynska (Poland), Vasilika Hysi (Albania), Marcelo F. Aebi (Spain, Database administrator), and Cynthia Tavares (United Kingdom, Secretariat).

5   See Marcelo F. Aebi, Martin Killias, Cynthia Tavares, "Comparing Crime Rates: International Crime (Victim) Survey, the European Sourcebook of Crime and Criminal Justice Statistics, and Interpol Statistics", International Journal of Comparative Criminology 2/1 (2002), 22-37.

16. Since 2001, the Dutch Ministry of Justice has provided the necessary resources to set up and maintain a website containing all the data published in the 1999 edition of the European Sourcebook (www.europeansourcebook.org) under the supervision of Mr. Paul Smit (WODC, Ministry of Justice of the Netherlands).

Offence definitions

17. Comparative criminology has to face the problem of national offence definitions that are often incompatible. The Group adopted the following procedure: For all offences included in the European Sourcebook, a standard definition was used and countries were invited to follow the standard definition where possible. Offence definitions and related commentaries are given in Appendix I to this book providing for each of the selected offences:
– the standard definition,
– a list of those countries which were not able to entirely meet this definition with an indication of which elements of the definition they were unable to meet. Countries not listed were able to fully conform to the standard definition.

The Structure of the European Sourcebook

18. Although the aim of the second European Sourcebook edition was to collect data for the period 1995 to 2000, it was clear that this would put an unduly heavy administrative burden on countries. The data was therefore divided into:
– Key items: crimes, suspects and convictions (selected offences only).
– Non-key items: number of minors, females, aliens and sanctions/measures, resources, and prison capacity.

19. The data for 1995-2000 was collected for key items. Data for 1999 was only collected for non-key items (the 2000 data was not available in many countries at the time of data collection). It was clearly a difficult decision to exclude time series data for sanctions/measures; however the Group felt that this decision was sensible as percentages for females, minors, and aliens, as well as legal rules on sanctions, sentencing practices and criminal justice resources change rather slowly over time. For the complete time-series from 1990, the reader will need to look at the first European Sourcebook edition.

20. The chapters are, in general, subdivided into four sections:
1. General comments
2. Tables
3. Technical information
4. Sources

21. The European Sourcebook is divided into five chapters:
A. *Police statistics* (offences and offenders recorded by the police and police staff). This chapter provides information on the volume of crime and the number of suspected offenders in each country. Most of the data is available as time series data for 1995-2000.

The selected offences focus almost exclusively (except for drug offences) on so-called *traditional* crimes. *Modern* crimes such as those relating to organised crime are not covered. The offences were:
a) Total offences,
   of which traffic violations which are punishable as offences, (traffic violations were thus excluded)
b) Homicide
   of which completed homicide (according to police and vital statistics)
c) Assault
d) Rape
e) Robbery
f) Theft
   of which theft of motor vehicle
   of which burglary
       of which domestic burglary
g) Drug offences
   of which drug trafficking

Compared with the first edition, total offences (and "criminal" traffic offences) have, thus, been added to the list, whereas armed robbery and bicycle theft have been abandoned. "Serious" drug trafficking has been replaced by drug trafficking in general. Other definitions were maintained, although clarified in a few instances (e.g., it was made clear that motor vehicle theft should include both taking away the vehicle with the intent to keep it permanently as well as to use it only temporarily).

B. *Prosecution statistics*. The chapter deals with the outcome of procedures at public prosecutor's level (prosecutors/examining magistrates) during the years 1995-2000. It also provides data on the staff of the prosecuting authorities in 1999. Unlike most other tables in the European Sourcebook, this chapter does not provide any breakdown of specific types of offences, but covers *all offences* dealt with by the prosecuting authorities.

C. *Conviction statistics*. The tables in this chapter concern persons who have been convicted, i.e. found guilty according to law, of having committed one of the selected offences. Information is presented by offence (1995-2000); the sex, age group, and nationality of the offender (1999); the type of sanctions imposed as well as the duration of unsuspended custodial sentences (1999). Sanctions were grouped under the following categories:

a) Fines
b) Non-custodial sanctions and measures
c) Suspended custodial sanctions and measures
d) Unsuspended custodial sentences
e) Death penalty
f) Other measures

D. *Correctional statistics.* The chapter contains data on prison populations (on "stock" and "flow") for the years 1995-2000 stemming from the European Sourcebook questionnaire on persons (both "stock" and "flow") under the supervision or care of an agent of the correctional services, or in community service. Data on electronic monitoring were available for fewer than ten countries (in 1999).

E. Survey data. The chapter presents data from the international crime victimisation surveys (ICVS) on crimes against individuals and households, conducted in 1992, 1996, and 2000. Given the small size of some of the national samples, average rates were indicated over all three sweeps taken together. The rates were given for the national level, urban and rural areas separately, in order to allow the inclusion of countries where the ICVS was conducted in major cities only. Also indicated are rates of offences reported to the police, as well as the assessment of offence seriousness by respondents.

Methodological issues

Data recording methods

22. Since the timing and method of recording can have a considerable impact on a statistical measure the Group paid much attention to the way in which national data were collected and recorded, and what operational definitions were applied at the several stages of the criminal justice process. Detailed information provided on this has been summarised in the form of tables and short comments.

Validation

23. Validation is often the most important and in many cases the most forgotten stage of the data collection process. As a first step, the Group identified and discussed obvious problems relating to this process. It then produced a series of check-tables to further assist validation. The function of these tables was:

A. To check whether individual cells added up to the totals given in the tables. It turned out that this was not always the case.

B. To compare figures and to ensure that they were consistent with those given in other sections of the European Sourcebook questionnaire. It had to be checked, for example, whether the number of persons sentenced to unsuspended custodial sentences was compatible with the figure contained in the sentence length tables.

C. To calculate rates per 100 000 population for the key items and to check for "outliers", i.e. extreme values which are difficult, if not impossible, to explain.

D. To look at the attrition process of recorded offences, suspects, convictions and imprisonment; to recheck "outliers" assuming that, starting with recorded crime (on an offence basis), the number of suspects (person's basis) will be lower and the number of convictions leading to an unsuspended custodial sentence will be lower still.

E. To compare the proportion of minors, females and aliens in the tables for the number of suspects and convictions. Did these proportions make sense (80% juvenile suspects would seem out of proportion) and were they consistent with other relevant figures?

24. This procedure resulted in the need to go back to many national correspondents for clarification and additional cross-checking. Although some errors were made when completing the questionnaire, it became apparent that the survey had identified many differences in national systems of criminal justice statistics, which had not become apparent in the previous edition. Part of this was due to the problems of language, as several national correspondents had to translate the questionnaire into their respective national languages and, in doing so, altered the definition of the information required. Other problems were related to the different criminal justice processes in the countries concerned. This is particularly true for the way attempts are classified in police statistics. As a rule, attempts are included in all offences throughout the European Sourcebook, although the proportion of attempts differs between offences and countries. For example, an aggression or threat will usually be counted as assault, injury or threat, whereas the police e.g. in the Netherlands classify such incidents relatively often as attempted murder. This not only substantially increases the overall rate of murder (i.e. including attempts), but also affects the severity of dispositions since sentences tend to be shorter for attempts than for completed offences. A similar difficulty arises from the treatment of minors who, in some countries and at some stages of the criminal procedure, are included in statistics, whereas in others they are not.

25. In some cases it was possible to correct the data, whilst in others more or less detailed explanations had to be given. However, despite the considerable efforts made by the Group to detect errors and inconsistencies in the data, not all of

these may have been identified; nor was it possible to deal with all errors and inconsistencies in a fully satisfactory way.

Presentational details

26. In order to increase the clarity of the present report, the Group took the following practical decisions:

A. To make *all* raw data and *all* comments available in a separate document through the Website www.europeansourcebook.org. Thus, the present document contains only a selection of all the data and commentaries submitted.

B. To eliminate, in general, tables where the number of reporting countries was very small.

C. To use decimals sparingly so as to avoid the impression of false precision.

D. To use the English notation for figures. The decimal marker is represented by a "point" (i.e. 1.5 means one and a half). The thousand marker is represented by a "space" (i.e. 1 500 means one thousand five hundred).

E. To translate comments (although left in the original language in the database that can be accessed through the European Sourcebook website)

F. To use the following symbols throughout the tables:

   a) "0" to indicate a number between 0 and 0.4;
   b) "…" to indicate that data is not (yet) available or that the question/concept as used in the European Sourcebook questionnaire does not apply;
   c) "> 1000" to indicate that the percentage change between 1995 and 2000 is above one thousand per cent.

G. To condense the vast amount of technical information on definitions, data collection methods, processing rules etc. into clearly arranged summary tables, listings and footnotes.

H. Whenever possible and reasonable, figures were transformed into rates per 100 000 population or indicated as percentages. The population figures used are contained in the appendix at the end of the publication.

I. To use the term "Eastern European countries" to refer to countries in Eastern Europe that formerly had a communist or socialist regime and were allied with the former USSR (except from the former German Democratic Republic which is included in the Western Europe). For all the remaining countries we use the term "Western European countries". Also, the term "Common Law" system countries is used to indicate Ireland and the UK countries.

J. To use the following measures throughout the tables to provide information on the data dispersion:
    – Mean: The arithmetic average; the sum of scores divided by the number of countries that provided data. The value of the mean is sensitive to the presence of very high or very low scores. For this reason the median was also included as an indicator of the central tendency of the data.
    – Median: The median is the score that divides the distribution of scores into two exact halves
    – Minimum: The lowest score in the table.
    – Maximum: The highest score in the table.
    – Percentage change 1995-2000 (based upon unrounded scores).

Comparability

27. The basic aim of the European Sourcebook data collection is to present comparable information on crime and criminal justice statistics in Europe. However, the issue of whether or not it is feasible to use official criminal justice statistics for decision-making in crime policy or for conducting scientific studies is one of the classic debates of criminology. The problems involved are even more serious when it comes to international comparisons, because nations differ widely in the way they organise their police and court systems, the way they define their legal concepts, and the way they collect and present their statistics. In fact, the lack of uniform definitions of offences, of common measuring instruments and of common methodology makes comparisons between countries extremely hazardous. This is the reason why criminologists in recent years have developed alternatives to complement the existing official statistics: international comparative victimisation studies on the one hand and international comparative self-report studies on the other (see chapter 5).

28. There can be no doubt that international comparisons based on official statistics give rise to delicate problems. The Fifth Criminological Colloquium of the Council of Europe in the beginning of the 1980's was exclusively devoted to these issues. The question, however, whether official data can be used or not, cannot be answered once and for all. The answer is *empirical* in nature. Thus, the purpose the data is intended to serve should determine whether or not it is suitable as a basis for analysis.

29. Comparative analyses generally fall into one of three categories:
(A) distributive comparisons, (B) level comparisons and, (C) trend comparisons.

A. *Distributive* comparisons are aimed at answering questions such as: Do theft offences dominate the crime picture in most countries? What is the age profile of convicted offenders in the various countries?
B. Relevant questions for *level* comparisons are of the following type: Which country reports the highest robbery rate? Which countries show low rates of incarcerated offenders?
C. In contrast, interpretations of *trends* deal with such questions as: Did the increase in rape offences differ over time in various countries? Did the number of community sentences increase in all countries between 1995 and 1999?

30. Before these and other questions can be answered, it should be noted that official crime and criminal justice statistics are fundamentally dependent upon three sets of circumstances:
A. *actual circumstances* such as the propensity of individuals to commit crimes, the opportunity structure, the risk of detection, the willingness of the public to report crimes, the efficiency of criminal justice authorities;
B. *legal circumstances* such as the design of the Criminal Code, the Code of Criminal Procedure and other relevant legislation; the formal organisation of criminal justice agencies and the informal application of the law in everyday life;
C. *statistical circumstances* such as the formal data collection and processing rules and their practical implementation.

31. To ensure comparability when making distribution and level comparisons, one must carefully control the legal and statistical circumstances before concluding that similarities or dissimilarities can be taken as real. The demands are somewhat different when it comes to ascertaining crime trends. For such analyses, the "real" crime level does not need to be known; it is sufficient to control for possible changes to the legal and statistical systems. This is of course a difficult task, and identifying informal changes in criminal justice procedures and in statistical routines is especially difficult.

32. In order to facilitate the use of the data contained in this European Sourcebook, comprehensive additional information concerning the definition of offences and sanctions, the data collection and processing rules was collected. This information is contained in section 3 of each chapter. More specifically, each table is accompanied by a list of questions intended to clarify the scope of data. For example, in some countries "assault" included legally and/or statistically not only "wounding" but also "causing bodily pain". Consequently, the latter will report a higher frequency of assault - *ceteris paribus*. By studying these specific questions carefully, it should be possible to identify those countries which tend to over-report (or to under-report) offence frequencies. However, it is not possible to easily quantify the extent to which over- or under-reporting occurs.

1 Police statistics

1.1 General comments

1.1.1 Police statistics as a measure of crime

1. This chapter provides information on offences recorded by the police, the number of and characteristics of suspected offenders and the number of police staff.

2. Police statistics are collected in every country but for several reasons do not always provide a good measure of crime.

3. Firstly, victims may choose not to report the crime to the police or may not be aware that they have been a victim of crime. In addition, reporting may be self-incriminating (e.g. when a victim is also an offender) or humiliating; or the victim may think that nothing will be gained by reporting (e.g. the victim does not think that the police will be able to solve the burglary or return the stolen goods). If a victim does not report a crime and the police do not learn about the offence from another source, the offence will not be recorded and therefore not counted in police statistics. Data given in chapter 5 (table 5.2.4) suggest that assault and rapes tend to be less reported than property offences.

4. Even when a crime is reported to the police, it might not be recorded in the official statistics. This occurs mainly after official enquiries, which lead the police to believe that the event reported did not actually constitute a crime. Research has shown that recording is less complete for personal offences than for property offences.

5. Not all crimes are reported by a victim or witness. The police themselves may report some violent crimes, for example homicide (a dead body is found), and "victimless" offences (i.e. offences against rules and regulations, such as illegal possession of arms, drink driving and most drug offences).

6. Readers should be aware that petty offences are not always recorded in police statistics. Also, countries differ in the way they consider certain offences as petty (example: theft of small value).

7. In assessing national differences, correlational analyses with other data sources (such as survey measures of crime provided by the ICVS in chapter 5) are equally helpful. Such correlations may be substantial, suggesting that both data sources catch international differences rather accurately, although the absolute volume of crime, as indicated by both sources, may differ for reasons which may be hard to explain.[1] Therefore, the data contained in this document should not be used for country by country (level) comparisons.

---

1   Marcelo F. Aebi, Martin Killias, Cynthia Tavares, "Comparing Crime Rates: *International Crime (Victim) Surveys*, the *European Sourcebook of Crime and Criminal Justice Statistics*, and *Interpol Statistics*", *International Journal of Comparative Criminology* 2/1 (2002), 22-37.

1.1.2 The position of the police in the criminal justice system

8. In most countries the police can be regarded as the first stage of the criminal justice process. However, this does not mean that the figures on recorded crime (i.e. in this chapter) give an accurate account of the total input to the criminal justice system. This is because, in a number of countries, the prosecuting authorities may initiate criminal proceedings without receiving a police report. For example, in some Eastern European countries serious violent offences will not always be recorded by the police but by the public prosecutor's office. Also, other agencies (military police, customs, border police, fiscal fraud squads) and individuals (foresters, judges, or even citizens) may have the power to initiate criminal proceedings by filing a complaint with the prosecution authorities or the court. Nevertheless, most of the offences covered by the Sourcebook will be reported to/detected by the police.

9. The position of the police in the criminal justice system may also directly influence the number of offences recorded and their classification. This is firstly because, in some countries the police may be quite independent in its activities, whilst in others they may work under the close supervision of the prosecutor or the court. Secondly, the police may have the power to "label" the incidents that they investigate as specific offences, or this may be done by the prosecutor. This difference may also have consequences for the relative distribution of the various types of offences dealt with in the Sourcebook.

10. When looking at police staff, and especially when trying to relate these to the "output" of the police in terms of reported or recorded crime, it is important to note that substantial differences exist between countries in the tasks that the police carry out. For example, in most countries the police deal with traffic offences like drink driving, causing bodily harm or petty traffic offences (like speeding and illegal parking). Also, in most countries, the police have the additional task of maintaining public order and of assisting the public in various situations (from providing information to rendering first aid). This might not apply, however, to all types of police or related agencies, which have been included in the tables on police staff. Therefore, care should be taken when relating police resources to the volume of recorded crime or the number of suspected offenders.

1.1.3 Counting offences and offenders

11. As well as problems of classification (e.g. is a dead body found in the road a victim of a traffic accident, an assault, a murder or one who died of natural causes?) other issues need to be considered when examining police statistics.
- The first is the point in time at which the offence was recorded in the statistics. This relates to whether it was following an initial report ("input" statistic) or following an initial investigation ("output" statistic).

- The second is the so-called "multiple offence problem". One offence can consist of several offences (e.g. rape, followed by a homicide and the use of an illegal weapon). Therefore, an awareness of whether the offences committed were counted separately or whether a principal offence rule was applied (i.e. only counting the most serious offence) is essential. In addition, in relation to serial or continuous offending, issues such as, whether a gang rape is counted as one rape or several, are important, as is a report of domestic violence experienced over a period of time, and whether this represents one offence or several offences.

12. Similar problems arise in connection with the counting of offenders. In most countries, a person will only be classed as an offender if his or her guilt has been proven and this verdict is usually the end-result of a judicial process. Therefore, at police level, it is common practice to speak of "suspects" or "suspected offenders" but this introduces new problems such as the point in time at which it is appropriate to record a person as a suspected offender. Again, major differences between countries exist and practices range from recording a person as a "suspected offender" as soon as the police are reasonably convinced that is the case (perhaps even before questioning) to recording a person as a "suspect" only after the prosecutor has started criminal proceedings.

1.1.4 Counting police officers

13. European countries organise their police systems in different ways. Most of them have more than one police force, e.g. state police, communal police, municipal police, gendarmerie or judicial police, all of which perform tasks in connection with the offences under consideration in this Sourcebook. In addition, there may also be special police forces or units which are less important in this context (e.g. tax and military police); the same might apply to certain categories of staff within the general police force (e.g. police reserves and cadet police officers).

14. Such differences should be kept in mind when comparing the number of police officers between countries. Therefore, the national correspondents were asked to use a standard definition for "police officer" which includes criminal police, traffic police, border police, gendarmerie and uniformed police but excludes customs police, tax police, military police, secret service police, part-time officers, police reserves, cadet police officers and court police (see tables 1.3.3.1-1.3.3.2).

1.1.5 Results

Definitions and counting rules
15. Police statistics for offences are available for thirty-nine countries. For two of them, data was not available for 2000. All countries could give data, with some

possible deviation from the standard definition, for homicide, assault, rape, robbery, total theft, drug offences, and total offences. However, problems arose for motor vehicle theft, burglary, domestic burglary and drug trafficking. Variations from the standard definition are important when comparing levels of recorded crime among European countries. These variations were listed at the end of this Sourcebook (appendix I) and the most significant are repeated within comments by offences.

16. Two countries reported not to have written counting rules (i.e. rules regulating the way in which the data shown in this table are recorded). For the other countries however, it should be kept in mind that the existence of counting rules is not a guarantee for consistency, but rather a stimulus.

17. The point at which the data is recorded also varies between countries. For example, in relation to the recording of total criminal offences, only sixteen countries reported that offences were recorded (immediately) when the offence was first reported to the police. Fourteen countries reported that recording is done subsequently, eight that recording occurs only after investigation. It is difficult to interpret these findings but it seems safe to assume that the answers "immediately" and "subsequently" imply that the legal labelling of the offence is the task of the police, whilst "after investigation" seems to indicate that the labelling is done by the prosecuting authorities (output statistics) once the police enquiry has been completed. This might explain some of the differences in levels between countries, in particular for offences such as homicide and assault.

18. The rules for recording both multiple and serial offences vary between countries. For example, with total criminal offences, twenty countries stated that they applied a principal offence rule and eighteen that they did not. In addition, multiple offences are counted as two or more offences in seventeen countries but as one offence in ten countries (the situation was uncertain or related to the type of offence in eight countries). (For details refer to tables 1.3.1.1 and 1.3.2.1).

19. Whilst, thirty-four countries answered the question on the number of police officers, very few were able to meet the standard definition for these figures (for details refer to tables 1.3.3.1. and 1.3.3.2).

General comments
20. For the total criminal offences at police level, differences in levels were substantial (even when traffic offences are removed). This partly reflects technical differences in the offences which are included or excluded and the point at which the statistics are recorded. Moreover, trends for total criminal offences cover quite different situations as regards the type of offences covered.

21. Trends in both recorded crime and suspected offenders over the years 1995–2000 vary from one type of offence to another. For a particular type, in

several central and eastern European countries, trends are quite different from those observed in other countries. These variations may not necessarily reflect actual increases or decreases in the rates under consideration, but could also be the result of improvements in data collection or important changes in the legal definition of offences.

22. For tables 1.2.3.1 to 1.2.3.3 (percentage of female, minor and alien suspected offenders) there was a wide variation between countries which could not be easily explained. However, for nearly all offences and countries, the proportion of female offenders was lower than 30%.

23. The highest proportions of suspected minor offenders (persons under 18) were found for domestic burglary, theft of motor vehicles and robbery and the lowest for homicide and traffic offences.

24. Only half of the total countries were able to provide figures on the percentage of suspected offenders who were aliens as, in practice, the nationality or ethnic origin of the suspected offender is not always recorded in the relevant statistics.

1.1.6 Comments by offences

Homicide
25. Homicide rates vary significantly between countries, even when attempted homicide is excluded. Other variations in definitions (for instance fifteen countries excluded assault leading to death) may influence homicide rates but do not explain by themselves these differences. In 1999, the highest rates of completed homicide were observed in Albania, Estonia, Latvia and Lithuania (more than 6 per 100 000) and the lowest in Austria, Denmark and Norway (less than 1 per 100 000). For half of the countries, these rates decreased during the period 1995-2000. No underlying increase was observed.

26. The highest proportion of suspected female offenders for completed homicide in 1995 was 15% (France). The overall proportion of suspected minor offenders was smaller than for all other offences with a maximum of 12% (Slovenia).

Assault
27. Assaults vary widely in definition, with six countries including threats, fifteen including assaults that only caused pain and two more including slapping or punching. In addition, five countries included sexual assault. It was also evident that several Eastern European countries counted some cases as public order offences rather than as assaults at police level. Rather low levels of assault rates in some countries may also be explained by the fact that a complaint from the victim is a condition for recording the case.

28. However, it is difficult to adequately explain the big differences between countries for assault rates in relation to these definition problems. For example, in principle, countries where "only causing pain" and "slapping/punching" were included in the definition of assault should have high rates of assault, as is the case for Finland, the Netherlands, Portugal, Sweden, England & Wales and Scotland. However, exceptions to this rule were evident in Cyprus, Estonia, Ireland (before 2000), and Latvia. In contrast, some countries have high rates without recording minor assaults (Belgium or Northern Ireland) and differences in the rules for counting multiple assaults may also be important here. The result is a distribution of countries where low and high rates are more frequent than rates in the middle.

29. Trends for assault rates between 1995 and 2000 are not uniform and seem to be increasing in countries where rates are already high (more than 100 per 100 000), with the exception of Luxembourg. In contrast, in countries where rates are already low, they appear to be decreasing. In addition, the proportion of suspected female offenders was, overall, higher than for completed homicide whereas the proportion of suspected minors was relatively low in relation to the number of minors in the total population.

Rape
30. Rape statistics are affected by the deviation from the standard definition proposed in the questionnaire: only two countries do not show any deviation. But many countries reported some changes in the legal definition of rape leading to more compliance with the standard definition (inclusion of violent intra-marital sexual intercourse).

31. According to the mean and median, rape offences recorded by the police remained steady between 1995 and 2000. However, just as can be seen for assault, rates in sixteen countries are increasing (with twelve showing rates above the median in 1999), rates in ten countries are decreasing (all under the median with the exception of the Czech Republic and Luxembourg) and of thirteen countries with steady or fluctuating rates (nine of them are under the median). However, as stated previously, changes may reflect differences in reporting practices.

32. In some countries females are counted among the offenders suspected of having committed rape offences (five countries reported figures of 1% or more). The most likely explanation is that suspected female offenders acted as accomplices in rape incidents. The proportion of minor suspects varied considerably between countries and was on average slightly lower than for most offences but slightly higher than for assault and twice as big in comparison to homicide. However, this may reflect the fact that some countries included sexual intercourse with a minor without force in their rape statistics.

Robbery

33. The differences in levels between countries are still important and may reflect variation in definition of robbery (eight countries excluded muggings and six excluded theft with violence). However, their distribution around the mean or the median is more concentrated. In 1999, six countries had a rate above 150 per 100 000; fourteen countries below 150 and above the median; another fifteen were below the median but above 10 per 100 000, and four were under 10.

34. Between 1995 and 2000, there was an increase in recorded robbery in twenty-six countries. There was an increase of more than 30% in 16 countries and an increase of more than 60% in Croatia, Cyprus, Latvia, Norway and Poland. For some countries, the increase occurred mainly at the end of the period. However, in Ireland there was a reduction of 64%. On the whole, the negative variations are not important and they range from -2% (Russia) to -20% for eight countries.

35. There was a low proportion of female offenders but a high proportion of minors (the highest proportion after burglary).

Theft

36. All theft (except robbery) is, in principle, included in this category. Differences between countries cannot be explained totally by a variation in offence definition. Even when thefts of small value are included, their exlusion does not produce a very significant reduction in the level of theft. This may be due to the fact that in some countries where theft of small value is, in principle, included, only cases prosecuted after a formal complaint are counted.

37. Variations in theft rates (from 40 per 100 000 in Albania to about 8 000 per 100 000 in Sweden in 2000) can be related to a ratio calculated by dividing the number of offenders by the number of offences. This ratio is different from the clearance rate but depends on it, as the higher the clearance rate, the higher this ratio is. It appears to be high for countries with a low rate of theft registered by the police (Albania, Armenia, Cyprus, Georgia, Latvia, Moldova, Romania, Russia, Turkey and the Ukraine). In contrast, several countries with a low ratio of offenders/ offences have a high rate for theft (France, Italy, the Netherlands, Norway, Sweden, Switzerland, England and Wales, exception: Greece and Malta). This could mean that, in some countries, either victims do not register theft with the police when they do not know the offender or the police do not necessarily record it.

38. In the majority of countries, there is no clear trend for the period 1995-2000, although there was an increase in twenty-one countries for the year 2000.

39. A relatively high percentage of female offenders is recorded for theft and this would be even higher if motor vehicle theft and burglary were exluded. The high percentages of minors are probably related to vehicle theft.

Theft of a motor vehicle
40. The differences in levels between countries can be related to the definition of these offences. For example, at least seven countries did not include joyriding, whereas five countries included only joyriding or an equivalent offence (vehicle theft being included within total theft). In addition, some countries mentioned that data referred to all vehicles (including bicycles) and other countries that it referred to cars only. The number of offences is also dependant on the number of vehicle owners.

41. The rates for motor vehicle theft decreased during the period 1995-2000 in fourteen countries. They increased by more than 20% in fourteen countries and fluctuated or steadied in the others. However, these three groups do not show any geographical or rate level consistency.

42. The proportion of females among offenders was low (under 10%), whilst the proportion of minors was high (mean value of 25% for the twenty-one countries where data are available).

Burglary
43. The concept of burglary varies widely between countries. For example, some countries adopt a relatively narrow definition whilst others apply the (continental law) concept of aggravated theft. Only thirty-one countries could give data for burglary and twenty-nine for domestic burglary (10 countries had no data at all). Fifteen countries include theft from a car as burglary and most of these also include theft from a container or a vending machine. Definitions for domestic burglary also show significant variations with seven countries out of twenty-nine excluding theft from a secondary residence and seven others excluding theft from an attic or basement in a multi-dwelling building.

44. For total burglary, a majority of countries reported a decrease in rates with only five countries reporting an increase. For domestic burglary, the mean rate seems to be decreasing and the median fluctuating.

45. The overall proportion of females amongst the suspected offenders was relatively low, whilst that of minors was relatively high.

Drug offences
46. From the 37 countries that provided figures for total drug offences only 25 provided figures for drug trafficking. The proportion of drug trafficking in the total figures varies widely between countries. For Russia, drug trafficking represents about 95% of the total drug offences and for the Netherlands the total figure refers to drug trafficking only. Spain provided figures only for drug trafficking but not total drug offences. Norway had very high figures in both categories and drug trafficking represents 43% of the total drug offences (in 1999). In other countries, where total drug offences appear to be low (e.g. the Czech Republic), the proportion of drug trafficking is also substantive.

Table 1.a: Trends in police data (percentage change of the rates between 1995 and 2000)

	Homicide		Assault	Rape	Robbery	Theft				Drug	Offences
	Total	Complete				Total Theft	Motor Vehicle Theft	Burglary		Total	Drug Trafficking
								Total	Domestic Burglary		
Albania	+	+	-	-	+	--	+	--	-	+	...
Armenia	-	-	+	--	+	+	+	...	...	-	...
Austria	o	o	+	+	+	+	+	o	o	+	-
Belgium	+	+	+	+	+	o	o	...	...	+	+
Bulgaria	-	-	--	-	-	-	o	--	...	++	...
Croatia	-	-	o	+	+	o	+	o	o	++	++
Cyprus	o	++	-	+	+	o	+	o	...	+	...
Czech Republic	o	...	-	-	+	o	o	-	-	++	++
Denmark	o	o	+	+	+	o	-	o	o	+	-
Estonia	-	-	o	-	+	+	+	+	o	++	++
Finland	o	o	+	+	+	o	+	-	-	+	...
France	-	-	+	+	+	o	-	-	-	+	-
Georgia	o	-	-	-	-	-	+	...	...	++	++
Germany	-	-	+	+	o	-	--	-	-	+	+
Greece	o	...	o	o	o	o	+	-	...	++	...
Hungary	-	-	o	-	+	o	+	-	+	++	++
Ireland	+	o	++	o	--	-	+	-	-	++	++
Italy	-	-	+	+	+	+	o	+	+	+	...
Latvia	-	-	-	-	++	+	+	...	...	++	...
Lithuania	-	-	+	o	+	+	+	...	+	++	...
Luxembourg	o	...	-	-	+	-	--	...	-	+	...
Moldova	o	...	-	o	o	o	...	+	...	++	...
Netherlands	...	-	+	+	+	o	...	o	...	...	...
Norway	+	o	+	+	+	o	o	-	--	+	+
Poland	o	o	+	+	++	+	+	+	+	++	++
Portugal	...	-	+	-	+	+	+	o	o	o	-
Romania	-	...	-	o	-	-	-	-	-	+	...
Russia	o	...	-	-	o	o	-	...	+	++	++
Slovakia	o	o	-	-	o	-	-	-	-	...	...
Slovenia	-	-	o	o	+	+	o	+	...	++	++
Spain	+	+	...	-	o	o	+	o	...	...	-
Sweden	...	...	o	+	+	o	+	o	o	+	-
Switzerland	o	o	+	+	+	-	-	-	-	o	o
Turkey	-	...	+	+	-	+	+	+	...	+	...
Ukraine	o	...	o	-	-	-	--	...	...	+	...
UK: England & Wales	o	o	++	+	+	-	-	-	-	...	o
UK: Northern Ireland	+	+	++	+	o	o	+	o	-	+	-
UK: Scotland	-	-	+	+	-	-	-	-	-	+	o

Note:

- -- : decrease of 50% or more
- - : decrease of [50, 10%]
- o : decrease or increase of less than 10%
- + : increase of [10, 100%]
- ++: increase of more than 100%

47. Norway, Belgium, Sweden, Switzerland and Scotland have the highest rates for total drug offences. However, in many countries drug trafficking accounts for less than 30% (e.g. 4% for Germany). The main differences come from the inclusion or exclusion of offences linked to personal use in the total drug offences and/or in drug trafficking.

48. There is a significant increase in registered drug offences in most European countries between 1995 and 2000.

49. The proportion of suspected female offenders is relatively high in comparison with other offences (except total theft) and the proportion of minors is relatively low.

Trends
50. The following table summarises trends (i.e. percentage changes between 1995 and 2000) in police data by types of offences. Its purpose is to give a general view of differences in trends for each offence; it should not be used to examine changes in specific offences for particular countries.

1.1.7 Police staff

51. The rate of police officers (excluding civilians) per 100 000 population (hereafter referred to as police density) varied between 150 and 1 200. In summary table 1.b, the distribution over five density categories is given.

Table 1.b: Number of police officers (excluding civilians) per 100 000 population (police density) in 2000

Under 200	200-299	300-399	400-499	500 and over
Denmark	Estonia	Austria	Albania	Croatia
Finland	the Netherlands (1999)	Belgium	the Czech Republic	Cyprus
Norway	Moldova	France	Greece	Georgia
Sweden	Poland	Hungary	Latvia	Italy (1999)
	Romania	Ireland	Lithuania	Russia
	Switzerland	Slovakia	Malta	UK: Northern Ireland
	Turkey	Slovenia	Portugal	
	UK: England & Wales	Spain		
	UK: Scotland			

52. Fourteen countries had a police density below 300 and fourteen between 300 and 500. Densities of more than 500 do not exceed 560 (Georgia) with the exeption of Russia (about 1 200). Overall there does not seem to be a clear relationship between police density and the level of recorded crime.

53. Twelve countries were unable to give data for civilian employees within the police. For other countries, there were some differences in the ratio of police officers/civilian employees. This proportion was under 10% in eight countries (Albania, Cyprus, France, Georgia, Greece, Moldova, Portugal and Romania) and more than 20% in 14 countries (Austria, Croatia, Czech Republic, Estonia, Finland, Hungary, Norway, Slovakia, Slovenia, Sweden, Switzerland, England & Wales, Northern Ireland and Scotland). In summary table 1.c civilian staff is included in police density and the distribution is given over five categories.

Table 1.c: Police staff (officers and civilians) per 100 000 population in 2000

Under 250	250-349	350-449	450-549	550 and over
Denmark	Estonia	Albania	Cyprus	Croatia
Finland	Moldova	Austria	Greece	the Czech Republic
Norway	the Netherlands (1999)	Belgium	Latvia	Georgia
Romania	Poland	France	Portugal	UK: Northern Ireland
Switzerland	Sweden	Hungary		
	UK: England & Wales	Ireland		
		Slovakia		
		Slovenia		
		UK: Scotland		

1.2 Tables

1.2.1 Offences per 100 000 population

Table 1.2.1.1: Offences per 100 000 population – Criminal offences: Total

	1995 R11TC95	1996 R11TC96	1997 R11TC97	1998 R11TC98	1999 R11TC99	2000 R11TC00	% change 1995-2000
Albania	196.8	159.2	192.7	176.8	163.0	148.9	-24
Armenia	297.1	367.7	365.8	319.8	299.8	360.3	21
Austria	6048.7	6026.0	5965.6	5930.3	6081.0	6890.9	14
Belgium	7439.1	7569.5	8268.2	8594.7	8557.6	...	...
Bulgaria	2373.5	2261.0	2822.9	1995.3	1746.9	1779.1	-25
Croatia	1414.5	1334.7	1275.2	1315.6	1367.8	1596.8	13
Cyprus	552.2	613.0	525.6	576.6	558.8	574.7	4
Czech Republic	3638.0	3823.0	3918.4	4138.9	4149.6	3811.0	5
Denmark	10300.1	10043.4	10051.0	9414.4	9290.1	9447.3	-8
Estonia	2666.9	2409.7	2810.0	3156.1	3579.1	4037.7	51
Finland	9777.9	9568.1	9369.2	9658.2	9879.2	10261.7	5
France	6336.5	6134.5	6001.7	6105.6	6086.4	6404.5	1
Georgia	...	311.2	291.2	291.6	297.3	269.3	...
Germany	8150.7	8105.6	8026.3	7870.8	7670.5	7615.8	-7
Greece	3137.6	3324.8	3587.4	3653.7	3532.4	3481.9	11
Hungary	4876.1	4536.4	5021.2	5882.1	4970.5	4445.0	-9
Ireland	2838.0	2774.3	2476.7	2307.5	2165.3	1929.7	-32
Italy	3959.8	4225.9	4249.9	4218.0	4123.0	...	...
Latvia	1551.6	1530.7	1492.2	1486.6	1812.8	2087.3	35
Lithuania	1655.9	1858.1	2076.1	2146.0	2123.4	2274.9	37
Luxembourg	6924.5	6629.6	5783.2	6367.0	6241.4	5216.4	-25
Malta	...	...	...	3834.0	4123.7	4344.5	...
Moldova	861.3	782.4	898.6	816.0	887.8	863.7	0
Netherlands	7910.6	7617.4	7807.0	7782.3	8128.4	8215.3	4
Norway	9189.5	9401.3	9796.7	10076.8	9814.0	10136.9	10
Poland	2525.5	2323.8	2567.2	2775.3	2901.2	3278.2	30
Portugal	3275.9	3229.1	3218.1	3407.1	3615.0	3615.5	10
Romania	1309.0	1421.5	1600.3	1773.1	1619.3	1578.4	21
Russia	1860.5	1776.6	1626.8	1756.9	2048.8	2022.2	9
Slovakia	2137.0	1850.0	1716.2	1740.5	1740.8	1642.3	-23
Slovenia	2018.6	1987.6	2015.3	2920.4	3283.2	3614.3	79
Spain	2284.9	2338.0	2318.9	2420.1	2407.3	2308.4	1
Sweden	12984.6	13266.9	13492.7	13318.5	13462.0	13692.8	5
Switzerland	4255.9	4348.6	4686.2	4594.9	4294.3	3731.6	-12
Turkey	479.3	553.9	617.3	562.9	681.0	711.5	48
Ukraine	1250.8	1213.2	1168.5	1152.2	1127.2	1126.3	-10
UK: England & Wales	9831.0	9675.1	8703.1	9752.7	10090.7	9817.3	0
UK: Northern Ireland	4284.4	4253.7	3706.2	6724.5	7323.9	7354.2	72
UK: Scotland	10784.6	10300.3	9673.0	9844.8	9921.6	9637.7	-11
Mean	4362	4209	4215	4381	4415	4333	
Median	3138	3002	3020	3407	3579	3614	
Minimum	197	159	193	177	163	149	
Maximum	12985	13267	13493	13318	13462	13693	

Table 1.2.1.2: Offences per 100 000 population – Criminal offences: Traffic offences

	1995 R11TT95	1996 R11TT96	1997 R11TT97	1998 R11TT98	1999 R11TT99	2000 R11TT00	% change 1995-2000
Albania	12.1	3.0	11.2	12.9	13.6	...	...
Armenia	17.6	24.2	23.7	19.9	19.0	16.9	-4
Austria	522.0	504.3	507.5	509.6	520.5	569.9	9
Belgium	...	...	...	...	...	...	...
Bulgaria	13.8	15.9	15.0	21.1	29.0	27.9	102
Croatia	186.9	170.0	157.3	62.2	58.0	60.0	-68
Cyprus	...	...	...	...	...	...	...
Czech Republic	...	...	...	...	...	...	...
Denmark	...	...	...	...	...	...	...
Estonia	31.3	25.0	32.4	32.7	86.5	149.7	379
Finland	2779.4	2680.2	2569.3	2684.9	2663.6	2795.8	1
France	...	...	...	...	...	...	...
Georgia	...	4.4	5.0	5.2	4.5	4.9	...
Germany	...	...	...	...	...	...	...
Greece	1049.4	1033.5	1131.5	1230.4	1182.3	1402.0	34
Hungary	239.3	201.4	207.0	219.6	201.5	193.0	-19
Ireland	0.7	0.9	0.7	0.9	1.1	1.0	48
Italy	2.6	2.4	2.2	2.3	2.0	...	...
Latvia	158.0	147.7	157.7	184.7	181.0	186.3	18
Lithuania	27.6	36.2	44.4	52.6	53.7	51.8	88
Luxembourg	...	...	...	...	...	...	...
Malta	...	...	...	...	...	...	...
Moldova	15.3	16.8	17.6	14.4	12.9	13.1	-15
Netherlands	577.0	634.1	638.6	671.1	741.1	741.2	28
Norway	1307.0	1277.8	1342.5	1390.5	1304.9	1337.9	2
Poland	90.7	90.2	104.0	89.1	53.0	51.5	-43
Portugal	81.8	101.1	100.2	125.4	270.9	292.8	258
Romania	129.2	130.6	104.2	153.8	134.5	96.8	-25
Russia	33.8	32.3	32.6	35.7	36.7	...	...
Slovakia	...	...	...	...	84.1	75.9	...
Slovenia	85.4	81.4	81.3	60.0	67.7	72.0	-16
Spain	...	...	75.0	78.1	81.2	75.9	...
Sweden	637.0	574.1	564.9	559.5	623.6	837.4	31
Switzerland	...	...	...	...	...	...	...
Turkey	...	...	...	...	...	...	...
Ukraine	28.8	26.2	25.4	23.9	22.1	20.8	-28
UK: England & Wales	...	...	...	...	...	...	...
UK: Northern Ireland	0.9	0.6	2.3	13.4	17.0	13.9	> 1000
UK: Scotland	...	...	...	...	...	...	...
Mean	334	313	306	317	314	379	
Median	84	81	78	61	68	76	
Minimum	1	1	1	1	1	1	
Maximum	2779	2680	2569	2685	2664	2796	

Table 1.2.1.3: Offences per 100 000 population – Intentional homicide: Total

	1995 R11HO95	1996 R11HO96	1997 R11HO97	1998 R11HO98	1999 R11HO99	2000 R11HO00	% change 1995-2000
Albania	15.7	18.4	77.0	29.9	25.3	17.4	11
Armenia	4.7	4.7	4.0	4.3	4.7	3.8	-18
Austria	2.3	2.4	2.1	2.2	1.5	2.5	7
Belgium	4.1	4.3	5.1	5.4	5.3	...	...
Bulgaria	10.1	9.1	8.8	8.0	7.7	6.7	-33
Croatia	9.4	7.5	7.3	7.2	7.1	6.9	-26
Cyprus	1.6	2.8	1.2	2.5	2.7	1.5	-11
Czech Republic	2.7	2.6	2.8	3.0	2.6	2.7	1
Denmark	3.9	4.3	5.2	3.9	4.1	4.1	5
Estonia	20.5	18.2	16.9	17.1	13.9	13.2	-36
Finland	10.3	10.1	9.6	8.8	8.9	9.9	-4
France	5.2	4.7	4.1	4.0	3.7	4.0	23
Georgia	...	7.8	7.6	7.3	7.2	7.8	...
Germany	5.5	5.0	4.6	4.2	3.8	3.8	-32
Greece	2.7	3.0	3.3	3.3	2.9	2.7	-2
Hungary	4.0	4.0	4.2	4.4	4.1	3.5	-12
Ireland	1.5	1.5	1.5	1.5	1.4	1.8	19
Italy	4.9	4.7	4.6	4.5	4.3	...	...
Latvia	11.1	10.3	10.5	9.7	8.8	9.1	-18
Lithuania	13.7	11.1	10.7	9.8	9.4	11.0	-20
Luxembourg	13.7	11.5	13.8	11.0	17.1	14.2	4
Malta	...	...	...	2.1	3.1	2.0	...
Moldova	9.0	8.9	9.3	8.5	8.8	9.3	3
Netherlands	17.5	17.2	...	...	...	...	...
Norway	2.2	2.6	2.0	1.9	2.3	2.6	19
Poland	3.5	3.4	3.4	3.2	3.1	3.7	7
Portugal	...	...	...	...	...	...	...
Romania	3.1	3.0	2.9	2.5	2.1	2.5	-19
Russia	21.4	19.9	19.9	20.1	21.3	21.8	2
Slovakia	2.4	2.5	2.6	2.4	2.6	2.6	11
Slovenia	4.8	5.4	4.2	3.4	3.6	4.0	-15
Spain	2.4	2.4	2.3	2.7	2.8	3.0	24
Sweden	...	...	...	...	...	...	...
Switzerland	2.3	2.8	2.6	2.6	2.7	2.2	-1
Turkey	2.9	2.9	2.7	2.6	2.4	...	...
Ukraine	9.3	9.6	9.0	9.1	9.3	9.8	5
UK: England & Wales	2.7	2.6	2.7	2.7	2.9	3.0	11
UK: Northern Ireland	3.7	6.8	10.0	9.9	5.8	10.5	187
UK: Scotland	15.0	15.5	13.9	14.3	16.2	13.3	-11
Mean	7	7	8	7	7	7	
Median	5	5	5	4	4	4	
Minimum	2	1	1	2	1	1	
Maximum	21	20	77	30	25	22	

Table 1.2.1.4: Offences per 100 000 population – Intentional homicide: Completed

	1995 R11HC95	1996 R11HC96	1997 R11HC97	1998 R11HC98	1999 R11HC99	2000 R11HC00	% change 1995-2000
Albania	6.5	7.6	46.5	17.0	14.4	7.9	21
Armenia	3.4	3.4	3.0	2.8	2.7	2.7	-20
Austria	1.1	1.4	1.1	1.1	0.8	1.2	7
Belgium	1.5	1.2	1.5	2.2	1.7	...	...
Bulgaria	5.6	4.9	4.6	4.6	3.9	4.1	-27
Croatia	4.2	3.2	3.3	2.8	2.8	2.6	-38
Cyprus	0.4	1.6	0.9	1.9	1.6	1.1	158
Czech Republic	1.8	1.7	...	...	...	...	...
Denmark	1.1	1.3	1.7	0.9	1.0	1.2	1
Estonia	16.6	14.6	12.2	13.5	10.9	10.0	-40
Finland	3.4	3.7	3.3	2.8	3.4	3.4	-1
France	3.0	2.7	2.1	1.9	1.9	2.1	-32
Georgia	...	4.3	4.1	4.7	4.8	3.1	...
Germany	2.4	2.2	2.0	1.9	1.6	1.6	-34
Greece	1.3	1.6	...	...	...	...	...
Hungary	2.9	2.6	2.8	2.8	2.5	2.0	-30
Ireland	1.5	1.3	1.4	1.4	1.3	1.5	0
Italy	1.8	1.8	1.6	1.6	1.5	...	...
Latvia	7.3	7.1	7.0	6.9	6.3	6.2	-15
Lithuania	12.1	10.0	9.2	8.5	8.5	10.2	-15
Luxembourg	...	...	...	...	1.4	1.1	...
Malta	...	...	...	1.3	2.6	1.0	...
Moldova	...	...	...	...	...	7.9	...
Netherlands	1.8	1.6	1.8	1.4	1.5	1.4	-18
Norway	1.0	1.0	0.9	0.9	0.8	1.1	11
Poland	2.6	2.6	2.6	2.3	2.2	2.5	-4
Portugal	4.1	3.9	3.8	3.4	3.0	2.5	-40
Romania	...	...	...	...	...	...	...
Russia	...	...	...	...	...	...	...
Slovakia	2.4	2.5	2.6	2.4	2.6	2.6	11
Slovenia	2.4	2.0	1.9	0.8	1.3	1.5	-38
Spain	1.0	1.0	0.9	1.1	1.0	1.2	19
Sweden	1.0	1.2	1.1	1.1	1.2	...	...
Switzerland	1.1	1.2	1.2	1.1	1.2	1.0	-17
Turkey	...	...	...	...	...	...	...
Ukraine	...	...	...	...	...	...	...
UK: England & Wales	1.4	1.3	1.4	1.4	1.5	1.6	12
UK: Northern Ireland	1.5	2.4	3.0	4.6	2.1	2.9	97
UK: Scotland	2.7	2.6	1.8	1.9	2.5	2.1	-22
Mean	3	3	4	3	3	3	
Median	2	2	2	2	2	2	
Minimum	0	1	1	1	1	1	
Maximum	17	15	46	17	14	10	

Table 1.2.1.5: Offences per 100 000 population – Intentional homicide according to Health Statistics

	1995	1996	1997	1998	1999	2000	% change 1995-2000
Albania	9.0	9.9	48.3	24.7	20.1	6.0	-33
Armenia	4.6	3.1	2.8	2.7	2.8	2.4	-48
Austria	1.0	1.2	0.9	1.1	0.8	0.9	-14
Belgium	1.6	2.0	...	...	...	...	...
Bulgaria	4.7	4.9	4.3	3.7	2.8	3.3	-29
Croatia	3.3	3.0	2.7	3.3	2.8	2.6	-19
Cyprus	...	...	...	...	...	...	...
Czech Republic	1.8	1.6	1.6	1.6	1.4	1.5	-15
Denmark	1.2	1.1	1.2	0.9	...	...	...
Estonia	22.1	19.9	15.9	18.0	15.8	13.6	-39
Finland	2.9	3.3	2.6	2.3	2.7	2.6	-10
France	1.1	1.0	0.9	0.7	0.7	...	...
Georgia	0.0	0.6	1.9	4.1	3.7	3.2	> 1000
Germany	1.1	1.1	0.9	0.9	0.9	...	...
Greece	1.3	1.5	1.5	1.3	1.2	...	...
Hungary	3.4	3.1	3.2	3.2	2.8	2.5	-26
Ireland	0.8	1.0	0.9	1.1	...	...	...
Italy	1.4	1.4	1.2	1.2	...	...	...
Latvia	18.1	15.5	16.2	12.8	12.5	12.4	-31
Lithuania	11.9	9.3	9.2	8.3	8.0	9.5	-20
Luxembourg	0.7	0.9	0.6	0.9	0.7	1.6	114
Malta	0.8	1.3	0.5	1.9	2.2	1.0	22
Moldova	17.9	14.6	14.1	12.4	11.9	12.7	-29
Netherlands	1.2	1.3	1.3	1.1	1.3	...	...
Norway	1.0	1.0	0.9	1.0	0.8	...	...
Poland	2.9	2.7	...	...	2.3	2.1	-28
Portugal	1.7	1.3	1.2	1.3	1.1	0.9	-46
Romania	4.3	3.8	3.8	3.3	3.6	3.6	-16
Russia	30.9	26.6	23.7	22.5	25.7	27.6	-11
Slovakia	2.1	2.1	2.6	2.1	2.4	2.2	1
Slovenia	2.3	2.2	2.2	1.0	1.4	...	...
Spain	0.9	0.8	0.8	0.8	...	...	...
Sweden	1.0	1.2	1.1	1.1	1.2	...	...
Switzerland	0.9	1.1	1.4	0.8	...	...	...
Ukraine	15.0	15.0	13.0	12.0	12.4	12.7	-15
United Kingdom	1.0	0.9	0.7	0.7	0.8	1.0	2
Mean	4.8	4.4	5.4	4.6	5.0	5.6	
Median	1.7	1.6	1.6	1.7	2.5	2.6	
Minimum	0.0	0.6	0.5	0.7	0.7	0.9	
Maximum	30.9	26.6	48.3	24.7	25.7	27.6	

Source: World Health Organization. "European health for all database": Homicide and intentional injury, all ages per 100 000. Available on line: http://www.who.dk/hfadb

Table 1.2.1.6: Offences per 100 000 population – Assault

	1995 R11AS95	1996 R11AS96	1997 R11AS97	1998 R11AS98	1999 R11AS99	2000 R11AS00	% change 1995-2000
Albania	7.7	7.3	10.4	5.6	5.6	4.4	-43
Armenia	28.0	28.0	33.8	35.2	36.0	37.5	34
Austria	402.6	387.9	385.5	385.5	397.5	459.9	14
Belgium	480.2	498.5	541.4	548.8	546.9	...	...
Bulgaria	15.1	14.3	16.5	5.2	4.6	3.9	-74
Croatia	24.8	25.6	29.9	26.8	24.8	23.1	-7
Cyprus	18.4	15.7	15.9	12.7	15.1	12.8	-31
Czech Republic	77.5	75.5	74.3	77.2	71.9	70.0	-10
Denmark	164.8	163.2	165.3	159.6	168.7	183.0	11
Estonia	27.4	26.5	30.0	28.2	26.3	28.9	5
Finland	434.0	478.6	483.2	497.8	507.7	537.8	24
France	122.2	129.3	140.2	148.3	162.2	180.5	48
Georgia	...	8.8	8.4	8.9	7.9	6.7	...
Germany	370.0	388.5	406.1	427.6	449.1	464.2	25
Greece	65.4	61.6	62.5	65.8	66.2	67.6	3
Hungary	103.3	97.5	103.1	108.0	105.6	107.5	4
Ireland	15.9	15.2	15.9	18.6	12.0	44.8	182
Italy	37.5	41.4	43.9	46.5	52.0	...	...
Latvia	23.7	18.7	20.2	17.5	17.7	17.6	-26
Lithuania	24.4	26.4	27.5	28.3	32.3	33.7	38
Luxembourg	291.3	290.5	235.1	250.2	271.1	260.0	-11
Malta	...	...	...	143.3	170.0	191.0	...
Moldova	13.4	11.4	11.8	9.5	11.9	10.1	-25
Netherlands	180.5	193.1	240.8	242.0	267.7	277.5	54
Norway	57.6	59.4	59.7	59.7	66.9	78.2	36
Poland	75.4	79.1	85.5	83.1	78.2	83.9	11
Portugal	348.3	355.2	371.8	410.4	408.4	433.2	24
Romania	33.2	31.6	32.6	28.3	27.6	27.6	-17
Russia	41.7	36.2	31.3	30.7	32.5	34.1	-18
Slovakia	83.3	80.9	73.5	74.8	72.8	69.0	-17
Slovenia	24.7	24.5	22.0	20.3	21.1	22.4	-10
Spain	...	...	32.5	45.2	45.9	43.2	...
Sweden	616.2	606.5	621.7	641.4	675.5	663.2	8
Switzerland	52.0	57.7	61.2	67.4	72.5	74.5	43
Turkey	67.5	79.4	83.2	89.0	87.4	...	...
Ukraine	33.3	32.8	30.9	29.9	31.0	30.2	-9
UK: England & Wales	392.2	439.2	467.6	732.5	836.2	856.1	118
UK: Northern Ireland	269.0	286.3	240.2	1021.7	1170.1	1133.4	321
UK: Scotland	1027.6	1044.5	1072.7	1096.6	1161.3	1171.2	14
Mean	168	168	168	198	211	215	
Median	66	62	62	67	72	70	
Minimum	8	7	8	5	5	4	
Maximum	1028	1045	1073	1097	1170	1171	

Table 1.2.1.7: Offences per 100 000 population – Rape

	1995 R11RA95	1996 R11RA96	1997 R11RA97	1998 R11RA98	1999 R11RA99	2000 R11RA00	% change 1995-2000
Albania	3.0	3.1	1.2	1.7	1.8	2.5	-15
Armenia	0.8	0.7	0.7	0.4	0.4	0.4	-41
Austria	10.7	10.5	10.8	12.0	12.2	14.3	34
Belgium	13.4	14.7	17.1	17.2	18.0	...	...
Bulgaria	9.1	7.6	8.2	8.3	8.1	7.0	-23
Croatia	2.6	3.4	3.4	3.7	4.1	4.8	86
Cyprus	1.2	2.0	1.6	1.5	1.5	1.6	29
Czech Republic	7.0	6.6	6.4	6.6	6.2	4.9	-31
Denmark	8.4	7.4	8.2	7.9	9.0	9.3	11
Estonia	6.9	6.4	6.7	3.7	4.1	5.1	-26
Finland	8.7	7.7	9.1	9.0	10.0	11.2	28
France	12.7	12.4	14.1	13.4	13.6	14.4	13
Georgia	...	1.7	1.4	1.4	1.2	1.4	...
Germany	7.5	7.6	8.1	9.6	9.2	9.1	21
Greece	2.2	1.7	2.1	2.0	2.3	2.2	-1
Hungary	4.1	4.1	3.8	3.4	3.3	2.9	-28
Ireland	23.4	21.6	26.1	25.5	18.8	23.6	1
Italy	1.7	2.0	2.8	3.2	3.3	...	...
Latvia	6.3	5.2	4.8	3.4	4.2	5.6	-11
Lithuania	5.4	4.6	4.5	4.6	6.2	5.1	-7
Luxembourg	11.2	9.9	6.2	10.6	6.7	6.9	-39
Malta	...	...	...	0.5	3.3	3.3	...
Moldova	5.2	6.2	5.3	5.2	5.5	5.3	1
Netherlands	9.1	9.2	9.9	10.4	11.2	10.4	13
Norway	8.5	9.7	9.6	10.3	10.5	12.4	46
Poland	6.1	5.4	6.2	6.0	5.8	6.7	9
Portugal	5.4	4.9	5.5	4.0	3.8	3.8	-28
Romania	6.5	6.0	6.1	5.6	6.5	6.1	-6
Russia	8.4	7.4	6.3	6.1	5.7	5.4	-36
Slovakia	3.9	3.9	3.2	2.8	3.2	2.4	-39
Slovenia	6.4	5.5	6.2	4.6	4.1	6.2	-4
Spain	4.3	...	3.1	3.7	3.2	3.5	-19
Sweden	19.3	18.2	19.1	22.2	23.7	22.8	18
Switzerland	4.2	4.8	5.1	5.3	6.2	5.6	32
Turkey	3.9	7.8	8.0	7.6	5.4	...	...
Ukraine	3.8	3.4	3.0	2.7	2.6	2.3	-38
UK: England & Wales	9.9	11.5	12.7	14.6	16.0	16.3	65
UK: Northern Ireland	16.1	18.1	16.8	20.0	19.1	14.2	-12
UK: Scotland	7.9	8.7	11.0	11.8	11.4	10.8	37
Mean	7	7	7	7	7	7	
Median	6	6	6	6	6	6	
Minimum	1	1	1	0.4	0.4	0.4	
Maximum	23	22	26	26	24	24	

Table 1.2.1.8: Offences per 100 000 population – Robbery

	1995 R11RO95	1996 R11RO96	1997 R11RO97	1998 R11RO98	1999 R11RO99	2000 R11RO00	% change 1995-2000
Albania	8.1	7.9	20.4	22.2	16.0	11.1	38
Armenia	5.8	6.0	6.3	7.5	6.9	7.6	30
Austria	26.3	25.8	24.7	27.6	28.1	37.3	42
Belgium	130.3	136.4	164.5	192.4	211.7	...	...
Bulgaria	69.4	68.7	80.2	63.3	52.9	55.4	-20
Croatia	10.4	11.9	12.5	17.1	15.7	18.7	80
Cyprus	3.0	2.6	3.4	3.6	4.2	5.7	89
Czech Republic	38.5	41.5	46.1	41.8	46.9	45.7	19
Denmark	39.0	43.3	47.8	49.1	52.3	59.3	52
Estonia	210.1	192.7	238.5	274.6	341.5	332.1	58
Finland	42.9	40.7	39.3	40.6	44.1	50.3	17
France	128.9	136.9	138.3	144.3	162.0	186.5	45
Georgia	...	7.5	6.1	6.0	5.7	6.7	...
Germany	77.6	82.4	84.8	78.5	74.8	72.2	-7
Greece	15.3	14.1	18.7	21.4	19.4	16.1	6
Hungary	25.8	26.2	29.8	29.9	31.1	34.5	34
Ireland	225.0	230.1	100.9	73.0	84.3	81.1	-64
Italy	50.0	54.5	57.3	65.7	68.4	...	...
Latvia	35.9	41.3	33.6	24.9	108.0	131.4	266
Lithuania	77.2	95.0	108.7	100.1	93.0	120.8	56
Luxembourg	61.5	62.5	68.4	87.2	81.5	70.2	14
Malta	...	...	...	82.4	54.5	37.3	...
Moldova	66.1	59.5	73.7	63.6	72.2	66.2	0
Netherlands	101.6	97.2	90.9	91.7	110.8	117.0	15
Norway	21.7	23.2	24.4	30.5	38.1	39.7	83
Poland	52.5	52.7	62.1	68.9	94.7	111.9	113
Portugal	144.4	129.2	139.1	124.3	160.2	170.7	18
Romania	18.3	17.1	17.8	15.8	14.9	14.6	-20
Russia	120.4	105.5	99.3	109.5	122.9	117.7	-2
Slovakia	24.4	23.7	22.3	22.8	26.6	23.4	-4
Slovenia	22.5	33.1	22.4	23.6	29.0	30.1	34
Spain	219.5	249.4	260.9	261.8	252.1	233.8	7
Sweden	65.1	65.7	74.9	75.7	97.3	101.4	56
Switzerland	46.3	52.5	56.7	59.1	59.2	51.7	12
Turkey	2.5	2.4	2.1	2.3	2.1	...	...
Ukraine	73.3	68.2	63.0	59.6	56.5	58.3	-20
UK: England & Wales	131.2	142.2	120.0	127.6	160.4	180.7	38
UK: Northern Ireland	75.2	79.8	63.8	70.7	79.4	97.2	29
UK: Scotland	103.9	102.1	86.8	95.6	97.7	84.9	-18
Mean	69	69	69	71	79	80	
Median	52	54	60	63	59	59	
Minimum	3	2	2	2	2	6	
Maximum	225	249	261	275	342	332	

Table 1.2.1.9: Offences per 100 000 population – Theft: Total

	1995 R11TH95	1996 R11TH96	1997 R11TH97	1998 R11TH98	1999 R11TH99	2000 R11TH00	% change 1995-2000
Albania	82.5	65.0	54.6	63.9	54.4	41.1	-50
Armenia	70.2	89.5	93.7	89.9	93.7	112.8	61
Austria	2658.1	2683.6	2643.8	2620.5	2650.5	3199.0	20
Belgium	3458.5	3334.4	3520.1	3736.8	3743.3	...	...
Bulgaria	1788.1	1670.8	2190.8	1340.0	1060.2	1120.9	-37
Croatia	656.5	568.4	508.1	582.5	572.1	698.2	6
Cyprus	239.5	299.1	267.4	291.1	255.4	244.3	2
Czech Republic	2588.3	2660.7	2677.4	2739.8	2625.9	2464.9	-5
Denmark	5390.3	5417.5	5559.3	5327.8	5339.4	5499.4	2
Estonia	1975.2	1751.6	1957.4	2202.8	2540.2	2781.4	41
Finland	4276.6	4106.2	4110.4	4293.7	4395.6	4417.5	3
France	3957.8	3821.1	3656.6	3712.9	3620.7	3722.4	-6
Georgia	...	94.0	86.2	84.9	85.2	81.1	...
Germany	4703.5	4478.2	4311.1	4051.8	3813.6	3626.7	-23
Greece	670.5	687.9	799.4	802.3	695.2	628.7	-6
Hungary	2265.1	2658.4	2798.7	2922.7	2538.9	2311.0	2
Ireland	2447.6	2385.1	2146.6	2093.9	1764.3	1997.3	-18
Italy	2337.3	2431.2	2440.3	2570.4	2571.8	...	...
Latvia	976.3	936.2	886.2	879.7	1021.4	1194.9	22
Lithuania	1133.1	1217.8	1292.3	1323.9	1318.1	1470.0	30
Luxembourg	3388.6	3108.5	2664.9	3124.8	2971.3	2773.7	-18
Malta	...	...	...	1620.9	1911.0	2203.4	...
Moldova	512.1	443.0	489.2	446.7	479.1	493.6	-4
Netherlands	5684.1	5205.1	5250.1	5193.3	5340.5	5403.3	-5
Norway	4531.3	4488.6	4533.0	4724.7	4564.1	4665.0	3
Poland	1338.0	1198.9	1315.2	1420.4	1575.1	1661.0	24
Portugal	1396.6	1409.9	1409.5	1510.8	1615.7	1633.5	17
Romania	517.0	510.4	566.9	583.6	423.1	444.1	-14
Russia	923.5	817.2	715.2	778.0	965.0	897.3	-3
Slovakia	1489.3	1234.4	1133.4	1146.6	1094.7	1019.4	-32
Slovenia	1038.2	956.7	924.3	1547.7	1850.3	2028.4	95
Spain	1555.3	1601.4	1575.1	1628.9	1638.3	1591.8	2
Sweden	7694.8	7045.5	8259.6	8048.6	7958.2	7831.3	2
Switzerland	3888.2	3986.4	4303.7	4194.2	3842.6	3329.1	-14
Turkey	146.8	192.1	210.9	193.0	165.5	...	...
Ukraine	673.4	615.4	541.1	538.2	530.0	561.5	-17
UK: England & Wales	7115.7	6816.6	5999.6	6002.7	5958.0	5660.4	-20
UK: Northern Ireland	3058.7	2998.0	2574.1	3107.9	3235.1	3210.5	5
UK: Scotland	5731.6	5219.4	4671.3	4760.7	4755.6	4424.7	-23
Mean	2496	2347	2346	2367	2350	2373	
Median	1975	1711	2052	1629	1850	2013	
Minimum	70	65	55	64	54	41	
Maximum	7695	7045	8260	8049	7958	7831	

Table 1.2.1.10: Offences per 100 000 population – Theft: Theft of a motor vehicle

	1995 R11TV95	1996 R11TV96	1997 R11TV97	1998 R11TV98	1999 R11TV99	2000 R11TV00	% change 1995-2000
Albania	2.8	4.3	5.7	13.8	13.6	5.6	97
Armenia	3.9	4.7	4.1	4.1	3.3	4.5	15
Austria	93.4	87.1	87.3	86.2	86.2	129.6	39
Belgium	519.8	467.1	484.9	501.4	482.6	...	...
Bulgaria	29.6	29.5	30.1	17.9	12.4	29.5	-1
Croatia	47.8	46.9	42.2	39.3	43.4	59.1	24
Cyprus	17.9	23.4	20.4	23.0	28.3	27.7	55
Czech Republic	264.7	287.4	304.1	289.4	281.5	248.6	-6
Denmark	702.1	820.7	808.2	733.1	661.6	603.9	-14
Estonia	131.8	111.8	120.8	145.4	170.5	162.2	23
Finland	387.2	395.6	428.7	512.9	574.0	510.7	32
France	784.0	764.8	717.0	712.2	675.4	681.0	-13
Georgia	...	6.2	6.9	7.7	6.3	8.2	...
Germany	321.0	275.3	232.3	198.1	171.2	155.3	-52
Greece	120.9	118.9	157.2	159.3	161.6	156.1	29
Hungary	124.8	165.3	196.8	204.2	163.8	141.0	13
Ireland	325.5	369.0	370.4	371.7	395.7	420.4	29
Italy	533.4	554.4	524.5	537.5	511.9	...	...
Latvia	110.0	88.8	84.3	101.5	127.9	121.9	11
Lithuania	183.4	171.1	183.4	190.7	183.7	248.7	36
Luxembourg	291.8	197.0	160.3	153.6	144.9	123.9	-58
Malta	...	...	...	302.2	276.8	268.3	...
Moldova	...	...	...	...	...	...	...
Netherlands	212.2	192.2	195.5	191.5	193.7	...	...
Norway	516.6	489.5	454.4	488.9	468.0	520.8	1
Poland	142.0	131.5	147.1	169.1	192.8	176.1	24
Portugal	173.9	200.3	228.0	269.3	280.8	263.0	51
Romania	11.8	8.0	9.4	10.1	10.4	9.6	-19
Russia	32.8	28.2	24.3	24.1	25.4	26.3	-20
Slovakia	143.5	124.4	138.2	142.5	131.9	112.3	-22
Slovenia	68.2	65.4	59.7	68.2	59.6	67.0	-2
Spain	248.7	286.1	334.5	346.0	347.8	336.5	35
Sweden	796.6	807.8	889.2	862.6	881.7	978.5	23
Switzerland	354.4	340.4	339.3	317.5	292.6	263.3	-26
Turkey	24.2	36.3	31.0	29.9	27.6	...	...
Ukraine	15.1	16.2	13.2	11.2	7.7	5.8	-62
UK: England & Wales	980.1	948.0	766.9	747.9	713.2	643.2	-34
UK: Northern Ireland	485.3	521.5	500.4	599.1	626.9	662.7	37
UK: Scotland	731.4	663.8	554.8	549.0	574.1	503.9	-31
Mean	276	266	261	267	263	255	
Median	179	171	183	191	177	159	
Minimum	3	4	4	4	3	4	
Maximum	980	948	889	863	882	978	

Table 1.2.1.11: Offences per 100 000 population – Theft: Burglary: Total

	1995 R11BU95	1996 R11BU96	1997 R11BU97	1998 R11BU98	1999 R11BU99	2000 R11BU00	% change 1995-2000
Albania	54.2	38.2	14.9	24.0	21.3	18.3	-66
Armenia	...	...	...	...	...	...	...
Austria	1065.8	1064.9	1041.9	1007.2	941.8	1077.4	1
Belgium	...	...	...	...	...	...	...
Bulgaria	975.2	857.2	1055.8	598.3	438.3	479.4	-51
Croatia	374.1	348.0	314.2	343.1	327.1	389.8	4
Cyprus	141.3	178.4	145.1	181.4	135.2	134.2	-5
Czech Republic	969.5	954.8	918.3	894.3	832.9	722.6	-25
Denmark	2035.9	2088.4	2110.3	1922.5	1896.7	1866.5	-8
Estonia	1385.1	1240.6	1274.5	1462.7	1653.9	1625.7	17
Finland	1109.9	1015.5	984.9	976.6	930.8	881.1	-21
France	749.1	752.1	699.9	678.0	631.3	629.9	-16
Georgia	...	...	...	...	...	...	...
Germany	836.5	795.9	750.5	700.0	625.5	564.8	-32
Greece	400.1	401.9	416.1	407.0	346.2	300.3	-25
Hungary	798.4	925.1	947.9	925.5	797.9	706.5	-12
Ireland	858.2	818.5	749.6	693.4	613.9	568.4	-34
Italy	371.1	401.6	413.4	429.2	406.8	...	...
Latvia	...	...	...	...	...	...	...
Lithuania	...	...	...	...	...	...	...
Luxembourg	...	...	...	...	...	...	...
Malta	...	...	...	165.9	173.6	200.2	...
Moldova	301.7	276.1	328.3	311.4	321.2	342.9	14
Netherlands	3445.9	3110.2	3122.4	3102.9	3037.9	3127.3	-9
Norway	1923.7	1860.5	1830.5	1830.7	1603.5	1560.8	-19
Poland	789.8	791.3	838.2	918.6	955.1	943.9	20
Portugal	504.8	503.3	508.8	481.4	487.7	471.0	-7
Romania	137.6	128.4	139.0	130.9	94.9	85.0	-38
Russia	...	...	...	...	...	...	...
Slovakia	730.6	585.3	535.8	519.9	529.7	471.8	-35
Slovenia	495.9	423.0	396.2	699.3	845.7	824.3	66
Spain	561.4	591.6	576.4	612.1	600.4	561.9	0
Sweden	1615.4	1635.6	1661.6	1557.1	1451.8	1470.7	-9
Switzerland	935.5	1032.6	1144.6	1154.5	1053.9	831.5	-11
Turkey	122.5	155.8	179.9	163.1	137.8	...	...
Ukraine	...	...	...	...	...	...	...
UK: England & Wales	2389.2	2237.1	1892.6	1819.5	1725.4	1587.3	-34
UK: Northern Ireland	1024.7	999.9	848.8	954.5	987.7	971.8	-5
UK: Scotland	1447.4	1252.7	1074.4	1093.6	1036.4	935.5	-35
Mean	952	915	897	863	827	840	
Median	817	807	794	699	631	707	
Minimum	54	38	15	24	21	18	
Maximum	3446	3110	3122	3103	3038	3127	

Table 1.2.1.12: Offences per 100 000 population – Theft: Burglary: Domestic Burglary

	1995 R11BD95	1996 R11BD96	1997 R11BD97	1998 R11BD98	1999 R11BD99	2000 R11BD00	% change 1995-2000
Albania	13.1	10.6	8.0	10.8	11.3	10.9	-17
Armenia	...	...	...	...	...	...	...
Austria	170.6	171.9	158.9	146.0	124.7	163.1	-4
Belgium	...	...	...	633.1	623.4	...	...
Bulgaria	...	...	...	...	...	...	...
Croatia	66.6	59.7	55.1	55.9	63.4	67.0	1
Cyprus	141.3	178.4	145.1	181.4	135.2	134.2	-5
Czech Republic	135.0	131.3	126.9	123.9	121.0	109.9	-19
Denmark	618.5	636.7	655.8	593.4	645.0	627.7	1
Estonia	551.0	467.1	453.3	485.0	527.0	508.9	-8
Finland	225.5	201.7	203.2	199.9	189.3	179.3	-20
France	410.8	407.2	366.9	354.9	326.0	316.7	-23
Georgia	...	...	...	...	...	...	...
Germany	396.0	380.3	364.0	351.1	314.0	281.6	-29
Greece	...	...	...	...	...	...	...
Hungary	217.3	293.1	305.2	298.9	293.9	265.0	22
Ireland	512.5	486.5	462.5	426.9	380.6	352.3	-31
Italy	371.1	401.6	413.4	429.2	406.8	...	...
Latvia	...	...	...	...	...	...	...
Lithuania	203.2	235.7	258.1	253.9	252.8	254.2	25
Luxembourg	791.0	758.1	573.7	621.1	484.4	475.8	-40
Malta	...	...	...	...	...	...	...
Moldova	...	...	...	...	...	...	...
Netherlands	...	...	...	...	...	...	...
Norway	295.2	292.9	248.8	218.8	169.3	138.7	-53
Poland	160.6	170.7	181.6	191.7	192.3	200.3	25
Portugal	220.4	228.4	242.1	214.9	221.6	210.5	-4
Romania	137.3	128.3	138.8	130.6	94.8	84.9	-38
Russia	204.1	181.4	182.1	199.0	255.8	238.4	17
Slovakia	83.6	71.8	71.6	67.5	66.7	60.1	-28
Slovenia	30.5	30.6	29.1	27.0	51.3	...	...
Spain	...	...	211.8	216.8	221.7	...	...
Sweden	189.2	190.0	207.1	197.7	189.8	198.1	5
Switzerland	396.5	497.8	551.5	526.6	462.7	338.8	-15
Turkey	...	...	...	...	...	...	...
Ukraine	...	...	...	...	...	...	...
UK: England & Wales	1240.7	1156.7	960.4	903.6	842.5	765.1	-38
UK: Northern Ireland	608.6	529.3	442.5	476.3	471.3	513.6	-16
UK: Scotland	667.7	613.9	547.6	557.7	528.0	478.7	-28
Mean	335	330	306	314	299	279	
Median	220	236	245	219	253	238	
Minimum	13	11	8	11	11	11	
Maximum	1241	1157	960	904	842	765	

Table 1.2.1.13: Offences per 100 000 population – Drug offences: Total

	1995 R11DR95	1996 R11DR96	1997 R11DR97	1998 R11DR98	1999 R11DR99	2000 R11DR00	% change 1995-2000
Albania	11.1	12.0	1.5	13.3	9.9	15.5	40
Armenia	18.3	14.6	17.1	19.0	14.3	14.4	-21
Austria	144.7	185.2	208.2	196.6	201.3	223.0	54
Belgium	323.7	381.7	463.2	434.7	438.0	...	...
Bulgaria	0.2	2.3	5.2	9.3	10.1	9.9	> 1000
Croatia	15.6	51.2	79.5	117.4	152.0	171.4	> 1000
Cyprus	21.3	24.8	32.1	38.1	33.4	38.1	79
Czech Republic	11.0	19.8	27.7	50.9	72.0	40.1	267
Denmark	15.0	17.5	14.2	18.3	15.6	17.1	14
Estonia	3.4	7.8	7.8	16.2	20.6	110.4	> 1000
Finland	177.3	153.6	162.1	183.8	226.3	260.2	47
France	136.7	137.2	149.4	159.0	173.7	176.1	29
Georgia	...	23.4	27.1	27.8	31.4	48.6	...
Germany	193.7	228.0	249.9	264.1	275.7	297.0	53
Greece	27.9	40.6	56.7	62.3	63.3	99.6	257
Hungary	4.2	4.3	9.2	20.3	28.1	34.0	715
Ireland	106.9	79.4	113.3	151.7	190.1	221.1	107
Italy	66.8	67.9	72.1	74.8	78.2	...	...
Latvia	10.7	14.5	17.2	15.9	21.1	27.2	154
Lithuania	10.8	14.0	17.3	17.0	19.2	25.6	138
Luxembourg	186.4	207.8	191.1	193.4	217.9	280.3	50
Malta	...	...	27.7	75.7	71.5	...	...
Moldova	12.2	16.3	18.1	19.7	47.4	45.8	276
Netherlands	...	...	...	49.0	48.1	47.2	...
Norway	535.2	626.6	784.1	874.7	919.3	982.5	84
Poland	11.1	17.5	20.5	42.5	40.4	50.2	353
Portugal	64.4	62.2	59.3	70.3	82.0	65.0	1
Romania	1.6	2.6	3.6	2.8	2.9	2.5	54
Russia	53.9	65.4	126.1	129.4	147.7	166.8	210
Slovakia	...	...	...	...	...	...	...
Slovenia	23.3	34.5	49.8	50.2	57.4	72.0	209
Spain	...	...	...	...	...	...	...
Sweden	322.6	348.5	342.7	356.0	411.7	365.4	13
Switzerland	586.1	592.2	625.2	632.8	612.3	641.1	9
Turkey	4.0	4.3	4.6	4.0	5.1	5.3	31
Ukraine	70.6	59.0	69.5	71.9	77.4	82.3	17
UK: England & Wales	41.0	42.5	44.7	259.5	232.0	215.4	425
UK: Northern Ireland	88.8	67.8	68.3	86.3	105.6	89.1	0
UK: Scotland	483.0	466.2	569.2	607.5	613.6	603.6	25
Mean	111	117	132	146	156	163	
Median	34	42	53	70	72	77	
Minimum	0	2	1	3	3	3	
Maximum	586	627	784	875	919	983	

Table 1.2.1.14: Offences per 100 000 population – Drug offences: Drug trafficking

	1995 R11DT95	1996 R11DT96	1997 R11DT97	1998 R11DT98	1999 R11DT99	2000 R11DT00	% change 1995-2000
Albania	...	3.0	...	...	...	...	...
Armenia	...	...	...	...	...	...	...
Austria	25.6	27.4	32.9	32.1	31.0	18.5	-28
Belgium	72.3	86.4	112.2	101.2	100.4	...	...
Bulgaria	...	...	...	...	...	...	...
Croatia	0.1	2.0	3.2	2.7	2.4	3.3	> 1000
Cyprus	21.3	24.8	32.1	38.1	33.4	38.1	79
Czech Republic	9.7	15.4	23.3	40.4	59.3	32.0	231
Denmark	5.6	6.7	3.2	3.4	2.4	4.2	-24
Estonia	0.8	2.0	2.1	8.1	12.5	21.4	> 1000
Finland	...	...	...	...	...	...	...
France	9.8	8.9	14.3	20.4	21.4	7.2	-26
Georgia	...	3.0	3.2	4.0	4.3	15.3	...
Germany	7.3	8.0	8.5	9.0	9.9	9.8	35
Greece	...	...	...	...	...	...	...
Hungary	0.5	0.2	0.5	1.2	3.8	5.7	> 1000
Ireland	21.5	25.0	44.0	47.6	52.5	44.9	109
Italy	...	...	...	...	...	...	...
Latvia	...	...	...	...	...	...	...
Lithuania	...	...	...	...	...	...	...
Luxembourg	...	...	...	...	...	28.8	...
Malta	...	...	9.7	22.8	25.7	...	...
Moldova	...	2.0	2.6	2.5	5.1	8.3	...
Netherlands	...	...	...	...	...	...	...
Norway	273.2	312.0	367.0	389.7	399.7	430.7	58
Poland	0.7	1.3	2.6	5.9	5.6	4.8	556
Portugal	45.2	38.9	33.9	35.3	40.8	32.0	-29
Romania	...	...	...	...	...	...	...
Russia	48.9	60.8	119.3	123.5	141.2	159.9	227
Slovakia	...	...	...	...	...	...	...
Slovenia	15.8	23.2	32.3	34.3	38.5	50.0	216
Spain	38.0	38.4	35.8	34.5	31.0	27.6	-27
Sweden	70.6	67.2	62.1	60.0	59.3	45.2	-36
Switzerland	105.4	112.5	112.0	111.5	110.1	99.6	-6
Turkey	...	...	...	...	...	...	...
Ukraine	...	...	...	...	...	...	...
UK: England & Wales	41.0	42.5	44.7	41.6	38.0	37.6	-8
UK: Northern Ireland	22.3	12.7	10.9	11.9	11.9	14.0	-37
UK: Scotland	155.5	135.2	158.4	163.9	166.9	168.3	8
Mean	45	42	51	54	56	54	
Median	22	23	32	34	31	28	
Minimum	0	0	0	1	2	3	
Maximum	273	312	367	390	400	431	

Notes on tables 1.2.1.1 to 1.2.1.14

Albania: For 1997, the data was not correct since the police statistics did not include all the crime for that year, because the police and other state institutions were not functioning normally.

France: Data for metropolitan France (i.e. excluding the overseas territories). Police statistics refer to cases sent to the prosecutors. According to French legal categories, "contraventions" are excluded. Although some of them should have been included to follow the Sourcebook definitions (see assault).

Greece: There is a discrepancy between data appearing in the European Sourcebook 1999 and the present one. This is due to the fact that the data previously used were provisional figures.

Ireland: 1999 Statistics cover only nine months (January to September inclusive) due to the introduction of a new IT system.

Italy: Data reported in the table refers to the offences recorded and sent to the prosecuting authority.

Portugal: Until 1993, each of the main three police forces in the country produced their own statistics, using different statistical rules. In January 1993, a new integrated statistical system came into effect, introducing a common standard list of offences and identical recording rules for all police forces. However, multiple recording offences is a problem which, so far, has not been satisfactorily resolved, as a substantial amount of the offences registered by two of the police forces are subsequently passed to the third one, "Polícia Judiciária", (the criminal police) for investigation. Due to practical difficulties in the registration of cases handed over to "Polícia Judiciária", this source of error persisted until at least 1998.

UK: England & Wales, UK: Northern Ireland: Change in the counting rules has had different impacts on different offences and offence groups, and hence figures before and after 1 April 1998 cannot be directly compared.

UK: England & Wales: 1998 refers to 1998/1999 financial year ending March, 1999 to 1999/2000, 2000 to 2000/2001.

Notes on table 1.2.1.1: total

Greece: Total offences: breaches of public order regulations excluded when penalty is below 30 days or between 30 and 587 Euros.

Ireland: The offence total for 2000 is not comparable to the indictable offence total of previous years since criminal damage offences are no longer included in total offences.

Luxembourg: Traffic offences defined as criminal by the law are included before 2000 but excluded from 2000.

Russia: Police usually refuse to initiate cases if the damage is small (less than 80 Euros).

Notes on table 1.2.1.2: traffic offences

Czech Republic: As traffic offences are not defined as offences in their own right, it is not possible to differentiate them from the total.

Estonia: Since 23 January 1999, repeat drink driving (two times or more during the last 12 months) is punishable as a criminal offence (previously it was an administrative offence). This has resulted in a substantial increase in the number of recorded criminal traffic offences.

Portugal: Traffic offences include driving under the influence of alcohol and, after 1998, driving without a driving licence.

Notes on table 1.2.1.3: intentional homicide (total)

Sweden: Intentional homicide – Total: the data are considered unreliable.

Notes on table 1.2.1.4: intentional homicide (completed)
Germany: Assault leading to death is now included. As the European Sourcebook 1999 excluded this item, the new figures differ slightly from the previous figures for 1995/1996.
Netherlands: Although "assault leading to death" is excluded, "non-negligent manslaughter" is included. A tendency to handle some cases (which will, in most other countries be seen as an assault (or even a threat)) as an attempted homicide probably explains the high number of homicide attempts.
Portugal: The fact that statistical data are collected shortly after the offence is reported to the police may inflate the true figures for homicide. From January 1998, deaths not likely to be intentional homicides (suicide, accident) have been classified under another heading.
Sweden: Completed: Data is provided from vital statistics.

Notes on table 1.2.1.6: assault
Bulgaria: Police figures refer only to cases where serious injury was inflicted.
Finland: Since 1995, the scope of assault was widened (to include offences commited in private places) and the definition of assault was broadened to include events where only pain or damage to health was caused regardless of whether or not there was direct physical contact.
France: Assault where the bodily injury only resulted in loss of the ability to work for less than 8 days are excluded from police statistics if there is no other aggravating circumstance.
Germany: The definition of assault has changed compared to European Sourcebook 1999 (assault leading to death is no longer included).
Lithuania: Some intentional body injuries (e.g. act of terrorism, hooliganism) are not included.
Norway: Change in definition from the last European Sourcebook 1999 (earlier: assault as a less serious crime).
Spain: Since 1997, domestic violence is included in assault and is the main explanatory factor for the increase registered in this offence.
UK: England & Wales: Assault on a constable and common assault are included in this category from 1998/1999 onwards. From 1 April 1999 racially aggravated offences are included.

Notes on table 1.2.1.7: rape
In the following countries the definition of rape was widened: Croatia (1998), Finland (1998), Germany (1998), Italy (1996) and Spain (1996, 1999) to include rape within marriage.
Turkey: Adultery is also included in "rape" statistics.

Notes on table 1.2.1.8: robbery
Croatia: Muggings and pick pocketing are not recorded separately. They might be included within theft or robbery depending on whether force was used.
Germany: Extortion accompanied by violence or threat of violence is included.
Latvia: After 1 April 1999 different kind of thefts, which contain elements of violence, have been classified as robberies and included in the data.
Luxembourg: Including a few theft of cars with force. Attempts were excluded.
Spain: See comments on "theft" below.

Notes on table 1.2.1.9: total theft
Austria: Joyriding is now included in the definition of theft. As it was excluded in European Sourcebook 1999, the figures reported for 1995/1996 are higher.
Denmark: Theft of a vehicle is not part of "theft" in Denmark, since most of these offences are joy-riding. The figure of "theft of motor vehicle"= joyriding is therefore not included in the total theft figure.
Finland: Including unauthorised use of motor vehicle.
Germany: Unauthorised use of electricity included.
Luxembourg: Computed as aggravated theft + simple theft - completed robbery.

Slovenia: The large increases in the figures for theft and burglary between 1997 and 1998 are due to a change in the counting rules used by the police.
Spain: According to the Spanish Penal Code, the definition and the different categories of theft are slightly different from the ones used in the Sourcebook. Although we have tried to adapt the legal categories to the Sourcebook categories, some differences persist. This is one of the reasons of the high robbery rate registered by the police in Spain.
UK: England & Wales: Handling stolen goods is included within all theft.

Notes on table 1.2.1.10: theft of motor vehicle
Belgium: New figures for 1995/1996 including cars and motorcycles.
In the European Sourcebook 1999 police data for motor vehicle theft only referred to theft of car.
Denmark: The figure relates to joyriding (not included in total theft).
Greece: Theft of a motor vehicle includes joyriding only. All other thefts of motor vehicles are included in the general category of thefts.
Hungary: Joyriding included since 1997 only.
Lithuania: Data includes the theft of different forms of the transport: cars, bicycles, motorcycles, motor-rollers, boats, tractors, trucks, etc.
Luxembourg: data refers to vehicles "actually stolen" (attempts excluded).
Poland: Theft of cars only.
Russia: Theft of motor vehicle statistics are collected by State Auto Inspection.
Slovakia: Theft of cars only.
Ukraine: Theft of any vehicle (including a motorcycle, a bicycle, a motor boat etc.)

Notes on table 1.2.1.11: burglary (total)
Armenia: No data available as burglary is not mentioned in the Penal Code of Armenia.
Slovenia: Before 1998, several burglaries presumed to have been committed by the same burglar were recorded as one single so-called "continued" act of burglary. From 1998, a "continued" act was recorded only in cases where there was no doubt that they have been committed by the same burglar. This explains the rise in the figures.

Notes on table 1.2.1.12: domestic burglary
Russia: Data for domestic burglaries in 1995 was estimated from the total amount of thefts using the percentage of domestic burglaries.
Switzerland: Estimated data on the basis of results for the canton of Zurich only.

Notes on table 1.2.1.13: drug offences (total)
New offences about drug possession or drug trafficking were included in Albania (1998), Austria (1998), Czech Republic (2000), Finland (1999), Hungary (1999), Poland (1997, 2000) and UK: England & Wales (1999).
UK: England and Wales: For drugs offences, only trafficking figures were collected up to March 1998.

Notes on table 1.2.1.14: drug trafficking
Denmark: The figure of drug trafficking includes production and acquisition of drugs.
Croatia: The decrease in traffic offences from 1997 to 1998 is due to change of the offence definition.
Estonia: Rapid increase in 2000 mainly reflects the polices' increased efforts in tackling drug crime. (Recording procedures were not changed).
Germany: The definition of drug trafficking is not the same as the definition for the former category of serious drug trafficking in the European Sourcebook 1999.
Ireland: Drug trafficking = possession of drugs for sale or supply regardless of quantity.

1.2.2 Offenders

Table 1.2.2.1: Offenders per 100 000 population – Criminal offences: Total

	1995 R12TC95	1996 R12TC96	1997 R12TC97	1998 R12TC98	1999 R12TC99	2000 R12TC00	% change 1995-2000
Albania	234	170	103	168	172	178	-24
Armenia	231	247	292	254	234	242	5
Austria	2475	2515	2516	2530	2531	2451	-1
Belgium	...	...	...	...	...	...	...
Bulgaria	928	986	1254	862	774	697	-25
Croatia	836	757	681	592	636	684	-18
Cyprus	544	706	562	634	609	575	6
Czech Republic	1112	1149	1149	1256	1244	1268	14
Denmark	...	...	...	...	...	...	...
Estonia	694	738	720	687	777	929	34
Finland	6435	6509	6174	6301	6341	6764	5
France	1372	1387	1370	1351	1363	1417	3
Georgia	...	370	434	407	376	351	...
Germany	2589	2699	2771	2828	2754	2779	7
Greece	2665	2827	3018	3096	3118	3115	17
Hungary	1176	1190	1278	1372	1294	1212	3
Ireland	1101	1130	1061	1023	914	805	-27
Italy	1326	1380	1366	1414	1385	...	...
Latvia	1552	1531	1492	1499	1813	2087	35
Lithuania	625	608	699	697	693	692	11
Luxembourg	...	...	...	...	...	2917	...
Malta	...	...	...	760	841	...	...
Moldova	359	360	369	387	399	455	27
Netherlands	1598	1638	1730	1699	1691	1688	6
Norway	1566	1572	1565	1592	1667	1754	12
Poland	1098	989	1063	1024	942	1049	-4
Portugal	2151	2111	2110	2270	2372	2457	14
Romania	868	933	1107	1173	1066	1072	24
Russia	1077	1095	931	1008	1172	1193	11
Slovakia	842	844	814	843	863	891	6
Slovenia	1586	1722	1639	2037	2085	2268	43
Spain	489	512	491	495	514	528	8
Sweden	1068	957	962	968	782	977	-9
Switzerland	783	782	807	807	786	721	-8
Turkey	205	485	509	470	382	...	...
Ukraine	663	667	670	660	640	629	-5
UK: England & Wales	4070	4203	4062	4242	4060	4042	-1
UK: Northern Ireland	...	...	...	...	...	...	...
UK: Scotland	...	...	...	...	...	...	...
Mean	1385	1387	1387	1394	1391	1528	
Median	1088	989	1063	1016	928	1061	
Minimum	205	170	103	168	172	178	
Maximum	6435	6509	6174	6301	6341	6764	

Table 1.2.2.2: Offenders per 100 000 population – Criminal offences: Traffic offences

	1995 R12TT95	1996 R12TT96	1997 R12TT97	1998 R12TT98	1999 R12TT99	2000 R12TT00	% change 1995-2000
Albania	13	3	...	...	...	...	...
Armenia	...	...	...	...	...	...	...
Austria	544	529	527	531	539	517	-5
Belgium	...	...	...	...	...	...	...
Bulgaria	12	14	13	20	27	22	80
Croatia	172	158	146	59	55	57	-67
Cyprus	...	...	...	...	...	...	...
Czech Republic	...	...	...	...	...	...	...
Denmark	...	...	...	...	...	...	...
Estonia	29	22	28	28	65	127	342
Finland	2730	2663	2530	2654	2618	2791	2
France	...	...	...	...	...	...	...
Georgia	...	4	5	5	5	4	...
Germany	...	...	...	...	...	...	...
Greece	105	1046	1145	1245	1200	1419	> 1000
Hungary	213	173	171	178	171	161	-24
Ireland	0	0	1	1	1	1	223
Italy	3	2	2	2	2	...	...
Latvia	121	124	134	151	171	157	30
Lithuania	...	...	...	...	...	...	...
Luxembourg	...	...	...	...	...	...	...
Malta	...	...	...	...	...	...	...
Moldova	11	10	11	12	10	10	-13
Netherlands	235	260	271	268	270	281	19
Norway	560	530	529	537	532	542	-3
Poland	85	84	97	82	49	48	-44
Portugal	82	98	99	125	155	293	257
Romania	94	95	104	112	68	68	-28
Russia	...	...	...	...	...	...	...
Slovakia	...	...	...	...	...	...	...
Slovenia	89	82	82	63	72	76	-15
Spain	...	...	69	72	77	73	...
Sweden	262	240	252	245	207	262	0
Switzerland	...	...	...	...	...	...	...
Turkey	...	...	...	...	...	...	...
Ukraine	18	18	18	19	16	14	-22
UK: England & Wales	1618	1606	1586	1601	1522	1476	-9
UK: Northern Ireland	...	...	...	...	...	...	...
UK: Scotland	...	...	...	...	...	...	...
Mean	333	353	355	364	356	400	
Median	94	97	102	97	75	127	
Minimum	0	0	1	1	1	1	
Maximum	2730	2663	2530	2654	2618	2791	

Table 1.2.2.3: Offenders per 100 000 population – Intentional homicide: Total

	1995 R12HO95	1996 R12HO96	1997 R12HO97	1998 R12HO98	1999 R12HO99	2000 R12HO00	% change 1995-2000
Albania	20	22	28	28	26	21	5
Armenia	...	...	...	...	...	...	...
Austria	2	2	2	2	1	2	0
Belgium	...	...	...	...	...	...	...
Bulgaria	8	8	7	7	7	6	-25
Croatia	9	8	7	7	7	6	-33
Cyprus	1	1	2	3	3	1	0
Czech Republic	3	3	3	3	3	3	0
Denmark	...	...	...	...	...	...	...
Estonia	20	18	18	14	12	13	-35
Finland	10	11	10	9	9	10	0
France	4	4	4	4	3	3	-25
Georgia	...	19	17	20	16	16	...
Germany	6	6	5	5	4	4	-33
Greece	3	3	3	3	3	3	0
Hungary	4	4	4	4	4	3	-15
Ireland	1	1	1	1	1	1	19
Italy	4	4	4	4	4	...	...
Latvia	12	11	11	10	9	10	-17
Lithuania	13	11	9	9	8	8	-39
Luxembourg	...	...	...	...	...	...	...
Malta	...	...	...	1	1	1	...
Moldova	7	6	7	6	5	9	35
Netherlands	17	17	...	...	...	...	...
Norway	2	1	1	1	1	1	-50
Poland	4	3	3	3	3	4	0
Portugal	...	...	...	...	...	...	...
Romania	...	...	...	...	...	...	...
Russia	...	16	16	17	18	18	...
Slovakia	...	...	...	...	...	...	...
Slovenia	5	6	4	4	4	5	0
Spain	3	3	2	3	3	4	33
Sweden	4	4	3	3	3	5	25
Switzerland	2	3	3	3	3	2	0
Turkey	...	...	...	...	...	...	...
Ukraine	8	8	8	9	9	10	25
UK: England & Wales	2	2	2	2	2	2	0
UK: Northern Ireland	...	...	...	...	...	...	...
UK: Scotland	...	...	...	...	...	...	...
Mean	7	7	7	7	6	6	
Median	4	5	4	4	4	4	
Minimum	1	1	1	1	1	1	
Maximum	20	22	28	28	26	21	

Table 1.2.2.4:   Offenders per 100 000 population – Intentional homicide: Completed

	1995 R12HC95	1996 R12HC96	1997 R12HC97	1998 R12HC98	1999 R12HC99	2000 R12HC00	% change 1995-2000
Albania	9	9	20	15	14	9	0
Armenia	...	...	...	...	...	...	...
Austria	...	...	...	...	...	...	...
Belgium	...	...	...	...	...	...	...
Bulgaria	4	4	4	4	4	4	0
Croatia	4	3	3	3	3	3	-25
Cyprus	0	1	1	2	1	1	100
Czech Republic	2	2	...	...	...	...	...
Denmark	...	...	...	...	...	...	...
Estonia	16	15	14	11	10	10	-37
Finland	3	4	3	3	3	4	33
France	3	3	2	2	2	2	-33
Georgia	...	7	8	10	7	7	...
Germany	...	...	...	...	...	...	...
Greece	...	...	...	...	...	...	...
Hungary	3	3	3	3	3	2	-33
Ireland	1	1	1	1	1	1	0
Italy	1	1	1	1	1	...	...
Latvia	7	7	7	7	6	6	-15
Lithuania	11	9	8	8	7	7	-36
Luxembourg	...	...	...	...	...	...	...
Malta	...	...	...	1	1	1	...
Moldova	...	...	...	...	...	...	...
Netherlands	...	...	...	1	...	...	...
Norway	1	1	1	1	1	1	0
Poland	...	...	...	...	...	...	...
Portugal	3	2	3	3	2	2	-33
Romania	...	...	...	...	...	...	...
Russia	...	...	...	...	...	...	...
Slovakia	...	...	...	...	...	...	...
Slovenia	2	2	2	1	1	2	0
Spain	...	...	...	...	...	...	...
Sweden	1	1	1	1	1	1	0
Switzerland	...	...	...	...	...	...	...
Turkey	...	4	4	4	4	...	...
Ukraine	7	8	7	8	8	9	28
UK: England & Wales	1	1	1	1	1	1	0
UK: Northern Ireland	...	...	...	...	...	...	...
UK: Scotland	...	...	...	...	...	...	...
Mean	4	4	5	4	4	4	
Median	3	3	3	3	3	2	
Minimum	0	1	1	1	1	1	
Maximum	16	15	20	15	14	10	

Table 1.2.2.5: Offenders per 100 000 population – Assault

	1995 R12AS95	1996 R12AS96	1997 R12AS97	1998 R12AS98	1999 R12AS99	2000 R12AS00	% change 1995-2000
Albania	9	8	5	5	6	5	-41
Armenia	25	31	37	38	37	41	64
Austria	365	351	343	341	340	293	-20
Belgium	...	...	...	...	...	...	...
Bulgaria	14	14	16	5	5	4	-74
Croatia	26	28	32	27	25	24	-6
Cyprus	24	19	21	16	22	13	-46
Czech Republic	65	65	64	69	63	63	-3
Denmark	...	...	...	...	...	...	...
Estonia	18	20	19	14	16	16	-9
Finland	385	461	445	469	487	489	27
France	97	103	112	119	126	136	40
Georgia	...	22	23	20	19	18	...
Germany	349	367	387	410	431	447	28
Greece	72	69	69	73	72	74	3
Hungary	64	59	63	64	61	59	-8
Ireland	12	12	13	15	10	35	191
Italy	37	40	42	45	50	...	...
Latvia	26	22	23	19	19	19	-26
Lithuania	17	19	19	20	21	22	27
Luxembourg	...	...	...	...	...	...	...
Malta	...	...	...	96	105	150	...
Moldova	9	8	8	7	7	8	-6
Netherlands	117	130	170	167	180	188	60
Norway	26	24	24	24	25	26	0
Poland	73	77	84	79	75	84	14
Portugal	426	441	460	509	506	534	25
Romania	30	31	36	30	30	32	6
Russia	...	27	24	24	24	27	...
Slovakia	...	...	...	...	...	...	...
Slovenia	26	27	25	23	23	25	-4
Spain	...	...	16	22	24	26	...
Sweden	142	124	115	124	116	125	-12
Switzerland	48	53	57	58	64	65	35
Turkey	...	135	141	156	161	...	...
Ukraine	34	34	36	36	36	38	12
UK: England & Wales	253	263	283	308	290	321	27
UK: Northern Ireland	...	...	...	...	...	...	...
UK: Scotland	...	...	...	...	...	...	...
Mean	100	100	100	104	105	110	
Median	35	34	37	38	37	38	
Minimum	9	8	5	5	5	4	
Maximum	426	461	460	509	506	534	

Table 1.2.2.6: Offenders per 100 000 population – Rape

	1995 R12RA95	1996 R12RA96	1997 R12RA97	1998 R12RA98	1999 R12RA99	2000 R12RA00	% change 1995-2000
Albania	4	4	1	2	2	3	-27
Armenia	...	...	...	...	...	...	...
Austria	7	7	8	8	8	9	27
Belgium	...	...	...	...	...	...	...
Bulgaria	10	9	9	11	9	9	-12
Croatia	3	4	2	2	3	3	15
Cyprus	3	2	3	3	3	2	-54
Czech Republic	5	5	4	5	4	4	-33
Denmark	...	...	...	...	...	...	...
Estonia	6	4	6	3	2	3	-50
Finland	5	5	6	6	7	7	32
France	10	10	11	10	10	9	-7
Georgia	...	4	3	3	3	4	...
Germany	6	6	6	7	7	7	27
Greece	2	1	2	2	2	2	15
Hungary	3	3	2	2	2	2	-39
Ireland	19	18	22	22	16	18	-9
Italy	2	2	3	3	3	...	...
Latvia	8	7	6	5	5	7	-14
Lithuania	5	4	4	4	6	5	-13
Luxembourg	...	...	...	...	...	...	...
Malta	...	...	...	0	0	0	...
Moldova	4	4	5	4	3	5	23
Netherlands	...	...	...	...	7	6	...
Norway	1	1	1	1	1	2	5
Poland	5	4	4	4	4	4	-12
Portugal	6	5	6	5	4	4	-30
Romania	7	7	6	6	7	6	-11
Russia	...	7	6	5	5	5	...
Slovakia	...	...	...	...	...	...	...
Slovenia	4	3	4	4	4	6	44
Spain	3	...	2	2	2	2	-22
Sweden	3	2	2	3	2	3	-1
Switzerland	3	3	4	4	4	4	28
Turkey	...	20	23	22	17	...	...
Ukraine	3	3	3	3	2	2	-37
UK: England & Wales	3	3	4	4	4	4	24
UK: Northern Ireland	...	...	...	...	...	...	...
UK: Scotland	...	...	...	...	...	...	...
Mean	5	5	6	5	5	5	
Median	4	4	4	4	4	4	
Minimum	1	1	1	0	0	0	
Maximum	19	20	23	22	17	18	

Table 1.2.2.7: Offenders per 100 000 population – Robbery

	1995 R12RO95	1996 R12RO96	1997 R12RO97	1998 R12RO98	1999 R12RO99	2000 R12RO00	% change 1995-2000
Albania	12	10	11	20	17	15	24
Armenia	...	...	...	...	...	...	...
Austria	14	14	14	17	14	13	-10
Belgium	...	...	...	...	...	...	...
Bulgaria	42	41	47	52	43	40	-5
Croatia	11	12	11	7	6	6	-42
Cyprus	4	2	...	3	4	6	30
Czech Republic	24	25	25	23	24	23	-4
Denmark	...	...	...	...	...	...	...
Estonia	83	87	82	72	89	92	11
Finland	32	30	26	31	30	37	17
France	35	37	38	38	39	39	10
Georgia	...	17	17	18	16	20	...
Germany	46	50	53	51	49	47	2
Greece	7	5	5	8	9	7	-2
Hungary	19	19	20	17	16	17	-11
Ireland	66	69	53	41	31	35	-46
Italy	15	16	16	19	22	...	...
Latvia	116	118	102	89	111	134	16
Lithuania	28	31	38	36	34	38	36
Luxembourg	...	...	...	...	...	32	...
Malta	...	...	...	12	11	11	...
Moldova	26	27	...	...	...	...	...
Netherlands	44	43	37	36	42	44	0
Norway	4	4	4	4	6	7	80
Poland	33	32	36	35	43	52	58
Portugal	104	112	120	201	259	312	199
Romania	13	15	20	17	16	18	38
Russia	...	67	63	68	78	74	...
Slovakia	...	...	...	...	...	...	...
Slovenia	24	44	23	22	31	31	32
Spain	44	48	45	44	46	48	9
Sweden	10	10	9	11	11	15	43
Switzerland	18	22	23	25	28	24	37
Turkey	...	3	3	4	3	...	...
Ukraine	24	24	25	25	25	26	6
UK: England & Wales	20	23	22	21	21	24	20
UK: Northern Ireland	...	...	...	...	...	...	...
UK: Scotland	...	...	...	...	...	...	...
Mean	33	34	34	34	38	43	
Median	24	25	25	23	25	28	
Minimum	4	2	3	3	3	6	
Maximum	116	118	120	201	259	312	

Table 1.2.2.8: Offenders per 100 000 population – Theft: Total

	1995 R12TH95	1996 R12TH96	1997 R12TH97	1998 R12TH98	1999 R12TH99	2000 R12TH00	% change 1995-2000
Albania	92	63	31	54	52	45	-51
Armenia	55	57	66	49	57	62	14
Austria	394	410	396	408	410	433	10
Belgium	...	...	...	...	...	...	...
Bulgaria	572	597	814	776	575	622	9
Croatia	228	187	139	125	127	132	-42
Cyprus	203	313	...	317	288	...	...
Czech Republic	463	454	426	438	398	399	-14
Denmark	...	...	...	...	...	...	...
Estonia	387	404	370	347	368	406	5
Finland	1564	1573	1496	1534	1517	1675	7
France	411	408	380	367	345	339	-17
Georgia	...	187	187	194	193	180	...
Germany	972	1010	1010	987	910	869	-11
Greece	83	59	67	77	80	77	-7
Hungary	431	466	494	512	430	370	-14
Ireland	779	781	779	734	545	577	-26
Italy	192	186	176	181	168	...	...
Latvia	959	903	847	843	1223	1426	49
Lithuania	352	308	307	296	287	325	-8
Luxembourg	...	...	...	...	...	455	...
Malta	...	...	...	165	222	229	...
Moldova	181	185	191	199	203	236	31
Netherlands	708	685	688	680	632	605	-15
Norway	312	334	318	307	313	328	5
Poland	338	268	275	274	253	269	-21
Portugal	337	318	315	330	324	340	1
Romania	361	382	438	416	303	339	-6
Russia	...	414	354	361	471	448	...
Slovakia	...	...	...	...	...	...	...
Slovenia	536	563	507	663	759	845	58
Spain	188	196	180	171	177	176	-6
Sweden	399	353	357	364	260	319	-20
Switzerland	518	515	524	522	477	440	-15
Turkey	...	96	96	89	84	...	...
Ukraine	289	270	249	249	256	278	-4
UK: England & Wales	549	529	433	524	513	490	-11
UK: Northern Ireland	...	...	...	...	...	...	...
UK: Scotland	...	...	...	...	...	...	...
Mean	443	421	416	411	401	443	
Median	387	367	357	347	313	340	
Minimum	55	57	31	49	52	45	
Maximum	1564	1573	1496	1534	1517	1675	

Table 1.2.2.9: Offenders per 100 000 population – Theft: Theft of a motor vehicle

	1995 R12TV95	1996 R12TV96	1997 R12TV97	1998 R12TV98	1999 R12TV99	2000 R12TV00	% change 1995-2000
Albania	3	3	2	8	8	5	81
Armenia	2	3	3	2	2	2	1
Austria	27	26	25	23	25	28	5
Belgium	...	...	...	...	...	...	...
Bulgaria	...	1	0	1	2	1	...
Croatia	28	23	18	13	17	20	-29
Cyprus	18	23	20	23	28	28	55
Czech Republic	52	51	50	47	39	37	-29
Denmark	...	...	...	...	...	...	...
Estonia	43	...	...	...	...	...	...
Finland	...	185	172	185	196	223	...
France	67	66	59	55	50	48	-29
Georgia	...	10	11	13	13	14	...
Germany	65	61	56	49	44	39	-40
Greece	14	6	9	9	12	12	-15
Hungary	10	12	16	13	12	9	-11
Ireland	49	59	69	68	85	24	-50
Italy	29	27	23	23	20	...	...
Latvia	147	103	88	106	130	124	-15
Lithuania	18	20	24	18	16	18	3
Luxembourg	...	...	...	...	...	...	...
Malta	...	...	...	9	22	19	...
Moldova	...	...	...	...	...	...	...
Netherlands	...	...	...	...	...	...	...
Norway	22	24	21	18	22	22	-1
Poland	14	14	15	15	15	14	1
Portugal	28	31	33	39	37	34	24
Romania	4	4	5	5	4	4	3
Russia	...	...	...	...	...	...	...
Slovakia	...	...	...	...	...	...	...
Slovenia	65	61	56	61	48	27	-58
Spain	27	31	35	37	41	42	53
Sweden	56	46	46	46	41	46	-17
Switzerland	...	...	...	...	...	...	...
Turkey	...	9	7	7	7	...	...
Ukraine	...	2	2	2	1	1	...
UK: England & Wales	32	31	29	28	28	26	-18
UK: Northern Ireland	...	...	...	...	...	...	...
UK: Scotland	...	...	...	...	...	...	...
Mean	36	35	34	33	35	33	
Median	28	25	23	18	22	23	
Minimum	2	1	0	1	1	1	
Maximum	147	185	172	185	196	223	

Table 1.2.2.10:   Offenders per 100 000 population – Theft: Burglary: Total

	1995 R12BU95	1996 R12BU96	1997 R12BU97	1998 R12BU98	1999 R12BU99	2000 R12BU00	% change 1995-2000
Albania	55	35	7	19	20	17	-70
Armenia	...	...	...	...	...	...	...
Austria	93	99	87	86	86	80	-14
Belgium	...	...	...	...	...	...	...
Bulgaria	220	209	279	284	180	216	-2
Croatia	85	84	64	55	51	52	-39
Cyprus	102	196	...	194	157	134	31
Czech Republic	191	181	163	154	136	127	-34
Denmark	...	...	...	...	...	...	...
Estonia	219	244	201	191	199	213	-3
Finland	...	362	307	277	269	266	...
France	82	85	75	68	59	57	-30
Georgia	...	...	...	...	...	...	...
Germany	119	118	115	109	100	91	-23
Greece	42	29	33	37	38	25	-40
Hungary	148	152	148	142	113	99	-33
Ireland	268	276	263	239	148	169	-37
Italy	34	33	31	31	26	...	...
Latvia	...	...	...	...	...	...	...
Lithuania	...	...	...	...	...	...	...
Luxembourg	...	...	...	...	...	...	...
Malta	...	...	...	23	24	33	...
Moldova	18	19	21	22	21	24	30
Netherlands	387	353	335	342	299	291	-25
Norway	107	106	92	87	90	87	-18
Poland	167	163	164	161	149	145	-13
Portugal	129	130	128	115	108	101	-21
Romania	75	74	86	75	53	51	-32
Russia	...	...	...	...	...	...	...
Slovakia	...	...	...	...	...	...	...
Slovenia	236	226	185	293	317	341	44
Spain	90	95	87	81	81	...	...
Sweden	72	60	59	57	45	51	-29
Switzerland	115	125	120	146	127	118	3
Turkey	...	...	...	...	...	...	...
Ukraine	...	...	...	...	...	...	...
UK: England & Wales	122	116	113	108	102	93	-24
UK: Northern Ireland	...	...	...	...	...	...	...
UK: Scotland	...	...	...	...	...	...	...
Mean	132	143	132	131	115	120	
Median	111	118	114	109	101	96	
Minimum	18	19	7	19	20	17	
Maximum	387	362	335	342	317	341	

Table 1.2.2.11: Offenders per 100 000 population – Theft: Burglary: Domestic Burglary

	1995 R12BD95	1996 R12BD96	1997 R12BD97	1998 R12BD98	1999 R12BD99	2000 R12BD00	% change 1995-2000
Albania	11	8	4	9	10	9	-25
Armenia	...	...	...	...	...	...	...
Austria	18	18	18	18	15	19	1
Belgium	...	...	...	...	...	...	...
Bulgaria	...	...	...	...	...	...	...
Croatia	18	16	12	7	8	7	-62
Cyprus	...	...	...	...	...	...	...
Czech Republic	29	29	25	24	21	21	-29
Denmark	...	...	...	...	...	...	...
Estonia	67	...	...	...	...	...	...
Finland	...	76	66	64	58	63	...
France	38	40	34	31	26	25	-35
Georgia	...	...	...	...	...	...	...
Germany	41	41	41	41	38	35	-15
Greece	...	...	...	...	...	...	...
Hungary	30	34	39	40	33	30	-1
Ireland	...	...	...	...	...	...	...
Italy	34	33	31	31	26	...	...
Latvia	...	...	...	...	...	...	...
Lithuania	45	47	48	37	42	43	-5
Luxembourg	...	...	...	...	...	48	...
Malta	...	...	...	...	...	...	...
Moldova	...	...	...	...	...	...	...
Netherlands	...	...	...	...	...	...	...
Norway	24	25	22	20	19	19	-21
Poland	...	...	...	...	...	...	...
Portugal	60	62	63	57	53	46	-23
Romania	75	73	86	75	53	51	-32
Russia	...	...	...	...	...	...	...
Slovakia	...	...	...	...	...	...	...
Slovenia	12	13	12	10	18	...	...
Spain	...	...	...	20	20	...	...
Sweden	11	10	11	10	8	10	-6
Switzerland	...	...	...	...	...	...	...
Turkey	...	...	...	...	...	...	...
Ukraine	...	...	...	...	...	...	...
UK: England & Wales	59	57	59	58	55	49	-18
UK: Northern Ireland	...	...	...	...	...	...	...
UK: Scotland	...	...	...	...	...	...	...
Mean	36	36	36	32	30	32	
Median	32	34	33	31	26	30	
Minimum	11	8	4	7	8	7	
Maximum	75	76	86	75	58	63	

Table 1.2.2.12: Offenders per 100 000 population – Drug offences: Total

	1995 R12DR95	1996 R12DR96	1997 R12DR97	1998 R12DR98	1999 R12DR99	2000 R12DR00	% change 1995-2000
Albania	12	15	2	15	12	18	46
Armenia	19	16	17	20	14	14	-25
Austria	143	187	203	196	196	208	45
Belgium	...	...	...	...	...	...	...
Bulgaria	0	2	4	9	13	11	> 1000
Croatia	12	58	92	91	120	127	925
Cyprus	29	33	...	48	47	38	29
Czech Republic	...	...	...	...	...	...	...
Denmark	...	...	...	...	...	...	...
Estonia	1	4	6	9	13	44	> 1000
Finland	188	169	185	186	235	277	48
France	137	148	156	157	166	177	29
Georgia	...	41	43	51	49	82	...
Germany	151	179	198	216	226	246	62
Greece	42	60	84	96	96	109	162
Hungary	4	5	9	17	25	30	582
Ireland	107	79	113	152	190	221	107
Italy	83	84	88	87	93	...	...
Latvia	11	15	18	17	21	28	156
Lithuania	7	11	12	12	12	15	116
Luxembourg	...	...	...	...	...	393	...
Malta	...	...	...	178	189	164	...
Moldova	...	10	11	12	33	43	...
Netherlands	...	...	...	76	73	73	...
Norway	90	102	118	146	179	205	127
Poland	9	10	11	13	12	17	84
Portugal	96	93	89	102	113	99	3
Romania	5	5	4	3	2	2	-53
Russia	...	42	69	79	88	92	...
Slovakia	...	...	...	...	...	...	...
Slovenia	28	38	55	59	64	84	203
Spain	...	...	...	...	...	...	...
Sweden	103	92	115	125	113	135	31
Switzerland	586	592	625	633	612	641	9
Turkey	...	...	...	10	10	10	...
Ukraine	30	51	54	56	60	61	102
UK: England & Wales	166	169	200	220	202	175	6
UK: Northern Ireland	...	...	...	...	...	...	...
UK: Scotland	...	...	...	...	...	...	...
Mean	83	82	96	100	106	124	
Median	30	47	69	76	73	84	
Minimum	0	2	2	3	2	2	
Maximum	586	592	625	633	612	641	

Table 1.2.2.13: Offenders per 100 000 population – Drug offences: Drug trafficking

	1995 R12DT95	1996 R12DT96	1997 R12DT97	1998 R12DT98	1999 R12DT99	2000 R12DT00	% change 1995-2000
Albania	...	3	...	...	...	...	...
Armenia	...	...	...	...	...	...	...
Austria	27	31	35	34	30	18	-35
Belgium	...	...	...	...	...	...	...
Bulgaria	...	...	...	...	...	...	...
Croatia	0	4	7	5	5	6	> 1000
Cyprus	...	...	...	...	...	...	...
Czech Republic	...	...	...	...	...	...	...
Denmark	...	...	...	...	...	...	...
Estonia	0	1	2	5	7	8	> 1000
Finland	...	...	...	...	...	...	...
France	18	20	22	24	22	12	-32
Georgia	...	6	7	8	9	25	...
Germany	8	9	9	10	11	11	42
Greece	...	...	...	...	...	...	...
Hungary	1	0	1	1	4	5	648
Ireland	21	25	44	48	53	45	109
Italy	...	...	...	...	...	...	...
Latvia	...	...	...	...	...	...	...
Lithuania	...	...	...	...	...	...	...
Luxembourg	...	...	...	...	...	...	...
Malta	...	...	...	...	...	...	...
Moldova	...	...	2	2	3	6	...
Netherlands	...	...	...	...	...	...	...
Norway	57	66	78	92	110	124	116
Poland	1	1	1	2	2	2	338
Portugal	71	61	55	54	59	53	-25
Romania	...	...	...	...	...	...	...
Russia	...	...	...	...	...	...	...
Slovakia	...	...	...	...	...	...	...
Slovenia	20	27	37	42	43	60	203
Spain	...	...	52	49	45	42	...
Sweden	19	19	22	22	19	19	-3
Switzerland	105	112	112	111	110	100	-6
Turkey	...	...	...	5	5	...	...
Ukraine	...	...	...	...	...	...	...
UK: England & Wales	33	34	36	28	27	29	-11
UK: Northern Ireland	...	...	...	...	...	...	...
UK: Scotland	...	...	...	...	...	...	...
Mean	27	26	31	30	31	33	
Median	20	20	22	23	20	19	
Minimum	0	0	1	1	2	2	
Maximum	105	112	112	111	110	124	

Notes on tables 1.2.2.1 to 1.2.2.13

France: Data for metropolitan France (excluding the overseas territories).
Ireland: The counting unit here is the offence when at least one suspect is found.
Latvia: Data refers to persons who have been prosecuted.
UK: England & Wales: Suspected offenders = persons proceeded against + cautioned.
From 1 June 2000, the Crime and Disorder Act 1998 removed the use of cautions for persons under 18 nationally, and replaced them with reprimands and final warnings. Piloting of reprimands and final warnings began in seven areas from the end of September 1998. These have been included with cautions. It is thought that the centrally recorded data for these new disposals may be subject to a small amount of under recording.

Notes on table 1.2.2.1: total
Greece: The "total" in this table is smaller than that of table 1.2.1.1 because it only counts cases where the suspected offender was known during the month that the offence was recorded.

Notes on table 1.2.2.3: intentional homicide
Finland: Year 1995 intentional homicide: Assault leading to death is not included.

Notes on table 1.2.2.5: assault
Norway: Change of series compared with previous period (1990-1995)

Notes on table 1.2.2.7: robbery
Luxembourg: Offenders figures include attempts (excluded from offences figures).

Notes on table 1.2.2.8: total theft
Norway: Change of series compared with previous period (1990-1995)

Notes on table 1.2.2.12: drug offences: total
UK: England & Wales: The fall in the number of prosecutions and cautions for total drug offences between 1998 and 1999 probably reflects less use of stop and search and a consequent decline in the number of arrests.

Notes on table 1.2.2.13: drug offences: drug trafficking
Switzerland: Mixed cases (trafficking and consumption) are included.

Table 1.2.3.1: Percentage of female offenders - 1999

	Criminal offences: Total	Traffic offences	Intentional homicide: Total	Intentional homicide: Completed	Assault	Rape	Robbery	Theft: Total	Theft: Theft of a motor vehicle	Theft: Burglary: Total	Theft: Burglary: Domestic Burglary	Drug offences: Total	Drug offences: Drug trafficking
	P13TCW99	P13TTW99	P13HOW99	P13HCW99	P13ASW99	P13RAW99	P13ROW99	P13THW99	P13TVW99	P13BUW99	P13BDW99	P13DRW99	P13DTW99
Albania	1.2	...	2.2	3.4	3.6	...	0.2	0.2	0.3	0.3	0.0	...	...
Armenia	8.2	...	...	...	12.2	...	...	5.2	0.0	...	...	4.0	...
Austria	21.4	25.9	19.6	...	13.3	1.2	9.8	23.3	5.1	7.1	10.9	17.1	10.8
Belgium	...	...	...	...	...	...	...	...	...	...	...	...	...
Bulgaria	10.9	7.0	10.6	9.9	1.4	0.4	3.3	6.7	4.3	3.6	...	7.2	...
Croatia	10.4	11.7	7.6	7.9	3.3	0.0	4.0	6.6	0.8	4.7	8.4	8.6	1.2
Cyprus	...	...	...	...	...	...	...	...	...	...	...	...	...
Czech Republic	11.9	...	16.4	...	7.5	0	7.1	8.0	2.6	4.6	9.3	...	...
Denmark	...	...	...	...	...	...	...	...	...	...	...	...	...
Estonia	9.0	4.7	7.6	6.9	7.5	...	5.8	8.8	...	4.0	...	19.1	27.1
Finland	15.3	12.8	10.9	7.0	11.0	0.0	9.4	18.9	7.2	7.5	10.6	13.3	...
France	14	...	13.6	15.3	10.2	2.4	6.5	15.8	3.3	6.7	9.4	8.2	9.6
Georgia	1.8	20.2	3.0	5.5	1.3	0.0	2.6	1.5	2.9	...	...	4.5	8.6
Germany	23.1	...	12.2	...	13.6	1.2	9.0	31.4	5.0	8.8	13.3	12.2	11.6
Greece	15.2	9.4	2.0	...	11.2	1.8	3.8	10.4	2.4	8.7	...	7.4	...
Hungary	12.7	5.2	13.3	12.7	9.2	0.0	9.0	10.2	1.6	4.3	6.7	12.8	11.5
Ireland	1.3	0.0	0.0	0.0	0.5	0.0	0.0	1.2	...	0.4	...	9.9	...
Italy	...	...	...	...	...	...	...	...	...	...	...	...	...
Latvia	4.1	3.7	8.0	0.0	7.9	0.0	2.0	2.7	0.6	...	...	10.8	...
Lithuania	13.0	...	10.1	10.4	8.9	0.0	3.8	8.8	1.6	...	8.6	22.9	...
Luxembourg	...	...	...	...	...	...	...	...	...	...	...	...	...

	Criminal offences: Total	Traffic offences	Intentional homicide: Total	Intentional homicide: Completed	Assault	Rape	Robbery	Theft: Total	Theft: Theft of a motor vehicle	Theft: Burglary: Total	Theft: Burglary: Domestic Burglary	Drug offences: Total	Drug offences: Drug trafficking
	P13TCW99	P13TTW99	P13HOW99	P13HCW99	P13ASW99	P13RAW99	P13ROW99	P13THW99	P13TVW99	P13BUW99	P13BDW99	P13DRW99	P13DTW99
Malta	9.5	...	...	...	...	...	...	...	...	...	...	...	...
Moldova	11.2	2.1	11.2	...	8.9	...	...	7.6	...	4.2	...	15.4	...
Netherlands	11.8	8.7	...	...	10.5	0	6	16.1	...	6.6	...	12.2	...
Norway	16.0	12.4	0.0	0.0	6.0	0.0	8.0	26.9	8.4	7.2	10.8	19.8	17.4
Poland	9.1	9.4	12.8	...	7.7	0.6	4.6	5.1	1.2	2.4	...	12.3	8.1
Portugal	15.0	1.8	...	7.7	18.9	1.9	3.3	14.1	3.9	11.4	14.9	11.0	14.2
Romania	11.0	2.5	...	...	5.6	0.1	5.3	...	...	...	...	11.9	...
Russia	15.2	...	12.3	...	12.6	0.8	7.8	9.9	...	...	...	14.2	...
Slovakia	...	...	...	...	...	...	...	...	...	...	...	...	...
Slovenia	11.7	16.5	12.2	4.0	2.9	0.0	5.8	8.8	1.6	2.1	3.1	8.7	6.8
Spain	9.3	3.0	10.9	...	5.9	1.1	11.0	9.1	6.1	7.3	9.7	...	15.3
Sweden	17.6	9.3	10.8	13.1	9.3	0.0	4.2	26.7	5.7	6.6	8.4	14.3	13.2
Switzerland	14.6	...	12.1	...	10.1	0.0	8.1	16.1	...	5.8	...	14.5	3.0
Turkey	12.2	...	...	...	6.0	53.7	3.1	7.5	1.0	...	...	...	...
Ukraine	...	...	...	...	...	...	...	...	...	...	...	...	...
UK: England & Wales	16.4	12.0	10.4	11.4	16.5	0.8	8.1	23.4	5.6	6.0	7.4	11.7	16.6
UK: Northern Ireland	...	...	...	...	...	...	...	...	...	...	...	...	...
UK: Scotland	...	...	...	...	...	...	...	...	...	...	...	...	...
Mean	12	9	10	7	8	3	6	12	3	5	9	12	12
Median	12	9	11	7	9	0	6	9	3	6	9	12	12
Minimum	1	0	0	0	1	0	0	0	0	0	0	1	1
Maximum	23	26	20	15	19	54	11	31	8	11	15	23	27

Table 1.2.3.2: Percentage of minors among offenders - 1999

	Criminal offences: Total	Traffic offences	Intentional homicide: Total	Intentional homicide: Completed	Assault	Rape	Robbery	Theft: Total	Theft: Theft of a motor vehicle	Theft: Burglary: Total	Theft: Burglary: Domestic Burglary	Drug offences: Total	Drug offences: Drug trafficking
	P13TCM99	P13TTM99	P13HOM99	P13HCM99	P13ASM99	P13RAM99	P13ROM99	P13THM99	P13TVM99	P13BUM99	P13BDM99	P13DRM99	P13DT99
Albania	13.5	...	8.6	7.8	16.8	2.4	19.7	27.0	5.1	33.1	37.7	4.2	...
Armenia	6.0	...	...	...	6.4	...	...	16.3	16.2	...	...	0.2	...
Austria	16.0	6.2	4.9	...	17.0	13.8	37.5	30.4	40.6	33.3	29.6	29.0	15.0
Belgium	...	...	...	...	...	...	...	...	...	...	...	...	...
Bulgaria	12.0	2.3	4.2	4.0	2.4	13.3	16.7	9.6	73.0	12.3	...	14.4	...
Croatia	9.5	2.3	2.9	1.8	8.2	7.9	13.2	20.6	12.2	26.7	28.8	14.8	1.2
Cyprus	...	...	...	...	...	...	...	...	...	...	...	...	...
Czech Republic	13.7	...	1.9	...	9.4	11.9	27.0	16.4	23.2	35.0	31.7	...	...
Denmark	...	...	...	...	...	...	...	...	...	...	...	...	...
Estonia	16.3	1.4	7.6	8.3	6.6	19.4	23.1	23.1	...	28.6	...	8.2	9.3
Finland	11.7	5.4	5.1	4.3	14.3	4.2	32.2	19.6	27.0	19.7	16.6	9.1	...
France	21.3	...	7.5	6.6	15.5	20.5	39.9	33.3	40.5	33.7	33.0	19.9	12.8
Georgia	1.2	1.8	0.9	1.2	1.8	8.9	3.5	1.3	6.3	...	...	0.8	0.2
Germany	19.3	...	7.6	...	20.1	11.1	40.1	32.8	42.4	34.0	32.7	17.3	6.7
Greece	16.7	32.1	9.6	...	4.6	18.2	28.5	29.2	33.8	26.9	...	24.1	...
Hungary	8.4	1.5	4.4	5.8	7.4	13.1	28.5	14.6	15.1	18.0	16.6	17.7	22.8
Ireland	1.5	6.5	0.0	0.0	0.5	0.0	0.1	1.9	...	1.9	...	4.4	...
Italy	2.8	0.7	2.7	2.7	2.6	6.0	6.7	8.9	6.4	4.9	18.6	5.2	...
Latvia	6.5	0.6	5.8	0.0	3.1	7.0	7.8	6.8	8.4	...	...	1.3	...
Lithuania	13.3	...	7.0	7.7	5.1	17.3	26.6	21.1	26.4	...	25.9	3.6	...
Luxembourg	...	...	...	...	...	...	...	...	...	...	...	...	...

	Criminal offences: Total	Traffic offences	Intentional homicide: Total	Intentional homicide: Completed	Assault	Rape	Robbery	Theft: Total	Theft: Theft of a motor vehicle	Theft: Burglary: Total	Theft: Burglary: Domestic Burglary	Drug offences: Total	Drug offences: Drug trafficking
	P13TCM99	P13TTM99	P13HOM99	P13HCM99	P13ASM99	P13RAM99	P13ROM99	P13THM99	P13TVM99	P13BUM99	P13BDM99	P13DRM99	P13DT99
Malta	5.5	...	...	...	...	...	...	...	...	...	...	...	...
Moldova	13.8	1.4	5.6	...	6.0	12.7	...	21.5	...	23.2	...	10.8	...
Netherlands	17.9	2.2	...	...	18.0	16.5	32.5	23.1	...	26.5	...	3.6	...
Norway	14.8	6.6	3.7	6.3	14.7	24.6	47.7	29.9	32.8	22.0	18.3	11.2	8.3
Poland	14.5	1.9	7.1	...	20.9	10.0	26.7	28.6	15.0	33.6	...	19.1	12.7
Portugal	...	...	...	...	...	...	...	...	...	...	...	...	...
Romania	6.3	2.9	...	...	12.7	7.8	19.9	...	...	...	...	6.8	...
Russia	10.7	...	5.5	...	6.1	14.3	19.5	16.2	...	...	...	5.7	...
Slovakia	19.5	...	...	...	...	...	...	...	...	...	...	...	...
Slovenia	16.6	4.4	5.4	12.0	9.9	5.5	38.7	29.6	14.6	31.6	36.2	15.3	12.8
Spain	12.6	...	4.5	...	...	...	22.8	...	27.3	16.8	...	...	5.8
Sweden	11.8	4.1	2.6	2.4	14.5	4.9	21.8	18.4	21.3	14.9	15.6	4.1	3.8
Switzerland	28.8	...	6.0	...	16.4	8.0	38.4	26.6	...	25.7	...	11.8	6.0
Turkey	...	...	...	...	...	...	...	...	...	...	...	...	...
Ukraine	...	...	...	...	...	...	...	...	...	...	...	...	...
UK: England & Wales	11.2	2.0	7.3	7.9	18.2	9.0	42.3	31.2	45.3	34.4	29.9	12.6	5.3
UK: Northern Ireland	...	...	...	...	...	...	...	...	...	...	...	...	...
UK: Scotland	...	...	...	...	...	...	...	...	...	...	...	...	...
Mean	12	5	5	5	10	11	25	21	25	24	27	10	11
Median	13	2	5	5	9	11	27	21	23	27	29	9	8
Minimum	1	1	0	0	1	0	0	1	5	2	16	0	0
Maximum	29	32	10	12	21	25	48	33	73	35	38	29	38

Table 1.2.3.3: Percentage of aliens among offenders - 1999

	Criminal offences: Total	Traffic offences	Intentional homicide: Total	Intentional homicide Completed	Assault	Rape	Robbery	Theft: Total	Theft: Theft of a motor vehicle	Theft: Burglary: Total	Theft: Burglary: Domestic Burglary	Drug offences: Total	Drug offences: Drug trafficking
	P13TCA99	P13TTA99	P13HOA99	P13HCA99	P13ASA99	P13RAA99	P13ROA99	P13THA99	P13TVA99	P13BUA99	P13BDA99	P13DRA99	P13DTA99
Albania	1.1	...	0.7	1.3	0.5	0.0	0.3	0.7	1.7	1.0	1.2	0.5	...
Armenia	1.1	...	...	...	0.4	...	...	0.5	1.4	...	...	1.0	...
Austria	22.9	13.9	27.0	...	20.5	28.6	34.4	32.0	33.4	36.1	37.0	17.5	37.6
Belgium	...	...	...	...	...	...	...	...	...	...	...	...	...
Bulgaria	1.2	1.8	2.0	0.7	0.0	0.3	1.1	0.5	2.6	0.3	...	2.7	...
Croatia	5.6	6.4	2.9	5.3	1.3	3.6	2.9	4.6	2.6	6.1	8.7	10.6	2.9
Cyprus	23.9	...	14.3	22.2	16.5	31.6	28.6	25.0	...	22.4	...	24.6	...
Czech Republic	5.6	...	19.5	...	3.6	10.0	12.8	3.2	2.5	3.7	4.2	...	...
Denmark	...	...	...	...	...	...	...	...	...	...	...	...	...
Estonia	33.4	15.1	47.1	49.3	43.2	54.8	45.0	34.9	...	34.7	...	66.5	61.7
Finland	6.2	4.6	4.3	1.6	6.2	16.6	15.1	9.7	1.9	2.2	2.0	3.7	...
France	19.1	...	16.4	16.5	15.9	12.0	14.0	14.4	7.7	9.8	12.5	9.1	18.4
Georgia	0.9	7.5	0.9	1.7	1.1	0.6	1.6	0.5	0.8	...	...	2.4	9.2
Germany	25.8	...	28.6	...	22.1	32.4	31.4	21.8	18.3	19.0	17.7	21.1	27.9
Greece	6.1	15.4	28.7	...	4.4	23.6	29.7	30.9	23.7	32.4	...	9.4	...
Hungary	4.4	3.5	3.5	1.9	0.8	2.1	5.2	1.6	1.1	0.8	1.3	4.6	4.9
Ireland	...	...	...	...	...	...	...	...	...	...	...	...	...
Italy	...	...	...	...	...	...	...	...	...	...	...	...	...
Latvia	0.5	0.8	0.4	0.0	0.2	0.8	0.3	0.1	0.1	...	...	1.0	...
Lithuania	1.8	...	2.1	1.9	0.0	0.5	0.6	0.3	1.2	...	0.1	2.7	...
Luxembourg	...	...	...	...	...	...	...	...	...	...	...	...	...

Police statistics

	Criminal offences: Total	Traffic offences	Intentional homicide: Total	Intentional homicide: Completed	Assault	Rape	Robbery	Theft: Total	Theft: Theft of a motor vehicle	Theft: Burglary: Total	Theft: Burglary: Domestic Burglary	Drug offences: Total	Drug offences: Drug trafficking
	P13TCA99	P13TTA99	P13HOA99	P13HCA99	P13ASA99	P13RAA99	P13ROA99	P13THA99	P13TVA99	P13BUA99	P13BDA99	P13DRA99	P13DTA99
Malta	...	...	...	...	...	...	...	...	...	...	...	...	...
Moldova	1.7	0.9	4.7	...	2.2	2.0	...	1.3	...	1.8	...	1.6	...
Netherlands	...	...	...	...	...	...	...	...	...	...	...	...	...
Norway	11.3	9.3	...	...	...	...	...	...	...	...	...	...	...
Poland	1.7	2.1	2.3	...	0.3	0.7	1.3	0.4	0.9	0.3	...	1.6	2.5
Portugal	...	...	...	...	...	...	...	...	...	...	...	...	...
Romania	0.5	2.2	...	...	0.6	0.3	0.7	...	...	...	...	16.2	...
Russia	...	...	...	...	...	...	...	...	...	...	...	3.5	...
Slovakia	...	...	...	...	...	...	...	...	...	...	...	...	...
Slovenia	6.8	5.8	13.5	4.0	3.6	8.2	5.8	6.2	5.6	7.0	12.5	4.6	6.3
Spain	16.5	...	17.9	...	...	...	...	...	...	15.5	...	...	...
Sweden	...	...	...	...	...	...	...	...	...	...	...	...	...
Switzerland	54.3	...	63.3	...	55.4	58.3	59.0	57.4	...	59.8	...	38.7	40.2
Turkey	...	...	...	...	...	...	...	...	...	...	...	...	...
Ukraine	...	...	...	...	...	...	...	...	...	...	...	...	...
UK: England & Wales	...	...	...	...	...	...	...	...	...	...	...	...	...
UK: Northern Ireland	...	...	...	...	...	...	...	...	...	...	...	...	...
UK: Scotland	...	...	...	...	...	...	...	...	...	...	...	...	...
Mean	11	6	15	9	9	14	15	12	7	15	10	12	21
Median	6	5	9	2	2	6	6	4	2	7	6	5	14
Minimum	1	1	0	0	0	0	0	0	0	0	0	0	2
Maximum	54	15	63	49	55	58	59	57	33	60	37	66	62

Notes on tables 1.2.3.1 to 1.2.3.3

Austria, Bulgaria, Croatia, Czech Republic, Finland and Germany: Year of data: 2000
Other countries: Year of data: 1999 except for homicide in the Netherlands: Year of data 1998.

Notes on table 1.2.3.1 (females)
Turkey: Figures high because they include adultery.

Notes on table 1.2.3.2 (minors)
Portugal: Number of minors: The number of suspects under 18 cannot be determined from the statistical information sent by the police. The age brackets given are: under 16; 16 to 24; 25 and over.

1.2.4 Police staff

Table 1.2.4.1:   Police staff: Number of police officers per 100 000 population

	1995 R14OP95	1996 R14OP96	1997 R14OP97	1998 R14OP98	1999 R14OP99	2000 R14OP00	% change 1995-2000
Albania	...	...	...	...	...	418	...
Armenia	...	...	...	...	...	...	...
Austria	321	329	326	331	331	330	3
Belgium	352	356	360	357	363	367	4
Bulgaria	...	...	...	...	...	...	...
Croatia	495	506	535	540	538	532	8
Cyprus	519	517	550	546	543	540	4
Czech Republic	443	427	424	426	429	436	-1
Denmark	191	189	186	188	189	195	2
Estonia	331	322	302	282	249	254	-23
Finland	152	151	153	153	154	156	2
France	...	368	...	...	...	396	...
Georgia	...	576	606	631	596	560	...
Germany	...	...	...	...	...	...	...
Greece	402	418	419	430	463	482	20
Hungary	307	307	337	313	311	309	1
Ireland	300	298	299	303	305	307	2
Italy	...	530	525	533	544	...	...
Latvia	353	370	448	445	441	443	26
Lithuania	456	477	493	501	498	485	6
Luxembourg	...	...	...	...	...	...	...
Malta	...	...	...	455	446	439	...
Moldova	270	268	261	261	265	259	-4
Netherlands	249	253	256	257	262	...	...
Norway	180	182	181	180	186	192	7
Poland	257	267	261	257	259	261	1
Portugal	374	438	445	454	466	478	28
Romania	219	228	223	217	214	204	-7
Russia	...	...	...	...	...	1219	...
Slovakia	371	366	364	369	368	382	3
Slovenia	354	357	355	327	336	357	1
Spain	...	...	...	...	...	310	...
Sweden	201	189	189	185	183	181	-10
Switzerland	198	197	197	199	195	200	1
Turkey	212	222	230	238	247	253	19
Ukraine	...	...	...	...	...	...	...
UK: England & Wales	244	244	243	242	239	237	-3
UK: Northern Ireland	524	523	525	521	519	507	-3
UK: Scotland	279	282	286	289	285	282	1
Mean	317	338	344	348	347	374	
Median	307	326	326	320	321	343	
Minimum	152	151	153	153	154	156	
Maximum	524	576	606	631	596	1219	

Table 1.2.4.2: Police staff: Number of civilians per 100 000 population

	1995 R14CP95	1996 R14CP96	1997 R14CP97	1998 R14CP98	1999 R14CP99	2000 R14CP00	% change 1995-2000
Albania	...	...	...	...	...	20	...
Armenia	...	...	...	...	...	...	...
Austria	...	71	70	75	75	75	...
Belgium	...	44	46	48	51	54	...
Bulgaria	...	...	...	...	...	...	...
Croatia	204	233	222	218	196	153	-25
Cyprus	5	5	5	5	5	5	8
Czech Republic	80	109	114	123	128	116	45
Denmark	38	37	37	38	37	39	4
Estonia	80	74	72	71	75	79	-1
Finland	67	43	43	47	49	51	-24
France	...	21	...	...	...	22	...
Georgia	...	40	39	39	39	35	...
Germany	...	...	...	...	...	...	...
Greece	14	13	13	13	12	12	-10
Hungary	90	91	90	91	89	90	0
Ireland	...	43	48	47	46	46	...
Italy	...	...	...	...	...	...	...
Latvia	...	...	44	72	74	70	...
Lithuania	...	...	...	...	...	...	...
Luxembourg	...	...	...	...	...	...	...
Malta	...	...	...	...	...	...	...
Moldova	22	22	22	22	24	22	-1
Netherlands	62	63	64	64	65	...	...
Norway	43	48	49	54	55	56	32
Poland	46	45	49	50	50	50	8
Portugal	18	29	33	37	36	37	110
Romania	18	18	18	17	16	12	-33
Russia	...	...	...	...	...	...	...
Slovakia	121	111	118	110	116	127	5
Slovenia	75	80	86	93	97	78	4
Spain	...	...	...	...	...	...	...
Sweden	84	81	67	65	70	75	-11
Switzerland	40	43	44	44	46	48	20
Turkey	...	...	...	...	...	...	...
Ukraine	...	...	...	...	...	...	...
UK: England & Wales	101	102	101	102	101	102	2
UK: Northern Ireland	209	206	208	207	204	205	-2
UK: Scotland	77	79	83	87	90	91	18
Mean	71	67	69	71	71	66	
Median	67	47	49	59	60	54	
Minimum	5	5	5	5	5	5	
Maximum	209	233	222	218	204	205	

Notes on tables 1.2.4.1 and 1.2.4.2
Austria: Number of civilians: Employees who also fulfil other duties than police related tasks are included (e.g. organisation of elections).
France: The data do not include local municipal police force.
Greece: From 1999 the figure includes the newly set up frontier guards and special guards for embassies, foreign missions in Greece and certain public offices and officials.
Hungary: Figures in the European Sourcebook 1999 for the year 1995 are not comparable as they included border police and excluded Secret Service police. The figures in the current Table 1.3 include Secret Service and exclude Border Police.
Latvia: Municipal police do not have grades of service and they are not included in the number of state police staff.
Lithuania: There is no exact statistical data on the number of civilians in the police, because some types of police (border police, tax police, etc.) are independent from the Police Department and at the moment it is not possible to provide all numbers of civilians from different police bodies.
Netherlands: Counting is in full time equivalent, not in persons.
Norway: The Norwegian raw data is presented in the following manner: Lawyers - civil servants [officers] - administrative personnel - others. Lawyers and civil servants have been classified as "police officers" Administrative personnel and others as "civilians".
Russia: Police staff includes internal armed forces of the Russian Ministry of Internal Affairs.
Turkey: There are two main law-enforcement agencies, these are police and the gendarmerie. While the police is responsible for all kinds of law-enforcement activities within the city limits, the gendarmerie is the counterpart of the police force in the rural areas. So, the figures presented in this study only include the police statistics.
UK: England & Wales: All the figures shown are full time equivalents.

1.3 Technical information

1.3.1 Data recording methods in connection with tables 1.2.1.1 to 1.2.1.14

Description of data recording methods in connection with tables 1.2.1.1 to 1.2.1.14

Question	Are there written rules regulating the way in which this data is recorded?	When is the data collected for the statistics?	What is the counting unit used in this table?	Is a principal offence rule applied?	How are multiple offences counted?	How is an offence committed by more than one person counted?	Have the data recording methods been substantially modified between 1995 & 2000?
Possible answers	1: Yes 2: No	1: When the offence is reported to the police 2: Subsequently 3: After investigation	1: Offence 2: Case 3: Decision 4: Other	1: Yes 2: No	1: As one offence 2: As two or more offences 3: Uncertain	1: As one offence 2: As two or more offences	1: Yes 2: No
Albania	1	2	1	1	1	1	2
Armenia	1	2	1	2	1	1	2
Austria	1	3	1	2	2	1	1
Belgium	1	2	1	2	3	1	2
Bulgaria	1	1	1	1	2	1	1
Croatia	1	2	1	2	2	1	2
Cyprus	1	1	2	1	2	1	2
Czech Republic	1	1	1	2	3	1	2
Denmark	2	1	1	2	2	1	2
Estonia	1	1	1	2	3	1	2
Finland	1	1	1	2	2	1	2
France	1	2	4	2	3	1	2
Georgia	1	1	1	1	2	1	2
Germany	1	3	1	1	3	1	2
Greece	1	1	1	1	3	1	2
Hungary	1	3	1	1	3	2	2
Ireland	1	1	1	1	1	1	1
Italy	1	3	1	2	2	1	2
Latvia	1	2	3	1	2	1	1
Lithuania	1	2	1	1	2	1	2
Luxembourg	...	...	2	...	...	1	1
Malta	1	1	2	1	1	...	1
Moldova	1	1	1	2	1	1	2
Netherlands	1	2	1	1	1	1	2
Norway	1	2	1	2	2	1	1

Question	Are there written rules regulating the way in which this data is recorded?	When is the data collected for the statistics?	What is the counting unit used in this table?	Is a principal offence rule applied?	How are multiple offences counted?	How is an offence committed by more than one person counted?	Have the data recording methods been substantially modified between 1995 & 2000?
Possible answers	1: Yes 2: No	1: When the offence is reported to the police 2: Subsequently 3: After investigation	1: Offence 2: Case 3: Decision 4: Other	1: Yes 2: No	1: As one offence 2: As two or more offences 3: Uncertain	1: As one offence 2: As two or more offences	1: Yes 2: No
Poland	1	3	1	1	1	1	2
Portugal	1	2	2	1	1	1	2
Romania	1	3	1	2	2	1	1
Russia	1	2	1	2	2	1	2
Slovakia	1	...	1	1	1	1	1
Slovenia	1	3	1	1	2	1	1
Spain	1	1	1	2	1	1	1
Sweden	1	1	1	2	2	1/2	2
Switzerland	...	2	4	2	3	1/2	2
Turkey	2	1	2	1	3	1	2
Ukraine	1	2	1	2	2	1	2
UK: England & Wales	1	1	1	1	3	1	1
UK: Northern Ireland	1	1	1	1	3	1	1
UK: Scotland	1	2	4	1	2	1	2

Notes on table 1.3.1.1

Answers to these questions were given for each offences. They are almost the same from one offence to the other. In some countries different rules are applied according to the offence type (counting unit, multiple offences, multiple offenders).

Written rules regulating the way in which the data are recorded
Switzerland: There are no general rules at the federal level, but most cantons use writen standards, largely following the rules of the Zurich police (who record about 30% of all offences known to the police in the country).

What is the counting unit used in tables 1.2.1
When the counting unit depends upon the type of offence, the answer is "other" (France, Scotland, Switzerland).

For many countries the counting unit for homicide is the *Case* not the *Victim*

Principal offence rule applied

This rule is "If the sequence of offences in an incident, or a complex crime, contains more than one type of offence, then count the most serious offence." (UK)

Some restrictions to this general principle are listed below.

Belgium: A sequence of offences may be reduced to a single one (the most serious) only if there is a common criminal intent.
France: The principal offence rule is applied to offence counting only in the sense that aggravating circumstances must not be counted as separate offences.
Germany: If one act violates several criminal rules, the registration refers to the offence with the severest penalty.
Hungary: The counting system used in cases of simultaneous offences depends on the character of offences in question. Statistics show one offence if the crimes committed are dependent on each other. For example, if an offender in the course of a rape also committs other violence, the statistics will show one offence. Causing aggravated violence – there will be a separate count for each offence, because the aggravated violence is not incidental to rape.
Ireland: One offence counted for a sequence of offences committed by the same offender against the same injured party.
Latvia: Criminal Code determines which offence is criminal and must be punished.
Lithuania: There is no one universal rule in Lithuanian criminal law. The rules depend on the type and characteristic of the offences. Legal precedents mainly provide the answer as to which two offences will be counted as one and which offences as two.
Russia: Since the beginning of 1997 the principal offence rule is not longer valid and does not influence police and prosecutor bodies statistics.
Switzerland: Among the 26 cantons of Switzerland five cantons (representing 23% of the total population) apply a principle offence rule, excluding car theft, drug offences and assault against police officers.
UK: England & Wales, UK: Northern Ireland: If the sequence of offences in an incident, or a complex crime, contains more than one type of offence, then the most serious offence is counted. These incidents must involve the same offender and victim.

How are multiple offences counted

When the counting unit depends on the offence type, the answer is "uncertain".

Belgium: Multiple offences are counted as one offence in case of routinely repeated offences.
Czech Republic: Multiple offences are counted as one offence if similar offences are directed against the same victim with the same criminal intent.
Estonia: There are no strict rules how offences of the same kind (serial offences) are recorded – it depends on concrete circumstances. Usually multiple offences are counted as one offence, but this is not always the practice.
Finland: Multiple drug offences are counted as one.
France: The rule applied for multiple offences is linked to the counting unit. For some offences type multiple offences are counted as one, for others they are counted as two or more.
Germany: Multiple offences against the same victim or without a victim are counted as one offence, multiple offences against different victims are counted as two offences.
Hungary: Cumulative crimes: all acts of perpetration are counted if they are not included as aggravating circumstances in the definition of one of the crimes. Crimes committed continuously are counted as one unit in the police statistics and in the court statistics as well. One act simultaneously victimising two or more persons has to be recorded and counted two or more times.

Norway: When more than one offence is committed by a single action, all offences should be reported if they could reasonably be constructed as offences.
UK: England & Wales: Multiple offences counted as two or more offences (1 per victim if reported to the police all at once) where possible.
UK: Northern Ireland: Where multiple offences against the same victim are reported simultaneously, only one offence is recorded.
UK: Scotland: For offences against the person, one crime is counted for each victim. For offences of dishonesty (including robbery) one crime is counted per incident, regardless of the number of victims.

How is an offence commited by more than one person counted?
The general rule is to count one offence (with the exception of Hungary). In Sweden, there is an exception to this general rule for rape and drug offences. In France and Switzerland and Scotland, one exception for some drug offences when two or more offences are counted.

Changes in data recording methods 1995-2000
Austria: The increased number of offences reported in 2000 is due to new electronic on-line data collection. Although the rules for offence-count did not change markedly, the figures rose strongly. The main reason may be "multiplication" of offences by a different count of units of offences.
Belgium: The geographical extent of police forces included in published statistics has been increasing from 1995 to 1999. Rates are estimated according to the correspondent population (94% of the total Belgian population in 1995, 98% in 1999). During this period, the conditions of statistical recording may have changed, due to the fact that communication of offences to the prosecuting authority is changing.
Bulgaria: In 1998 the police statistics modified its crime recording and counting methods. Cases that are still in the process of preliminary investigation are not included in the statistics.
Ireland: The main counting rules were retained, but there were changes to the offences that were recorded as serious and less serious offences. The changes commenced in 2000.
Latvia: A new Criminal Code and a new counting system came into force in 1 April 1999.
Malta: Since 1998, all data is inputted in the Police Incident Reporting System (FIRS) immediately upon the filing of a report at the local police station. The information is relayed to a central computer and is accessible over the local network.
Norway: When more than one offence is committed by one action, all offences should be reported if they, by reasonable evaluation, could cause a charge. During the autumn of 1994 and 1995, this directive was implemented by all police districts.
Portugal: At the beginning of 1998, a new counting rule was introduced, which was expected to avoid double counting in the future.
Slovenia: Since 1998, cases in which the prosecution of a crime depends on a complaint from the victim are counted on police level even if the victim does not make a complaint. Before 1998, cases without a complaint were not counted. There was an important change in the recording of burglaries as well.
Spain: On 1 January 1997, a new typology was introduced in order to adapt Police Statistics to the new Penal Code introduced on 1 January 1996. Since 1998, Police Statistics include data from the Autonomous Basque Police (representing slightly less than 5% of the total offences known to the police).
Sweden: Change of the rules on how traffic offences are gathered in 2000.
UK: England & Wales, UK: Northern Ireland: The counting rules which are standard for all police forces in England and Wales were revised with effect from 1 April 1998. They now include all indictable and triable either-way offences together with a few summary offences, closely linked to more serious ones. The new rules have changed the emphasis of measurement more towards one crime per victim, and have also increased the coverage of offences. The change has had different impacts on different offences and offence groups, and hence figures before and after 1 April 1998 cannot be directly compared.

1.3.2 Data recording methods in connection with tables 1.2.2.1 to 1.2.2.13 and 1.2.3.1 to 1.2.3.3

Description of data recording methods in connection with tables 1.2.2.1 to 1.2.2.13

Question	How is a person suspected of more than one offence in the same year counted?	Is a principal offence rule applied?	How is a person suspected of multiple offences counted?
Possible answers	1= As one person 2=As two or more people 3 = Other	1: Yes 2: No	1= As one person 2=As two or more people 3 = Other
Albania	3	1	1
Armenia	1	1	1
Austria	2	2	1
Belgium	...	...	...
Bulgaria	3	1	1
Croatia	1	2	2
Cyprus	2	1	2
Czech Republic	3	2	3
Denmark	...	...	...
Estonia	2	1	2
Finland	2	2	2
France	2	1	1
Georgia	1	...	1
Germany	3	1	3
Greece	3	1	1
Hungary	2	1	1
Ireland	...	...	...
Italy	2	2	2
Latvia	3	1	3
Lithuania	2	1	1
Luxembourg	...	...	...
Malta	2	1	1
Moldova	2	2	1
Netherlands	2	1	1
Norway	1	1	1
Poland	2	1	1
Portugal	2	1	1
Romania	1	1	1
Russia	...	2	1
Slovakia	1	1	1
Slovenia	2	1	2

Question	How is a person suspected of more than one offence in the same year counted?	Is a principal offence rule applied?	How is a person suspected of multiple offences counted?
Possible answers	1= As one person 2=As two or more people 3 = Other	1: Yes 2: No	1= As one person 2=As two or more people 3 = Other
Spain	2	2	2
Sweden	3	2	3
Switzerland	2	2	3
Turkey	1	1	1
Ukraine	...	...	...
UK: England & Wales	2	1	1
UK: Northern Ireland	...	...	...
UK: Scotland	...	...	...

Notes on table 1.3.2.1

How is a person suspected of more than one offence in the same year counted?

Albania, the Czech Republic: As two or more if the person commits a new offence after conviction for the first one, as one person if the existing criminal proceeding includes the new offence.

Bulgaria, Germany: Once for each type of offence and once in the total outcome.

Greece, Sweden: If the offence type is the same, as one offender. If the offender has committed two different offences, as two.

Is a principle offence rule applied?

The general rule is that when a person is suspected of multiple offences he or she is counted only once for the priciple offence. This offence may be:

- implicit (not descibed in the answer (Armenia, the Czech Republic, Estonia, Latvia, Poland, Slovenia)
- the most "serious" one (Albania, France, the Netherlands, Portugal)
- the offence with the maximum penalty (Austria, Greece, Norway)
- the offence for which the heaviest sentence was imposed or for which the statutory maximum penalty is the most severe if the same disposal is imposed (UK: England & Wales).

Person suspected of multiple offences

Germany: In this case, some offenders are counted only once in the total and once for each type of recorded offence.

Differences with tables 1.2.1.1 to 1.2.1.14

Do the offence definitions used in tables 1.2.2. differ from those in the "definitions" section?

Lithuania: the definition of the assault is narrower than that given in the definitions section. There is no statistical data for the number of persons suspected in making bodily injury in a state of affect. The given numbers cover grave bodily injury or infection or bodily injury or infection of lower degree. Actually, the missing numbers are too small to make a significant impact on the provided statistics.

Number of offenders for drug offences in 1995 cover only those suspected in illegal production, acquisition, possession, transportation, delivery, sale or other distribution of the narcotic or psychotropic substances.

Romania: In this table assault excludes violence and physical injuries leading to death and includes homicide offences (including the attempts), aggravated physical injuries and outrages.

Changes in recording methods 1995-2000.

No particular change besides those mentioned for tables 1.2.1 with exception of Austria (the principle offence rule terminated in 2000) and Bulgaria (principal offence rule since 1998).

Age brackets used in table 1.2.3.2

All countries count minors as persons who are not yet 18 years old. The only exception is Austria which included 18 year old (less than 19).

The lower limit varies widely among countries as far consideration in police statistics is concerned. Persons below the age of criminal responsibility will not be convicted and therefore not counted in conviction statistics (for details refer to 3.3.2.1). However, this is not necessarily the case for police statistics where persons below that age are sometimes included (minimum age = 0 in the following table), suggesting that all persons below 18 would be counted in police statistics. Yet, as in Austria, police will not register too young persons. All the countries in the following table include offences commited by minors in police statistics.

Table 1.3.2.3: Minimum age for consideration in police statistics

Country	Age	Country	Age
Albania	14	Lithuania	14
Armenia	14	Luxembourg	0
Austria	0	Malta	0
Bulgaria	14	Moldova	14
Croatia	14	Netherlands	0
Cyprus	7	Norway	5
Czech Republic	15	Poland	13
Estonia	13	Portugal	0
Finland	0	Romania	14
France	0	Russia	14
Georgia	14	Slovakia	0
Germany	0	Slovenia	14
Greece	7	Spain	14
Hungary	14	Sweden	15
Ireland	14	Switzerland	7
Italy	14	UK: England & Wales	10
Latvia	14		

Note:

Estonia: The minimum age for all offences is 13 years apart from rape and drug offences where it is 15 years of age.

Slovenia: The number of minors under 14 is counted by the police, but has been excluded from the total crime number. In 1999, the number of minors under 14 committing a criminal act was 840; they committed 569 criminal acts.

Definition of alien

Generally speaking, aliens are persons who do not have the nationality of the country concerned.

Bulgaria also counts persons having dual citizenship.
Hungary also counts Hungarian nationals with dual citizenship residing abroad.

1.3.3 Technical information on tables 1.2.4.1 & 1.2.4.2

Table 1.3.3.1: Police staff: Police officers

1=Included 2=Excluded	criminal police D14OPA00	traffic police D14OPB00	border police D14OPC00	gendarmerie D14OPD00	uniformed police D14OPE00	city guard, municipal police D14OPF00	customs officers D14OPG00	tax police D14OPH00	military police D14OPI00	secret service police D14OPJ00	part-time officers D14OPK00	police reserves D14OPL00	cadet police officers D14OPM00	court police D14OPN00
Albania	1	1	1	...	1	2	2	2	2	2	2	2	2	2
Armenia	...	...	...	...	...	...	...	...	...	...	...	...	...	...
Austria	1	1	1	1	1	1	2	2	2	1	2	2	1	2
Belgium	1	1	1	1	1	1	2	2	2	2	2	1	2	1
Bulgaria	...	...	...	...	...	...	...	...	...	...	...	...	...	...
Croatia	1	1	1	-3	1	-3	2	2	2	2	2	2	2	2
Cyprus	1	1	2	2	1	2	2	2	2	1	1	2	1	1
Czech Republic	1	1	1	...	1	2	...	...	2	2	2	2	1	2
Denmark	1	1	1	2	1	1	2	2	2	2	2	2	1	2
Estonia	1	1	...	...	1	...	2	2	2	2	2	2	1	...
Finland	1	1	2	-3	1	-3	2	-3	2	1	1	2	1	-3
France	1	1	1	1	1	2	2	2	2	...	1	2	1	...
Georgia	1	1	2	2	1	1	2	2	1	2	2	2	2	2
Germany	...	...	...	...	...	...	...	...	...	...	...	...	...	...
Greece	1	1	1	2	1	1	2	2	2	1	2	2	2	1
Hungary	1	1	2	-3	1	-3	2	2	2	1	2	2	1	...
Ireland	1	1	-3	-3	-3	-3	2	2	2	2	2	2	2	2
Italy	1	1	1	1	...	2	1	1	2	2	2	2	2	1
Latvia	1	1	2	2	1	2	2	2	2	1	1	1	1	1
Lithuania	1	1	1	1	1	1	1	1	2	2	1	2	2	1
Luxembourg	...	...	...	...	...	...	...	...	...	...	...	...	...	...
Malta	1	1	1	2	2	2	2	1	2	2	2	2	2	2
Moldova	1	1	2	1	1	1	2	2	2	2	2	2	2	2
Netherlands	1	1	1	-3	1	1	2	2	2	2	1	2	2	2
Norway	1	1	...	...	1	1	2	2	2	2	2	2	2	2
Poland	1	1	2	2	1	2	2	2	2	2	2	2	2	2
Portugal	1	1	1	1	1	1	2	2	2	2	2	2	1	2
Romania	1	1	2	2	1	1	2	1	2	2	2	2	2	1
Russia	1	1	-3	-3	1	1	2	2	-3	2	-3	-3	2	2
Slovakia	1	1	1	1	2	2	2	2	2	2	2	2	2	2
Slovenia	1	1	1	-3	1	2	2	2	2	2	2	2	2	2
Spain	1	1	2	1	1	1	2	2	2	2	2	2	2	2
Sweden	1	1	-3	-3	1	-3	2	-3	2	2	1	2	2	-3
Switzerland	1	-4	-4	1	1	1	-4	-4	2	2	-4	-4	2	2
Turkey	1	1	1	2	1	2	2	2	2	2	2	2	2	2
Ukraine	...	...	...	...	...	...	...	...	...	...	...	...	...	...
UK: England & Wales	1	1	-3	-3	1	-3	2	-3	2	-3	1	-3	2	2
UK: Northern Ireland	1	1	-3	-3	1	-3	2	2	2	2	2	2	2	1
UK: Scotland	1	1	2	2	1	2	2	2	2	2	1	2	2	2

Table 1.3.3.2: Police staff: Civilians

1=Included 2=Excluded	cadet police officers	clerical staff	technical staff	maintenance staff	traffic wardens	domestic staff
	D14CPA00	D14CPB00	D14CPC00	D14CPD00	D14CPE00	D14CPF00
Albania	1	1	1	1	2	2
Armenia	...	...	...	...	...	...
Austria	2	1	1	1	1	1
Belgium	...	1	1	1	...	...
Bulgaria	...	...	...	...	...	...
Croatia	2	1	1	1	2	1
Cyprus	1	1	1	1	2	2
Czech Republic	2	1	1	1	1	1
Denmark	2	1	1	1	2	-4
Estonia	2	1	1	1	...	...
Finland	2	1	1	1	-3	-4
France	2	1	1	1	2	1
Georgia	2	1	1	1	2	2
Germany	...	...	...	...	...	...
Greece	2	1	1	1	2	2
Hungary	...	1	1	1	2	2
Ireland	2	1	1	1	2	1
Italy	1	1	1	1	1	2
Latvia	2	1	1	1	2	1
Lithuania	...	...	...	...	...	...
Luxembourg	...	...	...	...	...	...
Malta	1	1	1	1	2	2
Moldova	2	1	1	2	2	2
Netherlands	1	1	1	1	2	1
Norway	1	1	1	1	2	2
Poland	2	1	1	1	2	1
Portugal	2	2	1	1	2	2
Romania	2	2	1	1	2	1
Russia	1	1	1	2	2	-3
Slovakia	...	...	...	...	...	...
Slovenia	2	1	1	1	2	1
Spain	...	...	...	...	...	...
Sweden	2	1	1	1	2	1
Switzerland	2	1	1	2	2	2
Turkey	1	2	2	2	2	2
Ukraine	...	...	...	...	...	...
UK: England & Wales	2	1	1	1	2	2
UK: Northern Ireland	2	1	1	1	2	1
UK: Scotland	2	1	1	2	1	2

1.4 Sources of the data used in chapter 1

Source of the data

Albania	Police State, Department of Statistics. Ministry of Public Order, Tirana, Albania, unpublished. Personnel Directory, Ministry of Public Order, Tirana, Albania.
Armenia	Ministry of Internal Affairs.
Austria	Ministry of Interior – Police Crime Statistics, 1995-1999. Ministry of Interior – Crime Report. Data, 2000. State budget legislation. Planned staff posts.
Belgium	Statistiques Criminelles Interpolicières Intégrées (SCII) – Annua comparative I reports – Service général d'appui policier (jusqu'a la parution du rapport 1997-1998) General service for the support of the police (up to the publication of the report 1997-1998). Police fédérale – Direction du Fonctionnement policier intégré.
Bulgaria	Police statistics.
Croatia	Ministry of Interior – Department for Analytics and Research. Internal data (unpublished).
Cyprus	Research & Development Department, Cyprus Police Headquarters. "Criminal Statistics" report for the years 1995–1999, Ministry of Finance. (unpublished data).
Czech Republic	Pocket Yearbook of Criminality in the Czech Republic - Police Presidium, Department of Systém Directory and Informatics, 1995-2000. The Criminal Statistic within the area of the Czech Republic. Year 1995-2000. Police Presidium, Department of System Management and Information. Published. The Ministry of Interior, Personnel Department. Unpublished.
Denmark	Based on data taken from "Kriminalstatistik 1995, 1996, 1997, 1998, 1999, 2000" (Crime statistics), Statistics Denmark. "Politiets årsberetning 1995, 1996, 1997, 1998, 1999" & "Politiets Virksomhedsregnskab 2000", Rigspolitiet.
Estonia	Police Board – Crime statistics – Not published. Police Board – Personnel and financial statistics – not published.
Finland	Crimes reported to the police/Statistics Finland. Ministry of the Interior, police department, administration unit.
France	Ministère de l'Intérieur, Direction Centrale de la Police Judiciaire, "Aspect de la criminalité et de la délinquance constatées en France". Annual publication, (document in French). Ministère de l'Intérieur. Ministère de la Défense.
Georgia	The Information Centre of the Ministry of Internal Affairs of Georgia.
Germany	Bundeskriminalamt (Hrsg.): Polizeiliche Kriminalstatistik Bundesrepublik Deutschland, 1995-2000, Wiesbaden 1996–2001.
Greece	Annual Statistical Bulletin of the Hellenic Police – Ministry of Public Order: 1995-1999.
Hungary	Unified Statistics of the Police and Prosecution.

Ireland	Annual Reports of An Garda Síochána (Police).
Italy	National Institute of Statistics – Istat.
	Ministerio dell'economia e delle finanze.
Latvia	Crimininal Statistic Unit of Information centre of Ministry of Home Affairs.
Lithuania	Ministry of Internal Affairs – Department of Informatics and Communication – Section of Statistics.
	"Criminality and the law enforcement activity", Annual publication.
Luxembourg	Activity report 2000, Police Grand-Ducale Luxembourg.
Malta	Office of the Attorney General. The data represents all reports received in our Police Stations.
Moldova	Ministère de l'Intérieur, Direction Information et Enregistrement operatif.
Netherlands	Ministry of Justice (WODC) and Central Bureau of Statistics. (Not published).
	Ministry of the Interior and Kingdom Relations, Directorate-General for Public Order and Safety, Department Police.
Norway	Statistics Norway, Division for Social Welfare Statistics.
	Department of Justice.
Poland	Police Headquarters, Statistical Information Bureau and the HR Department.
Portugal	Legal Policy and Planning Office, Ministry of Justice.
Romania	Ministry of Interior.
Russia	Russian Statistical Year-Book 2000.
	Russian Ministry of Internal Affairs.
Slovakia	Ministry of Interior Slovak Republic.
Slovenia	Ministry of the Interior of the Republic of Slovenia.
Spain	Ministerio del Interior: Secretaría General Técnica. *Anuario Estadístico del Ministerio del Interior.* Published annually.
Sweden	Official Swedish Criminal Statistics published by the National Crime Prevention Council.
	The Swedish Police Organization Annual Report.
Switzerland	Office fédéral de la police, Statistique policière de la criminalité, Berne: Office central des stupéfiants, Statistique suisse des stupéfiants, Berne: Office fédéral de la police.
	Office fédéral de la statistique.
Turkey	Turkish General Directorate of Security Statistics.
Ukraine	State committee of statistics of Ukraine – Statistical yearbook of Ukraine, 2000.
UK: England & Wales	"Criminal Statistics England and Wales".
	Police Forces.
UK: Northern Ireland	Police Service of Northern Ireland (Central Statistics Unit)
	Police Service of Northern Ireland (Personnel Branch).
UK: Scotland	Scottish Executive Justice Department – Justice Statistics Unit Branch 2.
	Police staff numbers from Quarterly Strength Return from all forces as at 31 March of each year.

2 Prosecution statistics

2.1 General Comments

2.1.1 Background

1. This chapter provides information on the outcome of criminal justice procedures at the prosecutorial level (prosecutors and examining judges) for the years 1995–2000. It also provides information on the staff numbers of the prosecuting authorities for the same years.

2. Five countries (Ireland, Luxembourg, Spain, Turkey and Ukraine) were not able to provide any data for this chapter and they are not listed in the tables. Four countries did not provide data on the number of cases but only on the number of prosecutors/employees of the prosecuting authority (Georgia, Greece, Malta, Sweden; see tables 2.2.4.1 and 2.2.4.2).

3. In the tables presented in this chapter raw data have been combined in some cases in order to make analysis possible. Data in the tables may not exactly match the raw data.

2.1.2 Definitions of the prosecution stage

4. In a narrow sense, the term *prosecution* refers only to the process of carrying out a trial in a criminal court. However, the term here is used in the broader sense of processing or disposing of cases (decision-making) by the prosecuting authorities. As such, it includes the decision to drop proceedings or to impose a sanction or measure, where this option is available to the prosecutor. However, in some countries even when a suspect has not been identified the case will be presented at the prosecuting authorities and therefore counted in the statistics used in table 2.2.3.

5. The term *prosecuting authority* refers to the legal body whose main task is to institute criminal proceedings, i.e. to decide, depending on national legislation and practice, whether or not to prosecute. The actual functions vary widely between countries. In most European countries, the prosecution of suspected offenders is dealt with by a special prosecuting authority, either a public prosecutor or an investigating judge.

6. The prosecutorial stage differs vastly between the European countries covered in this chapter. For the purpose of this chapter, the prosecution stage is considered to be an intermediate stage between the police and the court.

2.1.3 The role of the police in relation to the prosecution stage (case input)

7. In some countries, the input at the prosecutorial level is equal to the output at the police level (including specialised authorities of public order, such as

customs or tax authorities). This is the case in countries (such as France and Germany) in which the police are regarded purely as a supporting institution to the public prosecutor, with no powers of their own to dispose of a criminal case; they are obliged to transfer all cases to the prosecuting authority. This also applies to cases where no suspect has been identified. As a result, the prosecution input may appear disproportionally high in such systems, especially when cases without suspects are counted (e.g. in France).

8. However, in some European countries the actual practice deviates from the model and the input at prosecutorial level is not identical to police level output, because the police can exercise some discretion and decide on whether or not to prosecute. Thus, certain cases are not transferred to the prosecuting authority and are ended by a police decision. The following countries reported that, according to their criminal justice systems, the police can impose sanctions: the Czech Republic, Denmark, Finland, Greece, Hungary, Norway, UK: England & Wales, UK: Northern Ireland and UK: Scotland. However, the powers of the police are always limited to minor cases. In some countries, they involve only petty traffic offences (e.g. Finland).

9. The prosecution statistics are affected by the different structures in the criminal justice systems, which influence the number of suspects dealt with. Due to changes in definitions and counting rules, statistics at the prosecution level may also be different from the police level "output".

2.1.4 What is recorded?

10. Since most countries could only provide the total number of offences disposed of by prosecuting authorities, no offence breakdown is given in this chapter.

11. In order to make the data comparable, the figures exclude minor traffic offences (e.g. parking offences) and breach of police and administrative regulations. However, the data include drink driving and dangerous driving traffic offences. This rule was applied by the majority of the countries (for exceptions see technical table 2.3.2).

12. The counting unit used here is the *case* not the offence. Thus, one case may combine several offences or offenders. In general, such occurrences are counted as single cases (for exceptions see paragraph 19 below and technical table 2.3.4.1).

2.1.5 Discretion at prosecutor's level (output)

13. The data provided for the cases disposed of by the prosecuting authority (table 2.2.1) refer to the "output" at public prosecutor's level (tables 2.2.2.1 to 2.2.2.5), in

other words, the type of decision that was made. This means that pending cases are not included in the total of disposals. Some countries were not able to give data for the breakdown of the total (Italy, Russia, and Northern Ireland).

14. The prosecuting authorities vary from country to country. Three *basic structures* are possible:
– There are countries in which the prosecuting authority has neither the power to drop a case nor to impose conditions/sanctions upon an offender. In accordance with a strict principle of legality, the prosecuting authority merely has the function of preparing a case for court.
– In most of the countries included in this chapter, the prosecuting authority has the power to decide whether or not to prosecute (i.e. to drop a case completely).
– In some countries, the prosecuting authority has both the power to decide whether or not to prosecute and also the possibility of dropping the case with conditions, i.e. to bind or sanction the suspected offender (only possible if he/she agrees to the measure – otherwise the case will go to court), or to impose a fine of some sort.

15. The following *categories for disposal* are used in this chapter:
– Number of cases brought before a court.
– Number of cases ended by a sanction from the prosecution authorities with or without admission of guilt.
– Number of cases dropped.
– Number of other disposals.
Some of these categories may not apply to all countries.

16. The difference between "cases brought before a court" and "proceedings ended by a sanction from the prosecuting authority" depends on how far the court is involved in the public prosecutor's decision-making. In some countries, the court has to approve all decisions made by the prosecutor to end a prosecution without formally taking it to court, whereas in other countries the public prosecutor has more powers.

17. In tables 2.2.2.2 and 2.2.2.3, a distinction is made between sanctions imposed by the prosecutor with and without admission of guilt by the defendant. If there is admission of guilt, the penal order (*Strafbefehl*) is applied in some countries and the defendant is considered to be convicted (and to be counted as such in chapter 3). If guilt is not admitted, sanctions imposed without formal recognition of guilt are usually administered in a rather informal way. Usually, the defendant agrees to pay a fine or accepts restrictions in exchange of ending the prosecution, implying that he will not be considered as being convicted formally.

18. According to the questionnaire, "other disposals" (e.g. cases that were transferred to another competent domestic jurisdiction) should be included in the

total of cases handled by the prosecuting authorities. This can lead to some double counting and to significant differences between the total disposals and the sum of the police output. Some countries provided further information that clarifies this complexity and explains differences that occur. For further explanations on "other disposals" see technical table 2.3.3.4.

2.1.6 Statistical rules

19. Most of the countries reporting data on prosecution level apply written rules regulating the way in which data are recorded. Also, most countries count proceedings where more than one person is involved as one case, with the exception of Croatia, Denmark, the Netherlands, Slovakia, UK: England & Wales and UK: Northern Ireland. Most countries do the same for multiple offences. However, the majority of the countries record two cases if a person is subject to two proceedings in the same year. Usually, data collected by other agencies apart from the public prosecution authorities are not included, nor are cases disposed of by the police (see technical table 2.3.4.1 for more detailed information). Also, since data on pending cases and the input of persons and proceedings were rarely available, no separate input statistics are given in this chapter. For countries where output data were not available, input data were used instead (see notes on table 2.2.1).

2.1.7 Results

20. There is wide variation in the figures as regards the output, i.e. the total of cases disposed of by the prosecution authorities, from 218 disposals per 100 000 population in Albania to 5 878 per 100 000 in Italy for 1999 (see table 2.2.1). Similar differences can be found at police level. Depending on the different "workload" of the national prosecution authorities, different ways of handling of cases can be seen (see table 2.a for more information).

21. Wheras in many countries the rates of all cases disposed of by the prosecuting authorities appear to be stable between 1995 and 2000 (i.e. increase or decrease in case numbers of less than 10%), in other countries there is a remarkable increase of between 10% and 50% (Armenia, Latvia, Lithuania, Moldova, Norway, Poland, Romania, Slovenia) and in some Eastern European countries there is a high increase of more than 50% (Estonia, Slovakia). On the other hand, Albania (-27%) and Bulgaria (-10%) – Eastern European countries as well – are the only countries to show decreases of 10% or more.

Total of disposals by public prosecution and cases brought before a court
22. Table 2.a shows the rate of all cases disposed of and the percentage of cases brought before court in 1999. Several countries were excluded, as they could not provide this information. Table 2.a has been drawn up in order to illustrate the

relationship between the two factors. More specifically, where a prosecution authority has to deal with a relatively low number of cases, the percentage of cases brought before a court will be high (e.g. in Hungary), while, where the total of cases disposed is high, the percentage of cases brought before a court tends to be low (e.g. in Germany).

23. There are two groups of countries which do not follow the pattern mentioned above: the Common Law system countries on the one hand, where the percentage of cases brought before a court remains relatively high even when the total of cases disposed of is not low and some of the Eastern European countries on the other hand, where the percentage of cases brought before a court remains relatively low, although the number of cases disposed of is also low.

Table 2.a: Percentage of cases brought before a court by rate of all cases disposed of

		Cases brought before a court per 100 000 population in 1999		
		low: below 33% of total cases disposed of	middle: from 33% to under 66% of total cases disposed of	high: 66% and above of total cases disposed of
Cases disposed of per 100 000 population in 1999	low 33%: below 1200	Slovenia	Albania* Croatia Slovakia	Armenia the Czech Republic* Hungary* Latvia Lithuania
	middle 33%: from 1200 to under 2800	France Moldova Poland Romania*	the Netherlands	Finland (1998) UK: England & Wales
	high 33%: 2800 and above	Estonia* Germany Portugal* Switzerland	Austria UK: Scotland	

* Including cases transferred to the prosecutor where the offender is unknown.

Staff of the prosecuting authorities: workload
25. There is a wide variation in the number of public prosecutors per 100 000 inhabitants in European countries (from 27.2 in Latvia to 1.5 in Malta for the year 2000 (see table 2.2.4.2)).

26. Only Western European countries fall into the low category (less than 7 prosecutors per 100 000) and only Eastern European countries (with the exception of Portugal) fall into the high category (more than 10 prosecutors per 100 000). These rates do not correlate with the crime situation nor with the

number of police officers under the supervision of the prosecuting authorities and especially not with the amount of disposals made by public prosecution.

Table 2.b: Rate of prosecutors by rate of all cases disposed of

		Prosecutors per 100 000 population in 1999		
		low 33% below 7.0	middle 33%: from 7.0 to under 10.0	high 33%: 10.0 and above
Cases disposed of per 100 000 population in 1999	low 33%: below 1200		Albania* Croatia (2000) the Czech Republic* Slovenia	Hungary* Latvia Lithuania Slovakia
	middle 33%: from 1200 to under 2800	UK: England & Wales Finland (1998) the Netherlands UK: Northern Ireland	Romania*	Moldova Poland
	high 33%: 2800 and above	Austria Germany (2000) UK: Scotland	Switzerland Bulgaria	Estonia* Portugal*

* Including cases transferred to the prosecutor where the offender is unknown.

2.2 Tables

Output: Total number of cases disposed of by the prosecuting authorities

Table 2.2.1: Output: Total number of cases disposed of per 100 000 population

	1995	1996	1997	1998	1999	2000	% change 1995 - 2000
Albania	270	232	156	189	218	198	-27
Armenia	228	271	336	276	260	324	42
Austria	3215	3220	3115	3134	2955	...	...
Belgium	...	...	...	...	...	...	...
Bulgaria	3519	3418	3554	3531	3279	3185	-10
Croatia	676	685	661	807	709	704	4
Cyprus	...	...	...	...	...	...	...
Czech Republic	1052	1059	1051	1035	1049	1079	2
Denmark	...	...	...	...	...	...	...
Estonia	2595	2323	2682	3006	3409	3970	53
Finland	1359	1338	1322	1395	...	...	...
France	2870	2716	2649	2583	2693	2720	-5
Georgia	...	...	...	...	...	...	...
Germany	5143	5280	5398	5589	5474	...	...
Greece	...	...	...	...	...	...	...
Hungary	...	...	1076	1150	1128	1060	...
Italy	5131	5187	4973	5375	5878	...	...
Latvia	490	717	719	730	698	650	33
Lithuania	814	887	1004	1005	1010	1051	29
Malta	...	...	...	...	...	...	...
Moldova	1234	1382	1533	1505	1563	1618	31
Netherlands	1738	1637	1627	1530	1476	...	...
Norway	4119	4439	4581	4654	5050	...	...
Poland	1493	1444	1553	1576	1545	1697	14
Portugal	4054	4077	4245	4342	4230	...	...
Romania	1269	1329	1482	1629	1617	1662	31
Russia	...	938	817	865	1005	964	...
Slovakia	796	798	771	727	786	1575	98
Slovenia	886	788	835	1021	1089	1223	38
Sweden	...	...	...	...	...	...	...
Switzerland	3164	3088	3178	3476	3185	3125	-1
UK: England & Wales	2688	2565	2657	2731	2714	2587	-4
UK: Northern Ireland	2053	1904	1915	1658	1631	...	...
UK: Scotland	4940	4905	5078	5102	4809	4826	-2
Mean	2232	2178	2184	2245	2287	1801	
Median	1738	1541	1553	1576	1590	1575	
Minimum	228	232	156	189	218	198	
Maximum	5143	5280	5398	5589	5878	4826	

2.2.2 Types of disposals

Table 2.2.2.1: Cases brought before a court per 100 000 population

	1995	1996	1997	1998	1999	2000	% change 1995-2000
Albania	107	108	35	70	97	101	-6
Armenia	148	171	192	175	200	220	49
Austria	1154	1120	1271	1060	1039	...	...
Belgium	...	...	...	...	...	...	...
Bulgaria	227	374	427	389	346	507	124
Croatia	520	495	416	503	468	479	-8
Cyprus	303	383	365	388	394	...	...
Czech Republic	814	828	816	718	827	838	3
Denmark	...	...	...	...	...	...	...
Estonia	396	409	424	411	403	461	16
Finland	1013	980	974	1033	...	...	...
France	873	702	907	919	936	914	5
Georgia	...	...	...	...	...	...	...
Germany	686	697	708	738	741	...	...
Greece	...	...	...	...	...	...	...
Hungary	673	669	728	774	752	700	4
Italy	...	...	...	...	...	...	...
Latvia	355	429	474	489	479	443	25
Lithuania	604	672	787	761	740	787	30
Malta	...	...	...	...	...	...	...
Moldova	275	275	306	311	326	368	34
Netherlands	825	814	822	797	786	...	...
Norway	1363	1572	1596	1651	1888	...	...
Poland	573	552	588	571	558	623	9
Portugal	1066	1066	1017	736	757	...	...
Romania	375	374	387	333	248	218	-42
Russia	...	...	...	...	...	...	...
Slovakia	403	387	365	352	365	366	-9
Slovenia	533	455	498	635	649	666	25
Sweden	...	...	...	...	...	...	...
Switzerland	397	349	351	385	338	267	-33
UK: England & Wales	2526	2448	2542	2594	2588	2470	-2
UK: Northern Ireland	...	...	...	...	...	...	...
UK: Scotland	2923	2897	2781	2625	2409	2270	-22
Mean	765	769	791	777	764	705	
Median	573	552	588	635	603	493	
Minimum	107	108	35	70	97	101	
Maximum	2923	2897	2781	2625	2588	2470	

Table 2.2.2.2: Sanctions imposed by the prosecutor (or by the court, but without a formal court hearing), based on the defendant's admission of guilt per 100 000 population

	1995	1996	1997	1998	1999	2000	% change 1995-2000
Albania	...	...	...	...	...	...	...
Armenia	...	...	...	...	...	...	...
Austria	...	...	...	...	...	552	...
Belgium	...	...	...	...	...	...	...
Bulgaria	...	...	...	...	...	...	...
Croatia	...	...	...	...	...	...	...
Cyprus	...	...	...	...	...	...	...
Czech Republic	...	...	...	...	...	...	...
Denmark	...	...	...	...	...	...	...
Estonia	659	652	676	578	628	665	1
Finland	418	457	457	474	509	...	...
France	58	88	100	102	123	123	110
Georgia	...	...	...	...	...	...	...
Germany	817	823	829	804	755	...	...
Greece	...	...	...	...	...	...	...
Hungary	...	...	...	...	...	...	...
Italy	...	...	...	...	...	...	...
Latvia	...	...	...	...	...	...	...
Lithuania	...	...	...	...	...	...	...
Malta	...	...	...	...	...	...	...
Moldova	...	...	...	...	...	...	...
Netherlands	...	...	...	...	...	...	...
Norway	1102	1091	1155	1164	1268	...	...
Poland	58	52	61	...	...	...	...
Portugal	...	...	...	...	...	...	...
Romania	...	...	...	...	...	...	...
Russia	...	...	...	...	...	...	...
Slovakia	4	8	15	24	21	23	465
Slovenia	...	...	...	...	...	...	...
Sweden	...	...	...	...	...	...	...
Switzerland	696	715	734	781	796	851	22
UK: England & Wales	...	...	...	...	...	...	...
UK: Northern Ireland	...	...	...	...	...	...	...
UK: Scotland	...	...	...	...	...	...	...
Mean	477	486	503	561	586	443	
Median	539	555	567	578	628	552	
Minimum	4	8	15	24	21	23	
Maximum	1102	1091	1155	1164	1268	851	

Table 2.2.2.3: Sanctions negotiated between the prosecutor and the defendant without admission of guilt per 100 000 population

	1995	1996	1997	1998	1999	2000	% change 1995-2000
Albania	...	...	...	...	...	...	...
Armenia	...	...	...	...	...	...	...
Austria	...	...	...	...	...	...	...
Belgium	53	58	66	69	64	70	31
Bulgaria	...	...	...	...	...	...	...
Croatia	...	...	...	...	...	...	...
Cyprus	...	...	...	...	...	...	...
Czech Republic	...	...	...	...	...	...	...
Denmark	...	...	...	...	...	...	...
Estonia	...	...	...	...	...	...	...
Finland	...	...	...	...	...	...	...
France	139	151	169	273	355	413	196
Georgia	...	...	...	...	...	...	...
Germany	297	301	305	304	294	...	...
Greece	...	...	...	...	...	...	...
Hungary	114	105	114	130	117	102	-11
Italy	...	...	...	...	...	...	...
Latvia	...	...	...	...	...	...	...
Lithuania	...	...	...	...	...	...	...
Malta	...	...	...	...	...	...	...
Moldova	...	...	...	...	...	...	...
Netherlands	373	372	379	378	423	472	27
Norway	...	...	...	...	...	...	...
Poland	...	...	...	...	...	...	...
Portugal	...	...	...	...	...	...	...
Romania	...	...	...	...	...	...	...
Russia	...	...	...	...	...	...	...
Slovakia	...	...	...	...	...	...	...
Slovenia	...	...	...	...	...	...	...
Sweden	...	...	...	...	...	...	...
Switzerland	...	...	...	...	...	...	...
UK: England & Wales	...	...	...	...	...	...	...
UK: Northern Ireland	...	...	...	...	...	...	...
UK: Scotland	508	434	514	552	472	480	-5
Mean	247	237	258	284	288	307	
Median	218	226	237	288	324	413	
Minimum	53	58	66	69	64	70	
Maximum	508	434	514	552	472	480	

Table 2.2.2.4: Proceedings dropped: Total per 100 000 population

	1995	1996	1997	1998	1999	2000	% change 1995-2000
Albania	163	123	119	119	121	97	-40
Armenia	80	99	144	101	60	104	30
Austria	1352	1398	1496	1574	1605	...	...
Belgium	...	...	...	...	...	...	...
Bulgaria	153	210	205	218	267	372	143
Croatia	144	175	209	244	163	145	0
Cyprus	...	...	...	...	...	...	...
Czech Republic	163	159	164	262	163	180	11
Denmark	205	206	199	209	207	212	3
Estonia	2050	1809	2240	2296	2688	3373	65
Finland	...	...	...	...	...	...	...
France	1776	1551	1447	1263	1251	1240	-30
Georgia	...	...	...	...	...	...	...
Germany	2437	2557	2651	2655	2626	...	...
Greece	...	...	...	...	...	...	...
Hungary	139	143	154	162	156	141	1
Italy	101	...	...	...	...	...	...
Latvia	52	97	75	69	59	51	-2
Lithuania	210	216	217	244	270	264	26
Malta	...	...	...	...	...	...	...
Moldova	104	111	102	122	136	129	24
Netherlands	345	290	267	218	166	153	-56
Norway	1430	1196	1262	1242	1289	...	...
Poland	526	512	568	621	618	671	28
Portugal	2988	3011	3228	3606	3473	...	...
Romania	893	955	1095	1296	1369	1444	62
Russia	...	...	...	...	...	...	...
Slovakia	138	99	92	96	...	108	-21
Slovenia	350	323	317	369	426	532	52
Sweden	...	...	...	...	...	...	...
Switzerland	1006	982	931	1020	975	998	-1
UK: England & Wales	544	491	487	479	477	463	-15
UK: Northern Ireland	...	...	...	...	...	...	...
UK: Scotland	1056	1078	1148	1261	1325	1481	40
Mean	736	741	784	823	865	608	
Median	345	306	292	316	426	238	
Minimum	52	97	75	69	59	51	
Maximum	2988	3011	3228	3606	3473	3373	

Table 2.2.2.5: Other disposals: Total per 100 000 population

	1995	1996	1997	1998	1999	2000	% change 1995-2000
Albania	...	...	...	...	...	...	...
Armenia	...	...	...	...	...	...	...
Austria	...	...	...	...	...	...	...
Belgium	...	...	...	...	...	...	...
Bulgaria	...	...	...	...	...	...	...
Croatia	11	14	36	61	78	80	596
Cyprus	...	...	...	...	...	...	...
Czech Republic	76	72	71	55	60	60	-20
Denmark	...	...	...	...	...	...	...
Estonia	...	...	...	...	...	...	...
Finland	...	...	...	...	...	...	...
France	...	...	...	...	...	...	...
Georgia	...	...	...	...	...	...	...
Germany	906	902	898	881	849	...	...
Greece	...	...	...	...	...	...	...
Hungary	48	56	194	214	219	219	361
Italy	...	...	...	...	...	...	...
Latvia	83	191	170	172	159	156	88
Lithuania	...	...	...	...	...	...	...
Malta	...	...	...	...	...	...	...
Moldova	...	...	...	...	...	...	...
Netherlands	196	160	160	137	101	102	-48
Norway	...	...	...	...	...	...	...
Poland	337	329	336	383	369	402	20
Portugal	...	...	...	...	...	...	...
Romania	...	...	...	...	...	...	...
Russia	...	...	...	...	...	...	...
Slovakia	21	13	17	12	11	21	1
Slovenia	3	11	20	17	15	25	909
Sweden	...	...	...	...	...	...	...
Switzerland	1011	977	873	960	931	1024	1
UK: England & Wales	...	...	...	...	...	...	...
UK: Northern Ireland	...	...	...	...	...	...	...
UK: Scotland	82	89	79	76	65	58	-29
Mean	252	256	259	270	260	215	
Median	82	89	160	137	101	91	
Minimum	3	11	17	12	11	21	
Maximum	1011	977	898	960	931	1024	

Notes on table 2.2.1:

Albania, the Czech Republic, Estonia, Hungary, Portugal, Romania and Russia: Including proceedings against unknown offenders.

Armenia, Croatia, France, Norway, Poland and Slovenia: Proceedings against unknown offenders, which were initially included in the figures for this country, have been subtracted from the total for better comparability with the other countries. For the number of proceedings where the offender is unknown see table 2.2.3.

Albania: In 1996 the new Code of Criminal Procedure came into force.

Bulgaria, Italy: Figures represent the total input of proceedings instead of output.

France: Statistical domain: metropolitan and overseas territories.

Germany: Not all länder could provide data for calendar year, so for some of them estimate figures were used instead.

Russia, Slovenia: Figures represent the total input of persons instead of output.

Switzerland: As these data do not exist at the national level, figures from 3 cantonal prosecutors' offices (Geneva, Vaud and Zurich) which deal with 29% of the total convictions in Switzerland were used. The rates are very stable between 1995 and 1999 but a different rate has been used for each year.

UK: England & Wales: The total includes pre-charge advice and non-criminal proceedings.

UK: Scotland: All figures quoted relate to financial years.

Notes on table 2.2.2.1:

Austria: Until 1997 unit of counting is the person; from 1998 unit of counting is the case.

France: Statistical domain: metropolitan and overseas territories.

Germany: Not all länder could provide data for calendar year, so for some of them estimate figures were used instead.

Switzerland: See notes on table 2.2.1.

UK: England & Wales: Cases brought before a court include those dropped in court. As these cases are included in the total of proceedings dropped as well, the sum of the different disposal categories is higher than the total number of cases disposed of.

UK: Scotland: All figures quoted relate to financial years. Figures for cases brought before a court relate to total numbers of cases closed at various courts and not to proceedings raised.

Notes on table 2.2.2.2:

Austria: Until 1999, cases dropped because of no public interest also include successfully resolved out of court settlements. In 2000 these cases are included in sanctions imposed by prosecutor ("intervening diversion").

France: Statistical domain: metropolitan and overseas territories.

Germany: All cases in which the Public Prosecution Office applies by the court for a "Strafbefehl" (penal order) with a special sanction (mostly fines) are counted; it is not counted as a sanction imposed by the prosecutor. The court issues the penal order after a summary review of the case and without a court hearing. If the accused raises an objection, a court hearing takes place. Furthermore, not all länder could provide data for calendar year, so for some of them estimate figures were used instead.

Poland: Procedure not applicable from 1998 onwards.

Switzerland: See notes on table 2.2.1.

Notes on table 2.2.2.3:

France: Statistical domain: metropolitan and overseas territories.

Germany: Not all länder could provide data for calendar year, so for some of them estimate figures were used instead.

Hungary: The counting unit is the person sanctioned by the prosecuting authorities (not the number of cases). The number of proceedings (cases) ended in this way is not available separately. However, the total of proceedings dropped includes cases in which an offender was sanctioned by the prosecuting authorities. Due to the different counting unit and in order to avoid double counting, the figures presented in this table are not included in the total number of cases disposed of.
UK: Scotland: All figures quoted relate to financial years.

Notes on table 2.2.2.4:
Albania, the Czech Republic, Estonia, Hungary, Portugal and Romania: Including proceedings against unknown offenders.
Austria: Until 1999, cases dropped because of no public interest also include successfully resolved "out of court" settlements. In 2000, these cases are included in sanctions imposed by the prosecutor ("intervening diversion").
Czech Republic: The extraordinary high number of "proceedings dropped" for 1998 is due to a president's amnesty that year.
France: Statistical domain: metropolitan and overseas territories.
Germany: Not all länder could provide data for calendar year, so for some of them estimate figures were used instead.
Switzerland: As these data do not exist at the national level, figures from 3 cantonal prosecutors' offices (Geneva, Vaud and Zurich) which deal with 29% of the total convictions in Switzerland were used. The rates are very stable between 1995 and 1999 but a different rate has been used for each year.
UK: England & Wales: Cases brought before a court include those dropped in court. As these cases are included in the total of proceedings dropped as well, the sum of the different disposal categories is higher than the total number of cases disposed of.
UK: Scotland: All figures quoted relate to financial years.

Notes on table 2.2.2.5:
France: Statistical domain: metropolitan and overseas territories.
Germany: Not all länder could provide data for calendar year, so for some of them estimate figures were used instead.
Switzerland: For the output, the total of other disposals for Zurich are included in the output for Zurich in order to make it comparable with that of the other cantons (see Marguerat, C., 2002, "Essai d'analyse des données statistiques des autorités de poursuite pénale de quatre cantons suisses", Criminology thesis, University of Lausanne, Institut de criminologie et de droit pénal, page 11). For the total of other disposals, the data for the Zurich canton are not included and therefore are not comparable to the two other cantons that represent 13% of the total disposals in Switzerland.
UK: Scotland: All figures quoted relate to financial years.

2.2.3 Proceedings where the offender is unknown

Table 2.2.3: Proceedings where the offender is unknown per 100 000 population*

	1995	1996	1997	1998	1999	2000	% change 1995-2000
Albania	...	...	45	77	66	41	...
Armenia	33	41	48	39	43	44	33
Austria	3287	3258	3282	3315	3435	...	...
Belgium	...	...	...	...	...	...	...
Bulgaria	...	...	...	...	...	...	...
Croatia	367	399	339	333	346	358	-2
Cyprus	...	...	...	...	...	...	...
Czech Republic	...	...	...	...	...	...	...
Denmark	...	...	...	...	...	...	...
Estonia	...	...	...	...	...	...	...
Finland	...	...	...	...	...	...	...
France	5188	5342	5210	5175	5068	5052	-3
Georgia	...	...	...	...	...	...	...
Germany	...	4723	4489	4341	4211	...	...
Greece	...	...	...	...	...	...	...
Hungary	...	...	...	...	...	...	...
Italy	...	...	...	...	...	...	...
Latvia	...	...	...	...	...	...	...
Lithuania	...	...	...	...	...	...	...
Malta	...	...	...	...	...	...	...
Moldova	398	351	380	362	324	328	-18
Netherlands	...	...	...	...	...	...	...
Norway	4290	4212	4042	4417	4348	...	...
Poland	1241	1157	1293	1489	1718	1849	49
Portugal	...	...	...	...	...	...	...
Romania	...	...	...	...	...	...	...
Russia	...	...	...	...	...	...	...
Slovakia	1160	978	874	886	825	685	-41
Slovenia	993	941	791	825	1547	1741	75
Sweden	...	...	...	...	...	...	...
Switzerland	...	...	...	...	...	...	...
UK: England & Wales	...	...	...	...	...	...	...
UK: Northern Ireland	...	...	...	...	...	...	...
UK: Scotland	...	...	...	...	...	...	...
Mean	1884	2140	1890	1933	1994	1262	
Median	1160	1068	874	886	1547	522	
Minimum	33	41	45	39	43	41	
Maximum	5188	5342	5210	5175	5068	5052	

Notes on table 2.2.3:
* Unless stated otherwise in tables 2.2.1 and 2.2.2.4, the number of unknown offenders is not included in the total number of cases disposed of and in the total of proceedings dropped. For details see technical table 2.3.3.3.

France: Statistical domain: metropolitan and overseas territories.

Germany: Not all länder could provide data for calendar year, so for some of them estimate figures were used instead.

2.2.4 Staff of the prosecuting authority

Table 2.2.4.1: Staff of the prosecuting authority: Total number of employees per 100 000 population

	1995	1996	1997	1998	1999	2000	% change 1995-2000
Albania	27.8	27.4	27.1	26.7	26.1	25.8	-7
Armenia	...	...	...	...	...	...	...
Austria	...	...	...	...	...	...	...
Belgium	...	...	36.2	36.6	37.0	37.9	...
Bulgaria	...	...	...	...	...	...	...
Croatia	...	...	...	...	...	20.6	...
Cyprus	13.0	13.0	13.7	13.4	12.6	13.3	3
Czech Republic	8.1	8.6	8.7	9.5	9.6	9.5	17
Denmark	...	...	...	16.9	17.6	18.0	...
Estonia	19.9	20.3	20.4	18.1	18.3	18.9	-5
Finland	...	...	...	...	...	...	...
France	...	...	...	...	...	...	...
Georgia	...	...	...	34.3	26.8	26.5	...
Germany	...	...	...	...	...	...	...
Greece	...	...	...	...	...	...	...
Hungary	25.2	25.1	26.9	29.1	30.0	31.2	24
Italy	16.9	17.0	17.0	17.2	17.8	...	...
Latvia	38.6	39.0	39.4	39.8	42.1	42.2	9
Lithuania	...	...	...	...	...	...	...
Malta	2.4	2.6	2.6	2.6	2.3	2.3	-4
Moldova	19.7	16.7	19.8	19.1	18.5	22.1	12
Netherlands	14.3	14.7	16.0	16.8	17.9	...	...
Norway	...	...	...	...	...	...	...
Poland	22.5	24.4	25.2	25.3	26.6	26.5	18
Portugal	...	...	...	...	...	...	...
Romania	17.9	18.1	18.4	18.9	18.9	19.2	7
Russia	...	...	...	...	...	...	...
Slovakia	23.4	23.5	23.8	24.1	24.6	24.7	5
Slovenia	12.4	14.2	14.7	15.3	15.7	16.1	30
Sweden	...	14.8	13.4	11.4	11.6	11.9	...
Switzerland	19.6	18.9	18.6	20.4	19.5	20.3	3
UK: England & Wales	...	11.4	10.9	10.8	10.9	10.8	...
UK: Northern Ireland	10.6	10.5	10.5	10.5	10.5	10.4	-2
UK: Scotland	20.7	20.3	20.5	20.4	20.3	21.2	3
Mean	18	18	19	20	20	20	
Median	20	17	19	19	18	20	
Minimum	2	3	3	3	2	2	
Maximum	39	39	39	40	42	42	

Table 2.2.4.2: Staff of the prosecuting authority: Number of prosecutors per 100 000 population

	1995	1996	1997	1998	1999	2000	% change 1995-2000
Albania	16.9	8.0	7.9	7.8	7.6	7.5	-56
Armenia	...	...	...	...	...	...	...
Austria	2.5	2.5	2.5	2.4	2.5	2.6	4
Belgium	7.7	7.7	7.7	8.8	8.8	8.9	16
Bulgaria	7.8	7.6	7.6	7.3	7.4	8.1	3
Croatia	...	...	...	...	...	8.8	...
Cyprus	3.5	3.7	3.6	3.9	3.4	4.4	23
Czech Republic	7.5	8.0	7.9	8.4	8.7	9.0	20
Denmark	...	...	...	9.9	10.6	11.0	...
Estonia	8.8	9.0	9.1	10.8	10.4	11.0	25
Finland	...	1.8	1.8	1.7	1.7	1.7	...
France	...	...	...	...	...	...	...
Georgia	...	...	...	23.9	19.8	22.3	...
Germany	...	6.4	...	6.1	...	6.1	...
Greece	3.7	4.0	3.9	4.0	4.0	4.4	18
Hungary	12.4	10.8	11.4	12.3	12.4	12.8	3
Italy	...	...	...	...	...	...	...
Latvia	26.2	26.5	26.8	27.1	27.3	27.2	4
Lithuania	...	21.1	20.5	20.5	21.9	22.3	...
Malta	1.1	1.3	1.3	1.3	1.3	1.5	44
Moldova	10.7	13.1	13.2	13.8	14.8	16.6	55
Netherlands	2.7	2.7	2.8	2.9	3.1	...	...
Norway	...	...	...	...	...	...	...
Poland	11.5	12.3	12.9	13.0	13.9	13.8	20
Portugal	10.6	10.8	10.9	11.1	11.3	11.7	10
Romania	7.7	8.6	7.8	8.9	8.8	9.3	21
Russia	...	...	...	...	...	...	...
Slovakia	10.3	10.4	10.7	11.1	11.7	11.9	16
Slovenia	7.3	8.1	8.0	8.4	9.1	9.0	24
Sweden	...	7.9	7.7	7.7	7.6	8.1	...
Switzerland	9.2	9.2	9.0	9.8	9.3	9.3	0
UK: England & Wales	...	3.8	3.6	3.6	3.6	3.5	...
UK: Northern Ireland	2.7	2.7	2.7	2.7	2.6	2.6	-2
UK: Scotland	5.2	5.1	5.5	5.4	5.6	6.2	21
Mean	8	8	8	9	9	10	
Median	8	8	8	8	9	9	
Minimum	1	1	1	1	1	2	
Maximum	26	27	27	27	27	27	

Notes on table 2.2.4.1:
Albania, UK: Northern Ireland: The absolute number of employees has not changed during the period 1995-2000.
Italy: Data concerning "magistrati italiani" which includes judges and prosecutors.
Switzerland: Estimate of the total number of staff employed in 2000 in 3 cantons (Geneva, Vaud and Zurich) using the same methodology as that used for table 2.2.1, since these 3 cantons deal with 29% of all convictions in Switzerland.
UK: Northern Ireland: Figures are based on estimates.

Notes on table 2.2.4.2:
Albania, UK: Northern Ireland: The absolute number of prosecutors has not changed during the period 1995-2000.
Albania: The figure for 1995 presents the number of prosecutors and investigators ("hetues"). Since the new Code of Penal Procedure came into force (1 August 1995), "hetues" no longer exist; their duties are now exercised either by the judiciary police or the prosecutors. So the data from 1996 onwards shows the number of prosecutors and judiciary police.
Denmark: Figures for 1998 and 1999 are based on estimates.
Germany: The numbers of "Amtsanwälte" (special prosecutors responsible for minor offences only) are not included. The numbers of "Amtsanwälte" for both 1998 and 2000 are 965. No data on "Amtsanwälte" are available for 1996.
Moldova: According to the penal code, crimes (homicide, rape, etc) are investigated by investigators from the public prosecutor's office, which means that the investigators from the State Prosecution are counted twice: once as investigating personnel and again when included in the total number of prosecutors.
Portugal: The number of prosecutors includes those working at the Attorney General's Office. In most courts, prosecutors deal with criminal as well as non criminal cases.
Sweden: Figure for 1996 is estimated.
UK: Northern Ireland: Figures are based on estimates and relate to Director of Public Prosecutions (DPP) only. In addition to the 43 "in-house" lawyers in the DPP office, it should be noted that an additional number of barristers from the independent Bar of Northern Ireland were briefed by the Department to conduct prosecutions at Magistrates' courts and County Courts and also the Crown Court.

2.3 Technical information on tables 2.2.1–2.2.4.2

2.3.1 General remarks

Five countries (Ireland, Luxembourg, Spain, Turkey and Ukraine) were not able to provide any data for this chapter. They are not listed in this section.

For most countries, the counting unit in the prosecution statistics is the case (i.e. proceedings), which implies that there is more than one defendant, or more than one offence. For details see technical table 2.3.4.1.

As the data presented here is counted on an output basis, i.e. based on the total number of cases disposed of, pending cases are not included. The countries were asked for input data and information on pending cases but the respective tables have been left out because most countries did not provide all the required information.

The sum of the figures reported for the different disposal categories is not always equal to the total number of cases disposed for the same country. This is due to several reasons, especially because of double counting and counting rules differing between categories (e.g. input vs. output or persons count vs. case count).

The data presented in this chapter give an overview of the prosecution statistics of the different countries and only a section of the comments made by the different countries are given here. For more information on a certain country see the raw data of the European sourcebook on the website.

2.3.2 Offences/cases handled by the prosecuting authorities

For most countries, figures on cases handled by the prosecuting authority *include* cases reported to the prosecutor by other institutions (e.g. customs, other non-police authorities).

Regarding the criminal offences handled by the prosecuting authority, in most countries more serious traffic offences, such as drink driving (with or without accident) and dangerous driving (with or without accident) were *included* in the figures, while minor traffic offences (e.g. exceeding the speed limit or parking offences) and offences against police or administrative regulations were *excluded*.

The exceptions are presented in the following table.

Table 2.3.2: Offences/cases handled by the prosecuting authorities

	Cases reported by other institutions	Drink driving (with or without accident)	Dangerous driving (with or without accident)	Minor traffic offences	Offences against police or administrative regulations
Albania	Excluded				
Austria		Excluded			
Croatia		*	*		
Cyprus	Excluded	Excluded	Excluded		
Czech Republic		Excluded	Excluded		
Denmark		Excluded	Excluded		
France				*	*
Georgia		Excluded	Excluded		Included
Latvia			Excluded		
Lithuania		*	*		
Moldova					Included
Norway	*				*
Poland		*	*		
Romania			Excluded		Included
Russia		*	*		
Slovakia		Excluded			
Slovenia		Excluded	Excluded		Included
UK: England & Wales	Excluded			Included	Included
UK: Northern Ireland	Excluded			Included	Included
UK: Scotland				*	*

* Notes on table 2.3.2:

Croatia: With accident included, without accident excluded.

France: According to French law, less serious offences are called "contraventions". Contraventions from categories 1 to 4 (minor contraventions, for which the prosecuting authority is the Police) are excluded. Contraventions from category 5 (the most serious) are included.

Lithuania: Only dangerous driving with accident causing body injury or big material loss is criminalised. Drink driving without accident is an offence if it occurs more than once a year.

Norway: Regarding cases reported by other institutions, on the spot fines (relating to traffic misdemeanours and misdemeanours against the Duty Act) are excluded. Offences against police regulations included; offences against administrative regulations excluded.

Poland: Drink driving without accident is an offence since 1 December 2000. Dangerous driving is only an offence in connection with an accident.

Russia: Included if consequences are grave (health or life), otherwise excluded.

UK: Scotland: Minor traffic offences excluded if dealt with by police directly, included if they are referred to the Procurator Fiscal. Offences against police or administrative regulations included if they are referred to the Procurator Fiscal.

2.3.3 Disposal categories

General disposal categories
Countries were asked to *include* – if possible – the following disposal categories in their figures: Cases brought before a court (indictment, acte d'accusation, Anklageschrift); sanctions imposed by the prosecutor (or by the court, but without a formal court hearing) based on the defendant's admission of guilt (Ordonnance pénale, Strafbefehl); sanctions negotiated between the prosecutor and the defendant without admission of guilt; proceedings dropped; other disposals. While most countries stated that their figures *included* information on cases brought before a court, proceedings dropped and other disposals, the two categories on prosecutorial sanctions where very often excluded. The latter is generally due to the fact that the prosecution authorities of most countries do not themselves have the power to impose sanctions on a person.

The following table shows the countries that did not *include* all of the disposal categories.

Table 2.3.3.1: General disposal categories

	Cases brought before a court	Sanctions imposed by the prosecutor (or by the court, but without a formal court hearing), based on the defendant's admission of guilt	Sanctions negotiated between the prosecutor and the defendant without admission of guilt	Proceedings dropped	Other disposals
Albania		Excluded	Excluded		
Armenia		Excluded	Excluded		
Austria		*	Excluded		
Belgium	Excluded	Excluded		Excluded	Excluded
Bulgaria		Excluded	Excluded		Excluded
Croatia		Excluded	Excluded		
Cyprus		Excluded	Excluded	Excluded	Excluded
Czech Republic			Excluded		
Denmark	Excluded	Excluded	Excluded		Excluded
Estonia			Excluded		Excluded
Finland			Excluded	Excluded	
Georgia		Excluded	Excluded		
Hungary		Excluded	*		
Latvia		Excluded	Excluded		
Lithuania		Excluded	Excluded		Excluded
Moldova		Excluded	Excluded		Excluded
Netherlands		Excluded			
Norway			Excluded		
Poland		*	Excluded		
Portugal		Excluded	Excluded		
Romania		Excluded	Excluded		
Russia		Excluded	Excluded		
Slovakia			Excluded		
Slovenia		Excluded	Excluded		
Switzerland			Excluded		
UK: England & Wales		Excluded	Excluded		Excluded
UK: Northern Ireland		Excluded	Excluded		Excluded
UK: Scotland		Excluded			

* Notes on table 2.3.3.1:

Austria: Not applicable before 2000, included since 2000.

Hungary: Figures for this category refer to persons, not cases, and are therefore not included in the total number of cases disposed of.

Poland: Since 1998 not applicable.

Proceedings dropped

Proceedings dropped should *include* these sub-categories: No criminal responsibility/suspect not guilty; lack of evidence; act not an offence; no complaint from victim (where this is required for a prosecution) or complaint withdrawn; no public interest (expediency principle); offender not available. While many countries were able to *include* these categories in the total of proceedings dropped and the total number of cases disposed of, fewer countries were able to give a breakdown by sub-categories as well.

The following table shows the countries that had to exclude certain sub-categories from the total of proceedings dropped and the total number of cases disposed of.

Table 2.3.3.2: Proceedings dropped

	No criminal responsibility/ suspect not guilty	Lack of evidence	Act not an offence	No complaint from victim or complaint withdrawn	No public interest	Offender not available
Armenia						
Austria						
Bulgaria				Excluded	Excluded	Excluded
Croatia						
Denmark	Excluded		Excluded	Excluded		Excluded
Estonia					Excluded	
France						
Germany						
Hungary					Excluded	
Latvia				Excluded	Excluded	Excluded
Lithuania						Excluded
Moldova						Excluded
Netherlands						
Norway	*		Excluded			Excluded
Poland						
Portugal						Excluded
Romania		Excluded	Excluded		Excluded	Excluded
Russia			Excluded		Excluded	
Slovenia						Excluded
Switzerland				*		
UK: England & Wales						Excluded
UK: Northern Ireland		Excluded	Excluded	Excluded	Excluded	Excluded
UK: Scotland	Excluded			Excluded	Excluded	Excluded

* Notes on Table 2.3.3.2:

Norway: No criminal responsibility included; suspect not guilty excluded.
Switzerland: When no complaint from victim, excluded; when complaint withdrawn, included.

Unknown offenders
A special problem occurred regarding the proceedings where an offence has been committed but the offender has not been found (unknown offender). Seventeen countries included unknown offenders in their statistics, while thirteen others excluded them. To make it even more complex, three (Austria, Germany and Moldova) of the 17 countries that included unknown offenders counted them on another basis rather than in the "other categories" (i.e. input instead of output) and therefore were unable to include the figure in the total number of cases disposed of and proceedings dropped. In the case of Slovakia, the figures for unknown offenders were included in the total of proceedings dropped, but obviously not in the total number of cases disposed of.

As countries were only asked whether unknown offenders were included or excluded in the data, the reasons for inclusion/exclusion are not always evident. For some countries (e.g. UK: England & Wales or the Netherlands) cases do not enter the prosecution stage at all if no suspect can be found. For other countries the reason may simply be that figures on unknown offenders are unavailable. Therefore, countries listed in the last column of table 2.3.3.3 have had different reasons for excluding unknown offenders from their data.

For the most part, comparisons are on figures for known offenders if countries provided sufficient data to calculate this figure. If for a certain country data on unknown offenders were initially included in the figures, it was decided to subtract the number of unknown offenders from the total number of cases disposed of and the number of dropped proceedings. That was possible for countries that provided us with the number of unknown offenders (see second column of table 2.3.3.3), but impossible for some other countries (see first column of table 2.3.3.3) that did not provide that number. Comparisons between countries of the latter group and the other countries are therefore problematic, as the number of cases dropped because no offender could be found is usually high.

Table 2.3.3.3: Unknown offenders

Unknown offenders included in total figures	Unknown offenders excluded from total figures		
	Initially included in total but subtracted here	Separate data on known and unknown offenders provided	No data available on unknown offenders
Albania	Armenia	Austria	Bulgaria
the Czech Republic	Croatia	Germany	Cyprus
Estonia	France	Moldova	Denmark
Georgia	Norway		Finland
Hungary	Poland		Italy
Portugal	Slovakia		Latvia
Romania	Slovenia		Lithuania
Russia			the Netherlands
			Switzerland
			UK: England & Wales
			UK: Northern Ireland
			UK: Scotland

Notes on Table 2.3.3.3:
Total figures include total number of cases disposed of and total number of proceedings dropped.
Slovakia: Number of unknown offenders was only subtracted from the total number of proceedings dropped, as it was never included in the total number of cases disposed of for that country.

Other disposals
For other disposals, the following sub-categories should be *included*: No authority; transfer to another domestic authority; private criminal prosecution recommended; transfer to a foreign authority.

The following table shows the countries that were not able to *include* all of the sub-categories.

Table 2.3.3.4: Other disposals

	No authority	Transfer to another domestic authority	Private criminal prosecution recommended	Transfer to a foreign authority
Albania			Excluded	
Armenia			Excluded	
Croatia	Excluded	Excluded	Excluded	
Czech Republic	Excluded		Excluded	
Finland			Excluded	Excluded
France		Excluded		Excluded
Georgia		Excluded	Excluded	Excluded
Hungary			Excluded	
Latvia	Excluded	Excluded	Excluded	
Netherlands		Excluded	Excluded	
Norway			Excluded	Excluded
Poland	Excluded	Excluded	Excluded	Excluded
Portugal	Excluded	Excluded	Excluded	
Romania		Excluded	Excluded	
Russia	Excluded		Excluded	
Slovakia	Excluded		Excluded	
Slovenia			Excluded	
Switzerland			Excluded	
UK: Scotland	Excluded	*	Excluded	Excluded

* **Notes on Table 2.3.3.4:**

UK: Scotland: Diversion to Social Work Department or children's reporter included.

2.3.4 Data recording methods for prosecution statistics

Description of data recording methods for prosecution statistics

Table 2.3.4.1: Description of data recording methods for prosecution statistics

Questions	Are there written rules regulating the way in which the data shown in Table 2.1.1 are recorded?	How are individual proceedings counted if more than one person is involved?	How are multiple offences counted?	How is a person counted who is subject to two or more proceedings in one year?	Are data collected by other authorities (apart from the prosecutor or examining judge) included?	Are cases disposed of by the police under the responsibility of the prosecutor included?
Possible answers	1=Yes 2=No	1=As one case 2=As two or more cases	1=As one case 2=As two or more cases	1=As one case 2=As two or more cases	1=Included 2=Excluded	1=Included 2=Excluded
Albania	1	1	1	2	2	1
Armenia	1	1	1	1	1	1
Austria	1	1	1	2	2	...
Belgium	...	...	...	...	...	...
Bulgaria	1	1	1	2	1	1
Croatia	1	2	1	2	2	2
Cyprus	1	1	1	2	2	2
Czech Republic	1	1	1	2	2	1
Denmark	2	2	1	2	...	1
Estonia	1	1	*	1	1	...
Finland	2	1	1	2	2	...
France	1	1	1	2	2	1*
Georgia	...	...	...	...	...	...
Germany	1	1	1	2	2	2
Greece	...	...	...	...	...	...
Hungary	1	1	1	2	1	1
Italy	1	1	2	2	2	2
Latvia	1	1	1	2	2	1
Lithuania	1	1*	2*	2	1	1
Malta	...	...	...	...	...	...
Moldova	1	1	1	1	1	1
Netherlands	1	2	1	2	1	2
Norway	1	1	2	1	2	1
Poland	1	1	1	2	2	1
Portugal	1	1	1	2	2	2
Romania	2	1	1	2	2	2
Russia	1	1	1	1	1	2
Slovakia	1	2	1	1	1	1
Slovenia	1	1	1	2	2	2
Sweden	...	...	...	...	...	...
Switzerland	1	1	1	1	2	1
UK: England & Wales	1	2	1	2	2	2
UK: Northern Ireland	1	2	1	2	2	2
UK: Scotland	1	1	1	2	2	2

* Notes on table 2.3.4.1:
Estonia: When pre-trial investigation begins, each offence is handled as a separate criminal case, but in the course of the pre-trial investigation, separate cases are consolidated, and only one criminal case is brought before a court. There are no strict rules on how similar offences (serial offences) are calculated – it depends on the particular circumstances.
France: The cases dealt with by the police alone (under the responsibility of the public prosecutor) are included where some of them are discontinued at the police stage on the direction of the prosecutor. However, these cases are registered by the Public Prosecution (e.g. shoplifting or drug usage). The police classification is not used by either the Public Prosecutor or the police.
Lithuania: Cases may be split apart under special circumstances, e.g. when one of the suspects is not available, then his case may be separated from the case of the other accessories and stopped (or paused). Cases are consolidated: a) when few persons are suspected as accessories in one or more offences; b) when one person is suspected in two or more offences. But normally one case covers one offence.

Substantial modifications of data recording methods between 1995 and 2000
Albania: From 1998, data recording methods changed. Changes were two-fold: first, the presentation of the data is done following the criteria of the New Procedure Code, which added new categories for other disposals. Because the number of cases is small no data appear to have been recorded for these new categories.

Austria: Cases brought before a court – until 1997 the counting unit is the person, from 1998 it is the case.
Until 1999 cases dropped because of no public interest also include successfully resolved out of court settlements. In 2000 these cases are included in sanctions imposed by the prosecutor ("intervening diversion").

France: In 1998, there was a review of discontinued cases according to their reason. The official statistics commentary suggested the systematisation of the concept of "other disposals" (alternative to formal proceedings). These proceedings take place beside cases where the proceeding is declared impossible (e.g. unknown offender, unspecified breach) and other discontinued cases (expediency principle). In the new classification only the last cases are considered as "discontinued" (proceedings were possible, but the prosecutor decided not to proceed neither before a court, neither by an alternative way).
It is difficult to reconstruct a homogenous series for "other disposals" since the point of time when they are counted has changed (at the beginning of the alternative procedure until 1997, to the final decision from 1998). Moreover, a new category has been added among "other disposals" including "reminder of the law" (similar to English caution, but given by a prosecutor representative) and "warning", that affected around 62 500 cases out of 163 800 in 1998 that were counted under "alternative procedures" (in 1999 around 96 000 cases out of 214 100 and in 2000 around 117 000 cases out of 250 000). With this change in the terminology and the statistical classification, the traditional rate for discontinued cases (for which the unknown offenders exceed 80% of cases) is replaced with a rate for "penal response" that comprises cases brought before a

court and alternative procedures, this total being divided by the number of cases that are "processable".

Romania: In 1997, recording methods were modified by the inclusion of more offences from the Penal Code and offences provided by special penal laws.

2.4 Sources of the data used in chapter 2

Countries that could not provide any data are not mentioned.

2.4.1 Sources of the data in tables 2.2.1–2.2.3

Albania	Department of Statistics, General Prosecutor's Office of the Republic of Albania
	The data are unpublished. Only some sporadic data are published on the internet.
Armenia	Ministry of Internal Affairs.
Austria	National Bureau of Statistics (Österr. Statistisches Zentralamt).
	Statistics of Administration of Justice, 1995-1997.
	Ministry of Justice. Information System on Operation of Prosecutors, 1998-2000.
Belgium	Penal mediation data:
	Source 1: Rapports d'évaluation de la loi organisant une procédure de médiation pénale en Belgique portant sur les années 1995, 1996, Penal mediation advisors of the Appeal Court.
	Source 2: Rapport d'activité pour le Service des Maisons de Justice portant sur les années 1999 et 2000 (publication en cours).
	Service des Maisons de Justice from 1999.
Bulgaria	"Prosecutor's Offices Activities" – the data of the activities of the regional and district prosecutor's offices are sent annually to the Supreme Cassations Prosecutor's Office where they are summarised.
Croatia	State Bureau of Statistics – Department of Judicial and Administrative Statistics:
	Internal Documentation (unpublished – only selected data are published).
Cyprus	"Criminal Statistics" for the years 1995-1999, Tables 5 and 6.
Czech Republic	The Statistical Yearbook of Criminality. Ministry of Justice.
Denmark	Source: "Kriminalstatistikken 1995, 1996, 1997, 1998, 1999, 2000" (Crime statistics), Statistics Denmark.
Estonia	The State Prosecutor's Office.
Finland	Yearbook of Justice Statistics, Statistics Finland.
France	Ministère de la Justice, sous-direction de la statistique des études et de la documentation, annuaire statistique de la justice.
Germany	Statistisches Bundesamt (Hrsg.), Staatsanwaltschaften, 1995-1999, Wiesbaden 1996–2002.

Hungary	Chief Public Prosecutor's Office.
Italy	National Institute of Statistics – ISTAT
Latvia	Prosecution Office of the Republic of Latvia.
Lithuania	Ministry of Internal Affairs – Department of Informatics and Communication – Section of Statistics. (Taken from the statistical database of the Centre of Crime Prevention in Lithuania. Website: www.nplc.lt).
Moldova	Rapport statistique, Office du Procureur Général.
Netherlands	Ministry of Justice (WODC) and Central Bureau of Statistics. Not published.
Norway	Statistics Norway, Division for Social Welfare Statistics.
Poland	Ministry of Justice, Department of Statistics.
Portugal	Annual reports produced by the Attorney General's Office.
Romania	Public Prosecutor's Office attached to the Supreme Court of Justice statistics.
Slovakia	Internal statistical system of prosecutor´s Office.
Slovenia	State Prosecutor's Annual Report.
Switzerland	– Administrative statistics available on: http://www.ge.ch/tribunaux/en_general/compterendu.html – Vaud: Internal administrative statistics; – Zurich: Cantonal annual report and administrative report (unpublished).
UK: England & Wales	Crown Prosecution Service.
UK: Northern Ireland	Northern Ireland Office Statistics and Research Branch.
UK: Scotland	Monthly statistical returns from Procurators Fiscal to Crown Office.

2.4.2 Sources of the data in tables 2.2.4.1 and 2.2.4.2

Albania	Personnel Directory. General Prosecutor Office, Tirana, Albania, unpublished.
Armenia	Ministry of Internal Affairs.
Austria	State budget legislation. Planned staff posts.
Belgium	Service du personnel de la Direction générale de l'Organisation judiciaire – Ministère de la Justice.
Croatia	Annual Report of the Public Prosecutor's Office for 2001.
Cyprus	The Law Office of the Republic.
Czech Republic	Report about Prosecuting Authorities´ work, 1995-2000 years. Published.
Denmark	"Politiets virksomhedsregnskab 2000", Rigspolitiet.
Estonia	The State's Prosecutor's Office.
Finland	Statistics Finland.

Germany	Statistisches Bundesamt (Hrsg.), Rechtspflege, Fachserie 10, Reihe 1, Ausgewählte Zahlen für die Rechtspflege 1998, Wiesbaden 2000.
Greece	Ministry of Justice (personal communication).
Hungary	Chief Public Prosecutor's Office.
Italy	Ministerio dell'economia e delle finanze, Relazione generale sulla situazione economica del paese.
Latvia	Prosecutor General of the Republic of Latvia.
Lithuania	Source: *"Criminality and the law enforcement activity"*. Annual publication of the Statistics Department under the Government of Lithuania.
Malta	Attorney-General's Office.
Moldova	Rapport statistique Office du Procureur Général.
Netherlands	Ministry of Justice (unpublished data).
Poland	Ministry of Justice, HR Department.
Portugal	Legal Policy and Planning Office, Ministry of Justice.
Romania	Service of Human Resources from the Public Prosecutor's Office attached to the Supreme Court of Justice.
Slovenia	Annual report about the work of the public prosecutors for the years 1995–2000.
Sweden	The Swedish Prosecutor Organisation Annual Report.
Switzerland	Estimate based on data from 3 out of the 26 cantons (Geneva, Vaud, and Zurich) which comprise 31% of Switzerland's population. Marguerat, C., 2002, "Essai d'analyse des données statistiques des autorités de poursuite pénale de quatre cantons suisses", Mémoire de diplôme en criminologie, Lausanne: Université de Lausanne, Institut de criminologie et de droit pénal.
UK: England & Wales	Crown Prosecution Service.
UK: Scotland	Personnel Division.

3 Conviction statistics

3.1 General comments

3.1.1 Introduction

1. The tables in this chapter refer to persons who have been convicted, i.e. found guilty, according to the law, of having committed a criminal offence. Information is presented on the type of offence (1995-2000); the sex, age and nationality of the offender (1999); the type of sanctions imposed, as well as the duration of unsuspended custodial sentences (1999). Thirty-one countries submitted data on sanctions/measures for 1999 and 29 on convicted persons for 2000. An obvious problem in this chapter is related to the major differences in criminal procedures between countries and, although attempts have been made to compare data on sanctions/measures imposed, this has proved impossible for some countries. It is important to remember that three countries (Luxembourg, Malta and Turkey) did not provide any data on convictions.

3.1.2 Offence definitions

2. In comparisons with police statistics, offence definitions used in this chapter are not always identical to those referred to for crimes recorded by the police. Offence definitions adopted by the various police systems present some uniformity but definitions used for recorded sanctions/measures can vary substantially as they are based on the judicial system of each country and are entirely dependent on the offence definition provided in national penal statutes. For this reason, the breakdown of data in this chapter does not follow that in chapter 1. Thus, "burglary" and "car theft" were not identified separately for many countries but were merely included in the general categories "theft" or "drugs offences". Some countries reported differences between the definitions of offences used by the courts in the conviction statistics and in those used by police in the recorded crime statistics. This affected several countries; for example, in the Portuguese, Swiss and Danish conviction statistics, "robbery" (street robberies or muggings) were included in the theft category. Also, in the continental systems, "theft of a motor vehicle" only included those thefts where there was an intention to use the vehicle temporarily whereas if the intention was to keep the vehicle permanently the offence was recorded as "theft".

3.1.3 Definition of convictions

3. In the preparation of the questionnaire an attempt was made to provide definitions for "convictions" of offenders and subsequent "disposals" compatible between most criminal justice systems. The need for such advice was created by the fact that (a) offenders in certain jurisdictions are not always convicted by a court and (b) sanctions/measures may be imposed by another authority (Police or Prosecutor). Therefore, the suggested definition of "persons convicted" included sanctions/measures imposed by a prosecutor based on an admission of guilt by

the defendant. However, this definition did not include cases where (a) a prosecutor imposed sanctions/measures not based on the admission of guilt by the defendant, (b) sanctions imposed by the police (e.g. cautions in UK: England & Wales) and (c) where other state authorities imposed a sanction/measure. The high number of offenders (mainly minors) who admit their guilt but were subsequently cautioned by the police were therefore excluded in UK: England & Wales. Some countries found that they were not able to supply data on sanctions from the prosecutor.

3.1.4 Minimum age of convictions

4. Information collected on convictions and sanctions/measures imposed will be affected by the minimum age at which a conviction can be imposed. For the 34 countries supplying this information, eleven countries had a minimum age between 15 and 17, fourteen had a minimum age of 14 years, three countries had a minimum age between 11 and 13, whilst in 6 countries the age was below 10 years. Although this age will be important, many countries have other systems for dealing with minors which divert most minors from the formal Criminal Justice System. How minors are dealt with may also differ between offences.

3.1.5 Validation checks

5. Once the term "convictions" had been defined, it was expected that the number of convictions should be equal to the number of persons on whom sanctions/measures had been imposed, either by the courts only or by both courts and prosecutors. Data checks were carried out in order to ensure that, for the information included in the relevant tables, each offender would be counted only once for each offence, even if several sanctions/measures were imposed with respect to that particular offence. Despite this, data for certain countries still showed significant differences between the number of convictions and sanctions/measures; these discrepancies were not fully explained, although they may be partly due to the different counting units used for convictions and sanctions/measures. In addition, in some countries it is possible to have a conviction without sanction.

6. Initial data checks also showed differences in several countries between the number of persons sentenced to a custodial sentence and the information received on the sentence lengths of such sentences. This reflected three points: (a) the inclusion of suspended sentences within the sentence length tables, (b) differences in the statistical collection system used and (c) variations following appeal in the sentence imposed whose length was taken into consideration.

3.1.6 Methodology

7. This section focuses on the information provided by countries in the process of clarifying the meaning of data included in statistical tables. It should, therefore, be read in conjunction with the tables in this section.

Statistical rules
8. All countries applied some form of written rules to regulate the method used to collect data on both convictions and sanctions/measures. This included some form of "principal offence rule", so that an offender convicted of more than one offence at the same time will only be counted once in the statistics. While most countries count the most serious offence, it was not always clear for many countries whether they determined the seriousness of the offence based upon a) the nature of the offence or b) the punishment imposed. If more than one offender participated in the commission of an offence, then each perpetrator was counted separately in all countries.

9. There were two different procedures identified with respect to the point at which statistics on court decisions were recorded. Twelve countries replied that information related to the position before the convicted person made an appeal on either the verdict or the sentence. For the remaining twenty-three, information was collected only after any such appeal was completed. Variations in the point at which data was collected may have affected the size of the figures in the relevant tables.

10. When an offender is convicted for more than one offence in a year, the majority of countries indicated that each conviction would be counted separately. However, Armenia, Bulgaria, Georgia, Slovakia and Slovenia indicated that such convictions would only be counted once in their statistics, which suggests that there will be a lower conviction rate in such countries.

Provision of data on sanctions/measures
11. Many countries had difficulties in providing detailed information on the sanctions/measures given for a particular offence. This was due to data being collected from three different statistical recording sources (i.e. prosecution, courts and authorities recording non-custodial sanctions).

12. Sanctions/measures in all countries fall into four categories: fines, non-custodial sentences, suspended custodial sentences and unsuspended custodial sentences. However, the actual form of each type of disposal, and consequently the components of each category differ substantially from country to country. Few countries have the same non-custodial options and in some countries they are available as part of the execution of a custodial sentence.

3.1.7 Results

13. The tables show a detailed breakdown of convictions and sanctions/measures imposed between 1995 and 2000. A full analysis of the data would require more detailed research in each country. The commentary in this chapter looks at four offences (Homicide (completed), Rape, Total Thefts and Total Drugs) drawing on the definitional differences and the comparison with

the trends in the number of recorded offences. These offences were chosen in order to include as many countries as possible with relatively similar definitions. Completed homicides were selected rather than total homicides since the closeness between these two numbers (for some countries) suggest that little distinction is made between the two definitions. Figures for different types of theft are not shown separately, as they are often not separated by the criminal code.

3.1.8 Total crimes

14. Information on the total number of criminal convictions for the period 1995-2000 shows that the highest numbers per 100 000 population in 2000 were in Finland (3 351 per 100 000) and UK: England & Wales (2 684), with a median of 571 and the lowest level in Albania (117). These differences reflect, in part, the different number and way that traffic offences are dealt with in each country. However, even when traffic offences are excluded, UK: England & Wales (1 544) and Finland (1 417) still retain the highest levels of criminal convictions, followed by Sweden (1 072), Norway (888), Hungary (881) and Russia (802). The lowest levels were in Albania (113) and Ireland (192).

3.1.9 Homicides (excluding attempts)

Convictions
15. For 2000, information was available for convictions for intentional homicides (completed, i.e. excluding attempts) in 16 countries. Over the 1995-2000 period, the rate per 100 000 population for completed homicide convictions fell in all countries except Croatia, Germany and UK: England & Wales. The biggest increase was in Croatia (1.7 per 100 000 in 1995 to 2.8 per 100 000 in 2000) and the biggest fall in Norway (0.9 per 100 000 in 1995 to 0.5 per 100 000 in 2000).

16. In absolute terms, the highest rate of convictions for completed homicides in 2000 were recorded in Estonia (7.4 per 100 000). The lowest rate was recorded in Ireland (0.3 per 100 000). For most countries, less than 8% of convictions for completed homicides in 2000 were for minors (aged under 18), although this was higher in Slovakia (16%) and UK: England & Wales (10%). In addition, in most countries less than 14% of convictions for completed homicides in 2000 were for females, with the exception of Hungary (19%).

17. Information on the sanctions/measures imposed for completed homicides in 1999 was only available for 17 countries. Imprisonment was imposed for over 80% of convictions in most countries, the exceptions being Portugal, Finland, Denmark and Norway. In Portugal 21% and in Switzerland 17% of the sanctions/ measures imposed were suspended custodial sentences. Suspended custodial sentences may have been given where the offender had acted in self-defence but without complete justification. For those countries that provided data, only

Latvia imposed the death penalty (1% of all sanctions imposed). The length of prison sentence imposed varied. For some countries, life sentences are mandatory for murder (all parts of the United Kingdom), although not for manslaughter or infanticide.

3.1.10 Rape

Convictions
18. Most countries were able to supply information for convictions for rape. Twenty-six countries provided data for 2000 on rape convictions per 100 000 of population. The highest increase was in Ireland (140%) followed by Croatia (111%) but there were sharp falls in Portugal (50%), Romania (37%), Ukraine (34%) and Estonia (33%). In total, there were rises in nine countries and falls in fourteen. However, such changes may be the result of legal changes broadening the concept of rape.

19. In absolute terms, the highest rates for rape convictions (4 to 5 per 100 000 population) in 2000 were in Belgium, Russia and Slovenia with the lowest rates in Albania, Norway, Portugal and UK: England & Wales (at less than 1 per 100 000). However, almost all countries' statistics on rape will be affected by the extent to which the victims report these offences to the police. As expected, countries showed a low proportion of females convicted for this offence in 2000 (except for Turkey whose figures include adultery). Minors accounted for more than 10% of convictions in most countries.

Sanctions and measures
20. Although imprisonment is the main sanction for this offence in all countries, several countries also use suspended custodial sentences and non-custodial sanctions. In 1999, the average sentence length was about 4.5 years in most countries. Also, in some countries life sentences may be given (e.g. UK: England & Wales) or other indeterminate sentences. Lower average sentence lengths were found in the Netherlands, Bulgaria and Norway. In addition, in 1999, around 50% of those convicted received suspended custodial sentences in Slovakia, Finland and Germany, and over 30% in the Czech Republic, Poland, Bulgaria, Slovenia and Estonia.

3.1.11 Total thefts

Convictions
21. Although there is wide variation in the definition for component parts of "total theft" (e.g. theft of a motor vehicle, burglary), the definition of "total theft" is fairly uniform.

22. There was a rise in rate of convictions per 100 000 population for total thefts over the period 1995-2000 for 15 countries and a fall in convictions for 8

countries. The biggest rise was in Bulgaria (74 per 100 000 in 1995 to 195 in 2000) and the biggest fall in Romania (213 in 1995 to 122 in 2000).

23. In absolute terms, the highest rates for theft convictions in 2000 were in Finland (687 per 100 000), Russia (410), Hungary (340), UK: Scotland (337) and Estonia (306). There were much lower rates in Albania and Georgia (below 50). The reason for this wide variation is not known. In Austria, Denmark, Germany and Sweden 25% or more of those convicted in 2000 were females, and in Albania, Estonia, Greece, Latvia, Slovakia, Switzerland, and UK: England & Wales over 20% were minors.

Sanctions and measures
24. There was a wide variation in the types of sanctions/measures imposed with over 50% of those convicted sentenced to unsuspended custody in Italy, Georgia, Portugal and Romania whereas in a number of countries, theft convictions mainly resulted in a fine, for example Finland (89%), Denmark (70%) and Germany (59%). For the majority of countries, the sentences imposed were normally short (less than 6 months).

3.1.12 Drugs Offences (total)

Convictions
25. There are wide variations between countries in their drug enforcement policy. For some countries drug convictions will mainly mean drug trafficking, whereas in others it could include simple possession of drugs.

26. In absolute terms, the highest levels of convictions for drug offences in 2000 were recorded in Norway (186 per 100 000 population), Finland (113) and Scotland (103). The lowest levels were recorded in Romania, Bulgaria, Slovakia, Albania, Latvia and Poland (all less than 8 per 100 000). Less than 20% of persons convicted were minors in all countries except for Switzerland (37%).

27. The variation in the types of offences included within this category is reflected in the differences in the severity of sentences imposed. There were widespread differences between countries in the sanctions/measures imposed, with the fine being the most frequently used sentence in some countries (e.g. Norway, Finland and UK: England & Wales (60-70%)), suspended sentences in others (e.g. Estonia, Greece, Poland and Slovakia (60-80%)) and unsuspended custodial sentences in others (e.g. Denmark, Italy and Romania (90-100%)). Such statistics provide an interesting comparison of the offences included in the definition and the severity of sentences imposed but these figures alone are insufficient for making comparisons. Similarly, there are wide variations in the sentence lengths for custodial sentences for example, Hungary (41% life) and Cyprus (67% less than 6 months).

3.2 Tables

3.2.1 Persons convicted per 100 000 population

Table 3.2.1.1: Persons convicted per 100 000 population – Criminal offences: Total

	1995 R31TC95	1996 R31TC96	1997 R31TC97	1998 R31TC98	1999 R31TC99	2000 R31TC00	% change 1995-2000
Albania	52.9	136.2	43.0	...	138.7	117.2	122
Armenia	...	...	209.7	191.2	194.9	203.0	...
Austria	867.7	831.4	805.7	789.3	763.8	511.9	-41
Belgium	1506.8	1499.7	1572.4	1560.0	1442.2	1446.2	-4
Bulgaria	139.8	198.3	269.2	350.2	306.9	388.3	178
Croatia	342.4	321.5	301.9	298.9	397.3	402.9	18
Cyprus	86.2	121.0	126.7	124.9	125.5	...	...
Czech Republic	532.3	562.1	580.3	525.5	608.8	615.4	16
Denmark	926.3	856.9	818.2	812.0	766.6	...	...
Estonia	539.6	579.1	620.9	570.7	610.1	716.8	33
Finland	3353.0	3218.7	3064.7	3262.3	3127.6	3350.7	0
France	612.7	837.5	898.1	935.0	971.5	957.3	56
Georgia	...	193.7	195.0	204.0	168.7	172.8	...
Germany	1123.5	1125.1	1148.3	1168.9	1113.6	1071.1	-5
Greece	1075.6	1055.3	1116.1	...	...	...	...
Hungary	937.5	907.4	966.1	1075.2	1054.3	1033.8	10
Ireland	146.3	143.2	141.1	115.4	62.4	192.7	32
Italy	357.1	428.0	510.1	526.3	484.0	...	...
Latvia	388.4	417.8	517.0	529.3	530.3	527.6	36
Lithuania	499.4	508.9	495.6	536.5	541.7	571.2	14
Luxembourg	...	...	...	...	...	...	...
Malta	...	...	...	...	...	...	...
Moldova	327.4	304.1	312.8	310.1	329.6	360.4	10
Netherlands	628.8	640.9	648.4	637.9	669.5	658.2	5
Norway	1274.4	1270.7	1448.5	1354.6	1384.6	1427.0	12
Poland	506.3	589.5	544.8	566.6	537.0	576.6	14
Portugal	364.9	368.5	377.5	405.7	443.8	534.2	46
Romania	448.2	459.7	496.1	471.9	389.9	336.5	-25
Russia	699.3	752.0	687.7	728.8	834.9	810.7	16
Slovakia	...	...	...	...	384.2	399.2	...
Slovenia	207.4	232.0	291.6	331.3	337.2	357.7	72
Spain	293.7	278.4	260.0	277.3	...	...	...
Sweden	1603.4	1348.1	1396.8	1403.4	1304.6	1338.0	-17
Switzerland	937.3	930.9	951.2	1004.8	971.2	...	...
Turkey	...	...	...	...	...	...	...
Ukraine	414.9	475.9	471.6	465.3	448.4	469.8	13
UK: England & Wales	2589.1	2738.6	2631.8	2782.3	2661.6	2683.8	4
UK: Northern Ireland	2053.0	1903.5	1915.2	1657.6	1630.9	...	...
UK: Scotland	1474.6	1477.0	1440.9	1346.0	1247.0	1146.9	-22
Mean	828	815	808	828	794	806	
Median	540	584	580	567	575	571	
Minimum	53	121	43	115	62	117	
Maximum	3353	3219	3065	3262	3128	3351	

Table 3.2.1.2: Persons convicted per 100 000 population – Criminal offences: Traffic offences

	1995 R31TT95	1996 R31TT96	1997 R31TT97	1998 R31TT98	1999 R31TT99	2000 R31TT00	% change 1995-2000
Albania	...	8.4	1.3	2.8	4.3	4.0	...
Armenia	...	...	...	...	...	...	...
Austria	...	...	...	...	...	...	...
Belgium	1054.9	1080.2	1165.5	1162.4	1080.7	1085.7	3
Bulgaria	10.1	11.1	11.4	10.6	10.4	15.7	56
Croatia	94.6	89.8	90.8	50.6	56.8	52.3	-45
Cyprus	...	...	...	...	...	...	...
Czech Republic	54.2	57.4	58.7	56.5	59.0	57.5	6
Denmark	...	...	...	...	...	...	...
Estonia	...	5.5	6.1	7.6	34.2	90.8	...
Finland	2096.0	1958.8	1828.4	1958.6	1779.2	1933.8	-8
France	223.1	260.4	270.7	291.4	334.9	347.5	56
Georgia	...	...	...	...	...	...	...
Germany	387.4	371.1	368.1	350.6	314.0	306.8	-21
Greece	251.6	226.9	310.0	...	...	...	...
Hungary	207.1	163.6	162.2	162.5	159.6	152.8	-26
Ireland	0.1	0.1	0.1	0.1	0.1	0.6	299
Italy	0.3	0.8	1.0	1.1	1.2	...	...
Latvia	70.0	79.9	98.5	103.7	112.1	94.3	35
Lithuania	...	...	...	...	...	...	...
Luxembourg	...	...	...	...	...	...	...
Malta	...	...	...	...	...	...	...
Moldova	8.3	7.3	9.5	8.8	7.0	6.5	-22
Netherlands	126.2	134.2	152.2	145.4	145.6	154.5	22
Norway	413.2	502.0	540.9	540.5	529.6	538.7	30
Poland	30.9	45.4	45.5	43.0	29.1	27.1	-12
Portugal	75.8	89.7	91.1	113.6	202.3	246.2	225
Romania	42.0	45.6	46.8	43.1	32.5	23.4	-44
Russia	...	...	13.7	10.5	10.8	8.5	...
Slovakia	...	...	...	...	19.1	18.4	...
Slovenia	29.3	35.2	41.4	44.5	37.2	42.5	45
Spain	58.2	60.7	65.5	73.4	...	...	...
Sweden	284.6	215.5	243.8	240.8	235.9	265.7	-7
Switzerland	512.0	492.5	488.8	525.5	498.4	...	...
Turkey	...	...	...	...	...	...	...
Ukraine	9.6	10.3	10.9	9.6	7.1	7.0	-27
UK: England & Wales	1223.7	1230.6	1228.4	1253.8	1191.8	1140.5	-7
UK: Northern Ireland	1253.0	1127.9	1160.9	947.7	970.4	...	...
UK: Scotland	...	...	...	...	...	...	...
Mean	341	308	304	302	291	276	
Median	95	90	91	73	59	74	
Minimum	0	0	0	0	0	1	
Maximum	2096	1959	1828	1959	1779	1934	

Table 3.2.1.3: Persons convicted per 100 000 population – Intentional homicide: Total

	1995 R31HO95	1996 R31HO96	1997 R31HO97	1998 R31HO98	1999 R31HO99	2000 R31HO00	% change 1995-2000
Albania	1.9	8.8	3.7	11.5	10.4	13.1	593
Armenia	...	...	...	...	...	...	...
Austria	0.7	0.7	0.7	0.8	0.7	...	...
Belgium	1.4	1.2	1.3	1.5	1.4	1.5	8
Bulgaria	2.6	2.6	3.0	2.1	2.6	2.0	-21
Croatia	3.1	3.2	3.2	3.4	4.7	4.6	49
Cyprus	0.0	0.8	0.8	0.7	1.7	...	...
Czech Republic	1.3	2.0	1.6	1.8	1.8	1.6	22
Denmark	1.1	0.9	1.2	1.1	0.8	...	...
Estonia	13.5	10.8	10.5	9.3	8.9	7.7	-43
Finland	3.8	3.7	3.4	2.8	3.0	3.2	-17
France	1.4	1.3	1.3	1.3	1.4	1.1	-19
Georgia	...	15.1	15.7	19.6	20.9	21.4	...
Germany	1.2	1.3	1.3	1.4	1.2	1.1	-9
Greece	0.7	0.6	0.6	...	...	...	...
Hungary	2.8	3.5	3.3	2.8	2.7	3.0	5
Ireland	0.1	0.0	0.0	0.1	0.0	0.4	344
Italy	1.3	1.0	1.3	1.3	1.3	...	...
Latvia	7.4	3.9	5.4	4.1	4.7	4.0	-47
Lithuania	...	...	...	...	...	...	...
Luxembourg	...	...	...	...	...	...	...
Malta	...	...	...	...	...	...	...
Moldova	7.3	4.2	3.4	3.2	3.4	4.0	-45
Netherlands	6.3	6.9	6.6	7.1	6.9	...	...
Norway	...	...	0.9	0.6	0.6	0.6	...
Poland	1.7	1.9	1.7	1.8	1.7	1.6	-2
Portugal	3.4	3.2	2.9	2.9	2.6	2.6	-24
Romania	8.5	9.0	9.2	8.8	8.3	6.5	-23
Russia	...	12.5	12.1	12.7	12.8	13.3	...
Slovakia	...	...	...	...	1.0	1.2	...
Slovenia	1.9	1.9	2.0	2.0	1.5	2.5	31
Spain	1.3	1.1	0.5	0.7	...	...	...
Sweden	1.4	1.5	1.4	1.2	1.5	1.7	20
Switzerland	1.2	1.2	1.2	1.2	0.9	...	...
Turkey	...	...	...	...	...	...	...
Ukraine	6.0	7.0	6.7	6.8	7.0	7.8	30
UK: England & Wales	0.5	0.6	0.7	0.6	0.6	0.6	18
UK: Northern Ireland	4.3	0.9	0.3	1.2	1.1	...	...
UK: Scotland	2.6	3.1	2.4	1.9	2.2	2.6	1
Mean	3	4	3	4	4	4	
Median	2	2	2	2	2	3	
Minimum	0	0	0	0	0	0	
Maximum	13	15	16	20	21	21	

Table 3.2.1.4: Persons convicted per 100 000 population – Intentional homicide: Completed

	1995 R31HC95	1996 R31HC96	1997 R31HC97	1998 R31HC98	1999 R31HC99	2000 R31HC00	% change 1995-2000
Albania	...	...	...	...	...	...	...
Armenia	...	...	...	...	...	...	...
Austria	0.5	0.4	0.4	0.4	0.4	...	...
Belgium	0.8	0.8	0.7	0.7	0.7	0.7	-22
Bulgaria	2.1	2.1	2.4	1.5	2.1	1.7	-22
Croatia	1.7	1.9	1.7	1.4	3.1	2.8	61
Cyprus	0.0	0.7	0.4	0.4	1.7	...	...
Czech Republic	...	...	...	...	...	...	...
Denmark	0.8	0.9	0.8	0.8	0.6	...	...
Estonia	12.1	8.9	9.1	7.9	8.5	7.4	-39
Finland	1.9	2.1	1.9	1.6	1.8	1.6	-18
France	...	...	...	...	...	...	...
Georgia	...	...	...	...	...	...	...
Germany	0.8	0.8	0.9	0.9	0.8	0.8	3
Greece	0.6	0.6	0.5	...	...	...	...
Hungary	2.1	2.4	2.2	1.6	1.7	1.9	-9
Ireland	0.0	0.0	0.0	0.0	0.0	0.3	...
Italy	0.8	0.7	0.7	0.8	0.9	...	...
Latvia	6.3	3.6	4.4	3.4	4.2	3.6	-43
Lithuania	...	...	...	...	...	...	...
Luxembourg	...	...	...	...	...	...	...
Malta	...	...	...	...	...	...	...
Moldova	...	...	...	...	...	...	...
Netherlands	1.0	1.2	1.1	1.2	1.1	...	...
Norway	0.9	0.7	0.5	0.4	0.5	0.5	-48
Poland	1.4	1.6	1.4	1.4	1.4	1.3	-9
Portugal	1.9	1.9	1.7	1.6	1.6	1.5	-20
Romania	6.1	6.3	6.6	6.3	6.0	4.8	-21
Russia	...	...	...	...	...	...	...
Slovakia	...	...	...	...	0.9	1.1	...
Slovenia	...	...	...	...	...	...	...
Spain	...	...	...	...	...	...	...
Sweden	...	...	...	...	...	...	...
Switzerland	0.7	0.6	0.7	0.6	0.3	...	...
Turkey	...	...	...	...	...	...	...
Ukraine	...	...	...	...	...	...	...
UK: England & Wales	0.4	0.5	0.5	0.5	0.5	0.5	20
UK: Northern Ireland	1.2	0.8	0.2	1.0	0.9	...	...
UK: Scotland	1.7	2.2	1.6	1.3	1.3	1.4	-18
Mean	2	2	2	2	2	2	
Median	1	1	1	1	1	1	
Minimum	0	0	0	0	0	0	
Maximum	12	9	9	8	9	7	

Table 3.2.1.5: Persons convicted per 100 000 population – Assault

	1995 R31AS95	1996 R31AS96	1997 R31AS97	1998 R31AS98	1999 R31AS99	2000 R31AS00	% change 1995-2000
Albania	3.6	4.0	0.9	2.6	1.4	0.1	-98
Armenia	...	...	...	...	...	...	...
Austria	124.7	114.8	105.9	99.7	88.3	...	...
Belgium	46.2	40.8	40.0	41.0	41.3	42.8	-7
Bulgaria	1.3	1.3	1.7	1.8	2.1	2.8	118
Croatia	10.3	9.3	8.7	17.2	22.5	18.0	74
Cyprus	4.8	6.5	9.7	6.1	5.0	...	...
Czech Republic	21.9	25.0	29.7	20.6	25.4	32.5	48
Denmark	80.6	74.1	75.4	76.5	79.2	...	...
Estonia	16.8	14.8	20.5	18.1	20.5	18.4	9
Finland	153.4	160.9	160.4	152.2	160.9	181.1	18
France	35.4	66.2	77.5	84.1	87.6	87.4	147
Georgia	...	...	...	...	...	...	...
Germany	50.9	54.6	59.8	64.7	67.5	70.6	39
Greece	32.8	28.0	26.8	...	...	...	...
Hungary	60.9	54.2	55.1	55.5	51.8	52.5	-14
Ireland	1.9	1.6	1.7	1.9	1.0	16.9	786
Italy	5.0	6.1	7.5	8.4	8.2	...	...
Latvia	...	...	...	...	...	...	...
Lithuania	...	...	...	...	...	...	...
Luxembourg	...	...	...	...	...	...	...
Malta	...	...	...	...	...	...	...
Moldova	8.0	6.7	6.0	5.3	6.9	6.5	-19
Netherlands	35.7	37.2	39.6	41.6	49.1	48.6	36
Norway	16.8	16.6	16.1	15.3	15.2	14.3	-15
Poland	35.5	49.2	47.5	48.7	42.4	44.3	25
Portugal	27.0	30.8	31.6	34.5	39.0	53.5	98
Romania	8.9	9.8	11.9	12.6	10.9	11.5	29
Russia	...	22.2	22.1	21.7	34.5	24.0	...
Slovakia	...	...	...	...	30.1	30.8	...
Slovenia	15.4	19.5	29.1	31.1	34.2	32.8	113
Spain	8.6	9.4	8.7	10.1	...	...	...
Sweden	105.9	92.5	84.5	90.5	89.8	88.5	-16
Switzerland	14.0	15.6	16.8	17.9	18.2	...	...
Turkey	...	...	...	...	...	...	...
Ukraine	24.6	26.7	28.2	29.5	30.2	30.3	23
UK: England & Wales	109.4	112.1	123.9	134.6	135.8	134.6	23
UK: Northern Ireland	38.5	45.4	39.3	38.1	35.4	...	...
UK: Scotland	248.1	257.2	260.4	249.5	229.2	214.9	-13
Mean	45	46	47	48	49	52	
Median	26	27	29	30	34	33	
Minimum	1	1	1	2	1	0.1	
Maximum	248	257	260	250	229	215	

Table 3.2.1.6: Persons convicted per 100 000 population – Rape

	1995 R31RA95	1996 R31RA96	1997 R31RA97	1998 R31RA98	1999 R31RA99	2000 R31RA00	% change 1995-2000
Albania	0.5	1.8	0.4	0.4	0.3	0.7	51
Armenia	...	...	...	...	...	...	...
Austria	2.2	1.8	1.8	2.1	2.0	...	...
Belgium	3.7	4.2	4.8	4.7	4.5	4.5	21
Bulgaria	1.7	1.9	1.9	1.9	2.6	2.3	36
Croatia	0.8	0.5	1.3	0.9	1.3	1.7	111
Cyprus	0.0	0.7	0.3	0.4	0.5	...	...
Czech Republic	1.8	1.5	1.6	2.0	1.6	1.4	-23
Denmark	1.4	0.7	1.0	1.4	1.4	...	...
Estonia	4.0	3.1	3.2	3.7	2.6	2.7	-33
Finland	1.2	1.2	1.0	1.0	1.0	1.2	-3
France	1.8	2.1	2.4	2.7	3.1	2.9	59
Georgia	...	1.2	1.2	2.2	1.7	1.8	...
Germany	1.5	1.5	1.5	2.8	2.8	2.7	82
Greece	0.4	0.4	0.3	...	...	...	...
Hungary	2.3	1.9	2.2	2.0	1.7	1.6	-31
Ireland	0.6	0.4	1.2	0.4	0.2	1.4	140
Italy	1.7	2.1	2.2	2.2	2.1	...	...
Latvia	4.2	3.0	4.9	4.7	4.3	3.7	-12
Lithuania	...	...	...	...	...	...	...
Luxembourg	...	...	...	...	...	...	...
Malta	...	...	...	...	...	...	...
Moldova	3.7	3.3	3.3	3.6	3.4	2.5	-34
Netherlands	2.3	2.1	2.2	2.1	2.1	2.0	-12
Norway	0.8	0.7	0.8	0.9	0.7	0.6	-32
Poland	2.5	2.8	2.5	2.7	2.3	2.2	-14
Portugal	1.3	1.0	0.7	0.7	0.6	0.6	-50
Romania	4.4	4.3	4.4	3.4	3.2	2.8	-37
Russia	...	6.1	5.3	4.9	5.3	4.4	...
Slovakia	...	...	...	...	1.3	1.1	...
Slovenia	2.2	2.6	2.9	3.8	3.7	3.9	79
Spain	0.7	0.5	0.2	0.8	...	...	...
Sweden	1.5	1.1	1.3	1.5	1.1	1.4	-10
Switzerland	1.2	0.9	1.4	1.3	1.3	...	...
Turkey	...	...	...	...	...	...	...
Ukraine	2.8	2.6	2.3	2.2	2.2	1.8	-34
UK: England & Wales	1.1	1.1	1.2	1.3	1.3	1.1	4
UK: Northern Ireland	1.5	0.9	1.3	1.1	0.4	...	...
UK: Scotland	0.5	0.6	0.6	0.7	0.5	0.5	-5
Mean	2	2	2	2	2	2	
Median	2	1	1	2	2	2	
Minimum	0	0	0	0	0	1	
Maximum	4	6	5	5	5	5	

Table 3.2.1.7: Persons convicted per 100 000 population – Robbery

	1995 R31RO95	1996 R31RO96	1997 R31RO97	1998 R31RO98	1999 R31RO99	2000 R31RO00	% change 1995-2000
Albania	1.4	3.5	1.7	6.1	6.7	8.5	512
Armenia	...	...	...	...	...	...	...
Austria	5.7	5.7	5.4	5.6	5.4	...	...
Belgium	21.6	21.0	20.6	21.5	18.7	23.9	11
Bulgaria	7.1	7.8	9.4	12.9	11.8	17.4	145
Croatia	2.6	2.0	2.8	3.1	3.8	4.8	85
Cyprus	1.0	0.5	1.1	1.7	1.1	...	...
Czech Republic	11.6	13.7	13.1	15.7	14.5	13.9	19
Denmark	10.5	11.0	12.2	12.0	12.9	...	...
Estonia	60.9	63.7	68.8	60.3	64.0	75.9	25
Finland	9.3	9.8	8.6	7.9	8.7	10.5	13
France	9.5	10.5	10.3	10.0	9.2	8.7	-9
Georgia	...	...	...	...	...	6.5	...
Germany	11.1	12.9	14.3	15.0	13.8	13.1	18
Greece	1.9	1.6	2.1	...	...	...	...
Hungary	14.5	12.5	14.5	15.7	14.9	15.3	6
Ireland	4.2	3.1	2.0	1.5	0.8	9.0	113
Italy	9.9	11.1	12.4	12.8	11.5	...	...
Latvia	17.1	10.3	18.3	14.7	15.6	26.8	56
Lithuania	...	...	...	...	...	...	...
Luxembourg	...	...	...	...	...	...	...
Malta	...	...	...	...	...	...	...
Moldova	23.7	19.7	18.8	21.5	23.3	22.7	-5
Netherlands	22.4	22.8	22.8	22.1	23.2	24.6	10
Norway	3.9	4.0	3.3	2.8	4.1	5.0	28
Poland	14.2	17.9	16.6	16.8	20.7	22.8	60
Portugal	16.2	14.8	13.9	12.8	11.7	14.6	-10
Romania	14.0	13.5	12.2	14.1	13.6	11.9	-15
Russia	...	52.6	53.2	56.0	69.6	63.2	...
Slovakia	...	...	...	...	12.9	12.7	...
Slovenia	2.4	3.1	4.0	4.3	5.1	5.0	109
Spain	16.4	14.6	11.5	12.0	...	...	...
Sweden	6.4	5.8	6.2	6.8	6.9	9.0	40
Switzerland	4.8	5.0	4.9	4.8	5.2	...	...
Turkey	...	...	...	...	...	...	...
Ukraine	17.5	18.7	19.7	20.0	20.6	20.3	16
UK: England & Wales	10.0	11.3	10.7	10.6	10.7	11.2	12
UK: Northern Ireland	12.1	10.0	10.3	8.3	7.9	...	...
UK: Scotland	12.9	14.0	12.6	11.7	12.7	11.4	-12
Mean	12	13	14	14	15	18	
Median	11	11	12	12	12	13	
Minimum	1	1	1	2	1	5	
Maximum	61	64	69	60	70	76	

Table 3.2.1.8:   Persons convicted per 100 000 population – Theft: Total

	1995 R31TH95	1996 R31TH96	1997 R31TH97	1998 R31TH98	1999 R31TH99	2000 R31TH00	% change 1995-2000
Albania	17.6	45.7	7.9	16.7	20.2	28.0	59
Armenia	...	...	...	...	...	...	...
Austria	211.0	200.5	189.2	193.3	189.9	...	...
Belgium	89.4	83.4	76.3	71.7	65.9	75.4	-16
Bulgaria	73.5	105.4	153.6	202.6	164.8	195.3	166
Croatia	84.1	66.6	56.9	73.4	92.2	88.9	6
Cyprus	33.4	47.5	42.6	44.3	45.4	...	...
Czech Republic	169.9	170.0	173.7	150.4	165.6	160.8	-5
Denmark	473.2	439.1	414.4	416.6	382.8	...	...
Estonia	303.7	333.2	343.9	299.9	295.8	305.5	1
Finland	653.2	655.7	637.6	705.6	690.8	687.0	5
France	104.6	162.4	165.9	170.4	167.0	157.4	50
Georgia	...	44.2	38.8	37.2	38.3	32.2	...
Germany	228.1	233.7	239.8	242.6	224.4	208.6	-9
Greece	30.9	39.1	37.6	...	...	...	...
Hungary	328.2	337.6	356.4	395.8	380.8	339.9	4
Ireland	126.7	132.4	139.2	119.5	97.9	132.8	5
Italy	52.0	62.2	75.6	85.5	88.0	...	...
Latvia	180.1	200.1	244.5	246.1	240.6	232.9	29
Lithuania	...	...	...	...	...	...	...
Luxembourg	...	...	...	...	...	...	...
Malta	...	...	...	...	...	...	...
Moldova	183.6	165.7	165.2	165.7	177.3	199.7	9
Netherlands	179.4	179.5	161.2	162.9	169.3	171.3	-4
Norway	175.4	179.9	179.7	178.5	179.6	181.7	4
Poland	135.3	138.7	124.1	131.7	134.3	139.9	3
Portugal	80.3	60.6	51.9	49.5	48.0	55.4	-31
Romania	213.0	216.8	221.4	196.4	150.2	122.3	-43
Russia	...	325.8	315.6	320.6	417.4	409.9	...
Slovakia	...	...	...	...	49.7	131.8	...
Slovenia	65.6	63.6	72.1	81.5	83.8	88.4	35
Spain	105.7	98.3	91.8	96.3	...	...	...
Sweden	374.5	314.3	344.8	345.6	292.1	274.4	-27
Switzerland	87.4	91.4	100.4	100.9	90.5	...	...
Turkey	...	...	...	...	...	...	...
Ukraine	180.3	193.1	189.9	196.1	198.1	220.5	22
UK: England & Wales	249.4	246.4	253.0	266.2	276.2	267.3	7
UK: Northern Ireland	254.0	221.3	204.8	186.3	167.4	...	...
UK: Scotland	432.2	420.8	400.3	385.1	370.3	336.9	-22
Mean	190	190	190	198	192	202	
Median	175	170	166	174	167	177	
Minimum	18	39	8	17	20	28	
Maximum	653	656	638	706	691	687	

Table 3.2.1.9: Persons convicted per 100 000 population – Theft: Theft of a motor vehicle

	1995 R31TV95	1996 R31TV96	1997 R31TV97	1998 R31TV98	1999 R31TV99	2000 R31TV00	% change 1995-2000
Albania	...	...	...	...	...	...	...
Armenia	...	...	...	...	...	...	...
Austria	...	...	...	...	...	...	...
Belgium	...	...	...	...	...	...	...
Bulgaria	...	...	...	...	...	...	...
Croatia	2.8	2.7	3.0	...	...	...	...
Cyprus	...	...	...	...	...	...	...
Czech Republic	...	...	...	...	...	...	...
Denmark	36.1	36.2	39.8	36.6	35.4	...	...
Estonia	...	...	...	...	...	...	...
Finland	...	...	...	...	...	...	...
France	...	...	...	...	...	...	...
Georgia	...	6.2	6.0	9.9	11.8	6.7	...
Germany	...	...	...	...	...	...	...
Greece	0.4	0.3	0.3	...	...	...	...
Hungary	...	...	...	...	...	...	...
Ireland	33.9	46.9	53.6	51.9	62.8	23.2	-32
Italy	...	...	...	...	...	...	...
Latvia	...	...	...	...	...	...	...
Lithuania	...	...	...	...	...	...	...
Luxembourg	...	...	...	...	...	...	...
Malta	...	...	...	...	...	...	...
Moldova	...	...	...	...	...	...	...
Netherlands	...	...	...	...	...	...	...
Norway	10.6	10.5	12.0	8.5	8.4	7.2	-32
Poland	...	...	...	...	...	...	...
Portugal	...	...	...	...	...	...	...
Romania	...	...	...	...	...	0.6	...
Russia	...	...	...	...	...	...	...
Slovakia	...	...	...	...	6.4	2.1	...
Slovenia	5.9	6.4	6.6	7.7	5.5	7.3	24
Spain	12.8	10.0	6.8	8.7	...	...	...
Sweden	28.3	22.8	23.3	23.3	21.9	19.5	-31
Switzerland	...	...	...	...	...	...	...
Turkey	...	...	...	...	...	...	...
Ukraine	...	...	...	...	...	...	...
UK: England & Wales	17.1	16.4	16.0	15.4	15.2	13.5	-21
UK: Northern Ireland	33.7	26.5	28.6	25.8	18.2	...	...
UK: Scotland	47.0	45.8	41.6	35.8	31.6	27.7	-41
Mean	21	19	20	22	22	12	
Median	17	13	14	19	17	7	
Minimum	0	0	0	8	6	1	
Maximum	47	47	54	52	63	28	

Table 3.2.1.10: Persons convicted per 100 000 population – Theft: Burglary: Total

	1995 R31BU95	1996 R31BU96	1997 R31BU97	1998 R31BU98	1999 R31BU99	2000 R31BU00	% change 1995-2000
Albania	...	...	...	...	...	...	...
Armenia	...	...	...	...	...	...	...
Austria	28.6	25.3	23.6	21.7	22.4	...	...
Belgium	...	...	...	...	...	...	...
Bulgaria	...	...	...	...	...	...	...
Croatia	35.4	22.4	20.5	21.6	32.2	35.1	-1
Cyprus	14.5	19.6	18.4	15.5	17.6	...	...
Czech Republic	...	...	...	...	...	...	...
Denmark	70.7	67.2	63.5	55.6	50.0	...	...
Estonia	...	...	...	...	...	...	...
Finland	...	...	...	...	...	...	...
France	...	...	...	...	...	...	...
Georgia	...	...	...	...	...	...	...
Germany	36.8	35.4	35.2	32.5	27.8	23.4	-36
Greece	...	...	...	...	...	...	...
Hungary	...	...	...	...	...	...	...
Ireland	41.6	41.1	37.3	27.9	13.4	37.1	-11
Italy	...	...	...	...	...	...	...
Latvia	103.6	115.1	127.2	114.0	111.6	112.2	8
Lithuania	...	...	...	...	...	...	...
Luxembourg	...	...	...	...	...	...	...
Malta	...	...	...	...	...	...	...
Moldova	...	...	...	...	...	...	...
Netherlands	113.9	108.2	90.8	88.3	89.2	88.1	-23
Norway	63.9	62.3	59.7	55.9	56.7	47.7	-25
Poland	85.2	101.0	91.9	92.9	83.9	83.9	-2
Portugal	...	...	...	...	...	...	...
Romania	...	...	...	...	...	...	...
Russia	...	...	...	...	...	...	...
Slovakia	...	...	...	...	43.3	39.2	...
Slovenia	14.3	16.8	20.2	28.4	36.0	32.8	129
Spain	73.7	71.1	68.9	70.8	...	...	...
Sweden	15.1	13.8	14.4	14.8	13.3	13.3	-12
Switzerland	8.6	9.7	10.7	10.0	8.5	...	...
Turkey	...	...	...	...	...	...	...
Ukraine	...	...	...	...	...	...	...
UK: England & Wales	68.1	61.8	60.7	58.7	55.7	49.0	-28
UK: Northern Ireland	59.2	49.7	44.2	39.9	43.2	...	...
UK: Scotland	87.1	74.5	63.4	57.4	58.1	51.6	-41
Mean	54	53	50	47	45	51	
Median	59	50	44	40	43	43	
Minimum	9	10	11	10	8	13	
Maximum	114	115	127	114	112	112	

Table 3.2.1.11: Persons convicted per 100 000 population – Theft: Burglary: Domestic Burglary

	1995 R31BD95	1996 R31BD96	1997 R31BD97	1998 R31BD98	1999 R31BD99	2000 R31BD00	% change 1995-2000
Albania	...	...	...	...	...	...	...
Armenia	...	...	...	...	...	...	...
Austria	...	...	...	...	...	...	...
Belgium	...	...	...	...	...	...	...
Bulgaria	...	...	...	...	...	...	...
Croatia	...	...	...	...	...	...	...
Cyprus	...	...	...	...	...	...	...
Czech Republic	...	...	...	...	...	...	...
Denmark	20.1	19.2	20.1	17.0	16.2	...	...
Estonia	...	...	...	...	...	...	...
Finland	...	...	...	...	...	...	...
France	...	...	...	...	...	...	...
Georgia	...	...	...	...	...	...	...
Germany	...	...	...	...	...	...	...
Greece	...	...	...	...	...	...	...
Hungary	...	...	...	...	...	...	...
Ireland	...	...	...	...	...	...	...
Italy	...	...	...	...	...	...	...
Latvia	...	...	...	...	...	...	...
Lithuania	...	...	...	...	...	...	...
Luxembourg	...	...	...	...	...	...	...
Malta	...	...	...	...	...	...	...
Moldova	...	...	...	...	...	...	...
Netherlands	...	...	...	...	...	...	...
Norway	...	...	...	5.1	4.7	3.7	...
Poland	...	...	...	...	...	...	...
Portugal	...	...	...	...	...	...	...
Romania	...	...	...	...	...	...	...
Russia	...	...	...	...	...	...	...
Slovakia	...	...	...	...	31.0	19.4	...
Slovenia	...	...	...	...	...	...	...
Spain	...	...	...	...	...	...	...
Sweden	...	...	...	...	...	...	...
Switzerland	...	...	...	...	...	...	...
Turkey	...	...	...	...	...	...	...
Ukraine	...	...	...	...	...	...	...
UK: England & Wales	35.2	32.8	34.2	33.0	31.2	27.2	-23
UK: Northern Ireland	20.2	23.1	22.0	21.1	26.0	...	...
UK: Scotland	...	...	...	...	...	...	...
Mean	25	25	25	19	22	17	
Median	20	23	22	19	26	19	
Minimum	20	19	20	5	5	4	
Maximum	35	33	34	33	31	27	

Table 3.2.1.12: Persons convicted per 100 000 population – Drug offences: Total

	1995 R31DR95	1996 R31DR96	1997 R31DR97	1998 R31DR98	1999 R31DR99	2000 R31DR00	% change 1995-2000
Albania	0.2	6.1	1.5	2.3	4.5	6.6	> 1000
Armenia	...	...	...	...	...	...	...
Austria	40.5	42.9	47.0	41.1	41.4	...	...
Belgium	51.1	56.2	55.3	45.9	40.8	41.0	-20
Bulgaria	0.1	0.1	0.5	0.9	1.5	2.9	> 1000
Croatia	2.9	6.4	15.9	23.2	38.5	44.8	> 1000
Cyprus	12.7	13.3	16.3	19.6	23.0	...	...
Czech Republic	1.6	3.2	4.1	7.8	8.7	9.5	503
Denmark	6.5	7.8	7.6	9.4	8.5	...	...
Estonia	1.0	4.0	3.7	4.5	10.0	22.6	> 1000
Finland	46.1	56.2	60.0	77.4	88.2	112.5	144
France	33.4	39.6	40.1	40.1	40.0	37.8	13
Georgia	...	...	13.2	16.0	18.4	19.7	...
Germany	46.4	54.5	60.8	62.6	66.0	65.9	42
Greece	14.8	18.6	25.8	...	...	...	...
Hungary	1.9	2.3	4.2	9.0	10.4	15.4	723
Ireland	0.3	56.2	64.2	98.5	112.7	96.3	> 1000
Italy	28.6	35.3	34.2	36.0	31.5	...	...
Latvia	3.6	4.2	5.5	6.2	7.1	6.7	85
Lithuania	0.1	9.5	11.0	9.8	10.9	14.2	> 1000
Luxembourg	...	...	...	...	...	...	...
Malta	...	...	...	...	...	...	...
Moldova	5.0	8.6	11.2	12.7	22.4	30.4	511
Netherlands	29.8	33.1	39.7	43.2	43.8	42.9	44
Norway	94.9	102.3	98.3	157.3	183.3	186.2	96
Poland	4.8	4.5	3.8	4.3	5.9	7.4	54
Portugal	27.1	32.6	43.5	45.3	31.2	35.2	30
Romania	1.1	1.6	1.6	1.2	1.2	0.8	-25
Russia	26.0	30.9	44.3	69.1	78.6	67.9	161
Slovakia	...	...	...	...	2.1	6.5	...
Slovenia	1.5	4.9	5.3	10.4	11.4	12.5	749
Spain	18.8	17.7	12.4	18.1	...	...	...
Sweden	69.8	66.2	77.4	83.9	81.4	90.8	30
Switzerland	113.9	116.2	122.5	118.5	110.9	...	...
Turkey	...	...	...	...	...	...	...
Ukraine	34.8	42.4	44.5	47.4	49.5	52.1	50
UK: England & Wales	60.9	65.4	77.9	93.2	92.7	84.0	38
UK: Northern Ireland	41.8	41.3	32.5	36.3	35.7	...	...
UK: Scotland	109.2	120.1	135.7	133.6	123.2	103.4	-5
Mean	28	33	36	42	44	45	
Median	19	31	29	36	31	35	
Minimum	0	0	0	1	1	1	
Maximum	114	120	136	157	183	186	

Table 3.2.1.13: Persons convicted per 100 000 population – Drug offences: Drug trafficking

	1995 R31DT95	1996 R31DT96	1997 R31DT97	1998 R31DT98	1999 R31DT99	2000 R31DT00	% change 1995-2000
Albania	...	...	...	...	...	...	...
Armenia	...	...	...	...	...	...	...
Austria	14.0	12.7	12.8	13.8	13.9	...	...
Belgium	47.9	...	...	...	...	...	...
Bulgaria	0.0	0.0	0.0	0.1	0.0	0.0	0
Croatia	0.1	0.1	0.1	0.6	0.7	1.4	> 1000
Cyprus	...	...	...	...	...	...	...
Czech Republic	1.3	2.7	3.5	6.8	7.4	8.0	497
Denmark	2.8	3.1	2.9	2.7	2.3	...	...
Estonia	0.2	1.6	1.0	2.0	4.9	4.5	> 1000
Finland	...	...	...	...	...	...	...
France	12.7	14.4	14.6	13.2	13.0	12.4	-2
Georgia	...	...	3.8	4.8	8.0	8.9	...
Germany	5.3	5.6	6.6	6.3	6.5	6.8	27
Greece	3.7	5.0	6.0	...	...	...	...
Hungary	...	...	...	...	...	...	...
Ireland	0.3	0.6	0.7	0.6	0.3	18.1	> 1000
Italy	...	...	...	...	...	...	...
Latvia	...	...	...	...	...	...	...
Lithuania	...	...	...	...	...	...	...
Luxembourg	...	...	...	...	...	...	...
Malta	...	...	...	...	...	...	...
Moldova	...	...	...	...	...	...	...
Netherlands	...	...	...	...	...	...	...
Norway	55.0	62.0	64.9	88.7	104.3	99.3	81
Poland	0.1	0.2	0.5	0.8	1.2	1.3	982
Portugal	11.7	10.4	12.7	11.6	11.3	13.1	12
Romania	...	...	...	...	...	...	...
Russia	...	...	...	...	...	...	...
Slovakia	...	...	...	...	2.0	4.8	...
Slovenia	1.7	4.4	3.9	7.9	8.1	9.1	425
Spain	...	...	...	...	...	...	...
Sweden	...	...	...	...	...	...	...
Switzerland	75.6	74.0	80.1	74.3	71.3	...	...
Turkey	...	...	...	...	...	...	...
Ukraine	...	...	...	...	...	...	...
UK: England & Wales	20.0	21.8	23.9	23.7	21.8	19.4	-3
UK: Northern Ireland	12.0	16.4	12.8	10.5	6.5	...	...
UK: Scotland	22.9	29.9	31.3	31.3	29.9	24.5	7
Mean	15	15	15	17	16	15	
Median	5	5	6	7	7	9	
Minimum	0	0	0	0	0	0	
Maximum	76	74	80	89	104	99	

Table 3.2.2.1: Percentage of females convicted

	Criminal offences: Total	Traffic offences	Intentional homicide: Total	Intentional homicide: Completed	Assault	Rape	Robbery	Theft: Total	Theft: Theft of a motor vehicle	Theft: Burglary: Total	Theft: Burglary: Domestic Burglary	Drug offences: Total	Drug offences: Drug trafficking
	P32TCW99	P32TTW99	P32HOW99	P32HCW99	P32ASW99	P32RAW99	P32ROW99	P32THW99	P32TVW99	P32BUW99	P32BDW99	P32DRW99	P32DTW99
Albania	2.5	...	...	...	...	...	...	...	...	...	...	...	...
Armenia	6.7	...	...	...	...	...	...	...	...	...	...	...	...
Austria	19.7	...	5.6	6.3	6.2	1.2	8.4	29.1	...	7.0	...	12.0	11.9
Belgium	11.6	12.0	8.1	...	4.1	2.1	7.5	9.8	...	...	...	8.2	...
Bulgaria	9.5	4.3	8.3	9.5	2.5	0.0	4.0	5.6	...	...	...	8.6	50.0
Croatia	8.8	9.1	7.7	0.0	5.7	1.4	3.4	5.8	...	3.5	...	6.6	13.8
Cyprus	7.4	...	0.0	0.0	2.6	0.0	0.0	2.0	...	5.3	...	6.9	...
Czech Republic	11.0	...	8.0	...	3.1	...	5.8	9.7	...	...	...	12.2	12.9
Denmark	48.6	...	15.6	12.1	5.9	0.0	6.7	30.9	7.5	3.5	4.7	12.1	14.0
Estonia	7.9	2.2	9.1	...	8.0	...	5.3	8.3	...	...	...	...	...
Finland	16.1	13.8	11.5	7.6	11.2	0.0	5.8	22.4	...	...	...	16.1	...
France	9.7	7.4	11.8	...	8.1	3.0	5.4	11.3	...	...	...	6.1	6.8
Georgia	...	...	...	...	...	...	...	...	...	...	...	...	...
Germany	17.0	13.0	12.1	12.5	7.7	0.6	7.0	26.3	...	4.3	...	10.0	10.2
Greece	13.1	5.1	4.4	5.4	5.8	0.0	3.2	9.5	0.0	...	...	4.3	6.2
Hungary	13.4	5.8	16.6	19.2	9.6	0.6	9.4	11.8	...	...	...	10.5	...
Ireland	11.5	0.0	0.0	0.0	4.2	0.0	0.0	7.3	...	3.2	...	15.3	...
Italy	16.5	...	3.1	2.7	11.3	1.4	5.8	16.6	...	...	...	7.8	...
Latvia	8.1	3.5	11.6	11.5	...	1.1	5.9	8.4	...	4.4	...	22.2	...
Lithuania	...	...	...	...	...	...	...	...	...	...	...	...	...
Luxembourg	...	...	...	...	...	...	...	...	...	...	...	...	...

Conviction statistics 139

	Criminal offences: Total	Traffic offences	Intentional homicide: Total	Intentional homicide Completed	Assault	Rape	Robbery	Theft: Total	Theft: Theft of a motor vehicle	Theft: Burglary: Total	Theft: Burglary: Domestic Burglary	Drug offences: Total	Drug offences: Drug trafficking
	P32TCW99	P32TTW99	P32HOW99	P32HCW99	P32ASW99	P32RAW99	P32ROW99	P32THW99	P32TVW99	P32BUW99	P32BDW99	P32DRW99	P32DTW99
Malta	7.8	...	...	...	...	...	...	...	...	...	...	...	...
Moldova	11.2	1.3	15.3	...	8.5	0.0	2.1	6.7	...	...	...	14.0	...
Netherlands	13.6	6.8	...	...	7.7	1.5	7.4	15.8	...	11.5	...	10.8	...
Norway	7.1	11.4	3.7	4.8	3.4	0.0	6.6	22.5	4.0	5.7	19.4	18.9	16.7
Poland	7.0	6.8	16.9	10.8	5.3	0.8	3.8	4.2	...	1.6	...	10.0	10.2
Portugal	13.7	2.7	7.4	8.0	14.7	3.3	3.6	6.0	...	...	...	10.0	13.4
Romania	11.8	5.3	8.1	9.5	7.8	3.3	8.9	9.0	5.6	...	...	12.9	...
Russia	7.1	...	...	...	...	...	...	...	...	...	...	...	...
Slovakia	10.5	7.0	10.7	12.2	5.0	...	5.2	18.0	0.6	...	1.9	15.5	16.5
Slovenia	...	11.5	8.2	...	5.7	0.0	5.2	6.9	2.1	2.8	...	7.1	5.7
Spain	16.5	...	...	...	...	...	...	...	...	...	...	...	...
Sweden	14.2	10.4	11.7	...	9.4	1.0	2.3	30.5	4.3	...	...	16.6	...
Switzerland	...	11.4	4.8	8.3	6.9	0.0	8.3	17.9	...	...	...	12.6	12.5
Turkey	14.4	...	...	...	...	...	...	...	...	...	...	...	...
Ukraine	15.7	2.1	13.1	...	5.7	0.5	6.1	9.2	...	...	...	23.7	...
UK: England & Wales	11.5	12.2	8.2	9.2	12.4	0.2	7.8	16.8	4.5	3.6	4.4	10.6	14.3
UK: Northern Ireland	14.4	12.1	5.6	7.1	6.4	0.0	1.6	14.2	2.0	2.0	1.9	4.8	11.4
UK: Scotland		...	9.6	13.6	13.0	0.0	8.1	17.5	2.6	2.1	...	13.0	17.1
Mean	13	7	9	8	7	1	5	14	3	4	6	12	14
Median	12	7	8	8	6	0	6	11	3	4	4	11	13
Minimum	3	0	0	0	2	0	0	2	0	2	2	4	6
Maximum	49	14	17	19	15	3	9	31	8	11	19	24	50

Table 3.2.2.2: Percentage of minors among persons convicted

	Criminal offences: Total P32TCM99	Traffic offences P32TTM99	Intentional homicide: Total P32HOM99	Intentional homicide Completed P32HCM99	Assault P32ASM99	Rape P32RAM99	Robbery P32ROM99	Theft: Total P32THM99	Theft: Theft of a motor vehicle P32TVM99	Theft: Burglary: Total P32BUM99	Theft: Burglary: Domestic Burglary P32BDM99	Drug offences: Total P32DRM99	Drug offences: Drug trafficking P32DTM99
Albania	8.1	2.7	6.4	...	10.6	9.1	18.3	30.5	...	...	...	1.3	...
Armenia	5.1	...	...	...	...	...	...	...	...	...	...	...	...
Austria	6.1	...	5.6	3.1	11.8	12.3	37.1	11.7	...	28.7	...	12.4	8.6
Belgium	0.5	...	...	...	...	...	...	...	...	...	...	...	...
Bulgaria	13.5	3.9	6.8	7.7	0.6	7.7	30.1	19.4	...	...	...	17.2	0.0
Croatia	4.6	0.9	4.6	5.0	5.6	8.2	19.0	10.1	...	18.3	...	6.1	1.7
Cyprus	2.9	...	0.0	0.0	0.0	0.0	0.0	5.6	...	7.5	...	0.0	...
Czech Republic	6.6	...	3.1	...	5.4	8.6	19.8	11.1	...	...	...	14.2	13.8
Denmark	9.7	...	...	...	...	...	...	...	...	...	...	...	...
Estonia	15.8	...	2.7	...	4.9	20.5	22.7	21.2	...	...	...	...	...
Finland	7.1	4.0	5.7	4.3	13.2	4.0	23.9	11.8	...	...	...	11.5	...
France	6.7	0.3	8.4	...	10.2	22.5	22.1	19.9	...	...	...	6.8	4.6
Georgia	...	...	...	...	...	...	...	...	...	...	...	...	...
Germany	6.8	2.3	5.8	...	18.2	12.1	37.4	13.4	93.3	25.9	...	8.0	2.9
Greece	10.5	24.2	4.4	5.4	3.8	9.1	31.2	33.4	...	...	...	14.6	12.6
Hungary	9.1	1.8	4.0	3.6	7.2	12.3	29.0	16.1	...	...	...	6.2	...
Ireland	13.4	40.0	0.0	0.0	4.2	0.0	1.8	11.6	...	16.2	...	6.8	...
Italy	0.0	...	0.0	0.0	0.0	0.0	0.3	0.1	...	...	...	0.1	...
Latvia	14.2	1.1	7.4	8.0	...	16.9	20.5	23.3	...	27.3	...	3.7	...
Lithuania	11.4	...	...	...	...	...	...	...	...	...	...	...	...
Luxembourg	...	...	...	...	...	...	...	...	...	...	...	...	...

	Criminal offences: Total	Traffic offences	Intentional homicide: Total	Intentional homicide Completed	Assault	Rape	Robbery	Theft: Total	Theft: Theft of a motor vehicle	Theft: Burglary: Total	Theft: Burglary: Domestic Burglary	Drug offences: Total	Drug offences: Drug trafficking
	P32TCM99	P32TTM99	P32HOM99	P32HCM99	P32ASM99	P32RAM99	P32ROM99	P32THM99	P32TVM99	P32BUM99	P32BDM99	P32DRM99	P32DTM99
Malta	...	...	...	...	...	...	...	...	...	...	...	...	...
Moldova	10.5	0.6	3.3	...	3.9	0.0	17.4	14.1	...	...	...	6.4	...
Netherlands	7.4	0.6	...	...	9.3	16.3	28.7	10.4	...	16.6	...	2.4	...
Norway	7.6	5.7	3.7	4.8	8.4	12.9	25.3	11.3	25.8	11.4	15.6	9.1	7.0
Poland	7.1	2.5	8.6	...	9.6	4.0	16.2	14.6	...	18.7	...	12.5	10.0
Portugal	5.0	6.1	2.3	3.1	2.2	11.5	11.4	9.6	15.2	...	...	2.8	2.5
Romania	8.9	2.3	4.1	4.1	3.2	9.7	19.2	18.3	...	...	...	4.5	...
Russia	12.0	...	5.8	...	3.8	13.5	18.4	15.9	...	...	...	5.2	...
Slovakia	12.8	4.6	14.3	16.3	2.8	16.7	22.0	44.2	4.0	...	4.7	6.0	6.4
Slovenia	8.6	1.1	10.2	...	5.1	13.2	25.8	19.0	17.7	20.6	...	11.3	10.9
Spain	...	...	...	...	...	...	...	...	...	...	...	...	...
Sweden	10.4	6.5	4.4	...	18.2	5.1	44.0	17.8	30.9	17.0	...	6.2	...
Switzerland	14.9	4.0	0.0	0.0	18.0	11.8	35.5	38.2	...	...	...	37.3	16.6
Turkey	...	...	...	...	...	...	...	...	...	...	...	...	...
Ukraine	9.0	1.7	7.4	...	15.4	9.8	16.2	14.1	...	...	...	2.8	...
UK: England & Wales	6.5	2.0	8.8	10.0	16.3	8.5	36.3	25.0	42.1	26.7	25.6	6.4	3.9
UK: Northern Ireland	3.2	0.6	0.0	0.0	5.9	0.0	5.4	12.8	15.5	16.6	16.8	1.9	1.9
UK: Scotland	0.1	...	0.9	1.5	0.2	3.7	1.1	0.1	0.9	0.1	...	0.0	0.0
Mean	8	5	5	4	8	9	21	17	27	18	16	8	6
Median	8	2	4	4	6	9	21	14	18	18	16	6	6
Minimum	0	0	0	0	0	0	0	0	1	0	5	0	0
Maximum	16	40	14	16	18	22	44	44	93	29	26	37	17

Table 3.2.2.3: Percentage of aliens among persons convicted

	Criminal offences: Total	Traffic offences	Intentional homicide: Total	Intentional homicide Completed	Assault	Rape	Robbery	Theft: Total	Theft: Theft of a motor vehicle	Theft: Burglary: Total	Theft: Burglary: Domestic Burglary	Drug offences: Total	Drug offences: Drug trafficking
	P32TCA99	P32TTA99	P32HOA99	P32HCA99	P32ASA99	P32RAA99	P32ROA99	P32THA99	P32TVA99	P32BUA99	P32BDA99	P32DRA99	P32DTA99
Albania	...	...	...	...	...	...	...	...	...	...	...	...	...
Armenia	...	...	...	...	...	...	...	...	...	...	...	...	...
Austria	22.0	...	24.1	18.8	19.7	21.0	34.4	29.7	...	29.8	...	21.4	27.2
Belgium	15.5	...	...	...	...	...	...	...	...	...	...	...	...
Bulgaria	1.5	1.7	0.0	0.0	0.0	0.0	1.3	0.4	...	...	...	11.2	...
Croatia	3.6	5.3	2.6	0.0	1.3	0.0	7.3	3.5	...	4.6	...	2.8	1.7
Cyprus	26.2	...	15.4	15.4	44.7	0.0	0.0	29.8	...	32.3	...	34.7	...
Czech Republic	7.2	...	16.6	...	3.9	18.7	14.7	7.2	...	...	...	11.7	2.0
Denmark	...	...	...	...	...	...	...	...	...	...	...	...	...
Estonia	31.9	12.7	58.2	...	41.7	38.5	45.9	33.2	...	...	...	...	...
Finland	6.8	5.2	3.2	3.3	5.4	20.0	9.6	9.4	...	...	...	5.3	...
France	12.3	8.4	13.3	...	13.0	9.4	12.9	12.4	...	...	...	14.5	22.3
Georgia	...	...	...	...	...	...	...	...	...	...	...	...	...
Germany	24.8	17.1	32.3	...	26.4	33.4	34.0	27.9	...	24.8	...	24.5	30.9
Greece	2.3	...	...	...	...	...	...	...	...	...	...	4.9	...
Hungary	4.5	3.8	2.3	3.1	1.1	1.8	3.6	1.6	...	...	...	6.5	...
Ireland	...	...	...	...	...	...	...	...	...	...	...	...	...
Italy	14.2	...	12.1	...	...	16.2	16.4	22.2	...	...	...	31.9	...
Latvia	...	...	...	...	...	...	...	...	...	...	...	...	...
Lithuania	...	...	...	...	...	...	...	...	...	...	...	...	...
Luxembourg	...	...	...	...	...	...	...	...	...	...	...	...	...

Conviction statistics

	Criminal offences: Total:	Traffic offences	Intentional homicide: Total	Intentional homicide: Completed	Assault	Rape	Robbery	Theft: Total	Theft: Theft of a motor vehicle	Theft: Burglary: Total	Theft: Burglary: Domestic Burglary	Drug offences: Total	Drug offences: Drug trafficking
	P32TCA99	P32TTA99	P32HOA99	P32HCA99	P32ASA99	P32RAA99	P32ROA99	P32THA99	P32TVA99	P32BUA99	P32BDA99	P32DRA99	P32DTA99
Malta	...	...	...	...	...	...	...	...	...	...	...	...	...
Moldova	...	...	...	...	...	...	...	...	...	...	...	...	...
Netherlands	...	...	...	...	...	...	...	...	...	...	...	...	...
Norway	9.5	8.0	14.8	9.5	9.7	12.9	12.1	23.4	4.5	7.6	9.0	11.3	14.0
Poland	1.0	1.6	1.8	...	0.2	1.0	1.9	0.4	...	0.4	...	10.0	2.5
Portugal	2.8	3.0	6.2	6.2	1.5	4.9	3.8	2.0	...	...	...	4.8	8.5
Romania	1.5	...	...	...	...	...	...	...	...	...	...	...	...
Russia	...	...	...	...	...	...	...	...	...	...	...	...	...
Slovakia	0.8	...	...	...	0.1	2.8	0.6	0.3	...	...	0.1	1.7	1.8
Slovenia	5.7	3.8	10.2	...	0.5	5.3	5.2	4.6	14.9	4.0	...	5.4	7.4
Spain	...	...	...	...	...	...	...	...	...	...	...	...	...
Sweden	...	...	...	...	...	...	...	...	...	...	...	...	...
Switzerland	47.4	35.6	59.7	37.5	59.4	61.9	52.4	62.4	...	...	...	49.0	56.0
Turkey	...	...	...	...	...	...	...	...	...	...	...	...	...
Ukraine	1.8	1.3	4.6	...	2.7	1.8	2.2	1.7	...	...	...	1.8	...
UK: England & Wales	...	...	...	...	...	...	...	...	...	...	...	...	...
UK: Northern Ireland	...	...	...	...	...	...	...	...	...	...	...	...	...
UK: Scotland	...	...	...	...	...	...	...	...	...	...	...	...	...
Mean	12	8	16	10	14	14	14	15	10	15	5	14	16
Median	7	5	12	6	4	7	8	8	10	8	5	11	9
Minimum	1	1	0	0	0	0	0	0	5	0	0	2	2
Maximum	47	36	60	38	59	62	52	62	15	32	9	49	56

Notes on Tables 3.2.2.1-3.2.2.3
Belgium and Greece: Data relates to the year 1997 (instead of 1999).
Ireland: Data relates to the year 1998 (instead of 1999).
Croatia, the Czech Republic, Estonia, France, Germany, Hungary, Latvia, Romania and Slovenia: Data relates to the year 2000 (instead of 1999).

Table 3.2.3.1: Types of sanctions/measures imposed in 1999 – Criminal offences: Total

	Total sanctions & measures per 100 000 population	of which: % of Fines	of which: % of Non-custodial sanctions & measures	of which: % of Suspended custodial sanctions & measures	of which: % of Unsuspended custodial sanctions & measures	of which: % of Death penalty	of which: % of Other measures
	R33TCT99	P33TCF99	P33TCN99	P33TCS99	P33TCU99	P33TCH99	P33TCO99
Albania	138.7	23.1	4.9	0.0	75.1	0.1	0.4
Armenia	...	...	...	...	...	...	...
Austria	761.4	62.8	1.5	22.0	13.7	...	...
Belgium	...	...	...	...	...	...	...
Bulgaria	306.9	20.7	4.7	52.2	46.5	...	...
Croatia	469.2	14.6	3.8	56.0	12.7	...	12.9
Cyprus	125.5	46.0	2.9	13.4	37.7	...	...
Czech Republic	609.4	5.4	5.3	61.0	24.5	...	3.8
Denmark	766.6	52.8	7.8	17.5	20.5	...	1.4
Estonia	612.2	25.8	0.4	45.6	24.2	...	4.0
Finland	5670.8	91.3	1.3	4.3	2.6	...	0.3
France	957.3	35.0	16.0	31.8	17.1	...	...
Georgia	197.3	2.8	4.2	7.5	85.5	...	...
Germany	1071.1	70.1	10.4	13.1	6.5	...	...
Greece	1116.1	3.6	5.6	81.1	4.8	...	5.0
Hungary	937.6	43.5	23.3	20.6	12.6	...	...
Ireland	...	...	...	...	...	...	...
Italy	484.0	32.4	...	27.9	39.7	0.0	...
Latvia	530.3	15.8	1.4	57.6	22.3	0.0	2.8
Lithuania	547.2	3.4	4.4	52.9	38.4	0.0	1.0
Luxembourg	...	...	...	...	...	...	...
Malta	...	...	...	...	...	...	...
Moldova	329.6	21.1	27.7	35.2	16.0	...	...
Netherlands	665.5	40.2	...	...	26.0	0.0	...
Norway	1384.6	70.6	1.5	12.8	15.0	...	0.1
Poland	537.0	18.4	7.5	61.4	12.6	...	0.1
Portugal	443.8	73.2	4.1	11.8	10.8	...	0.2
Romania	389.9	21.9	23.1	1.3	51.9	...	1.8
Russia	834.9	5.3	...	...	31.8	0.0	...
Slovakia	384.2	5.0	...	72.1	20.1	...	2.8
Slovenia	357.7	5.1	10.8	68.1	16.1	...	...
Spain	...	...	...	...	...	...	...
Sweden	1304.6	61.5	24.8	1.9	11.8	...	...
Switzerland	971.2	32.7	...	52.1	15.3	...	...
Turkey	...	...	...	...	...	...	...
Ukraine	...	...	...	...	...	...	...
UK: England & Wales	2660.7	70.3	20.1	0.2	7.5	...	1.8
UK: Northern Ireland	1630.9	68.2	19.0	5.3	7.4	...	0.1
UK: Scotland	1254.4	52.2	28.9	...	18.9	...	...
Mean	918	35	10	32	24	0	2
Median	612	32	5	25	17	0	2
Minimum	126	3	0	0	3	0	0
Maximum	5671	91	29	81	85	0	13

Table 3.2.3.2: Types of sanctions/measures imposed in 1999 – Criminal offences: Traffic offences

	Total sanctions & measures per 100 000 population	of which: % of Fines	of which: % of Non-custodial sanctions & measures	of which: % of Suspended custodial sanctions & measures	of which: % of Unsuspended custodial sanctions & measures	of which: % of Death penalty	of which: % of Other measures
	R33TTT99	P33TTF99	P33TTN99	P33TTS99	P33TTU99	P33TTH99	P33TTO99
Albania	...	...	...	...	...	...	...
Armenia	...	...	...	...	...	...	...
Austria	...	...	...	...	...	...	...
Belgium	...	...	...	...	...	...	...
Bulgaria	10.4	25.6	7.7	61.1	38.9	...	...
Croatia	59.6	23.8	0.8	55.5	7.9	...	12.1
Cyprus	...	...	...	...	...	...	...
Czech Republic	59.1	...	...	66.9	...	...	19.8
Denmark	...	...	...	...	...	...	...
Estonia	34.1	40.9	0.0	51.7	6.3	...	1.0
Finland	1937.2	88.4	2.0	7.4	2.2	...	0.1
France	347.5	48.9	16.1	30.0	5.1	...	...
Georgia	...	...	...	...	...	...	...
Germany	306.8	85.3	5.4	6.8	2.4	...	...
Greece	310.0	8.4	13.2	67.0	0.3	...	11.0
Hungary	157.3	81.3	6.3	10.4	2.0	...	...
Ireland	...	...	...	...	...	...	...
Italy	...	...	...	...	...	...	...
Latvia	112.1	40.8	2.8	51.8	2.8	...	1.8
Lithuania	...	...	...	...	...	...	...
Luxembourg	...	...	...	...	...	...	...
Malta	...	...	...	...	...	...	...
Moldova	7.0	27.6	36.2	33.7	2.6	...	...
Netherlands	...	...	...	...	...	...	...
Norway	529.6	77.8	0.2	10.6	11.4	...	0.0
Poland	29.1	23.4	1.8	70.0	4.8	...	0.1
Portugal	202.3	94.6	1.8	3.1	0.5	...	0.0
Romania	32.5	25.8	51.9	4.0	17.1	...	1.2
Russia	...	...	...	...	...	...	...
Slovakia	19.1	7.2	...	55.9	8.7	...	15.0
Slovenia	42.5	15.5	4.0	67.1	13.4	...	...
Spain	...	...	...	...	...	...	...
Sweden	235.9	57.2	22.9	4.2	15.7	...	...
Switzerland	498.4	43.3	...	43.8	12.9	...	...
Turkey	...	...	...	...	...	...	...
Ukraine	...	...	...	...	...	...	...
UK: England & Wales	1191.8	89.2	7.1	0.1	2.5	...	1.1
UK: Northern Ireland	970.4	91.1	5.2	1.5	2.1	...	0.1
UK: Scotland	...	...	...	...	...	...	...
Mean	338	50	10	33	8	...	5
Median	157	42	5	34	5	...	1
Minimum	7	7	0	0	0	0	0
Maximum	1937	95	52	70	39	0	20

Table 3.2.3.3: Types of sanctions/measures imposed in 1999 – Intentional homicide: Total

	Total sanctions & measures per 100 000 population	of which: % of Fines	of which: % of Non-custodial sanctions & measures	of which: % of Suspended custodial sanctions & measures	of which: % of Unsuspended custodial sanctions & measures	of which: % of Death penalty	of which: % of Other measures
	R33HOT99	P33HOF99	P33HON99	P33HOS99	P33HOU99	P33HOH99	P33HOO99
Albania	...	...	...	...	...	...	...
Armenia	...	...	...	...	...	...	...
Austria	0.8	0.0	0.0	0.0	100.0	...	...
Belgium	...	...	...	...	...	...	...
Bulgaria	2.6	0.0	0.0	14.1	85.9	...	...
Croatia	6.4	0.0	1.8	2.6	84.6	...	11.0
Cyprus	1.7	0.0	0.0	0.0	100.0	...	...
Czech Republic	1.8	0.0	0.0	0.5	99.5	...	0.0
Denmark	0.8	0.0	2.2	0.0	66.7	...	31.1
Estonia	9.2	0.8	...	0.8	90.2	...	5.3
Finland	3.0	0.0	0.0	0.6	92.4	...	7.0
France	1.1	0.0	0.1	2.7	97.2	...	...
Georgia	4.5	...	...	...	100.0	...	...
Germany	1.1	0.5	0.1	8.7	90.6	...	...
Greece	0.7	0.0	1.4	0.0	95.8	...	2.8
Hungary	2.7	0.0	0.7	11.3	88.0	...	...
Ireland	...	...	...	...	...	...	...
Italy	1.3	0.0	...	...	100.0	0.0	...
Latvia	4.7	0.0	0.0	0.9	96.5	0.9	1.7
Lithuania	...	...	...	...	...	...	...
Luxembourg	...	...	...	...	...	...	...
Malta	...	...	...	...	...	...	...
Moldova	3.3	0.0	7.5	2.7	89.8	...	...
Netherlands	...	...	...	...	...	...	...
Norway	0.6	0.0	0.0	0.0	74.1	...	25.9
Poland	1.7	1.5	1.0	4.9	92.6	...	...
Portugal	2.6	2.7	2.3	21.3	73.6	...	0.0
Romania	8.3	0.1	2.6	0.0	97.1	...	0.1
Russia	13.8	...	...	...	89.5	0.1	2.4
Slovakia	1.0	...	...	7.1	92.9	...	...
Slovenia	2.5	0.0	16.3	8.2	75.5	...	...
Spain	...	...	...	...	...	...	...
Sweden	1.5	0.0	4.4	0.0	95.6	...	...
Switzerland	0.9	0.0	...	12.9	87.1	...	...
Turkey	...	...	...	...	...	...	...
Ukraine	...	...	...	...	...	...	...
UK: England & Wales	0.6	0.0	2.4	0.3	94.5	...	2.7
UK: Northern Ireland	1.1	0.0	0.0	0.0	22.2	...	0.0
UK: Scotland	2.2	0.0	13.0	...	87.0	...	...
Mean	3	0	3	4	88	0	7
Median	2	0	1	1	91	0	3
Minimum	1	0	0	0	22	0	0
Maximum	14	3	16	21	100	1	31

Table 3.2.3.4: Types of sanctions/measures imposed in 1999 – Intentional homicide: Completed

	Total sanctions & measures per 100 000 population	of which: % of Fines	of which: % of Non-custodial sanctions & measures	of which: % of Suspended custodial sanctions & measures	of which: % of Unsuspended custodial sanctions & measures	of which: % of Death penalty	of which: % of Other measures
	R33HCT99	P33HCF99	P33HCN99	P33HCS99	P33HCU99	P33HCH99	P33HCO99
Albania	...	...	...	...	...	...	...
Armenia	...	...	...	...	...	...	...
Austria	0.5	0.0	0.0	0.0	100.0	...	...
Belgium	...	...	...	...	...	...	...
Bulgaria	2.1	0.0	0.0	7.7	92.3	...	...
Croatia	...	...	...	...	...	...	...
Cyprus	1.7	0.0	0.0	0.0	100.0	...	...
Czech Republic	...	...	...	...	...	...	...
Denmark	0.6	0.0	0.0	0.0	72.7	...	27.3
Estonia	...	...	...	...	...	...	...
Finland	1.8	0.0	0.0	1.1	72.8	...	14.1
France	...	...	...	...	...	...	...
Georgia	2.9	...	...	...	...	...	...
Germany	...	...	...	...	...	...	...
Greece	0.6	0.0	1.7	0.0	98.3	...	0.0
Hungary	1.7	0.0	1.1	9.2	89.7	...	...
Ireland	...	...	...	...	...	...	...
Italy	...	...	...	...	...	...	...
Latvia	4.2	0.0	0.0	1.0	96.0	1.0	2.0
Lithuania	...	...	...	...	...	...	...
Luxembourg	...	...	...	...	...	...	...
Malta	...	...	...	...	...	...	...
Moldova	...	...	...	...	...	...	...
Netherlands	...	...	...	...	...	...	...
Norway	0.5	0.0	0.0	0.0	71.4	...	28.6
Poland	...	...	...	...	...	...	...
Portugal	2.6	2.7	2.3	21.3	73.6	...	0.0
Romania	5.9	0.2	2.7	0.0	97.0	...	0.2
Russia	...	...	...	...	...	...	...
Slovakia	0.8	...	...	...	100.0	...	...
Slovenia	...	...	...	...	...	...	...
Spain	...	...	...	...	...	...	...
Sweden	...	...	...	...	...	...	...
Switzerland	0.3	0.0	...	16.7	83.3	...	...
Turkey	...	...	...	...	...	...	...
Ukraine	...	...	...	...	...	...	...
UK: England & Wales	0.5	0.0	2.7	0.0	96.9	...	0.4
UK: Northern Ireland	0.9	0.0	0.0	0.0	100.0	...	0.0
UK: Scotland	1.3	0.0	9.1	...	90.9	...	...
Mean	2	0	1	4	90	1	8
Median	1	0	0	0	94	1	0
Minimum	0	0	0	0	71	1	0
Maximum	6	3	9	21	100	1	29

Conviction statistics **149**

Table 3.2.3.5: Types of sanctions/measures imposed in 1999 – Assault

	Total sanctions & measures per 100 000 population	of which: % of Fines	of which: % of Non-custodial sanctions & measures	of which: % of Suspended custodial sanctions & measures	of which: % of Unsuspended custodial sanctions & measures	of which: % of Death penalty	of which: % of Other measures
	R33AST99	P33ASF99	P33ASN99	P33ASS99	P33ASU99	P33ASH99	P33ASO99
Albania	...	...	...	...	...	...	...
Armenia	...	...	...	...	...	...	...
Austria	87.9	73.5	2.5	13.9	10.1	...	...
Belgium	...	...	...	...	...	...	...
Bulgaria	2.1	20.2	1.8	63.2	36.8	...	...
Croatia	18.2	12.0	5.4	73.2	7.4	...	1.9
Cyprus	5.0	36.8	2.6	10.5	52.6	...	...
Czech Republic	25.5	7.3	4.1	73.0	13.2	...	2.4
Denmark	79.2	5.9	11.1	28.9	51.2	...	2.9
Estonia	20.5	13.6	...	43.7	31.2	...	5.1
Finland	161.0	67.8	4.4	15.8	29.8	...	1.8
France	87.4	25.5	14.2	40.4	19.9	...	...
Georgia	6.7	...	17.3	24.0	58.7	...	...
Germany	70.6	44.1	24.8	22.7	8.4	...	...
Greece	26.8	0.2	1.1	92.0	3.8	...	2.9
Hungary	49.8	28.5	22.7	36.7	12.0	...	...
Ireland	...	...	...	...	...	...	...
Italy	8.2	25.3	...	...	74.7	0.0	...
Latvia	...	...	...	...	...	...	...
Lithuania	...	...	...	...	...	...	...
Luxembourg	...	...	...	...	...	...	...
Malta	...	...	...	...	...	...	...
Moldova	6.9	1.0	32.0	27.8	39.2	...	...
Netherlands	...	...	...	...	...	...	...
Norway	15.2	0.7	2.8	13.8	81.7	...	0.9
Poland	42.4	15.8	7.4	68.8	7.9	...	0.0
Portugal	1.6	1.9	0.6	14.8	82.7	...	0.0
Romania	...	...	...	...	...	...	...
Russia	21.8	...	...	...	68.1	...	31.9
Slovakia	30.1	7.9	...	78.8	12.0	...	1.3
Slovenia	32.8	2.7	8.4	81.5	7.4	...	...
Spain	...	...	...	...	...	...	...
Sweden	89.8	25.6	38.9	9.8	25.8	...	...
Switzerland	18.2	11.1	...	68.0	20.9	...	...
Turkey	...	...	...	...	...	...	...
Ukraine	...	...	...	...	...	...	...
UK: England & Wales	65.0	12.9	53.7	1.3	29.2	...	2.8
UK: Northern Ireland	35.4	19.5	28.0	25.0	23.8	...	3.7
UK: Scotland	229.2	50.8	34.0	...	15.2	...	...
Mean	48	21	15	40	32	0	4
Median	28	15	8	29	25	0	2
Minimum	2	0	1	1	4	0	0
Maximum	229	73	54	92	83	0	32

Table 3.2.3.6: Types of sanctions/measures imposed in 1999 – Rape

	Total sanctions & measures per 100 000 population	of which: % of Fines	of which: % of Non-custodial sanctions & measures	of which: % of Suspended custodial sanctions & measures	of which: % of Unsuspended custodial sanctions & measures	of which: % of Death penalty	of which: % of Other measures
	R33RAT99	P33RAF99	P33RAN99	P33RAS99	P33RAU99	P33RAH99	P33RAO99
Albania	...	...	...	...	...	...	...
Armenia	...	...	...	...	...	...	...
Austria	2.1	1.7	3.4	28.7	66.1	...	...
Belgium	...	...	...	...	...	...	...
Bulgaria	2.6	0.0	0.0	36.7	63.3	...	...
Croatia	1.8	0.0	7.8	9.1	83.1	...	0.0
Cyprus	0.5	0.0	0.0	0.0	100.0	...	...
Czech Republic	1.6	0.0	0.0	43.6	54.5	...	1.8
Denmark	1.4	0.0	0.0	13.9	62.5	...	23.6
Estonia	2.6	...	...	35.1	64.9	...	0.0
Finland	1.1	0.0	3.4	51.7	48.3	...	0.0
France	2.9	0.0	1.0	9.8	89.2	...	...
Georgia	1.3	...	...	9.4	90.6	...	...
Germany	2.7	0.3	5.7	48.6	45.4	...	...
Greece	0.3	0.0	3.0	3.0	84.8	...	9.1
Hungary	1.7	0.0	1.2	16.2	82.7	...	...
Ireland	...	...	...	...	...	...	...
Italy	2.1	0.2	...	...	99.8	0.0	...
Latvia	4.3	0.0	0.0	28.8	69.2	...	1.9
Lithuania	...	...	...	...	...	...	...
Luxembourg	...	...	...	...	...	...	...
Malta	...	...	...	...	...	...	...
Moldova	3.4	3.4	24.8	8.1	63.8	...	...
Netherlands	...	...	...	...	...	...	...
Norway	0.7	0.0	0.0	0.0	100.0	...	0.0
Poland	2.3	0.6	0.3	40.8	58.3	...	0.0
Portugal	39.0	82.8	5.6	9.4	2.1	...	0.1
Romania	3.2	0.3	2.6	0.1	97.0	...	0.0
Russia	5.1	...	...	...	73.9	...	16.8
Slovakia	1.3	1.4	...	58.3	40.3	...	...
Slovenia	3.9	0.0	11.8	32.9	55.3	...	...
Spain	...	...	...	...	...	...	...
Sweden	1.1	0.0	8.2	0.0	91.8	...	...
Switzerland	1.3	0.0	...	29.9	70.1	...	...
Turkey	...	...	...	...	...	...	...
Ukraine	...	...	...	...	...	...	...
UK: England & Wales	1.2	0.0	2.3	0.2	96.3	...	1.2
UK: Northern Ireland	0.4	0.0	0.0	0.0	100.0	...	0.0
UK: Scotland	0.5	0.0	3.7	...	96.3	...	...
Mean	3	4	4	21	73	0	4
Median	2	0	2	14	72	0	0
Minimum	0	0	0	0	2	0	0
Maximum	39	83	25	58	100	0	24

Table 3.2.3.7: Types of sanctions/measures imposed in 1999 – Robbery

	Total sanctions & measures per 100 000 population	of which: % of Fines	of which: % of Non-custodial sanctions & measures	of which: % of Suspended custodial sanctions & measures	of which: % of Unsuspended custodial sanctions & measures	of which: % of Death penalty	of which: % of Other measures
	R33ROT99	P33ROF99	P33RON99	P33ROS99	P33ROU99	P33ROH99	P33ROO99
Albania	...	...	...	...	...	...	...
Armenia	...	...	...	...	...	...	...
Austria	5.5	0.4	0.2	22.5	76.8	...	...
Belgium	...	...	...	...	...	...	...
Bulgaria	11.7	0.0	1.3	53.4	46.6	...	...
Croatia	5.6	0.0	13.7	13.3	64.7	...	8.3
Cyprus	1.1	37.5	0.0	0.0	62.5	...	...
Czech Republic	14.5	0.0	0.0	39.2	58.4	...	2.4
Denmark	12.9	0.1	8.5	11.7	74.1	...	5.6
Estonia	64.5	12.2	...	42.8	42.4	...	1.7
Finland	8.5	0.9	6.8	34.5	98.9	...	1.4
France	8.7	1.4	11.4	27.3	59.9	...	...
Georgia	10.4	...	3.8	10.6	85.6	...	...
Germany	13.1	0.7	25.6	35.8	37.9	...	...
Greece	2.1	0.0	11.9	6.9	61.9	...	19.3
Hungary	14.8	0.1	4.2	20.5	75.1	...	...
Ireland	...	...	...	...	...	...	...
Italy	11.5	0.4	...	...	99.6	0.0	...
Latvia	15.6	0.5	0.0	33.9	65.6	...	0.0
Lithuania	...	...	...	...	...	...	...
Luxembourg	...	...	...	...	...	...	...
Malta	...	...	...	...	...	...	...
Moldova	23.3	12.7	28.0	21.8	37.6	...	...
Netherlands	...	...	...	...	...	...	...
Norway	4.1	0.0	9.3	14.3	75.3	...	1.1
Poland	20.7	0.2	0.4	41.4	58.0	...	0.0
Portugal	0.6	3.3	3.3	11.5	82.0	...	0.0
Romania	13.6	0.6	3.8	0.1	94.1	...	1.4
Russia	62.2	0.8	0.0	4.7	60.0	0.0	34.4
Slovakia	12.8	1.0	...	51.7	46.4	...	0.9
Slovenia	5.0	0.0	24.7	14.4	60.8	...	...
Spain	...	...	...	...	...	...	...
Sweden	6.9	1.1	29.1	5.7	64.0	...	...
Switzerland	5.2	0.0	...	57.1	42.9	...	...
Turkey	...	...	...	...	...	...	...
Ukraine	...	...	...	...	...	...	...
UK: England & Wales	10.8	0.2	25.6	0.6	72.3	...	1.3
UK: Northern Ireland	7.9	0.8	31.8	14.7	52.7	...	0.0
UK: Scotland	12.7	4.9	24.8	...	70.4	...	...
Mean	14	3	11	23	65	0	5
Median	11	1	8	18	63	0	1
Minimum	1	0	0	0	38	0	0
Maximum	65	38	32	57	100	0	34

Table 3.2.3.8: Types of sanctions/measures imposed in 1999 – Theft: Total

	Total sanctions & measures per 100 000 population	of which: % of Fines	of which: % of Non-custodial sanctions & measures	of which: % of Suspended custodial sanctions & measures	of which: % of Unsuspended custodial sanctions & measures	of which: % of Death penalty	of which: % of Other measures
	R33THT99	P33THF99	P33THN99	P33THS99	P33THU99	P33THH99	P33THO99
Albania	...	...	...	...	...	...	...
Armenia	...	...	...	...	...	...	...
Austria	190.1	57.3	2.6	19.7	20.4	...	...
Belgium	...	...	...	...	...	...	...
Bulgaria	164.8	7.9	3.7	61.5	38.5	...	...
Croatia	96.9	10.6	9.1	59.3	14.4	...	6.7
Cyprus	45.4	38.9	4.1	17.3	39.8	...	...
Czech Republic	165.8	3.0	6.6	53.0	32.3	...	5.1
Denmark	382.8	70.3	6.2	11.2	11.4	...	0.5
Estonia	296.8	26.4	...	47.4	23.5	...	2.4
Finland	663.8	88.7	1.6	3.8	11.0	...	0.2
France	157.4	9.4	20.7	36.8	33.1	...	...
Georgia	78.7	...	3.8	7.2	89.0	...	...
Germany	208.6	58.9	17.6	8.8	14.7	...	...
Greece	37.6	0.1	16.1	50.2	30.9	...	2.8
Hungary	351.9	32.0	29.3	20.1	18.5	...	...
Ireland	...	...	...	...	...	...	...
Italy	88.1	0.0	...	...	100.0	0.0	...
Latvia	240.6	4.9	0.9	62.9	29.0	...	2.3
Lithuania	...	...	...	...	...	...	...
Luxembourg	...	...	...	...	...	...	...
Malta	...	...	...	...	...	...	...
Moldova	177.3	19.6	30.4	37.8	12.2	...	...
Netherlands	...	...	...	...	...	...	...
Norway	179.6	53.4	4.3	14.7	27.6	...	0.1
Poland	134.3	12.9	7.3	60.6	19.2	...	0.0
Portugal	11.7	2.8	7.8	32.7	56.4	...	0.3
Romania	150.2	1.1	8.4	0.6	81.0	...	3.4
Russia	403.8	3.9	...	58.3	31.6	...	0.7
Slovakia	49.7	4.0	...	68.7	26.2	...	1.1
Slovenia	88.4	2.2	19.6	59.9	18.4	...	...
Spain	...	...	...	...	...	...	...
Sweden	292.1	48.2	40.6	0.2	11.0	...	...
Switzerland	90.5	1.4	...	63.9	34.6	...	...
Turkey	...	...	...	...	...	...	...
Ukraine	...	...	...	...	...	...	...
UK: England & Wales	290.2	20.4	52.8	0.4	24.4	...	2.1
UK: Northern Ireland	167.4	17.7	42.2	12.3	25.6	...	2.1
UK: Scotland	370.3	36.5	32.2	...	31.3	...	...
Mean	199	23	16	33	32	0	2
Median	167	13	8	35	27	0	2
Minimum	12	0	1	0	11	0	0
Maximum	664	89	53	69	100	0	7

Table 3.2.3.9: Types of sanctions/measures imposed in 1999 – Theft: Theft of a motor vehicle

	Total sanctions & measures per 100 000 population	of which: % of Fines	of which: % of Non-custodial sanctions & measures	of which: % of Suspended custodial sanctions & measures	of which: % of Unsuspended custodial sanctions & measures	of which: % of Death penalty	of which: % of Other measures
	R33TVT99	P33TVF99	P33TVN99	P33TVS99	P33TVU99	P33TVH99	P33TVO99
Albania	...	...	...	...	...	...	...
Armenia	...	...	...	...	...	...	...
Austria	...	...	...	...	...	...	...
Belgium	...	...	...	...	...	...	...
Bulgaria	...	...	...	...	...	...	...
Croatia	...	...	...	...	...	...	...
Cyprus	...	...	...	...	...	...	...
Czech Republic	...	...	...	...	...	...	...
Denmark	35.4	49.9	10.7	12.4	26.4	...	0.6
Estonia	...	...	...	...	...	...	...
Finland	...	...	...	...	...	...	...
France	...	...	...	...	...	...	...
Georgia	3.3	...	18.9	23.1	58.0	...	...
Germany	...	...	...	...	...	...	...
Greece	0.3	0.0	3.3	93.3	3.3	...	0.0
Hungary	...	...	...	...	...	...	...
Ireland	...	...	...	...	...	...	...
Italy	...	...	...	...	...	...	...
Latvia	...	...	...	...	...	...	...
Lithuania	...	...	...	...	...	...	...
Luxembourg	...	...	...	...	...	...	...
Malta	...	...	...	...	...	...	...
Moldova	...	...	...	...	...	...	...
Netherlands	...	...	...	...	...	...	...
Norway	8.4	23.9	4.3	33.0	38.8	...	0.0
Poland	...	...	...	...	...	...	...
Portugal	48.0	27.0	6.8	31.7	33.2	...	1.3
Romania	...	...	...	...	...	...	...
Russia	...	...	...	...	...	...	...
Slovakia	6.4	7.8	...	72.0	18.2	...	2.0
Slovenia	7.3	1.4	18.4	70.2	9.9	...	...
Spain	...	...	...	...	...	...	...
Sweden	21.9	9.8	66.6	0.6	23.0	...	...
Switzerland	...	...	...	...	...	...	...
Turkey	...	...	...	...	...	...	...
Ukraine	...	...	...	...	...	...	...
UK: England & Wales	15.5	5.6	48.1	0.3	34.7	...	11.2
UK: Northern Ireland	18.2	17.2	39.9	8.4	32.1	...	2.4
UK: Scotland	31.6	25.1	44.0	...	30.9	...	...
Mean	18	17	26	35	28	...	3
Median	16	14	19	27	31	...	1
Minimum	0	0	3	0	3	0	0
Maximum	48	50	67	93	58	0	11

Table 3.2.3.10: Types of sanctions/measures imposed in 1999 – Theft Burglary: Total

	Total sanctions & measures per 100 000 population	of which: % of Fines	of which: % of Non-custodial sanctions & measures	of which: % of Suspended custodial sanctions & measures	of which: % of Unsuspended custodial sanctions & measures	of which: % of Death penalty	of which: % of Other measures
	R33BUT99	P33BUF99	P33BUN99	P33BUS99	P33BUU99	P33BUH99	P33BUO99
Albania	...	...	...	...	...	...	...
Armenia	...	...	...	...	...	...	...
Austria	22.3	11.5	5.5	41.2	41.9	...	...
Belgium	...	...	...	...	...	...	...
Bulgaria	...	...	...	...	...	...	...
Croatia	37.7	0.0	16.6	55.6	22.1	...	5.6
Cyprus	17.6	11.3	6.0	25.6	57.1	...	...
Czech Republic	...	...	...	...	...	...	...
Denmark	50.0	3.7	17.1	37.6	40.8	...	0.8
Estonia	251.3	...	...	...	...	...	1.2
Finland	...	...	...	...	...	...	...
France	...	...	...	...	...	...	...
Georgia	...	...	...	...	...	...	...
Germany	23.4	11.0	29.9	33.2	26.0	...	...
Greece	...	...	...	...	...	...	...
Hungary	...	...	...	...	...	...	...
Ireland	...	...	...	...	...	...	...
Italy	...	...	...	...	...	...	...
Latvia	111.6	2.6	0.3	64.8	31.0	...	1.3
Lithuania	...	...	...	...	...	...	...
Luxembourg	...	...	...	...	...	...	...
Malta	...	...	...	...	...	...	...
Moldova	...	...	...	...	...	...	...
Netherlands	...	...	...	...	...	...	...
Norway	56.7	7.3	8.3	24.0	60.2	...	0.2
Poland	83.9	2.8	3.3	68.5	25.4	...	0.0
Portugal	...	...	...	...	...	...	...
Romania	...	...	...	...	...	...	...
Russia	...	...	...	...	...	...	...
Slovakia	43.3	3.4	...	68.2	27.4	...	1.0
Slovenia	32.8	0.2	19.9	54.9	25.0	...	...
Spain	...	...	...	...	...	...	...
Sweden	13.3	3.7	43.2	2.3	50.8	...	...
Switzerland	...	...	...	...	...	...	...
Turkey	...	...	...	...	...	...	...
Ukraine	...	...	...	...	...	...	...
UK: England & Wales	55.8	3.8	45.6	0.5	48.9	...	1.2
UK: Northern Ireland	43.2	5.8	39.4	13.1	40.1	...	1.6
UK: Scotland	58.1	15.2	34.3	...	50.5	...	...
Mean	60	6	21	38	39	...	1
Median	43	4	17	38	40	...	1
Minimum	13	0	0	1	22	0	0
Maximum	251	15	46	69	60	0	6

Table 3.2.3.11: Types of sanctions/measures imposed in 1999 – Theft Burglary: Domestic Burglary

	Total sanctions & measures per 100 000 population	of which: % of Fines	of which: % of Non-custodial sanctions & measures	of which: % of Suspended custodial sanctions & measures	of which: % of Unsuspended custodial sanctions & measures	of which: % of Death penalty	of which: % of Other measures
	R33BDT99	P33BDF99	P33BDN99	P33BUS99	P33BUU99	P33BDH99	P33BDO99
Albania	...	...	...	...	...	...	...
Armenia	...	...	...	...	...	...	...
Austria	...	...	...	...	...	...	...
Belgium	...	...	...	...	...	...	...
Bulgaria	...	...	...	...	...	...	...
Croatia	...	...	...	...	...	...	...
Cyprus	...	...	...	...	...	...	...
Czech Republic	...	...	...	...	...	...	...
Denmark	16.2	1.9	14.8	32.2	50.1	...	1.0
Estonia	...	...	...	...	...	...	...
Finland	...	...	...	...	...	...	...
France	...	...	...	...	...	...	...
Georgia	...	...	...	...	...	...	...
Germany	...	...	...	...	...	...	...
Greece	...	...	...	...	...	...	...
Hungary	...	...	...	...	...	...	...
Ireland	...	...	...	...	...	...	...
Italy	...	...	...	...	...	...	...
Latvia	...	...	...	...	...	...	...
Lithuania	...	...	...	...	...	...	...
Luxembourg	...	...	...	...	...	...	...
Malta	...	...	...	...	...	...	...
Moldova	...	...	...	...	...	...	...
Netherlands	...	...	...	...	...	...	...
Norway	4.7	5.7	9.5	19.0	65.9	...	0.0
Poland	...	...	...	...	...	...	...
Portugal	...	...	...	...	...	...	...
Romania	...	...	...	...	...	...	...
Russia	...	...	...	...	...	...	...
Slovakia	31.0	3.9	...	68.0	27.1	...	1.0
Slovenia	...	...	...	...	...	...	...
Spain	...	...	...	...	...	...	...
Sweden	...	...	...	...	...	...	...
Switzerland	...	...	...	...	...	...	...
Turkey	...	...	...	...	...	...	...
Ukraine	...	...	...	...	...	...	...
UK: England & Wales	32.0	1.7	36.7	0.7	60.0	...	1.0
UK: Northern Ireland	26.0	4.7	39.2	13.5	41.4	...	1.2
UK: Scotland	...	...	...	...	...	...	...
Mean	22	4	25	27	49	...	1
Median	26	4	26	19	50	...	1
Minimum	5	2	9	1	27	0	0
Maximum	32	6	39	68	66	0	1

Table 3.2.3.12: Types of sanctions/measures imposed in 1999 – Drug offences: Total

	Total sanctions & measures per 100 000 population	of which: % of Fines	of which: % of Non-custodial sanctions & measures	of which: % of Suspended custodial sanctions & measures	of which: % of Unsuspended custodial sanctions & measures	of which: % of Death penalty	of which: % of Other measures
	R33DRT99	P33DRF99	P33DRN99	P33DRS99	P33DRU99	P33DRH99	P33DRO99
Albania	...	...	...	...	...	...	...
Armenia	...	...	...	...	...	...	...
Austria	40.8	38.6	3.4	26.3	31.8	...	...
Belgium	...	...	...	...	...	...	...
Bulgaria	1.5	...	...	58.6	41.4	...	...
Croatia	56.4	9.9	4.7	44.8	18.8	...	21.8
Cyprus	23.0	43.4	0.6	13.9	42.2	...	...
Czech Republic	8.7	0.7	3.7	56.9	34.0	...	4.7
Denmark	8.5	0.0	7.9	5.3	84.4	...	6.6
Estonia	9.7	4.3	...	60.7	34.3	...	0.7
Finland	88.2	70.6	2.7	11.9	27.3	...	2.1
France	37.8	15.2	10.2	38.1	36.4	...	...
Georgia	25.3	6.1	5.6	13.2	64.3	...	...
Germany	65.9	39.0	16.7	27.6	16.7	...	...
Greece	25.8	0.3	5.1	69.3	16.4	...	8.9
Hungary	6.9	31.8	31.8	23.7	12.8	...	...
Ireland	...	...	...	...	...	...	...
Italy	31.5	1.7	...	...	98.3	0.0	...
Latvia	7.1	9.9	1.2	58.7	29.1	...	1.2
Lithuania	...	...	...	...	...	...	...
Luxembourg	...	...	...	...	...	...	...
Malta	...	...	...	...	...	...	...
Moldova	22.4	37.9	10.5	39.5	12.1	...	...
Netherlands	...	...	...	...	...	...	...
Norway	183.3	65.1	1.8	19.1	14.0	...	0.0
Poland	5.9	12.4	5.2	63.8	18.5	...	0.0
Portugal	31.2	33.5	8.3	18.7	39.5	...	0.0
Romania	1.2	7.5	8.2	0.7	83.1	...	0.4
Russia	73.9	1.7	...	18.3	36.8	...	...
Slovakia	2.1	0.9	...	75.0	23.3	...	0.9
Slovenia	12.5	0.0	11.3	55.8	32.9	...	...
Spain	...	...	...	...	...	...	...
Sweden	82.2	50.4	29.1	0.5	20.0	...	...
Switzerland	110.9	6.3	...	55.3	38.4	...	...
Turkey	...	...	...	...	...	...	...
Ukraine	...	...	...	...	...	...	...
UK: England & Wales	93.2	47.4	33.0	0.7	17.8	...	1.0
UK: Northern Ireland	35.7	48.2	20.0	16.4	15.3	...	0.2
UK: Scotland	123.2	63.2	22.0	...	14.8	...	...
Mean	43	24	11	34	34	0	3
Median	28	12	8	27	30	0	1
Minimum	1	0	1	1	12	0	0
Maximum	183	71	33	75	98	0	22

Table 3.2.3.13: Types of sanctions/measures imposed in 1999 – Drug offences: Drug trafficking

	Total sanctions & measures per 100 000 population	of which: % of Fines	of which: % of Non-custodial sanctions & measures	of which: % of Suspended custodial sanctions & measures	of which: % of Unsuspended custodial sanctions & measures	of which: % of Death penalty	of which: % of Other measures
	R33DTT99	P33DTF99	P33DTN99	P33DTS99	P33DTU99	P33DTH99	P33DTO99
Albania	...	...	...	...	...	...	...
Armenia	...	...	...	...	...	...	...
Austria	13.8	6.3	0.1	26.6	66.9	...	...
Belgium	...	...	...	...	...	...	...
Bulgaria	0.0	...	...	0.0	100.0	...	...
Croatia	1.8	0.0	1.3	0.0	96.1	...	2.6
Cyprus	...	...	...	...	...	...	...
Czech Republic	7.4	0.5	3.0	56.5	36.5	...	3.5
Denmark	2.3	0.0	8.3	2.5	87.6	...	1.7
Estonia	...	...	...	...	...	...	...
Finland	...	...	...	...	...	...	...
France	12.4	5.4	6.1	37.3	51.3	...	...
Georgia	2.7	...	...	5.8	94.2	...	...
Germany	6.8	2.6	4.1	51.2	42.1	...	...
Greece	6.0	0.6	8.4	33.1	57.8	...	0.0
Hungary	...	...	...	...	...	...	...
Ireland	...	...	...	...	...	...	...
Italy	...	...	...	...	...	...	...
Latvia	...	...	...	...	...	...	...
Lithuania	...	...	...	...	...	...	...
Luxembourg	...	...	...	...	...	...	...
Malta	...	...	...	...	...	...	...
Moldova	...	...	...	...	...	...	...
Netherlands	...	...	...	...	...	...	...
Norway	104.3	41.3	2.9	32.1	23.7	...	0.0
Poland	1.2	8.5	4.0	52.5	34.7	...	0.2
Portugal	11.3	1.8	3.7	16.1	78.5	...	0.0
Romania	...	...	...	...	...	...	...
Russia	18.5	...	...	...	...	...	...
Slovakia	2.0	0.9	...	75.2	22.9	...	0.9
Slovenia	9.1	0.0	10.9	46.9	42.3	...	...
Spain	...	...	...	...	...	...	...
Sweden	...	...	...	...	...	...	...
Switzerland	71.3	6.5	...	57.5	36.0	...	...
Turkey	...	...	...	...	...	...	...
Ukraine	...	...	...	...	...	...	...
UK: England & Wales	17.7	9.7	24.8	2.1	63.0	...	0.4
UK: Northern Ireland	6.5	13.3	17.1	30.5	39.0	...	0.0
UK: Scotland	29.9	15.7	37.4	...	46.8	...	...
Mean	17	7	9	31	57	...	1
Median	7	4	5	32	49	...	0
Minimum	0	0	0	0	23	0	0
Maximum	104	41	37	75	100	0	4

Notes on Tables 3.2.3.1-3.2.3.13

Greece: Data relates to the year 1997 (instead of 1999).

Croatia, the Czech Republic, France, Germany and Slovenia: Data relates to the year 2000 (instead of 1999).

Table 3.2.4.1: Number of convictions by length of unsuspended custodial sanctions and measures imposed in 1999 – Criminal offences: Total

Criminal offences: Total	Total unsuspended custodial sanctions per 100 000 pop R34TC A99	of which: % under 1 month P34TC B99	of which: % 1 month & less than 12 months P34TC C99	of which: % 3 months & less than 12 months P34TC D99	of which: % under 6 months P34TC E99	of which: % 6 months & less than 12 months P34TC F99	of which: % 6 months & less than 18 months P34TC G99	of which: % under 12 months P34TC H99	of which: % 12 months & less than 24 months P34TC I99	of which: % 12 months & less than 36 months P34TC J99	of which: % 12 months & less than 60 months P34TC K99	of which: % 18 months & less than 36 months P34TC L99	of which: % 24 months & less than 48 months P34TC M99	of which: % 24 months & less than 60 months P34TC N99	of which: % 36 months & less than 60 months P34TC O99	of which: % 48 months & over P34TC P99	of which: % 60 months & less than 120 months P34TC Q99	of which: % 60 months & less than 144 months P34TC R99	of which: % 60 months & less than 180 months P34TC S99	of which: % 60 months & over P34TC T99	of which: % 120 months & over P34TC U99	of which: % 120 months & less than 240 months P34TC V99	of which: % 144 months & over P34TC W99	of which: % 180 months & over P34TC X99	Average length of custodial sanction/measure (in months) T34TC Y99	of which: % Life P34TC Z99	of which: % Indeterminate sanctions/measures P34TC 99
Albania	101.7	23.3	39.4	...	...	...	...	...	21.0	...	...	...	...	...	...	...	6.8	...	...	...	2.6	...	...	...	...	...	8.2
Armenia	...	...	...	...	...	...	...	...	...	...	...	...	...	...	...	...	...	...	...	...	...	...	...	...	...	...	...
Austria	104.5	...	...	...	36.8	14.1	...	...	14.4	...	...	...	...	2.5	...	...	...	...	...	1.7	...	...	...	...	...	0.1	1.7
Belgium	107.9	...	...	...	68.7	14.2	...	...	10.3	...	...	...	...	2.0	...	...	0.8	...	...	...	0.3	...	...	...	...	0.4	3.3
Bulgaria	142.6	...	...	...	7.7	11.6	...	...	20.6	...	...	...	...	...	...	...	...	...	...	...	...	...	...	...	16.0	0.2	...
Croatia	59.6	...	...	...	33.0	22.2	...	...	14.3	...	...	...	...	8.7	...	...	3.3	...	...	...	2.9	...	...	...	22.0	...	15.6
Cyprus	47.4	...	...	...	44.5	...	31.9	...	...	8.4	...	...	...	...	7.3	...	...	...	...	5.9	...	...	...	...	15.7	1.7	...
Czech Republic	149.3	...	...	...	...	...	...	64.7	...	...	30.8	...	...	...	...	...	...	...	4.4	...	...	...	0.1	...	...	0.0	4.4
Denmark	156.8	...	31.6	...	79.0	11.3	...	...	5.8	...	...	...	...	2.9	...	...	...	0.9	...	...	...	0.1	...	...	...	0.0	...
Estonia	148.1	...	...	...	...	...	...	...	35.8	...	...	...	...	19.3	...	...	11.9	...	...	...	1.4	...	...	...	...	0.2	6.2
Finland	154.6	...	...	...	68.1	13.4	...	...	7.4	...	...	...	...	5.2	...	...	1.4	...	...	...	0.3	...	...	...	7.5	0.1	4.2
France	163.9	...	...	...	61.8	19.7	...	...	12.3	...	...	...	...	...	2.7	...	2.0	...	...	...	1.4	...	...	...	9.9	0.0	...
Georgia	168.7	...	...	...	...	9.0	...	...	15.0	...	...	...	...	25.2	...	...	20.4	...	...	...	14.7	...	...	...	...	0.2	4.4
Germany	69.4	...	...	...	33.3	23.6	...	...	18.8	...	...	...	...	20.6	...	...	3.1	...	...	...	0.4	...	...	...	...	0.2	6.2
Greece	53.8	...	...	...	...	...	...	...	...	...	84.8	...	...	...	...	...	...	...	...	8.3	...	...	...	...	...	0.8	...
Hungary	118.5	...	...	...	31.3	28.7	...	...	20.3	...	...	...	...	15.5	...	...	3.6	...	...	...	0.6	...	...	...	19.0	0.1	...
Ireland	...	...	...	...	...	...	...	...	...	...	...	...	...	...	...	...	...	...	...	...	...	...	...	...	...	...	...
Italy	327.2	...	...	...	64.4	17.9	...	...	12.2	...	...	...	...	4.1	...	...	1.0	...	...	...	0.4	...	...	...	...	0.1	...
Latvia	118.1	...	...	...	...	...	...	10.8	...	...	...	...	...	...	15.5	...	10.7	...	...	...	...	1.3	...	...	...	0.0	2.3
Lithuania	210.1	...	...	...	...	...	...	...	61.7	...	...	...	...	...	...	...	...	...	...	...	...	...	...	...	...	...	...
Luxembourg	...	...	...	...	...	...	...	...	...	...	...	...	...	...	...	...	...	...	...	...	...	...	...	...	...	...	...

Conviction statistics 159

Criminal offences: Total	Total unsuspended custodial sanctions per 100 000 pop R34TC A99	of which: % under 1 month P34TC B99	of which: % 1 month & less than 12 months P34TC C99	of which: % 3 months & less than 12 months P34TC D99	of which: % under 6 months P34TC E99	of which: % 6 months & less than 12 months P34TC F99	of which: % 6 months & less than 18 months P34TC G99	of which: % under 12 months P34TC H99	of which: % 12 months & less than 24 months P34TC I99	of which: % 12 months & less than 36 months P34TC J99	of which: % 12 months & less than 60 months P34TC K99	of which: % 18 months & less than 36 months P34TC L99	of which: % 24 months & less than 48 months P34TC M99	of which: % 24 months & less than 60 months P34TC N99	of which: % 36 months & less than 60 months P34TC O99	of which: % 48 months & over P34TC P99	of which: % 60 months & less than 120 months P34TC Q99	of which: % 60 months & less than 144 months P34TC R99	of which: % 60 months & less than 180 months P34TC S99	of which: % 60 months & over P34TC T99	of which: % 120 months & over P34TC U99	of which: % 120 months & less than 240 months P34TC V99	of which: % 144 months & over P34TC W99	of which: % 180 months & over P34TC X99	Average length of custodial sanction/measure (in months) T34TC Y99	of which: % Life P34TC Z99	of which: % Indeterminate sanctions/measures P34TC_99
Malta	52.7	:	:	:	:	:	:	:	:	:	:	:	:	:	:	:	:	:	:	:	:	:	:	:	:	:	:
Moldova	173.1	:	:	:	:	:	:	13.6	8.2	:	:	:	:	34.9	:	:	35.4	:	:	:	7.8	:	:	:	5.9	0.0	0.0
Netherlands	208.3	:	:	:	77.3	10.4	:	:	6.3	:	:	:	4.5	:	:	1.4	:	:	:	:	:	:	:	:	:	:	:
Norway	67.7	:	:	:	78.5	12.2	:	:	5.9	:	:	:	:	2.7	:	:	0.4	:	:	:	0.2	:	:	:	4.7	:	0.9
Poland	47.7	:	:	:	5.7	15.9	:	:	41.1	:	:	:	:	32.7	:	:	3.2	:	:	:	1.5	:	:	:	:	0.0	:
Portugal	202.2	:	:	:	7.3	13.9	:	:	18.7	:	:	:	:	37.2	:	:	18.5	:	:	:	4.3	:	:	:	44.0	:	0.8
Romania		:	:	:	:	:	:	27.8	:	:	53.5	:	:	:	:	:	7.0	:	:	:	1.6	:	:	:	:	0.0	:
Russia		:	:	:	:	:	:	:	:	:	:	:	:	:	:	:	:	:	:	:	:	:	:	:	:	:	:
Slovakia		:	:	:	:	:	:	:	:	:	:	:	:	:	:	:	:	:	:	:	:	:	:	:	:	:	:
Slovenia	57.5	:	:	:	46.4	21.3	:	:	17.3	:	:	:	:	12.2	:	:	2.0	:	:	:	0.8	:	:	:	7.2	:	3.1
Spain	144.4	:	:	:	67.0	16.5	:	:	11.4	:	:	:	3.2	:	:	1.8	:	:	:	:	:	:	:	:	:	:	:
Sweden	148.5	:	:	:	79.6	4.9	:	:	4.0	:	:	:	:	6.9	:	:	0.8	:	:	:	0.1	:	:	:	5.5	0.0	3.6
Switzerland		:	:	:	:	:	:	:	:	:	:	:	:	:	:	:	:	:	:	:	:	:	:	:	:	:	:
Turkey		:	:	:	:	:	:	:	:	:	:	:	:	:	:	:	:	:	:	:	:	:	:	:	:	:	:
Ukraine		:	:	:	:	:	:	:	:	:	:	:	:	:	:	:	:	:	:	0.5	:	:	:	:	:	:	:
UK: E & W	200.5	:	:	:	57.7	13.3	:	:	13.1	:	:	8	4	12.0	6	2	2.8	1	4	4	0.8	1	0	0	11.4	0.5	0.4
UK: N-Ireland	120.3	:	:	:	52.7	26.7	:	:	8.4	:	:	8	4	7.9	3	2	2.4	1	4	4	:	1	0	0	10.0	0.6	:
UK: Scotland	237.0	:	:	:	68.2	15.7	:	:	6.7	:	:	8	3	6.3	:	1	2.5	1	4	1	0.3	0	0	0	8.0	0.3	0.0
Mean	135	23	39	32	51	16	32	29	15	25	48	8	4	15	6	2	7	1	4	4	2	1	0	0	13	0	4
Median	143	23	39	32	58	14	32	21	13	13	42	8	4	12	3	2	3	1	4	4	1	1	0	0	10	0	3
Minimum	47	23	39	32	6	5	32	11	4	10	21	8	3	3	2	1	0	1	4	1	0	0	0	0	5	0	0
Maximum	327	23	39	32	80	29	32	65	41	62	85	8	5	37	16	2	35	1	4	8	15	1	0	0	44	2	16

Table 3.2.4.2: Number of convictions by length of unsuspended custodial sanctions and measures imposed in 1999 – Criminal offences: Traffic offences

Criminal offences: Traffic offences	Total unsuspended custodial sanctions per 100 000 pop R34TT A99	of which: % under 1 month P34TT B99	of which: % 1 month & less than 12 months P34TT C99	of which: % 3 months & less than 12 months P34TT D99	of which: % under 6 months P34TT E99	of which: % 6 months & less than 12 months P34TT F99	of which: % 6 months & less than 18 months P34TT G99	of which: % under 12 months P34TT H99	of which: % 12 months & less than 24 months P34TT I99	of which: % 12 months & less than 36 months P34TT J99	of which: % 12 months & less than 60 months P34TT K99	of which: % 18 months & less than 36 months P34TT L99	of which: % 24 months & less than 48 months P34TT M99	of which: % 24 months & less than 60 months P34TT N99	of which: % 36 months & less than 60 months P34TT O99	of which: % 48 months & over P34TT P99	of which: % 60 months & less than 120 months P34TT Q99	of which: % 60 months & less than 144 months P34TT R99	of which: % 60 months & less than 180 months P34TT S99	of which: % 60 months & over P34TT T99	of which: % 120 months & over P34TT U99	of which: % 120 months & less than 240 months P34TT V99	of which: % 144 months & over P34TT W99	of which: % 180 months & over P34TT X99	Average length of custodial sanction/measure (in months) T34TT Y99	of which: % Life P34TT Z99	of which: % Indeterminate sanctions/measures P34TT _99
Albania	2.3	25.0	40.0	:	:	:	:	:	:	11.3	:	:	:	:	:	:	2.5	:	:	:	8.8	:	:	:	:	:	:
Armenia	:	:	:	:	:	:	:	:	:	:	:	:	:	:	:	:	:	:	:	:	:	:	:	:	:	:	:
Austria	:	:	:	:	:	:	:	:	:	:	:	:	:	:	:	:	:	:	:	:	:	:	:	:	:	:	:
Belgium	4.0	:	:	:	2.8	2.5	:	:	5.6	:	:	:	:	:	:	:	:	:	:	:	:	:	:	:	14.0	0.0	:
Bulgaria	4.7	:	:	:	42.8	33.8	:	:	17.4	:	:	:	3.5	:	:	:	0.0	:	:	:	0.0	:	:	:	9.0	:	2.5
Croatia	:	:	:	:	:	:	:	:	:	:	:	:	:	:	:	:	:	:	:	:	:	:	:	:	:	:	:
Cyprus	:	:	:	:	:	:	:	:	:	:	:	:	:	:	:	:	:	:	:	:	:	:	:	:	:	:	:
Czech Republic	:	:	:	:	:	:	:	:	:	:	:	:	:	:	:	:	:	:	:	:	:	:	:	:	:	:	:
Denmark	2.2	:	43.8	:	:	:	:	:	31.3	:	:	:	18.8	:	:	6.3	:	:	:	0.0	:	:	:	3.1	0.0	1.9
Estonia	42.0	:	:	:	88.5	8.6	:	:	0.9	:	:	:	0.0	:	:	0.0	:	:	:	0.0	:	:	:	:	:	:
Finland	17.6	:	:	:	86.4	11.1	:	:	2.4	:	:	:	0.0	:	:	0.0	:	:	:	0.0	:	:	:	2.9	0.0	:
France	:	:	:	:	:	:	:	:	:	:	:	:	:	:	:	:	:	:	:	:	:	:	:	:	:	:	:
Georgia	:	:	:	:	:	:	:	:	:	:	:	:	:	:	:	:	:	:	:	:	:	:	:	:	:	:	:
Germany	7.5	:	:	:	64.3	26.9	:	:	6.9	:	:	:	1.9	:	:	0.0	:	:	:	0.0	:	:	:	:	0.0	1.8
Greece	0.8	:	:	:	:	:	:	94.3	:	:	:	:	:	:	:	:	:	:	1.1	:	:	:	:	:	1.1	3.4
Hungary	3.2	:	:	:	38.8	31.7	:	:	17.4	:	:	:	10.9	:	:	1.2	:	:	:	0.0	:	:	:	14.0	0.0	:
Ireland	:	:	:	:	:	:	:	:	:	:	:	:	:	:	:	:	:	:	:	:	:	:	:	:	:	:	:
Italy	:	:	:	:	:	:	:	:	:	:	:	:	:	:	:	:	:	:	:	:	:	:	:	:	:	:	:
Latvia	3.1	:	:	:	26.7	:	:	:	65.3	:	:	:	:	6.7	:	1.3	:	:	:	0.0	:	:	:	:	:	:
Lithuania	:	:	:	:	:	:	:	:	:	:	:	:	:	:	:	:	:	:	:	:	:	:	:	:	:	:	:
Luxembourg	:	:	:	:	:	:	:	:	:	:	:	:	:	:	:	:	:	:	:	:	:	:	:	:	:	:	:

Conviction statistics 161

Criminal offences: Traffic offences

	Total unsuspended custodial sanctions per 100 000 pop R34TT A99	of which: % under 1 month P34TT B99	of which: % 1 month & less than 12 months P34TT C99	of which: % 3 months & less than 12 months P34TT D99	of which: % under 6 months P34TT E99	of which: % 6 months & less than 12 months P34TT F99	of which: % 6 months & less than 18 months P34TT G99	of which: % under 12 months P34TT H99	of which: % 12 months & less than 24 months P34TT I99	of which: % 12 months & less than 36 months P34TT J99	of which: % 12 months & less than 60 months P34TT K99	of which: % 18 months & less than 36 months P34TT L99	of which: % 24 months & less than 48 months P34TT M99	of which: % 24 months & less than 60 months P34TT N99	of which: % 36 months & less than 60 months P34TT O99	of which: % 48 months & over P34TT P99	of which: % 60 months & less than 120 months P34TT Q99	of which: % 60 months & less than 144 months P34TT R99	of which: % 60 months & less than 180 months P34TT S99	of which: % 60 months & over P34TT T99	of which: % 120 months & over P34TT U99	of which: % 120 months & less than 240 months P34TT V99	of which: % 144 months & over P34TT W99	of which: % 180 months & over P34TT X99	Average length of custodial sanction/measure (in months) T34TT Y99	of which: % Life P34TT Z99	of which: % Indeterminate sanctions/measures P34TT _99
Malta	...	...	...	...	...	...	...	...	...	...	...	...	...	...	...	...	...	...	...	...	...	...	...	...	...	...	...
Moldova	0.2	25	40	44	...	...	...	12.5	0.0	...	...	...	...	62.5	...	...	25.0	...	...	...	0.0	...	...	...	...	...	...
Netherlands	6.7	...	...	...	97.6	0.9	...	...	0.5	...	...	...	0.0	...	...	0.0	0.0	...	...	...	0.0	...	...	...	1.1	0.0	0.0
Norway	60.3	...	...	...	98.8	1.0	...	...	0.1	...	...	...	...	0.0	...	...	0.0	...	...	...	0.0	...	...	...	1.1	...	0.2
Poland	1.4	...	...	...	0.6	5.4	...	...	29.7	...	...	...	...	55.4	...	...	9.0	...	...	...	0.0	...	...	...	...	...	...
Portugal	0.9	...	...	...	72.4	21.8	...	...	3.4	...	...	...	...	1.1	...	...	1.1	...	...	...	0.0	...	...	...	7.0	0.0	8.0
Romania	5.6	...	...	...	...	...	...	33.6	...	...	60.1	...	...	...	...	...	3.7	...	...	...	...	...	...	...	...	...	...
Russia	...	...	...	...	...	...	...	...	...	...	...	...	...	...	...	...	...	...	...	...	...	...	...	...	...	...	...
Slovakia	...	...	...	...	...	...	...	...	...	...	...	...	...	...	...	...	...	...	...	...	...	...	...	...	...	...	...
Slovenia	5.7	...	...	...	70.0	21.8	...	...	7.3	...	...	...	...	0.9	...	...	0.0	...	...	...	0.0	...	...	...	...	...	...
Spain	...	...	...	...	...	...	...	...	...	...	...	...	...	...	...	...	...	...	...	...	...	...	...	...	...	...	...
Sweden	35.5	...	...	...	97.3	2.6	...	...	0.1	...	...	...	...	...	...	...	0.1	...	...	...	0.1	...	...	...	1.5	...	0.3
Switzerland	64.3	...	...	...	89.2	2.7	...	...	1.9	...	...	...	...	2.5	...	...	...	...	...	...	...	...	...	...	2.8	0.0	3.4
Turkey	...	...	...	...	...	...	...	...	...	...	...	...	...	...	...	...	...	...	...	...	...	...	...	...	...	...	...
Ukraine	...	...	...	...	...	...	...	...	...	...	...	...	...	...	...	...	...	...	...	...	...	...	...	...	...	...	...
UK: E & W	30.0	...	...	...	91.2	8.8	...	...	0.0	...	...	...	...	0.0	...	...	0.0	...	...	...	0.0	...	...	...	3.4	0.0	0.0
UK: N.-Ireland	20.5	...	...	...	66.5	31.1	...	...	0.3	...	...	...	...	1.2	...	...	0.6	...	...	...	0.3	...	...	...	5.0	0.0	0.0
UK: Scotland	...	...	...	...	...	...	...	...	...	...	...	...	...	...	...	...	...	...	...	...	...	...	...	...	...	...	...
Mean	15	25	40	44	67	14	...	24	8	34	55	...	0	11	7	0	3	...	...	1	1	...	...	...	5	0	2
Median	6	25	40	44	72	9	...	27	3	34	60	...	0	2	7	0	1	...	...	1	0	...	...	...	3	0	2
Minimum	0	25	40	44	1	1	...	13	0	2	11	...	0	0	0	0	0	...	...	1	0	...	...	...	1	0	0
Maximum	64	25	40	44	99	34	...	34	31	65	94	...	0	63	7	0	25	...	...	1	9	...	...	...	14	1	8

Table 3.2.4.3: Number of convictions by length of unsuspended custodial sanctions and measures imposed in 1999 – Intentional Homicide: Total

Intentional Homicide: Total	Total unsuspended custodial sanctions per 100 000 pop R4HO A99	of which: % under 1 month B99	of which: % 1 month & less than 12 months C99	of which: % 3 months & less than 12 months D99	of which: % under 6 months E99	of which: % 6 months & less than 12 months F99	of which: % 6 months & less than 18 months G99	of which: % under 12 months H99	of which: % 12 months & less than 24 months I99	of which: % 12 months & less than 36 months J99	of which: % 12 months & less than 60 months K99	of which: % 18 months & less than 36 months L99	of which: % 24 months & less than 48 months M99	of which: % 24 months & less than 60 months N99	of which: % 36 months & less than 60 months O99	of which: % 48 months & over P99	of which: % 60 months & less than 120 months Q99	of which: % 60 months & less than 144 months R99	of which: % 60 months & less than 180 months S99	of which: % 60 months & over T99	of which: % 120 months & over U99	of which: % 120 months & less than 240 months V99	of which: % 144 months & over W99	of which: % 180 months & over X99	Average length of custodial sanction/measure (in months) Y99	of which: % Life Z99	of which: % Indeterminate sanctions/measures P34HO_99
Albania	8.0	13.5	19.7	:	:	:	:	:	:	:	31.0	:	:	:	:	19.3	:	:	:	13.1	:	:	:	:	:	:	3.3
Armenia	0.9	:	:	:	2.7	0.0	:	:	:	:	:	:	:	:	2.7	:	:	:	:	:	:	:	:	:	:	:	:
Austria	:	:	:	:	:	:	:	:	6.8	:	:	:	:	:	:	:	:	:	36.5	:	:	:	:	:	:	16.2	33.8
Belgium	:	:	:	:	:	:	:	:	:	:	:	:	:	:	:	:	:	:	:	:	:	:	:	:	:	:	:
Bulgaria	2.2	:	:	:	0.0	4.5	:	:	9.0	:	:	:	:	:	:	:	:	:	:	:	:	:	:	:	24	8.5	:
Croatia	5.4	:	:	:	2.6	12.2	:	:	11.7	:	:	:	:	21.3	:	19.1	:	:	:	12.6	:	:	:	:	64	46.2	20.4
Cyprus	1.7	:	:	:	0.0	:	0.0	:	:	:	:	0.0	:	:	:	:	:	:	53.8	:	:	:	:	:	156	2.2	:
Czech Republic	1.8	:	:	:	:	:	:	0.0	0.0	:	11.0	:	:	:	0.0	:	:	:	80.7	:	:	:	6.1	:	:	0.0	:
Denmark	0.5	:	:	:	:	:	:	:	:	:	:	:	:	10.3	:	61.3	:	79.3	:	:	10.3	:	:	:	:	:	:
Estonia	8.3	:	0.8	:	0.0	0.0	:	:	1.7	:	:	:	:	11.8	:	32.2	:	:	:	24.4	:	:	:	:	:	:	:
Finland	2.8	:	:	:	0.0	0.0	:	:	0.0	:	:	:	:	49.7	4.5	21.8	:	:	:	13.3	:	:	:	:	70.3	4.9	0.0
France	1.1	:	:	:	0.0	2.8	:	:	:	:	:	7.3	:	:	:	20.9	:	:	:	60.0	:	:	:	:	143.7	3.7	:
Georgia	4.5	:	:	:	:	:	:	:	:	:	:	:	:	3.1	:	:	:	:	:	68.4	:	:	:	:	:	7.6	:
Germany	1.0	:	:	:	0.1	0.7	:	:	1.4	:	:	:	:	32.2	:	37.0	:	:	:	13.9	:	:	:	:	:	14.6	27.9
Greece	0.6	:	:	:	:	:	:	:	:	:	1.5	:	:	:	:	:	:	:	60.3	:	:	:	:	:	:	36.8	4.4
Hungary	2.4	:	:	:	0.0	1.2	:	:	2.1	:	:	:	:	30.7	:	36.1	:	:	:	24.9	:	:	:	:	95	5.0	:
Ireland	:	:	:	:	:	:	:	:	:	:	:	:	:	:	:	:	:	:	:	:	:	:	:	:	:	:	:
Italy	1.3	:	:	:	0.0	0.0	:	:	4.0	:	:	:	:	15.5	:	19.2	:	:	:	61.4	:	:	:	:	:	:	:
Latvia	4.6	:	:	:	:	:	0.0	0.0	:	:	:	:	3.6	:	9.0	57.7	:	:	:	:	27.9	:	:	:	:	1.8	:
Lithuania	:	:	:	:	:	:	:	:	:	:	:	:	:	:	:	:	:	:	:	:	:	:	:	:	:	:	:
Luxembourg	:	:	:	:	:	:	:	:	:	:	:	:	:	:	:	:	:	:	:	:	:	:	:	:	:	:	:

Conviction statistics **163**

Intentional Homicide: Total

	Total unsuspended custodial sanctions per 100 000 pop A99	of which: % under 1 month B99	of which: % 1 month & less than 12 months C99	of which: % 3 months & less than 12 months D99	of which: % under 6 months E99	of which: % 6 months & less than 12 months F99	of which: % 6 months & less than 18 months G99	of which: % under 12 months H99	of which: % 12 months & less than 24 months I99	of which: % 12 months & less than 36 months J99	of which: % 12 months & less than 60 months K99	of which: % 18 months & less than 36 months L99	of which: % 24 months & less than 48 months M99	of which: % 24 months & less than 60 months N99	of which: % 36 months & less than 60 months O99	of which: % 48 months & over P99	of which: % 60 months & less than 120 months Q99	of which: % 60 months & less than 144 months R99	of which: % 60 months & less than 180 months S99	of which: % 60 months & over T99	of which: % 120 months & over U99	of which: % 120 months & less than 240 months V99	of which: % 144 months & over W99	of which: % 180 months & over X99	Average length of custodial sanction/measure (in months) Y99	of which: % Life Z99	of which: % Indeterminate sanctions/measures P34HO_99
Malta	3.0	...	...	...	...	...	...	...	...	...	...	...	...	...	...	...	...	...	...	...	...	...	...	...	...	...	...
Moldova	...	...	...	...	...	...	...	2.3	0.0	...	...	...	...	4.5	...	...	50.8	...	...	...	42.4	...	...	...	...	...	...
Netherlands	0.4	...	...	...	5.0	0.0	...	...	0.0	...	...	...	...	15.0	...	...	50.0	...	...	...	30.0	...	...	...	100.6	...	35.0
Norway	1.6	...	...	...	0.2	0.5	...	...	0.6	...	...	...	...	12.5	...	...	30.1	...	...	...	54.9	...	...	...	...	1.3	...
Poland	1.9	...	...	...	0.0	1.1	...	...	2.7	...	...	...	...	24.7	...	...	23.1	...	...	...	48.4	...	...	...	127	...	2.2
Portugal	8.0	...	...	...	...	...	...	0.6	...	31.0	...	...	...	...	...	...	34.2	...	...	...	29.4	...	...	...	...	0.7	...
Romania	...	...	...	...	...	...	...	...	...	...	...	...	...	...	...	...	...	...	...	...	...	...	...	...	...	...	...
Russia	...	...	...	...	...	...	...	...	...	...	...	...	...	...	...	...	...	...	...	...	...	...	...	...	...	...	...
Slovakia	1.9	...	...	...	0.0	2.7	...	...	18.9	...	...	...	...	45.9	...	...	13.5	...	...	...	18.9	...	...	...	...	...	...
Slovenia	...	...	...	...	...	...	...	...	...	...	...	3.2	...	...	...	55.9	...	...	...	...	...	...	...	...	81.4	19.4	35.5
Spain	1.0	...	...	...	...	...	...	...	4.3	...	...	...	...	35.2	...	...	29.6	...	...	...	9.3	...	...	...	70.7	0.0	16.7
Sweden	0.7	...	...	...	1.9	1.9	...	...	5.6	...	...	...	...	...	...	...	...	...	...	...	...	...	...	...	...	...	...
Switzerland	...	...	...	...	...	...	...	...	...	...	...	...	...	...	...	...	...	...	...	...	...	...	...	...	...	...	...
Turkey	0.6	...	...	...	0.0	0.0	...	0.0	0.0	...	...	...	...	0.3	...	...	7.7	...	...	...	6.7	...	...	...	108.4	85.3	...
Ukraine	1.1	...	...	...	0.0	5.6	...	...	0.0	...	...	...	...	5.6	...	...	5.6	...	...	...	16.7	...	...	...	152	66.7	0.0
UK: E & W	1.9	...	...	...	0.0	1.0	...	2	2.0	...	...	...	...	22.0	...	...	30.0	...	...	...	10.0	...	...	...	75	32.0	3.0
UK: N.-Ireland																											
UK: Scotland																											
Mean	3	14	20	1	1	0	0	1	4	6	19	0	3	20	4	56	30	79	81	50	29	28	10	6	98	19	15
Median	2	14	20	1	0	1	0	0	2	7	21	0	3	15	4	56	30	79	81	54	24	28	10	6	95	8	11
Minimum	0	14	20	1	0	0	0	0	0	4	1	0	3	0	0	56	6	79	81	36	7	28	10	6	24	0	0
Maximum	8	14	20	1	5	12	0	2	19	7	31	0	3	50	9	56	61	79	81	60	68	28	10	6	156	85	35

Table 3.2.4.4: Number of convictions by length of unsuspended custodial sanctions and measures imposed in 1999 – Intentional Homicide: Completed

Intentional Homicide: Completed	Total unsuspended custodial sanctions per 100 000 pop R34HC A99	of which: % under 1 month P34HC B99	of which: % 1 month & less than 12 months P34HC C99	of which: % 3 months & less than 12 months P34HC D99	of which: % under 6 months P34HC E99	of which: % 6 months & less than 12 months P34HC F99	of which: % 6 months & less than 18 months P34HC G99	of which: % under 12 months P34HC H99	of which: % 12 months & less than 24 months P34HC I99	of which: % 12 months & less than 36 months P34HC J99	of which: % 12 months & less than 60 months P34HC K99	of which: % 18 months & less than 36 months P34HC L99	of which: % 24 months & less than 48 months P34HC M99	of which: % 24 months & less than 60 months P34HC N99	of which: % 36 months & less than 60 months P34HC O99	of which: % 48 months & over P34HC P99	of which: % 60 months & less than 120 months P34HC Q99	of which: % 60 months & less than 144 months P34HC R99	of which: % 60 months & less than 180 months P34HC S99	of which: % 60 months & over P34HC T99	of which: % 120 months & over P34HC U99	of which: % 120 months & less than 240 months P34HC V99	of which: % 144 months & over P34HC W99	of which: % 180 months & over P34HC X99	Average length of custodial sanction/measure (in months) T34HC Y99	of which: % Life P34HC Z99	of which: % Indeterminate sanctions/measures P34HC 99
Albania	:	:	:	:	:	:	:	:	:	:	:	:	:	:	:	:	:	:	:	:	:	:	:	:	:	:	:
Armenia	:	:	:	:	:	:	:	:	:	:	:	:	:	:	:	:	:	:	:	:	:	:	:	:	:	:	:
Austria	0.6	:	:	:	4.0	0.0	:	:	:	8.0	:	:	:	:	0.0	:	:	:	34.0	:	:	:	:	:	20.0	32.0
Belgium	:	:	:	:	:	:	:	:	:	:	:	:	:	:	:	:	:	:	:	:	:	:	:	:	:	:	:
Bulgaria	2.0	:	:	:	0.0	0.0	:	:	4.5	:	:	:	:	:	:	:	:	:	:	:	:	:	:	24.0	9.6	:
Croatia	:	:	:	:	:	:	0.0	:	:	:	:	:	:	:	:	:	:	:	:	:	:	:	:	:	:	:
Cyprus	1.7	:	:	:	0.0	:	:	:	0.0	:	0.0	:	:	:	0.0	:	:	:	53.8	:	:	:	:	156.0	46.2	:
Czech Republic	:	:	:	:	:	:	:	:	:	:	:	:	:	:	:	:	:	:	:	:	:	:	:	:	:	:	:
Denmark	0.4	:	:	:	0.0	0.0	:	:	0.0	:	:	:	:	4.3	:	:	82.6	:	:	:	:	13.0	:	:	0.0	:
Estonia	:	:	:	:	:	:	:	:	:	:	:	:	:	:	:	:	:	:	:	:	:	:	:	:	:	:	:
Finland	1.3	:	:	:	0.0	0.0	:	:	0.0	:	:	:	:	4.5	:	:	56.7	:	:	:	28.4	:	:	103.9	10.4	0.0
France	:	:	:	:	:	:	:	:	:	:	:	:	:	:	:	:	:	:	:	:	:	:	:	:	:	:	:
Georgia	2.9	:	:	:	:	:	:	:	:	:	:	:	:	:	:	:	:	:	:	:	:	:	:	:	:	:	:
Germany	:	:	:	:	:	:	:	:	:	:	:	:	:	:	:	:	:	:	:	:	:	:	:	:	:	:	:
Greece	0.6	:	:	:	:	:	:	:	:	:	0.0	:	:	:	:	:	:	:	53.4	:	:	:	:	:	41.4	5.2
Hungary	1.5	:	:	:	0.0	1.3	:	:	0.6	:	:	:	:	21.8	:	:	37.2	:	:	:	31.4	:	:	108.0	7.7	:
Ireland	:	:	:	:	:	:	:	:	:	:	:	:	:	:	:	:	:	:	:	:	:	:	:	:	:	:	:
Italy	:	:	:	:	:	:	:	:	:	:	:	:	:	:	:	:	:	:	:	:	:	:	:	:	:	:	:
Latvia	4.2	:	:	:	:	:	:	:	:	:	:	:	:	:	:	:	:	:	:	:	:	:	:	:	:	:	:
Lithuania	:	:	:	:	:	:	:	:	:	:	:	:	:	:	:	:	:	:	:	:	:	:	:	:	:	:	:
Luxembourg	:	:	:	:	:	:	:	:	:	:	:	:	:	:	:	:	:	:	:	:	:	:	:	:	:	:	:

Conviction statistics

Intentional Homicide: Completed

	Total unsuspended custodial sanctions per 100 000 pop (R34HC A99)	of which: % under 1 month (P34HC B99)	of which: % 1 month & less than 12 months (P34HC C99)	of which: % 3 months & less than 12 months (P34HC D99)	of which: % under 6 months (P34HC E99)	of which: % 6 months & less than 12 months (P34HC F99)	of which: % 6 months & less than 18 months (P34HC G99)	of which: % under 12 months (P34HC H99)	of which: % 12 months & less than 24 months (P34HC I99)	of which: % 12 months & less than 36 months (P34HC J99)	of which: % 12 months & less than 60 months (P34HC K99)	of which: % 18 months & less than 36 months (P34HC L99)	of which: % 24 months & less than 48 months (P34HC M99)	of which: % 24 months & less than 60 months (P34HC N99)	of which: % 36 months & less than 60 months (P34HC O99)	of which: % 48 months & over (P34HC P99)	of which: % 60 months & less than 120 months (P34HC Q99)	of which: % 60 months & less than 144 months (P34HC R99)	of which: % 60 months & less than 180 months (P34HC S99)	of which: % 60 months & over (P34HC T99)	of which: % 120 months & over (P34HC U99)	of which: % 120 months & less than 240 months (P34HC V99)	of which: % 144 months & over (P34HC W99)	of which: % 180 months & over (P34HC X99)	Average length of custodial sanction/measure (in months) (T34HC Y99)	of which: % Life (P34HC Z99)	of which: % Indeterminate sanctions/measures (P34HC _99)
Malta	...	...	...	...	...	...	...	...	...	...	...	...	...	...	...	...	...	...	...	...	...	...	...	...	...	...	...
Moldova	1.1	...	...	...	1.2	3.0	...	...	6.5	...	...	...	...	...	...	79.8	...	...	...	...	...	...	...	...	82.9	...	0.0
Netherlands	0.3	...	...	...	0.0	0.0	...	...	0.0	...	...	...	9.5	0.0	...	...	60.0	...	...	...	40.0	...	...	...	119.1	0.0	40.0
Norway	...	...	...	...	...	...	...	...	...	...	...	...	...	...	...	...	...	...	...	...	...	...	...	...	...	...	...
Poland	1.3	...	...	...	0.0	1.5	...	...	0.8	...	...	...	...	9.9	...	...	20.6	...	...	...	67.2	...	...	...	157.0	...	2.3
Portugal	5.7	...	...	...	...	...	...	0.5	...	...	24.7	...	...	...	...	...	30.8	...	...	...	38.9	...	...	...	...	0.9	...
Romania	...	...	...	...	...	...	...	...	...	...	...	...	...	...	...	...	...	...	...	...	...	...	...	...	...	...	...
Russia	...	...	...	...	...	...	...	...	...	...	...	...	...	...	...	...	...	...	...	...	...	...	...	...	...	...	...
Slovakia	...	...	...	...	...	...	...	...	...	...	...	...	...	...	...	...	...	...	...	...	...	...	...	...	...	...	...
Slovenia	...	...	...	...	...	...	...	...	...	...	...	...	...	...	...	...	...	...	...	...	...	...	...	...	...	...	...
Spain	...	...	...	...	...	...	...	...	...	...	...	...	...	...	...	...	...	...	...	...	...	...	...	...	...	...	...
Sweden	0.3	...	...	...	0.0	5.0	...	...	10.0	...	...	...	10	10.0	...	...	30.0	...	...	...	20.0	...	...	...	96.3	0.0	25.0
Switzerland	...	...	...	...	...	...	...	...	...	...	...	...	...	...	...	...	...	...	...	...	...	...	...	...	...	...	...
Turkey	...	...	...	...	...	...	...	...	...	...	...	...	...	...	...	...	...	...	...	...	...	...	...	...	...	...	...
Ukraine	0.5	...	...	...	0.0	0.0	...	...	0.0	...	...	...	10	0.0	0	80	0.0	83	...	0	0.0	...	...	...	0.0	100.0	0.0
UK: E & W	0.9	...	...	...	0.0	7.1	...	...	0.0	...	...	...	10	0.0	0	80	7.1	83	...	53	0.0	...	13	...	45.0	85.7	0.0
UK: N.-Ireland	1.2	...	...	...	0.0	1.7	...	...	1.7	...	...	...	10	13.3	0	80	23.3	83	...	54	3.3	...	13	...	73.0	51.7	5.0
UK: Scotland																											
Mean	2	...	...	...	0	2	0	1	2	...	8	0	10	7	0	80	30	83	...	47	25	...	13	...	88	29	12
Median	1	...	...	...	0	1	0	1	1	...	8	0	10	4	0	80	30	83	...	53	28	...	13	...	96	10	5
Minimum	0	...	...	...	0	0	0	0	0	...	8	0	10	0	0	80	0	83	...	34	0	...	13	...	0	0	0
Maximum	6	...	...	...	4	7	0	1	10	...	25	0	10	22	0	80	60	83	...	54	67	...	13	...	157	100	40

Table 3.2.4.5: Number of convictions by length of unsuspended custodial sanctions and measures imposed in 1999 – Assault

Assault	Total unsuspended custodial sanctions per 100 000 pop R34AS A99	of which: % under 1 month P34AS B99	of which: % 1 month & less than 12 months P34AS C99	of which: % 3 months & less than 12 months P34AS D99	of which: % under 6 months P34AS E99	of which: % 6 months & less than 12 months P34AS F99	of which: % 6 months & less than 18 months P34AS G99	of which: % under 12 months P34AS H99	of which: % 12 months & less than 24 months P34AS I99	of which: % 12 months & less than 36 months P34AS J99	of which: % 12 months & less than 60 months P34AS K99	of which: % 18 months & less than 36 months P34AS L99	of which: % 24 months & less than 48 months P34AS M99	of which: % 24 months & less than 60 months P34AS N99	of which: % 36 months & less than 60 months P34AS O99	of which: % 48 months & over P34AS P99	of which: % 60 months & less than 120 months P34AS Q99	of which: % 60 months & less than 144 months P34AS R99	of which: % 60 months & less than 180 months P34AS S99	of which: % 60 months & over P34AS T99	of which: % 120 months & over P34AS U99	of which: % 120 months & less than 240 months P34AS V99	of which: % 144 months & over P34AS W99	of which: % 180 months & over P34AS X99	Average length of custodial sanction/measure (in months) T34AS Y99	of which: % Life P34AS Z99	of which: % Indeterminate sanctions/measures P34AS _99
Albania	1.5	22.0	40.0	...	...	...	...	...	...	...	16.0	...	...	...	...	...	6.0	...	...	...	0.0	...	...	...	...	...	16.0
Armenia	...	...	...	...	...	...	...	...	...	...	...	...	...	...	...	...	...	...	...	...	...	...	...	...	...	...	...
Austria	8.9	...	...	...	70.8	10.1	...	...	...	6.2	...	...	...	...	0.8	...	...	...	...	0.3	...	...	...	...	...	0.0	2.4
Belgium	...	...	...	...	...	...	...	...	...	...	...	...	...	...	...	...	...	...	...	...	...	...	...	...	...	...	...
Bulgaria	0.8	...	...	...	8.3	1.7	...	...	15.0	...	...	...	...	3.4	...	...	0.0	0.2	...	...	0.0	...	...	...	16.0	0.0	...
Croatia	1.4	...	...	...	56.9	19.0	...	...	6.9	...	...	...	...	...	...	...	...	...	...	...	...	...	...	...	7.0	0.0	...
Cyprus	2.7	...	...	...	60.0	...	30.0	...	...	...	...	0.0	...	...	...	...	...	...	...	10.0	...	...	...	...	11.2	...	13.8
Czech Republic	3.4	...	...	...	...	...	...	43.2	...	...	51.6	...	...	...	...	...	...	...	5.2	...	0.0	...	...	...	...	0.0	...
Denmark	40.5	...	...	10.9	90.6	6.2	...	...	2.2	...	...	...	...	0.7	...	...	...	...	...	...	...	...	0.0	...	...	0.0	...
Estonia	6.4	...	...	...	54.5	21.4	...	...	16.3	...	...	...	...	40.2	...	...	32.6	...	...	...	0.0	...	...	...	...	0.0	...
Finland	17.0	...	...	...	61.1	22.6	...	...	14.5	...	...	...	...	7.7	...	...	0.3	...	...	...	0.0	...	...	...	8.0	0.0	1.6
France	17.4	...	...	...	...	...	...	...	...	13.1	...	...	...	...	2.1	...	0.7	...	...	...	0.4	...	...	...	7.3	0.0	...
Georgia	...	...	...	...	...	...	...	...	...	...	...	...	...	...	...	...	...	...	...	...	...	...	...	...	...	...	...
Germany	5.9	...	...	...	23.0	33.9	...	...	24.1	...	...	...	...	17.9	...	...	1.0	...	...	...	0.0	...	...	...	...	0.0	9.0
Greece	1.0	...	...	...	...	...	...	...	...	...	86.1	...	...	...	...	...	...	...	...	13.0	...	...	...	...	...	0.0	0.9
Hungary	6.0	...	...	...	23.2	32.2	...	...	19.9	...	...	...	...	21.5	...	...	3.0	...	...	...	0.3	...	...	...	20.0	0.0	...
Ireland	...	...	...	...	...	...	...	...	...	...	...	...	...	...	...	...	...	...	...	...	...	...	...	...	...	...	...
Italy	6.2	...	...	...	82.0	11.1	...	...	5.7	...	...	...	...	1.1	...	...	0.1	...	...	...	0.0	...	...	...	...	...	...
Latvia	...	...	...	...	...	...	...	...	...	...	...	...	...	...	...	...	...	...	...	...	...	...	...	...	...	...	...
Lithuania	...	...	...	...	...	...	...	...	...	...	...	...	...	...	...	...	...	...	...	...	...	...	...	...	...	...	...
Luxembourg	...	...	...	...	...	...	...	...	...	...	...	...	...	...	...	...	...	...	...	...	...	...	...	...	...	...	...

Conviction statistics

Assault

	Total unsuspended custodial sanctions per 100 000 pop (A99)	of which: % under 1 month (B99)	of which: % 1 month & less than 12 months (C99)	of which: % 3 months & less than 12 months (D99)	of which: % under 6 months (E99)	of which: % 6 months & less than 12 months (F99)	of which: % 6 months & less than 18 months (G99)	of which: % under 12 months (H99)	of which: % 12 months & less than 24 months (I99)	of which: % 12 months & less than 36 months (J99)	of which: % 12 months & less than 60 months (K99)	of which: % 18 months & less than 36 months (L99)	of which: % 24 months & less than 48 months (M99)	of which: % 24 months & less than 60 months (N99)	of which: % 36 months & less than 60 months (O99)	of which: % 48 months & over (P99)	of which: % 60 months & less than 120 months (Q99)	of which: % 60 months & less than 144 months (R99)	of which: % 60 months & less than 180 months (S99)	of which: % 60 months & over (T99)	of which: % 120 months & over (U99)	of which: % 120 months & less than 240 months (V99)	of which: % 144 months & over (W99)	of which: % 180 months & over (X99)	Average length of custodial sanction/measure (in months) (Y99)	of which: % Life (Z99)	of which: % Indeterminate sanctions/measures (P34AS_99)
Malta	...	...	...	...	...	...	...	...	...	...	...	...	...	...	...	...	...	...	...	...	...	...	...	...	...	...	...
Moldova	2.7	...	...	...	...	...	...	7.5	6.7	...	...	...	...	44.2	...	...	35.8	...	...	...	5.8	...	...	...	...	...	...
Netherlands	7.5	...	...	...	80.6	12.7	...	...	4.6	...	...	...	1.7	...	...	0.0	...	...	...	...	...	...	...	...	3.9	0.0	0.0
Norway	12.4	...	...	...	78.9	12.8	...	...	6.7	...	...	...	...	1.4	...	...	0.2	...	...	...	0.0	...	...	...	4.2	...	0.9
Poland	3.4	...	...	...	3.4	24.6	...	...	36.4	...	...	...	...	26.9	...	...	8.2	...	...	...	0.5	...	...	...	...	...	...
Portugal	0.8	...	...	...	11.4	24.1	...	...	32.9	...	...	...	...	25.3	...	...	5.1	...	...	...	1.3	...	...	...	27.0	...	5.1
Romania	...	...	...	...	...	...	...	...	...	...	...	...	...	...	...	...	...	...	...	...	...	...	...	...	...	...	...
Russia	...	...	...	...	...	...	...	...	...	...	...	...	...	...	...	...	...	...	...	...	...	...	...	...	...	...	...
Slovakia	2.4	...	...	...	57.4	25.5	...	...	8.5	...	...	...	...	8.5	...	...	0.0	...	...	...	0.0	...	...	...	...	...	...
Slovenia	...	...	...	...	...	...	...	...	...	...	...	...	...	...	...	...	...	...	...	...	...	...	...	...	...	...	...
Spain	21.4	...	...	...	63.5	16.6	...	...	17.4	...	...	...	2.2	...	...	0.3	...	...	...	...	...	...	...	...	6.3	...	6.4
Sweden	3.8	...	...	...	56.5	10.1	...	...	8.3	...	...	...	...	17.4	...	...	0.7	...	...	...	0.4	...	...	...	10.8	0.0	6.5
Switzerland	...	...	...	...	...	...	...	...	...	...	...	...	...	...	...	...	...	...	...	...	...	...	...	...	...	...	...
Turkey	...	...	...	...	...	...	...	...	...	...	...	...	...	...	...	...	...	...	...	...	...	...	...	...	...	...	...
Ukraine	19.0	...	...	...	38.5	20.5	...	25	20.5	10	51	0	2	16.5	1	0	2.9	0	5	8	0.3	...	0	0	14.1	0.7	0.0
UK: E & W	8.4	...	...	...	29.2	32.8	30	25	13.1	10	52	0	2	17.5	1	0	3.6	0	5	10	3.6	...	0	0	20.0	0.0	0.0
UK: N-Ireland	34.9	...	...	...	57.3	17.6	30	43	12.1	13	86	0	2	9.4	2	0	3.4	0	5	13	0.1	...	0	0	10.0	0.1	0.0
UK: Scotland	...	...	...	...	...	...	30	8	...	6	16	0	2	...	0	0	...	0	5	0	...	...	0	0	...	...	...
Mean	9	22	40	11	50	19	30	25	14	10	51	0	2	16	1	0	6	0	5	8	1	...	0	0	12	0	5
Median	6	22	40	11	57	19	30	25	13	10	52	0	2	17	1	0	3	0	5	10	0	...	0	0	10	0	2
Minimum	1	22	40	11	3	2	30	8	2	6	16	0	2	1	0	0	0	0	5	0	0	...	0	0	4	0	0
Maximum	40	22	40	11	91	34	30	43	36	13	86	0	2	44	2	0	36	0	5	13	6	...	0	0	27	1	16

Table 3.2.4.6: Number of convictions by length of unsuspended custodial sanctions and measures imposed in 1999 – Rape

Rape	Total unsuspended custodial sanctions per 100 000 pop R34RA A99	of which: % under 1 month R34RA B99	of which: % 1 month & less than 12 months R34RA C99	of which: % 3 months & less than 12 months R34RA D99	of which: % under 6 months R34RA E99	of which: % 6 months & less than 12 months R34RA F99	of which: % 6 months & less than 18 months R34RA G99	of which: % under 12 months R34RA H99	of which: % 12 months & less than 24 months R34RA I99	of which: % 12 months & less than 36 months R34RA J99	of which: % 12 months & less than 60 months R34RA K99	of which: % 18 months & less than 36 months R34RA L99	of which: % 24 months & less than 48 months R34RA M99	of which: % 24 months & less than 60 months R34RA N99	of which: % 36 months & less than 60 months R34RA O99	of which: % 48 months & over R34RA P99	of which: % 60 months & less than 120 months R34RA Q99	of which: % 60 months & less than 144 months R34RA R99	of which: % 60 months & less than 180 months R34RA S99	of which: % 60 months & over R34RA T99	of which: % 120 months & over R34RA U99	of which: % 120 months & less than 240 months R34RA V99	of which: % 144 months & over R34RA W99	of which: % 180 months & over R34RA X99	Average length of custodial sanction/measure (in months) T34RA Y99	of which: % Life P34RA Z99	of which: % Indeterminate sanctions/measures P34RA 99_99
Albania	0.6	38.1	42.9	...	...	...	...	...	...	...	9.5	...	...	...	...	...	...	...	...	...	...	...	...	...	...	...	9.5
Armenia	...	...	...	...	...	...	...	...	...	...	...	...	...	...	...	...	...	...	...	...	...	...	...	...	...	...	...
Austria	1.4	...	...	...	1.7	8.7	...	...	29.6	...	...	...	...	...	11.3	...	...	...	...	7.0	0.0	...	...	...	...	0.0	12.2
Belgium	...	...	...	...	...	...	...	...	...	...	...	...	...	...	...	...	...	...	...	...	...	...	...	...	...	...	...
Bulgaria	1.7	...	...	...	0.8	3.1	...	...	42.7	...	...	...	...	43.8	...	...	10.9	...	...	...	...	...	...	...	23.0	0.0	...
Croatia	1.5	...	...	...	6.3	10.9	...	...	18.8	...	...	...	...	...	...	...	...	...	...	...	...	...	...	...	36.0	0.0	9.4
Cyprus	0.5	...	...	...	0.0	...	25.0	...	...	...	...	0.0	...	...	25.0	...	...	...	...	50.0	0.0	...	...	...	62.3	0.0	...
Czech Republic	0.9	...	...	...	...	...	...	2.2	40.0	...	68.9	...	...	11.1	...	...	28.9	...	...	...	...	...	...	...	0.0	...
Denmark	0.8	...	...	...	17.8	31.1	...	...	40.0	...	...	...	...	...	...	...	20.8	0.0	...	...	...	0.0	...	...	...	0.0	...
Estonia	1.7	...	...	4.2	...	...	...	...	12.5	...	...	...	...	62.5	...	...	3.7	...	...	...	0.0	...	...	...	27.0	0.0	0.0
Finland	0.5	...	...	...	0.0	18.5	...	...	22.2	...	...	...	...	55.6	...	...	33.5	...	...	...	0.0	...	...	...	...	...	...
France	2.6	...	...	...	0.0	5.1	...	...	...	6.9	...	...	...	...	9.1	...	44.8	...	...	...	45.2	...	...	...	104.2	0.2	0.0
Georgia	1.7	...	...	...	...	...	...	...	2.3	...	...	...	...	24.1	...	...	44.8	...	...	...	17.2	...	...	...	...	...	...
Germany	1.2	...	...	...	0.6	4.2	...	...	12.3	...	...	...	...	65.2	...	...	16.6	...	...	...	0.9	...	...	...	...	0.1	14.9
Greece	0.3	...	...	...	...	...	...	...	...	...	42.9	...	...	...	...	...	...	...	...	50.0	...	...	...	...	...	0.0	...
Hungary	1.4	...	...	...	0.7	0.7	...	...	13.3	...	...	...	...	49.7	29.2	...	35.0	...	...	...	0.7	...	...	...	56.0	0.0	7.1
Ireland	...	...	...	...	...	...	...	...	...	...	...	...	...	...	...	...	...	...	...	...	...	...	...	...	...	...	...
Italy	2.1	...	...	...	...	...	...	...	41.8	...	...	...	...	29.6	...	...	7.3	...	...	...	0.8	...	...	...	...	...	...
Latvia	3.0	...	...	...	1.1	19.3	...	38.9	29.2	...	...	...	...	...	29.2	...	2.8	...	...	...	...	...	...	...	...	...	...
Lithuania	...	...	...	...	...	...	...	...	...	...	...	...	...	...	...	...	...	...	...	...	...	...	...	...	...	...	...
Luxembourg	...	...	...	...	...	...	...	...	...	...	...	...	...	...	...	...	...	...	...	...	...	...	...	...	...	...	...

Conviction statistics

Rape

	Total unsuspended custodial sanctions per 100 000 pop R34RA A99	of which: % under 1 month P34RA B99	of which: % 1 month & less than 12 months P34RA C99	of which: % 3 months & less than 12 months P34RA D99	of which: % under 6 months P34RA E99	of which: % 6 months & less than 12 months P34RA F99	of which: % 6 months & less than 18 months P34RA G99	of which: % under 12 months P34RA H99	of which: % 12 months & less than 24 months P34RA I99	of which: % 12 months & less than 36 months P34RA J99	of which: % 12 months & less than 60 months P34RA K99	of which: % 18 months & less than 36 months P34RA L99	of which: % 24 months & less than 48 months P34RA M99	of which: % 24 months & less than 60 months P34RA N99	of which: % 36 months & less than 60 months P34RA O99	of which: % 48 months & over P34RA P99	of which: % 60 months & less than 120 months P34RA Q99	of which: % 60 months & less than 144 months P34RA R99	of which: % 60 months & less than 180 months P34RA S99	of which: % 60 months & over P34RA T99	of which: % 120 months & over P34RA U99	of which: % 120 months & less than 240 months P34RA V99	of which: % 144 months & over P34RA W99	of which: % 180 months & over P34RA X99	Average length of custodial sanction/measure (in months) T34RA Y99	of which: % Life P34RA Z99	of which: % Indeterminate sanctions/measures P34RA_99
Malta	:	:	:	:	:	:	:	:	:	:	:	:	:	:	:	:	:	:	:	:	:	:	:	:	:	:	:
Moldova	2.1	:	:	:	:	:	:	0.0	2.1	:	:	:	:	30.5	:	:	52.6	:	:	:	14.7	:	:	:	:	:	:
Netherlands	1.4	:	:	:	7.0	25.6	:	:	32.6	:	:	:	27.9	:	:	7.0	:	:	:	:	:	:	:	:	22.6	0.0	0.0
Norway	0.7	:	:	:	19.4	12.9	:	:	16.1	:	:	:	:	51.6	:	:	0.0	:	:	:	0.0	:	:	:	23.4	:	0.0
Poland	1.3	:	:	:	0.2	1.0	:	:	21.5	:	:	:	:	65.0	:	:	12.0	:	:	:	0.4	:	:	:	:	:	:
Portugal	0.5	:	:	:	0.0	0.0	:	:	6.4	:	:	:	:	40.4	:	:	40.4	:	:	:	12.8	:	:	:	76.0	:	6.4
Romania	3.1	:	:	:	:	:	:	1.3	:	:	39.0	:	:	:	:	:	35.0	:	:	:	10.9	:	:	:	:	0.0	:
Russia	:	:	:	:	:	:	:	:	:	:	:	:	:	:	:	:	:	:	:	:	:	:	:	:	:	:	:
Slovakia	2.2	:	:	:	9.5	19.0	:	:	33.3	:	:	:	:	28.6	:	:	9.5	:	:	:	0.0	:	:	:	:	:	:
Slovenia	:	:	:	:	:	:	:	:	:	:	:	:	:	:	:	:	:	:	:	:	:	:	:	:	:	:	:
Spain	:	:	:	:	:	:	:	:	:	:	:	:	39.0	:	:	10.4	:	:	:	:	:	:	:	:	29.7	:	16.9
Sweden	0.9	:	:	:	1.3	6.5	25	:	42.9	:	:	:	:	:	:	:	:	:	:	:	4.4	:	:	:	46.2	0.0	11.8
Switzerland	0.9	:	:	:	0.0	1.5	25	:	2.9	:	:	:	:	72.1	:	:	7.4	:	:	:	:	:	:	:	:	:	:
Turkey	:	:	:	:	:	:	:	:	:	:	:	:	:	:	:	:	:	:	:	:	:	:	:	:	:	:	:
Ukraine	:	:	:	:	:	:	:	:	:	:	:	:	:	:	:	:	:	:	:	:	:	:	:	:	:	:	:
UK: E & W	1.2	:	:	:	0.0	1.1	:	11	1.7	22	:	0	33	16.9	19	9	56.8	0	29	36	13.4	:	0	:	79.8	10.0	:
UK: N.-Ireland	0.4	:	:	:	0.0	0.0	:	2	14.3	29	:	0	33	0.0	18	9	28.6	0	29	50	42.9	:	0	:	91.0	0.0	0.0
UK: Scotland	0.5	:	:	:	0.0	0.0	25	0	0.0	7	:	0	28	30.8	9	7	50.0	0	29	7	19.2	:	0	:	81.0	0.0	0.0
Mean	1	38	43	4	3	9	25	39	19	30	69	0	39	40	19	9	23	0	29	50	10	:	0	0	54	1	7
Median	1	38	43	4	1	5	25	2	15	29	41	0	33	40	18	9	19	0	29	50	1	:	0	0	51	0	7
Minimum	0	38	43	4	0	0	25	0	0	7	10	0	28	0	9	7	0	0	29	7	0	:	0	0	23	0	0
Maximum	3	38	43	4	19	31	25	39	43	30	69	0	39	72	29	10	57	0	29	50	45	:	0	0	104	10	17

Table 3.2.4.7: Number of convictions by length of unsuspended custodial sanctions and measures imposed in 1999 – Robbery

Robbery	Total unsuspended custodial sanctions per 100 000 pop R34RO A99	of which: % under 1 month P34RO B99	of which: % 1 month & less than 12 months C99	of which: % 3 months & less than 12 months D99	of which: % under 6 months E99	of which: % 6 months & less than 12 months F99	of which: % 6 months & less than 18 months G99	of which: % under 12 months H99	of which: % 12 months & less than 24 months I99	of which: % 12 months & less than 36 months J99	of which: % 12 months & less than 60 months K99	of which: % 18 months & less than 36 months L99	of which: % 24 months & less than 48 months M99	of which: % 24 months & less than 60 months N99	of which: % 36 months & less than 60 months O99	of which: % 48 months & over P99	of which: % 60 months & less than 120 months Q99	of which: % 60 months & less than 144 months R99	of which: % 60 months & less than 180 months S99	of which: % 60 months & over T99	of which: % 120 months & over U99	of which: % 120 months & less than 240 months V99	of which: % 144 months & over W99	of which: % 180 months & over X99	Average length of custodial sanction/measure (in months) T34RO Y99	of which: % Life P34RO Z99	of which: % Indeterminate sanctions/measures P34RO _99
Albania	7.4	36.7	25.0	:	:	:	:	:	:	18.0	:	:	:	:	:	:	11.3	:	:	:	3.9	:	:	:	:	:	5.1
Armenia	:	:	:	:	:	:	:	:	:	:	:	:	:	:	:	:	:	:	:	:	:	:	:	:	:	:	:
Austria	4.3	:	:	:	0.9	5.8	:	:	24.1	:	:	:	:	:	18.3	:	:	:	:	17.4	:	:	:	:	:	:	:
Belgium	:	:	:	:	:	:	:	:	:	:	:	:	:	:	:	:	:	:	:	:	:	:	:	:	:	:	:
Bulgaria	5.4	:	:	:	0.0	6.1	:	:	38.2	:	:	:	:	:	:	:	:	:	:	:	:	:	:	:	22	:	3.8
Croatia	3.6	:	:	:	8.3	21.8	:	:	32.7	:	:	:	17.3	:	:	:	1.9	:	:	:	0.0	:	:	:	21	1.6	17.9
Cyprus	0.7	:	:	:	20.0	:	0.0	:	:	:	:	20.0	:	:	20.0	:	:	:	:	40.0	:	:	:	:	38.3	0.0	:
Czech Republic	8.5	:	:	:	:	:	:	3.4	:	:	79.5	:	:	:	:	:	:	17.0	:	:	:	:	:	:	:	0.0	:
Denmark	9.5	:	:	:	20.6	31.2	:	:	30.8	:	:	:	16.2	:	:	:	:	:	:	:	:	0.0	:	:	:	0.2	:
Estonia	11.0	:	0.6	:	:	:	:	:	6.9	:	:	:	24.5	:	:	:	67.3	1.0	:	:	0.6	:	:	:	18.2	0.0	0.3
Finland	5.7	:	:	:	16.7	30.7	:	:	22.9	:	:	:	26.3	:	:	:	2.4	:	:	:	0.7	:	:	:	:	0.0	:
France	5.2	:	:	:	36.5	24.9	:	:	:	23.2	:	:	:	:	5.5	:	6.0	:	:	:	4.0	:	:	:	19.9	0.0	:
Georgia	11.0	:	:	:	:	:	:	:	5.8	:	:	:	15.3	:	:	:	42.1	:	:	:	9.9	:	:	:	:	:	:
Germany	5.0	:	:	:	1.9	10.9	:	:	28.6	:	:	:	46.9	:	:	:	10.2	:	:	:	1.5	:	:	:	:	0.1	10.8
Greece	1.3	:	:	:	:	:	:	:	:	:	62.2	:	:	:	:	:	:	:	:	31.1	:	:	:	:	:	0.7	5.9
Hungary	11.1	:	:	:	0.4	3.5	:	:	21.4	:	:	:	56.3	:	:	:	18.0	:	:	:	0.4	:	:	:	45	0.0	:
Ireland	:	:	:	:	:	:	:	:	:	:	:	:	:	:	:	:	:	:	:	:	:	:	:	:	:	:	:
Italy	11.5	:	:	:	3.1	15.9	:	:	51.9	:	:	:	26.2	:	:	:	2.6	:	:	:	0.3	:	:	:	:	:	:
Latvia	10.2	:	:	:	:	:	0.0	:	35.9	:	:	:	:	30.2	:	:	32.3	:	:	:	:	1.6	:	:	:	:	:
Lithuania	:	:	:	:	:	:	:	:	:	:	:	:	:	:	:	:	:	:	:	:	:	:	:	:	:	:	:
Luxembourg	:	:	:	:	:	:	:	:	:	:	:	:	:	:	:	:	:	:	:	:	:	:	:	:	:	:	:

Conviction statistics

Robbery

	A99 Total unsuspended custodial sanctions per 100 000 pop	B99 of which: % under 1 month	C99 of which: % 1 month & less than 12 months	D99 of which: % 3 months & less than 12 months	E99 of which: % under 6 months	F99 of which: % 6 months & less than 12 months	G99 of which: % 6 months & less than 18 months	H99 of which: % under 12 months	I99 of which: % 12 months & less than 24 months	J99 of which: % 12 months & less than 36 months	K99 of which: % 12 months & less than 60 months	L99 of which: % 18 months & less than 36 months	M99 of which: % 24 months & less than 48 months	N99 of which: % 24 months & less than 60 months	O99 of which: % 36 months & less than 60 months	P99 of which: % 48 months & over	Q99 of which: % 60 months & less than 120 months	R99 of which: % 60 months & less than 144 months	S99 of which: % 60 months & less than 180 months	T99 of which: % 60 months & over	U99 of which: % 120 months & over	V99 of which: % 120 months & less than 240 months	W99 of which: % 144 months & over	X99 of which: % 180 months & over	Y99 Average length of custodial sanction/measure (in months)	Z99 of which: % Life	_99 of which: % Indeterminate sanctions/measures
Malta	8.8	:	:	:	:	:	:	3.6	2.1	:	:	:	:	:	:	:	:	:	:	:	13.7	:	:	:	:	:	:
Moldova	12.6	:	:	:	41.4	24.6	:	:	18.0	:	:	:	12.0	31.7	:	4.0	49.0	:	:	:	:	:	:	:	13.8	0.0	0.0
Netherlands	3.1	:	:	:	24.8	17.5	:	:	40.1	:	:	:	:	16.1	:	:	0.7	:	:	:	0.7	:	:	:	14.8	:	1.5
Norway	12.0	:	:	:	0.2	1.6	:	:	10.3	:	:	:	:	81.2	:	:	6.1	:	:	:	0.5	:	:	:	:	0.0	:
Poland	6.6	:	:	:	1.2	5.8	:	2.0	21.5	:	:	:	:	46.7	:	:	19.1	:	:	:	5.6	:	:	:	50	:	0.3
Portugal	12.8	:	:	:	:	:	:	:	:	:	39.9	:	:	:	:	:	39.2	:	:	:	2.5	:	:	:	:	0.0	:
Romania	:	:	:	:	:	:	:	:	:	:	:	:	:	:	:	:	:	:	:	:	:	:	:	:	:	:	:
Russia	3.1	:	:	:	10.2	20.3	:	:	33.9	:	:	:	:	28.8	:	:	5.1	:	:	:	1.7	:	:	:	:	:	:
Slovakia	:	:	:	:	:	:	:	:	:	:	:	:	:	:	:	:	:	:	:	:	:	:	:	:	:	:	:
Slovenia	3.9	:	:	:	12.8	6.7	:	:	54.1	:	:	:	18.9	:	:	7.6	:	:	:	:	:	:	:	:	22	:	3.2
Spain	2.2	:	:	:	2.5	18.1	:	:	10.0	:	:	:	:	32.5	:	:	2.5	:	:	:	1.9	:	:	:	30	0.0	32.5
Sweden	:	:	:	:	:	:	:	:	:	:	:	:	:	:	:	:	:	:	:	:	:	:	:	:	:	:	:
Switzerland	:	:	:	:	:	:	:	:	:	:	:	:	:	:	:	:	:	:	:	:	:	:	:	:	:	:	:
Turkey	:	:	:	:	:	:	:	:	:	:	:	:	:	:	:	:	:	:	:	:	:	:	:	:	:	:	:
Ukraine	7.8	:	:	:	5.0	5.9	:	:	20.7	:	:	:	15	51.5	18	6	14.2	1	17	30	1.9	2	0	0	35.7	0.9	0.0
UK: E & W	4.2	:	:	:	0.0	8.8	:	:	38.2	:	:	:	15	39.7	19	6	10.3	1	17	31	2.9	2	0	0	31	0.0	0.0
UK: N-Ireland	8.9	:	:	:	19.2	16.2	:	:	21.8	:	:	:	12	24.6	5	4	17.3	1	17	17	0.6	2	0	0	28	0.0	0.0
UK: Scotland																											
Mean	7	37	25	1	11	15	0	2	25	28	50	20	15	34	18	8	18	:	17	40	3	2	0	0	28	0	6
Median	7	37	25	1	7	16	0	3	22	24	51	20	15	29	19	6	11	:	17	31	2	2	0	0	25	0	3
Minimum	1	37	25	1	0	2	0	0	2	23	18	20	12	15	5	4	1	:	17	17	0	2	0	0	14	0	0
Maximum	13	37	25	1	41	31	0	4	54	36	80	20	19	81	30	8	67	:	17	40	14	2	0	0	50	2	33

172 *European Sourcebook of Crime and Criminal Justice Statistics - 2003*

Table 3.2.4.8: Number of convictions by length of unsuspended custodial sanctions and measures imposed in 1999 – Theft: Total

Theft: Total	Total unsuspended custodial sanctions per 100 000 pop R34TH A99	of which: % under 1 month P34TH B99	of which: % 1 month & less than 12 months P34TH C99	of which: % 3 months & less than 12 months P34TH D99	of which: % under 6 months P34TH E99	of which: % 6 months & less than 12 months P34TH F99	of which: % 6 months & less than 18 months P34TH G99	of which: % under 12 months P34TH H99	of which: % 12 months & less than 24 months P34TH I99	of which: % 12 months & less than 36 months P34TH J99	of which: % 12 months & less than 60 months P34TH K99	of which: % 18 months & less than 36 months P34TH L99	of which: % 24 months & less than 48 months P34TH M99	of which: % 24 months & less than 60 months P34TH N99	of which: % 36 months & less than 60 months P34TH O99	of which: % 48 months & over P34TH P99	of which: % 60 months & less than 120 months P34TH Q99	of which: % 60 months & less than 144 months P34TH R99	of which: % 60 months & less than 180 months P34TH S99	of which: % 60 months & over P34TH T99	of which: % 120 months & over P34TH U99	of which: % 120 months & less than 240 months P34TH V99	of which: % 144 months & over P34TH W99	of which: % 180 months & over P34TH X99	Average length of custodial sanction/measure (in months) T34TH Y99	of which: % Life P34TH Z99	of which: % Indeterminate sanctions/measures P34TH _99
Albania	20.7	23.4	33.7	...	...	...	...	...	...	30.4	...	...	...	...	...	...	6.2	...	...	0.6	...	...	...	...	...	5.8
Armenia	...	...	...	...	...	...	...	...	...	...	...	...	...	...	...	...	...	...	...	...	...	...	...	...	...	...
Austria	38.7	...	...	47.2	26.3	23.3	...	...	16.3	...	...	...	...	...	0.8	...	...	...	0.1	...	...	...	...	...	...	0.8
Belgium	...	...	...	...	...	...	...	...	...	...	...	...	...	...	...	...	...	...	...	...	...	...	...	...	...	...
Bulgaria	63.4	...	...	...	8.2	19.8	...	...	34.8	...	...	...	...	3.2	...	...	0.0	...	...	0.0	...	...	...	16.0	0.0	...
Croatia	13.9	...	...	...	41.5	29.3	...	...	12.7	...	...	...	...	...	...	...	...	...	...	...	...	...	...	9.0	0.0	13.2
Cyprus	18.0	...	...	...	54.4	...	33.1	...	...	...	...	6.6	...	...	4.4	...	...	...	1.5	...	...	...	...	9.2	0.0	...
Czech Republic	53.6	...	...	...	85.7	11.2	...	72.3	2.7	...	26.5	...	...	0.4	...	...	...	0.0	...	...	...	0.0	...	...	0.0	...
Denmark	43.4	...	...	...	85.7	11.2	...	...	2.7	...	...	...	...	0.4	...	...	1.5	...	...	0.0	...	0.0	...	...	0.0	...
Estonia	69.7	...	...	...	77.5	10.8	...	...	38.3	...	...	...	...	13.1	...	...	0.0	...	...	0.0	...	...	...	3.6	0.0	5.9
Finland	45.0	...	...	...	77.5	10.8	...	...	5.0	...	...	...	...	0.8	1.2	...	0.6	...	...	0.2	...	...	...	6.0	0.0	...
France	52.1	...	...	...	66.4	21.7	...	...	...	9.9	...	...	...	...	...	...	...	...	...	...	...	...	...	...	...	...
Georgia	98.7	...	...	...	...	0.5	...	...	9.1	...	...	...	...	55.0	...	...	24.7	...	...	...	...	...	...	...	...	...
Germany	20.7	...	...	...	41.3	28.1	...	...	20.7	...	...	...	...	9.5	...	...	0.5	...	...	0.0	...	...	...	...	0.0	1.6
Greece	11.6	...	...	...	...	...	...	...	...	...	74.3	...	...	...	...	...	...	...	7.4	...	...	...	...	...	0.1	18.2
Hungary	65.1	...	...	...	40.1	34.6	...	...	19.2	...	...	...	...	5.9	...	...	0.1	...	...	0.0	...	...	...	12.0	0.0	...
Ireland	...	...	...	...	...	...	...	...	...	...	...	...	...	...	...	...	...	...	...	...	...	...	...	...	...	...
Italy	88.0	...	...	...	86.2	11.9	...	...	1.7	...	...	...	...	0.2	...	...	0.0	...	...	0.0	...	...	...	...	0.0	...
Latvia	69.9	...	...	...	...	...	...	9.4	...	70.4	...	...	...	...	14.6	...	5.6	...	...	0.1	0.1	...	...	...	...	...
Lithuania	...	...	...	...	...	...	...	...	...	...	...	...	...	...	...	...	...	...	...	...	...	...	...	...	...	...
Luxembourg	...	...	...	...	...	...	...	...	...	...	...	...	...	...	...	...	...	...	...	...	...	...	...	...	...	...

Conviction statistics

Theft: Total

	Total unsuspended custodial sanctions per 100 000 pop R34TH A99	of which: % under 1 month P34TH B99	of which: % 1 month & less than 12 months P34TH C99	of which: % 3 months & less than 12 months P34TH D99	of which: % under 6 months P34TH E99	of which: % 6 months & less than 12 months P34TH F99	of which: % 6 months & less than 18 months P34TH G99	of which: % under 12 months P34TH H99	of which: % 12 months & less than 24 months P34TH I99	of which: % 12 months & less than 36 months P34TH J99	of which: % 12 months & less than 60 months P34TH K99	of which: % 18 months & less than 36 months P34TH L99	of which: % 24 months & less than 48 months P34TH M99	of which: % 24 months & less than 60 months P34TH N99	of which: % 36 months & less than 60 months P34TH O99	of which: % 48 months & over P34TH P99	of which: % 60 months & less than 120 months P34TH Q99	of which: % 60 months & less than 144 months P34TH R99	of which: % 60 months & less than 180 months P34TH S99	of which: % 60 months & over P34TH T99	of which: % 120 months & over P34TH U99	of which: % 120 months & less than 240 months P34TH V99	of which: % 144 months & over P34TH W99	of which: % 180 months & over P34TH X99	Average length of custodial sanction/measure (in months) T34TH Y99	of which: % Life P34TH Z99	of which: % Indeterminate sanctions/measures P34TH 99
Malta	:	:	:	:	:	:	:	:	:	:	:	:	:	:	:	:	:	:	:	:	:	:	:	:	:	:	:
Moldova	21.6	:	:	:	:	4.8	:	6.8	7.8	:	:	:	:	42.5	:	:	40.6	:	:	:	2.3	:	:	:	:	:	:
Netherlands	78.2	:	:	:	93.0	26.8	:	:	1.6	:	:	:	0.5	1.3	:	0.0	0.0	:	:	:	0.0	:	:	:	2.0	0.0	0.0
Norway	49.5	:	:	:	63.0	12.0	:	:	8.8	:	:	:	:	21.9	:	:	0.2	:	:	:	0.0	:	:	:	5.3	:	0.5
Poland	25.7	:	:	:	2.9	18.9	:	:	63.0	:	:	:	:	42.1	:	:	9.5	:	:	:	2.4	:	:	:	:	:	:
Portugal	15.9	:	:	:	6.8	:	:	26.5	20.4	:	:	:	:	:	:	:	3.2	:	:	:	0.1	:	:	:	34.0	:	0.1
Romania	121.6	:	:	:	:	:	:	:	:	:	57.5	:	:	:	:	:	:	:	:	:	:	:	:	:	:	0.0	:
Russia	:	:	:	:	:	:	:	:	:	:	:	:	:	:	:	:	:	:	:	:	:	:	:	:	:	:	:
Slovakia	:	:	:	:	:	:	:	:	:	:	:	:	:	:	:	:	:	:	:	:	:	:	:	:	:	:	:
Slovenia	16.2	:	:	:	51.8	23.3	:	:	15.3	:	:	:	:	8.3	:	:	1.3	:	:	:	0.0	:	:	:	:	:	:
Spain	:	:	:	:	:	:	:	:	:	:	:	:	:	:	:	:	:	:	:	:	:	:	:	:	:	:	1.6
Sweden	30.4	:	:	:	64.3	26.4	:	:	8.6	:	:	:	0.6	:	:	0.1	:	:	:	:	:	:	:	:	5.2	0.0	7.3
Switzerland	31.3	:	:	:	67.5	10.5	:	:	7.9	:	:	:	:	6.3	:	:	0.4	:	:	:	0.1	:	:	:	6.0	0.0	:
Turkey	:	:	:	:	:	:	:	:	:	:	:	:	:	:	:	:	:	:	:	:	:	:	:	:	:	:	:
Ukraine	:	:	:	:	:	:	:	:	:	:	:	:	:	:	:	:	:	:	:	:	:	:	:	:	:	:	:
UK: E & W	70.7	:	:	:	61.3	11.9	:	:	15.8	:	:	7	1	10.3	:	0	0.7	:	:	:	0.0	:	:	:	8.5	0.0	:
UK: N._Ireland	42.9	:	:	:	53.2	36.7	:	:	4.7	:	44	7	1	3.9	:	0	0.6	:	:	:	0.1	:	:	:	7.0	0.0	0.7
UK: Scotland	115.7	:	:	:	76.3	17.9	:	:	3.8	:	:	7	0	2.0	:	0	0.0	:	:	:	0.0	:	:	:	5.0	0.0	0.0
Mean	50	23	34	47	53	19	33	29	15	32	47	7	1	13	5	0	5	0	1	3	0	0	0	0	9	0	4
Median	44	23	34	47	58	19	33	18	9	16	44	7	1	6	3	0	1	1	1	1	0	0	0	0	7	0	2
Minimum	12	23	34	47	3	0	33	7	2	10	26	7	0	0	0	0	0	0	0	0	0	0	0	0	2	0	0
Maximum	122	23	34	47	93	37	33	72	63	70	74	7	1	55	15	0	41	0	1	7	2	0	0	0	34	0	18

Table 3.2.4.9: Number of convictions by length of unsuspended custodial sanctions and measures imposed in 1999 – Theft: Theft of a motor vehicle

Theft: Theft of a motor vehicle	Total unsuspended custodial sanctions per 100 000 pop	of which: % under 1 month	of which: % 1 month & less than 12 months	of which: % 3 months & less than 12 months	of which: % under 6 months	of which: % 6 months & less than 12 months	of which: % 6 months & less than 18 months	of which: % under 12 months	of which: % 12 months & less than 24 months	of which: % 12 months & less than 36 months	of which: % 12 months & less than 60 months	of which: % 18 months & less than 36 months	of which: % 24 months & less than 48 months	of which: % 24 months & less than 60 months	of which: % 36 months & less than 60 months	of which: % 48 months & over	of which: % 60 months & less than 120 months	of which: % 60 months & less than 144 months	of which: % 60 months & less than 180 months	of which: % 60 months & over	of which: % 120 months & over	of which: % 120 months & less than 240 months	of which: % 144 months & over	of which: % 180 months & over	Average length of custodial sanction/measure (in months)	of which: % Life	of which: % Indeterminate sanctions/measures
	R34TV A99	P34TV B99	P34TV C99	P34TV D99	P34TV E99	P34TV F99	P34TV G99	P34TV H99	P34TV I99	P34TV J99	P34TV K99	P34TV L99	P34TV M99	P34TV N99	P34TV O99	P34TV P99	P34TV Q99	P34TV R99	P34TV S99	P34TV T99	P34TV U99	P34TV V99	P34TV W99	P34TV X99	T34TV Y99	P34TV Z99	P34TV _99
Albania	:	:	:	:	:	:	:	:	:	:	:	:	:	:	:	:	:	:	:	:	:	:	:	:	:	:	:
Armenia	:	:	:	:	:	:	:	:	:	:	:	:	:	:	:	:	:	:	:	:	:	:	:	:	:	:	:
Austria	:	:	:	:	:	:	:	:	:	:	:	:	:	:	:	:	:	:	:	:	:	:	:	:	:	:	:
Belgium	:	:	:	:	:	:	:	:	:	:	:	:	:	:	:	:	:	:	:	:	:	:	:	:	:	:	:
Bulgaria	:	:	:	:	:	:	:	:	:	:	:	:	:	:	:	:	:	:	:	:	:	:	:	:	:	:	:
Croatia	:	:	:	:	:	:	:	:	:	:	:	:	:	:	:	:	:	:	:	:	:	:	:	:	:	:	:
Cyprus	:	:	:	:	:	:	:	:	:	:	:	:	:	:	:	:	:	:	:	:	:	:	:	:	:	:	:
Czech Republic	9.3	:	:	:	90.9	7.6	:	:	1.4	:	:	:	:	0.0	:	:	:	0.0	:	:	:	:	0.0	:	:	0.0	:
Denmark	:	:	:	:	:	:	:	:	:	:	:	:	:	:	:	:	:	:	:	:	:	:	:	:	:	:	:
Estonia	:	:	:	:	:	:	:	:	:	:	:	:	:	:	:	:	:	:	:	:	:	:	:	:	:	:	:
Finland	:	:	:	:	:	:	:	:	:	:	:	:	:	:	:	:	:	:	:	:	:	:	:	:	:	:	:
France	10.0	:	:	:	0.2	:	:	13.8	:	:	:	:	73.8	:	:	12.4	:	:	:	:	:	:	:	:	:	:	:
Georgia	:	:	:	:	:	:	:	:	:	:	:	:	:	:	:	:	:	:	:	:	:	:	:	:	:	:	:
Germany	0.0	:	:	:	:	:	:	:	:	100.0	:	:	:	:	:	:	:	:	0.0	:	:	:	:	:	0.0	0.0	:
Greece	:	:	:	:	:	:	:	:	:	:	:	:	:	:	:	:	:	:	:	:	:	:	:	:	:	:	:
Hungary	:	:	:	:	:	:	:	:	:	:	:	:	:	:	:	:	:	:	:	:	:	:	:	:	:	:	:
Ireland	:	:	:	:	:	:	:	:	:	:	:	:	:	:	:	:	:	:	:	:	:	:	:	:	:	:	:
Italy	:	:	:	:	:	:	:	:	:	:	:	:	:	:	:	:	:	:	:	:	:	:	:	:	:	:	:
Latvia	:	:	:	:	:	:	:	:	:	:	:	:	:	:	:	:	:	:	:	:	:	:	:	:	:	:	:
Lithuania	:	:	:	:	:	:	:	:	:	:	:	:	:	:	:	:	:	:	:	:	:	:	:	:	:	:	:
Luxembourg	:	:	:	:	:	:	:	:	:	:	:	:	:	:	:	:	:	:	:	:	:	:	:	:	:	:	:

Conviction statistics

Theft: Theft of a motor vehicle

	Total unsuspended custodial sanctions per 100 000 pop	% under 1 month	% 1 month & less than 12 months	% 3 months & less than 12 months	% under 6 months	% 6 months & less than 12 months	% 6 months & less than 18 months	% under 12 months	% 12 months & less than 24 months	% 12 months & less than 36 months	% 12 months & less than 60 months	% 18 months & less than 36 months	% 24 months & less than 36 months	% 24 months & less than 48 months	% 36 months & less than 60 months	% 48 months & over	% 60 months & less than 120 months	% 60 months & less than 144 months	% 60 months & less than 180 months	% 60 months & over	% 120 months & over	% 120 months & less than 240 months	% 144 months & over	% 180 months & over	Average length of custodial sanction/measure (in months)	% Life	% Indeterminate sanctions/measures
	R34TV A99	P34TV B99	P34TV C99	P34TV D99	P34TV E99	P34TV F99	P34TV G99	P34TV H99	P34TV I99	P34TV J99	P34TV K99	P34TV L99	P34TV M99	P34TV N99	P34TV O99	P34TV P99	P34TV Q99	P34TV R99	P34TV S99	P34TV T99	P34TV U99	P34TV V99	P34TV W99	P34TV X99	T34TV Y99	P34TV Z99	P34TV _99
Malta	...	...	...	...	...	...	...	...	...	...	...	...	...	...	...	...	...	...	...	...	...	...	...	...	...	...	...
Moldova	...	...	...	...	...	...	...	...	...	...	...	...	...	...	...	...	...	...	...	...	...	...	...	...	...	...	...
Netherlands	...	...	...	...	...	...	...	...	...	...	...	...	...	...	...	...	...	...	...	...	...	...	...	...	...	...	...
Norway	3.3	...	...	...	80.8	15.1	...	...	3.4	...	...	...	...	0.7	...	...	0.0	...	...	...	0.0	...	...	...	3.3	...	1.4
Poland	...	...	...	...	...	...	...	...	...	...	...	...	...	...	...	...	...	...	...	...	...	...	...	...	...	...	...
Portugal	...	...	...	...	...	...	...	...	...	...	...	...	...	...	...	...	...	...	...	...	...	...	...	...	...	...	...
Romania	...	...	...	...	...	...	...	...	...	...	...	...	...	...	...	...	...	...	...	...	...	...	...	...	...	...	...
Russia	...	...	...	...	...	...	...	...	...	...	...	...	...	...	...	...	...	...	...	...	...	...	...	...	...	...	...
Slovakia	0.7	...	...	...	85.7	0.0	...	...	0.0	...	...	...	...	0.0	...	...	...	...	...	...	...	...	...	...	...	...	...
Slovenia	...	...	...	...	...	...	...	...	...	...	...	...	...	...	...	...	14.3	...	...	...	0.0	...	...	...	...	...	...
Spain	...	...	...	...	...	...	...	...	...	...	...	...	...	...	...	...	...	...	...	...	...	...	...	...	...	...	...
Sweden	4.8	...	...	...	77.3	18.9	...	...	3.7	...	...	...	...	...	...	...	...	...	...	...	...	...	...	...	3.9	...	2.1
Switzerland	...	...	...	...	...	...	...	...	...	...	...	...	...	...	...	...	...	...	...	...	...	...	...	...	...	...	...
Turkey	...	...	...	...	...	...	...	...	...	...	...	...	...	...	...	...	...	...	...	...	...	...	...	...	...	...	...
Ukraine	...	...	...	...	...	...	...	...	...	...	...	...	...	...	...	...	...	...	...	...	...	...	...	...	...	...	...
UK: E & W	4.6	...	...	...	86.1	10.6	...	...	2.7	...	...	...	...	0.6	...	...	0.0	...	...	...	0.0	...	...	...	3.8	0.0	...
UK: N-Ireland	5.8	...	...	...	63.2	34.7	...	...	1.1	...	...	...	...	0.0	...	...	0.0	...	...	...	0.0	...	...	...	4.0	0.0	1.1
UK: Scotland	9.8	...	...	...	75.2	18.9	...	...	3.9	...	...	...	...	2.0	...	...	0.0	...	...	...	0.0	...	...	...	5.0	0.0	0.0
Mean	5				80	13			4		100			11			4			0	0		0		4	0	1
Median	5				81	13			3		100			1			0			0	0		0		4	0	1
Minimum	0				63	0			0		100			0			0			0	0		0		3	0	0
Maximum	10				91	35			14		100			74			14			0	0		0		5	0	2

176 European Sourcebook of Crime and Criminal Justice Statistics - 2003

Table 3.2.4.10: Number of convictions by length of unsuspended custodial sanctions and measures imposed in 1999 – (Theft) Burglary: Total

(Theft) Burglary: Total	Total unsuspended custodial sanctions per 100 000 pop R34BU A99	of which: % under 1 month P34BU B99	of which: % 1 month & less than 12 months P34BU C99	of which: % 3 months & less than 12 months P34BU D99	of which: % under 6 months P34BU E99	of which: % 6 months & less than 12 months P34BU F99	of which: % 6 months & less than 18 months P34BU G99	of which: % under 12 months P34BU H99	of which: % 12 months & less than 24 months P34BU I99	of which: % 12 months & less than 36 months P34BU J99	of which: % 12 months & less than 60 months P34BU K99	of which: % 18 months & less than 36 months P34BU L99	of which: % 24 months & less than 48 months P34BU M99	of which: % 24 months & less than 60 months P34BU N99	of which: % 36 months & less than 60 months P34BU O99	of which: % 48 months & over P34BU P99	of which: % 60 months & less than 120 months P34BU Q99	of which: % 60 months & less than 144 months P34BU R99	of which: % 60 months & less than 180 months P34BU S99	of which: % 60 months & over P34BU T99	of which: % 120 months & over P34BU U99	of which: % 120 months & less than 240 months P34BU V99	of which: % 144 months & over P34BU W99	of which: % 180 months & over P34BU X99	Average length of custodial sanction/measure (in months) T34BU Y99	of which: % Life P34BU Z99	of which: % Indeterminate sanctions/measures P34BU _99
Albania	:	:	:	:	:	:	:	:	:	:	:	:	:	:	:	:	:	:	:	:	:	:	:	:	:	:	:
Armenia	:	:	:	:	:	:	:	:	:	:	:	:	:	:	:	:	:	:	:	:	:	:	:	:	:	:	:
Austria	9.3	:	:	:	15.3	35.8	:	:	16.6	:	:	:	:	:	0.3	:	:	:	0.0	:	:	:	:	:	:	0.0	0.9
Belgium	:	:	:	:	:	:	:	:	:	:	:	:	:	:	:	:	:	:	:	:	:	:	:	:	:	:	:
Bulgaria	:	:	:	:	:	:	:	:	:	:	:	:	:	:	:	:	:	:	:	:	:	:	:	:	:	:	:
Croatia	8.3	:	:	:	30.5	34.5	:	:	17.1	:	:	:	:	4.5	:	:	0.0	:	:	:	:	:	:	:	10.0	:	13.4
Cyprus	10.1	:	:	:	44.7	:	38.2	:	:	9.2	:	:	:	:	6.6	:	:	:	1.3	:	:	:	:	:	11.0	0.0	:
Czech Republic	:	:	:	:	:	:	:	:	:	:	:	:	:	:	:	:	:	:	:	:	:	:	:	:	:	:	:
Denmark	20.3	:	:	:	79.5	15.2	:	:	4.9	:	:	:	:	0.4	:	:	0.0	:	:	:	0.0	:	0.0	:	:	0.0	:
Estonia	67.2	:	:	:	:	:	:	:	:	:	:	:	:	:	:	:	0.0	:	:	:	:	:	:	:	:	:	:
Finland	:	:	:	:	:	:	:	:	:	:	:	:	:	:	:	:	:	:	:	:	:	:	:	:	:	:	:
France	:	:	:	:	:	:	:	:	:	:	:	:	:	:	:	:	:	:	:	:	:	:	:	:	:	:	:
Georgia	6.1	:	:	:	12.2	33.5	:	:	35.6	:	:	:	:	18.0	:	:	0.6	:	:	:	0.0	:	:	:	:	0.0	2.8
Germany	:	:	:	:	:	:	:	:	:	:	:	:	:	:	:	:	:	:	:	:	:	:	:	:	:	:	:
Greece	:	:	:	:	:	:	:	:	:	:	:	:	:	:	:	:	:	:	:	:	:	:	:	:	:	:	:
Hungary	:	:	:	:	:	:	:	:	:	:	:	:	:	:	:	:	:	:	:	:	:	:	:	:	:	:	:
Ireland	:	:	:	:	:	:	:	:	:	:	:	:	:	:	:	:	:	:	:	:	:	:	:	:	:	:	:
Italy	34.6	:	:	:	:	:	:	6.0	:	72.7	:	:	:	:	16.3	:	5.0	:	:	:	:	:	:	:	:	:	:
Latvia	:	:	:	:	:	:	:	:	:	:	:	:	:	:	:	:	:	:	:	:	0.0	:	:	:	:	:	:
Lithuania	:	:	:	:	:	:	:	:	:	:	:	:	:	:	:	:	:	:	:	:	:	:	:	:	:	:	:
Luxembourg	:	:	:	:	:	:	:	:	:	:	:	:	:	:	:	:	:	:	:	:	:	:	:	:	:	:	:

Conviction statistics

(Theft) Burglary: Total

	Total unsuspended custodial sanctions per 100 000 pop R34BU A99	of which: % under 1 month P34BU B99	of which: % 1 month & less than 12 months P34BU C99	of which: % 3 months & less than 12 months P34BU D99	of which: % under 6 months P34BU E99	of which: % 6 months & less than 12 months P34BU F99	of which: % 6 months & less than 18 months P34BU G99	of which: % under 12 months P34BU H99	of which: % 12 months & less than 24 months P34BU I99	of which: % 12 months & less than 36 months P34BU J99	of which: % 12 months & less than 60 months P34BU K99	of which: % 18 months & less than 36 months P34BU L99	of which: % 24 months & less than 48 months P34BU M99	of which: % 24 months & less than 60 months P34BU N99	of which: % 36 months & less than 60 months P34BU O99	of which: % 48 months & over P34BU P99	of which: % 60 months & less than 120 months P34BU Q99	of which: % 60 months & less than 144 months P34BU R99	of which: % 60 months & less than 180 months P34BU S99	of which: % 60 months & over P34BU T99	of which: % 120 months & over P34BU U99	of which: % 120 months & less than 240 months P34BU V99	of which: % 144 months & over P34BU W99	of which: % 180 months & over P34BU X99	Average length of custodial sanction/measure (in months) T34BU Y99	of which: % Life P34BU Z99	of which: % Indeterminate sanctions/measures P34BU_99
Malta	...	...	...	...	...	...	...	...	...	...	...	...	...	...	...	...	...	...	...	...	...	...	...	...	...	...	...
Moldova	...	...	...	...	...	...	...	...	...	...	...	...	...	...	...	...	...	...	...	...	...	...	...	...	...	...	...
Netherlands	40.2	...	...	...	87.1	8.7	...	...	3.1	...	...	...	0.9	...	...	0.1	0.0	...	...	...	0.0	...	...	...	3.2	0.0	0.0
Norway	34.2	...	...	...	57.6	29.4	...	...	11.2	...	...	...	...	1.8	...	...	0.3	...	...	...	0.0	...	...	...	5.9	0.0	0.5
Poland	21.3	...	...	...	1.3	5.7	...	...	67.4	...	...	...	...	25.3	...	...	...	...	...	...	...	...	...	...	...	...	...
Portugal	...	...	...	...	...	...	...	...	...	...	...	...	...	...	...	...	...	...	...	...	...	...	...	...	...	...	...
Romania	...	...	...	...	...	...	...	...	...	...	...	...	...	...	...	...	...	...	...	...	...	...	...	...	...	...	...
Russia	...	...	...	...	...	...	...	...	...	...	...	...	...	...	...	...	...	...	...	...	...	...	...	...	...	...	...
Slovakia	8.2	...	...	...	42.4	29.1	...	...	20.9	...	...	...	...	7.0	...	...	0.6	...	...	...	0.0	...	...	...	...	...	...
Slovenia	...	...	...	...	...	...	...	...	...	...	...	...	...	...	...	...	...	...	...	...	...	...	...	...	...	...	...
Spain	6.6	...	...	...	13.1	54.2	...	...	29.8	...	...	...	2.6	...	...	0.3	...	...	...	...	...	...	...	...	10.1	...	1.5
Sweden	...	...	...	...	...	...	...	...	...	...	...	...	...	...	...	...	...	...	...	...	...	...	...	...	...	...	...
Switzerland	...	...	...	...	...	...	...	...	...	...	...	...	...	...	...	...	...	...	...	...	...	...	...	...	...	...	...
Turkey	...	...	...	...	...	...	...	...	...	...	...	...	...	...	...	...	...	...	...	...	...	...	...	...	...	...	...
Ukraine	...	...	...	...	...	...	...	...	...	...	...	...	...	...	...	...	...	...	...	...	...	...	...	...	...	...	...
UK: E & W	27.3	...	...	...	27.3	15.6	...	...	31.1	...	...	...	...	24.2	...	...	1.7	...	...	...	0.1	...	...	...	15.7	0.0	0.4
UK: N.-Ireland	17.3	...	...	...	40.8	45.4	...	...	7.4	...	...	...	...	5.0	...	...	0.7	...	...	...	0.4	...	...	...	8.0	0.0	0.0
UK: Scotland	29.4	...	...	...	63.8	19.9	...	...	9.8	...	...	...	...	6.4	...	...	0.1	...	...	...	0.0	...	...	...	7.0	0.0	0.0
Mean	23	...	...	...	40	27	38	6	22	45	...	9	2	10	8	0	1	1	...	1	0	0	0	...	9	0	2
Median	20	...	...	...	41	29	38	6	17	45	...	9	2	6	7	0	1	0	...	1	0	0	0	...	9	0	1
Minimum	6	...	...	...	1	6	38	6	3	17	...	9	1	0	0	0	0	0	...	0	0	0	0	...	3	0	0
Maximum	67	...	...	...	87	54	38	6	67	73	...	9	3	25	16	0	5	0	...	1	0	0	0	...	16	0	13

Table 3.2.4.11: Number of convictions by length of unsuspended custodial sanctions and measures imposed in 1999 – (Theft) Burglary: Domestic Burglary

(Theft) Burglary: Domestic Burglary	Total unsuspended custodial sanctions per 100 000 pop	of which: % under 1 month	of which: % 1 month & less than 12 months	of which: % 3 months & less than 12 months	of which: % under 6 months	of which: % 6 months & less than 12 months	of which: % 6 months & less than 18 months	of which: % under 12 months	of which: % 12 months & less than 24 months	of which: % 12 months & less than 36 months	of which: % 12 months & less than 60 months	of which: % 18 months & less than 36 months	of which: % 24 months & less than 48 months	of which: % 24 months & less than 60 months	of which: % 36 months & less than 60 months	of which: % 48 months & over	of which: % 60 months & less than 120 months	of which: % 60 months & less than 144 months	of which: % 60 months & less than 180 months	of which: % 60 months & over	of which: % 120 months & over	of which: % 120 months & less than 240 months	of which: % 144 months & over	of which: % 180 months & over	Average length of custodial sanction/measure (in months)	of which: % Life	of which: % Indeterminate sanctions/measures
	R34BD A99	P34BD B99	P34BD C99	P34BD D99	P34BD E99	P34BD F99	P34BD G99	P34BD H99	P34BD I99	P34BD J99	P34BD K99	P34BD L99	P34BD M99	P34BD N99	P34BD O99	P34BD P99	P34BD Q99	P34BD R99	P34BD S99	P34BD T99	P34BD U99	P34BD V99	P34BD W99	P34BD X99	T34BD Y99	P34BD Z99	P34BD 99_99
Albania	...	...	...	...	...	...	...	...	...	...	...	...	...	...	...	...	...	...	...	...	...	...	...	...	...	...	...
Armenia	...	...	...	...	...	...	...	...	...	...	...	...	...	...	...	...	...	...	...	...	...	...	...	...	...	...	...
Austria	...	...	...	...	...	...	...	...	...	...	...	...	...	...	...	...	...	...	...	...	...	...	...	...	...	...	...
Belgium	...	...	...	...	...	...	...	...	...	...	...	...	...	...	...	...	...	...	...	...	...	...	...	...	...	...	...
Bulgaria	...	...	...	...	...	...	...	...	...	...	...	...	...	...	...	...	...	...	...	...	...	...	...	...	...	...	...
Croatia	...	...	...	...	...	...	...	...	...	...	...	...	...	...	...	...	...	...	...	...	...	...	...	...	...	...	...
Cyprus	...	...	...	...	...	...	...	...	...	...	...	...	...	...	...	...	...	...	...	...	...	...	...	...	...	...	...
Czech Republic	...	...	...	...	...	...	...	...	...	...	...	...	...	...	...	...	...	...	...	...	...	...	...	...	...	...	...
Denmark	8.1	...	...	...	75.9	18.1	...	...	5.6	...	...	...	...	0.5	...	...	...	0.0	...	...	...	...	0.0	...	...	0.0	...
Estonia	...	...	...	...	...	...	...	...	...	...	...	...	...	...	...	...	...	...	...	...	...	...	...	...	...	...	...
Finland	...	...	...	...	...	...	...	...	...	...	...	...	...	...	...	...	...	...	...	...	...	...	...	...	...	...	...
France	...	...	...	...	...	...	...	...	...	...	...	...	...	...	...	...	...	...	...	...	...	...	...	...	...	...	...
Georgia	...	...	...	...	...	...	...	...	...	...	...	...	...	...	...	...	...	...	...	...	...	...	...	...	...	...	...
Germany	...	...	...	...	...	...	...	...	...	...	...	...	...	...	...	...	...	...	...	...	...	...	...	...	...	...	...
Greece	...	...	...	...	...	...	...	...	...	...	...	...	...	...	...	...	...	...	...	...	...	...	...	...	...	...	...
Hungary	...	...	...	...	...	...	...	...	...	...	...	...	...	...	...	...	...	...	...	...	...	...	...	...	...	...	...
Ireland	...	...	...	...	...	...	...	...	...	...	...	...	...	...	...	...	...	...	...	...	...	...	...	...	...	...	...
Italy	...	...	...	...	...	...	...	...	...	...	...	...	...	...	...	...	...	...	...	...	...	...	...	...	...	...	...
Latvia	...	...	...	...	...	...	...	...	...	...	...	...	...	...	...	...	...	...	...	...	...	...	...	...	...	...	...
Lithuania	...	...	...	...	...	...	...	...	...	...	...	...	...	...	...	...	...	...	...	...	...	...	...	...	...	...	...
Luxembourg	...	...	...	...	...	...	...	...	...	...	...	...	...	...	...	...	...	...	...	...	...	...	...	...	...	...	...

Conviction statistics

(Theft) Burglary: Domestic Burglary

	Total unsuspended custodial sanctions per 100 000 pop R34BD A99	of which: % under 1 month P34BD B99	of which: % 1 month & less than 12 months P34BD C99	of which: % 3 months & less than 12 months P34BD D99	of which: % under 6 months P34BD E99	of which: % 6 months & less than 12 months P34BD F99	of which: % 6 months & less than 18 months P34BD G99	of which: % under 12 months P34BD H99	of which: % 12 months & less than 24 months P34BD I99	of which: % 12 months & less than 36 months P34BD J99	of which: % 12 months & less than 60 months P34BD K99	of which: % 18 months & less than 36 months P34BD L99	of which: % 24 months & less than 48 months P34BD M99	of which: % 24 months & less than 60 months P34BD N99	of which: % 36 months & less than 60 months P34BD O99	of which: % 48 months & over P34BD P99	of which: % 60 months & less than 120 months P34BD Q99	of which: % 60 months & less than 144 months P34BD R99	of which: % 60 months & less than 180 months P34BD S99	of which: % 60 months & over P34BD T99	of which: % 120 months & over P34BD U99	of which: % 120 months & less than 240 months P34BD V99	of which: % 144 months & over P34BD W99	of which: % 180 months & over P34BD X99	Average length of custodial sanction/measure (in months) P34BD Y99	of which: % Life P34BD Z99	of which: % Indeterminate sanctions/measures P34BD _99
Malta	:	:	:	:	:	:	:	:	:	:	:	:	:	:	:	:	:	:	:	:	:	:	:	:	:	:	:
Moldova	:	:	:	:	:	:	:	:	:	:	:	:	:	:	:	:	:	:	:	:	:	:	:	:	:	:	:
Netherlands	3.1	:	:	:	55.4	28.1	:	:	15.1	:	:	:	:	1.4	:	:	0.0	:	:	:	0.0	:	:	:	7.5	:	0.0
Norway																											
Poland	:	:	:	:	:	:	:	:	:	:	:	:	:	:	:	:	:	:	:	:	:	:	:	:	:	:	:
Portugal	:	:	:	:	:	:	:	:	:	:	:	:	:	:	:	:	:	:	:	:	:	:	:	:	:	:	:
Romania	:	:	:	:	:	:	:	:	:	:	:	:	:	:	:	:	:	:	:	:	:	:	:	:	:	:	:
Russia	:	:	:	:	:	:	:	:	:	:	:	:	:	:	:	:	:	:	:	:	:	:	:	:	:	:	:
Slovakia	:	:	:	:	:	:	:	:	:	:	:	:	:	:	:	:	:	:	:	:	:	:	:	:	:	:	:
Slovenia	:	:	:	:	:	:	:	:	:	:	:	:	:	:	:	:	:	:	:	:	:	:	:	:	:	:	:
Spain	:	:	:	:	:	:	:	:	:	:	:	:	:	:	:	:	:	:	:	:	:	:	:	:	:	:	:
Sweden	:	:	:	:	:	:	:	:	:	:	:	:	:	:	:	:	:	:	:	:	:	:	:	:	:	:	:
Switzerland	:	:	:	:	:	:	:	:	:	:	:	:	:	:	:	:	:	:	:	:	:	:	:	:	:	:	:
Turkey	:	:	:	:	:	:	:	:	:	:	:	:	:	:	:	:	:	:	:	:	:	:	:	:	:	:	:
UK: E & W	19.2	:	:	:	13.9	15.4	:	:	37.1	:	:	:	:	31.3	:	:	2.2	:	:	:	0.1	:	:	:	18.9	0.0	0.6
UK: N.-Ireland	10.8	:	:	:	40.6	43.4	:	:	9.7	:	:	:	:	4.0	:	:	1.1	:	:	:	0.6	:	:	:	6	0.0	0.6
UK: Scotland	:	:	:	:	:	:	:	:	:	:	:	:	:	:	:	:	:	:	:	:	:	:	:	:	:	:	:
Mean	10				46	26			17					9			1				0		0		11	0	0
Median	9				48	23			12					3			1				0		0		8	0	0
Minimum	3				14	15			6					0			0				0		0		6	0	0
Maximum	19				76	43			37					31			2				1		0		19	0	1

Table 3.2.4.12: Number of convictions by length of unsuspended custodial sanctions and measures imposed in 1999 – Drug offences: Total

Drug offences: Total	Total unsuspended custodial sanctions per 100 000 pop R34DR A99	of which: % under 1 month P34DR B99	of which: % 1 month & less than 12 months P34DR C99	of which: % 3 months & less than 12 months P34DR D99	of which: % under 6 months P34DR E99	of which: % 6 months & less than 12 months P34DR F99	of which: % 6 months & less than 18 months P34DR G99	of which: % under 12 months P34DR H99	of which: % 12 months & less than 24 months P34DR I99	of which: % 12 months & less than 36 months P34DR J99	of which: % 12 months & less than 60 months P34DR K99	of which: % 18 months & less than 36 months P34DR L99	of which: % 24 months & less than 48 months P34DR M99	of which: % 24 months & less than 60 months P34DR N99	of which: % 36 months & less than 60 months P34DR O99	of which: % 48 months & over P34DR P99	of which: % 60 months & less than 120 months P34DR Q99	of which: % 60 months & less than 144 months P34DR R99	of which: % 60 months & less than 180 months P34DR S99	of which: % 60 months & over P34DR T99	of which: % 120 months & over P34DR U99	of which: % 120 months & less than 240 months P34DR V99	of which: % 144 months & over P34DR W99	of which: % 180 months & over P34DR X99	Average length of custodial sanction/measure (in months) T34DR Y99	of which: % Life P34DR Z99	of which: % Indeterminate sanctions/measures P34DR _99
Albania	8.9	13.6	63.3	:	:	:	:	:	4.2	:	:	:	:	:	:	:	5.2	:	:	:	0.6	:	:	:	:	:	13.0
Armenia	:	:	:	:	:	:	:	:	:	:	:	:	:	:	:	:	:	:	:	:	:	:	:	:	:	:	:
Austria	13.0	:	:	20.1	18.7	:	:	:	31.4	:	:	4.3	:	:	:	1.9	:	:	:	:	:	:	:	:	:	0.0
Belgium	:	:	:	:	:	:	:	:	:	:	:	:	:	:	:	:	:	:	:	:	:	:	:	:	:	:	:
Bulgaria	0.6	:	:	0.0	4.2	:	29.2	:	:	:	:	:	:	:	:	:	:	:	:	:	:	:	:	:	:	:	:
Croatia	10.6	:	:	24.5	18.3	:	18.5	:	:	:	:	:	11.9	:	:	:	0.4	:	:	:	0.2	:	:	15.0	0.0	26.0
Cyprus	9.7	:	:	67.1	:	13.7	:	:	:	8.2	:	6.8	:	:	:	4.1	:	:	:	:	:	:	:	10.8	0.0	:
Czech Republic	2.9	:	:	:	:	:	26.4	:	65.7	:	:	:	:	:	:	:	:	:	:	:	:	:	:	:	0.0	:
Denmark	7.2	:	:	19.6	26.1	:	23.2	:	:	:	:	:	21.1	:	:	:	:	9.1	7.9	:	:	0.8	:	:	0.0	:
Estonia	3.3	:	:	:	:	:	:	:	:	:	:	:	:	:	:	:	:	:	:	:	:	:	:	:	:	:
Finland	17.2	:	:	51.2	12.9	:	10.4	:	24.0	:	:	:	13.6	:	:	:	5.8	:	:	:	0.2	:	:	14.5	:	6.0
France	13.8	:	:	40.7	19.5	:	:	:	:	:	:	9.6	:	:	:	:	5.7	:	:	:	0.6	:	:	15.4	0.0	:
Georgia	21.8	:	:	:	10.2	:	29.1	:	:	:	:	:	49.2	:	:	:	14.2	:	:	:	4.0	:	:	:	:	:
Germany	11.0	:	:	19.1	14.9	:	21.7	:	:	:	:	:	39.2	:	:	:	4.8	:	:	:	0.4	:	:	:	0.0	3.5
Greece	4.2	:	:	:	:	:	:	:	57.8	:	:	:	:	:	:	10.8	:	:	:	:	:	:	:	:	0.2	31.2
Hungary	0.9	:	:	10.0	7.8	:	25.6	:	:	:	:	:	42.2	:	:	:	14.4	:	:	:	14.4	:	:	0.0	41.1	:
Ireland	:	:	:	:	:	:	:	:	:	:	:	:	:	:	:	:	:	:	:	:	:	:	:	:	:	:
Italy	31.0	:	:	22.1	33.0	:	:	:	24.0	:	:	:	13.0	:	:	:	6.6	:	:	:	1.1	:	:	:	:	:
Latvia	2.1	:	:	:	:	:	22.0	:	72.0	:	:	6.0	:	:	:	0.0	:	:	:	0.0	:	:	:	:	:	:
Lithuania	:	:	:	:	:	:	:	:	:	:	:	:	:	:	:	:	:	:	:	:	:	:	:	:	:	:
Luxembourg	:	:	:	:	:	:	:	:	:	:	:	:	:	:	:	:	:	:	:	:	:	:	:	:	:	:

Conviction statistics

Drug offences: Total

	Total unsuspended custodial sanctions per 100 000 pop R34DR A99	of which: % under 1 month P34DR B99	of which: % 1 month & less than 12 months P34DR C99	of which: % 3 months & less than 12 months P34DR D99	of which: % under 6 months P34DR E99	of which: % 6 months & less than 12 months P34DR F99	of which: % 6 months & less than 18 months P34DR G99	of which: % under 12 months P34DR H99	of which: % 12 months & less than 24 months P34DR I99	of which: % 12 months & less than 36 months P34DR J99	of which: % 12 months & less than 60 months P34DR K99	of which: % 18 months & less than 36 months P34DR L99	of which: % 24 months & less than 48 months P34DR M99	of which: % 24 months & less than 60 months P34DR N99	of which: % 36 months & less than 60 months P34DR O99	of which: % 48 months & over P34DR P99	of which: % 60 months & less than 120 months P34DR Q99	of which: % 60 months & less than 144 months P34DR R99	of which: % 60 months & less than 180 months P34DR S99	of which: % 60 months & over P34DR T99	of which: % 120 months & over P34DR U99	of which: % 120 months & less than 240 months P34DR V99	of which: % 144 months & over P34DR W99	of which: % 180 months & over P34DR X99	Average length of custodial sanction/measure (in months) T34DR Y99	of which: % Life P34DR Z99	of which: % Indeterminate sanctions/measures P34DR _99
Malta	...																										
Moldova	2.7							47.5	19.2					26.7			6.7				0.0						
Netherlands	20.1				47.1	20.3			15.0				14.5			3.1									13.0	0.0	0.0
Norway	25.7				66.0	9.5			10.8					10.1			2.4				1.1				10.7		0.4
Poland	1.1				2.4	10.5			35.3					45.1			6.0				0.7						
Portugal	12.3				3.2	3.7		38.7	18.4					40.4			33.3				1.1				52.0		0.0
Romania	1.0										46.8						4.1				5.0					0.0	
Russia																											
Slovakia																											
Slovenia	4.1				13.9	24.1			41.8					19.0			1.3				0.0				15.3		0.7
Spain																7.5											
Sweden	15.7				41.7	23.7			18.9				8.2				2.2				0.2				10.9	0.0	9.0
Switzerland	41.9				60.2	6.6			7.9					15.3													
Turkey																											
UK: E & W	16.6				23.0	14.0			18.0			8	11	30.6	7	5	11.5	9	8	6	2.9	0	1	0	28.7	0.0	0.0
UK: N.-Ireland	5.5				14.6	19.1			37.1					25.8			3.4				0.0				18.0	0.0	0.0
UK: Scotland	18.3				42.4	15.8			10.9					22.9			6.9				0.9				19.0	0.0	0.0
Mean	12	14	63		29	16	14	34	22	42	44	8	11	27	7	5	7	9	8	6	2	0	1	0	17	3	7
Median	10	14	63		23	15	14	33	19	31	52	8	11	24	6	5	6	9	8	4	1	0	1	0	15	0	1
Minimum	1	14	63		0	4	14	22	8	24	4	8	8	10	4	3	0	9	8	2	0	0	0	0	0	0	0
Maximum	42	14	63		67	33	14	48	42	72	66	8	14	49	10	8	33	9	8	11	14	0	1	0	52	41	31

Table 3.2.4.13: Number of convictions by length of unsuspended custodial sanctions and measures imposed in 1999 – Drug offences: Drug trafficking

Drug offences: Drug trafficking	Total unsuspended custodial sanctions per 100 000 pop R34DT A99	of which: % under 1 month P34DT B99	of which: % 1 month & less than 12 months P34DT C99	of which: % 3 months & less than 12 months P34DT D99	of which: % under 6 months P34DT E99	of which: % 6 months & less than 12 months P34DT F99	of which: % 6 months & less than 18 months P34DT G99	of which: % under 12 months P34DT H99	of which: % 12 months & less than 24 months P34DT I99	of which: % 12 months & less than 36 months P34DT J99	of which: % 12 months & less than 60 months P34DT K99	of which: % 18 months & less than 36 months P34DT L99	of which: % 24 months & less than 48 months P34DT M99	of which: % 24 months & less than 60 months P34DT N99	of which: % 36 months & less than 60 months P34DT O99	of which: % 48 months & over P34DT P99	of which: % 60 months & less than 120 months P34DT Q99	of which: % 60 months & less than 144 months P34DT R99	of which: % 60 months & less than 180 months P34DT S99	of which: % 60 months & over P34DT T99	of which: % 120 months & over P34DT U99	of which: % 120 months & less than 240 months P34DT V99	of which: % 144 months & over P34DT W99	of which: % 180 months & over P34DT X99	Average length of custodial sanction/measure (in months) T34DT Y99	of which: % Life P34DT Z99	of which: % Indeterminate sanctions/measures P34DT _99
Albania	:	:	:	:	:	:	:	:	:	:	:	:	:	:	:	:	:	:	:	:	:	:	:	:	:	:	:
Armenia	:	:	:	:	:	:	:	:	:	:	:	:	:	:	:	:	:	:	:	:	:	:	:	:	:	:	:
Austria	9.3	:	:	:	3.9	21.6	:	:	:	43.3	:	:	:	:	6.0	:	:	:	:	2.7	:	:	:	:	:	0.0	:
Belgium	:	:	:	:	:	:	:	:	:	:	:	:	:	:	:	:	:	:	:	:	:	:	:	:	:	:	:
Bulgaria	0.0	:	:	:	0.0	0.0	:	:	:	:	:	:	:	:	:	:	:	:	:	:	:	:	:	:	:	0.0	0.0
Croatia	1.7	:	:	:	0.0	16.2	:	:	20.3	:	:	:	:	36.5	:	:	2.7	:	:	:	1.4	:	:	:	24.0	0.0	23.0
Cyprus	:	:	:	:	:	:	:	:	:	:	:	:	:	:	:	:	:	:	:	:	:	:	:	:	32.0	:	:
Czech Republic	2.7	:	:	:	:	:	:	22.6	:	:	68.8	:	:	:	:	:	:	:	8.6	:	:	:	:	0.0	:	:	:
Denmark	2.0	:	:	:	5.7	18.9	:	:	27.4	:	:	:	:	25.5	:	:	:	20.8	:	:	:	:	1.9	:	:	0.0	:
Estonia	:	:	:	:	:	:	:	:	:	:	:	:	:	:	:	:	:	:	:	:	:	:	:	:	:	0.0	:
Finland	:	:	:	:	:	:	:	:	:	:	:	:	:	:	:	:	:	:	:	:	:	:	:	:	:	:	:
France	6.4	:	:	:	27.8	21.0	:	:	:	28.5	:	:	:	18.1	13.6	:	8.1	:	:	:	1.0	:	:	:	20.1	0.0	:
Georgia	4.7	:	:	:	:	:	:	:	:	:	:	:	:	:	:	:	70.2	:	:	:	18.5	:	:	:	:	:	4.7
Germany	2.9	:	:	:	2.0	7.0	:	:	17.6	:	:	:	:	62.2	:	:	10.4	:	:	:	0.8	:	:	:	:	0.0	:
Greece	3.4	:	:	:	:	:	:	:	:	:	59.2	:	:	:	:	:	:	:	:	31.7	:	:	:	:	:	1.9	7.2
Hungary	:	:	:	:	:	:	:	:	:	:	:	:	:	:	:	:	:	:	:	:	:	:	:	:	:	:	:
Ireland	:	:	:	:	:	:	:	:	:	:	:	:	:	:	:	:	:	:	:	:	:	:	:	:	:	:	:
Italy	:	:	:	:	:	:	:	:	:	:	:	:	:	:	:	:	:	:	:	:	:	:	:	:	:	:	:
Latvia	:	:	:	:	:	:	:	:	:	:	:	:	:	:	:	:	:	:	:	:	:	:	:	:	:	:	:
Lithuania	:	:	:	:	:	:	:	:	:	:	:	:	:	:	:	:	:	:	:	:	:	:	:	:	:	:	:
Luxembourg	:	:	:	:	:	:	:	:	:	:	:	:	:	:	:	:	:	:	:	:	:	:	:	:	:	:	:

Conviction statistics

Drug offences:
Drug trafficking

	Total unsuspended custodial sanctions per 100 000 pop R34DT A99	of which: % under 1 month P34DT B99	of which: % 1 month & less than 12 months P34DT C99	of which: % 3 months & less than 12 months P34DT D99	of which: % under 6 months P34DT E99	of which: % 6 months & less than 12 months P34DT F99	of which: % 6 months & less than 18 months P34DT G99	of which: % under 12 months P34DT H99	of which: % 12 months & less than 24 months P34DT I99	of which: % 12 months & less than 36 months P34DT J99	of which: % 12 months & less than 36 months P34DT K99	of which: % 18 months & less than 36 months P34DT L99	of which: % 24 months & less than 48 months P34DT M99	of which: % 24 months & less than 60 months P34DT N99	of which: % 36 months & less than 60 months P34DT O99	of which: % 48 months & over P34DT P99	of which: % 60 months & less than 120 months P34DT Q99	of which: % 60 months & less than 144 months P34DT R99	of which: % 60 months & less than 180 months P34DT S99	of which: % 60 months & over P34DT T99	of which: % 120 months & over P34DT U99	of which: % 120 months & less than 240 months P34DT V99	of which: % 144 months & over P34DT W99	of which: % 180 months & over P34DT X99	Average length of custodial sanction/measure (in months) T34DT Y99	of which: % Life P34DT Z99	of which: % Indeterminate sanctions/measures P34DT _99
Malta	:	:	:	:	:	:	:	:	:	:	:	:	:	:	:	:	:	:	:	:	:	:	:	:	:	:	:
Moldova	:	:	:	:	:	:	:	:	:	:	:	:	:	:	:	:	:	:	:	:	:	:	:	:	:	:	:
Netherlands	:	:	:	:	:	:	:	:	:	:	:	:	:	:	:	:	:	:	:	:	:	:	:	:	:	:	0.5
Norway	24.7	:	:	:	64.8	9.8	:	:	11.3	:	:	:	:	10.5	:	:	2.5	:	:	:	1.2	:	:	:	11.1	:	:
Poland	0.4	:	:	:	0.0	2.4	:	:	18.9	:	:	:	:	64.0	:	:	12.8	:	:	:	1.8	:	:	:	:	:	:
Portugal	8.9	:	:	:	0.4	1.9	:	:	9.3	:	:	:	:	43.8	:	:	43.2	:	:	:	1.3	:	:	:	61.0	:	0.0
Romania	:	:	:	:	:	:	:	:	:	:	:	:	:	:	:	:	:	:	:	:	:	:	:	:	:	:	:
Russia	:	:	:	:	:	:	:	:	:	:	:	:	:	:	:	:	:	:	:	:	:	:	:	:	:	:	:
Slovakia	:	:	:	:	8.1	25.7	:	:	44.6	:	:	:	:	20.3	:	:	1.4	:	:	:	0.0	:	:	:	:	:	:
Slovenia	3.8	:	:	:	:	:	:	:	:	:	:	:	:	:	:	:	:	:	:	:	:	:	:	:	:	:	:
Spain	:	:	:	:	:	:	:	:	:	:	:	:	:	:	:	:	:	:	:	:	:	:	:	:	:	:	:
Sweden	:	:	:	:	:	:	:	:	:	:	:	:	:	:	:	:	:	:	:	:	:	:	:	:	:	:	:
Switzerland	25.7	:	:	:	43.0	7.6	:	:	11.3	:	:	:	:	23.7	:	:	3.4	:	:	:	0.3	:	:	:	14.4	0.0	10.6
Turkey	:	:	:	:	:	:	:	:	:	:	:	:	:	:	:	:	:	:	:	:	:	:	:	:	:	:	:
Ukraine	:	:	:	:	:	:	:	:	:	:	:	:	:	:	:	:	:	:	:	:	:	:	:	:	:	:	:
UK: E & W	11.2	:	:	:	7.5	11.0	:	:	18.9	:	:	:	:	41.6	:	:	16.7	:	:	:	4.3	:	:	:	38.6	0.0	0.0
UK: N.-Ireland	2.5	:	:	:	2.4	22.0	:	:	53.7	:	:	:	:	17.1	:	:	4.9	:	:	:	0.0	:	:	:	18.0	0.0	0.0
UK: Scotland	14.0	:	:	:	27.4	18.7	:	:	13.8	:	:	:	:	29.8	:	:	9.1	:	:	:	1.2	:	:	:	24.0	0.0	0.0
Mean	7	:	:	:	14	13	:	23	22	36	64	:	:	33	10	:	15	21	9	17	3	:	2	0	27	0	5
Median	4	:	:	:	5	14	:	23	19	36	64	:	:	28	10	:	9	21	9	17	1	:	2	0	24	0	0
Minimum	0	:	:	:	0	0	:	23	9	29	59	:	:	11	6	:	1	21	9	3	0	:	2	0	11	0	0
Maximum	26	:	:	:	65	26	:	23	54	43	69	:	:	64	14	:	70	21	9	32	18	:	2	0	61	2	23

Notes on Tables 3.2.4.1-3.2.4.13
Belgium and Greece: Data relates to the year 1997 (instead of 1999).
Croatia, the Czech Republic, France, Germany and Slovenia: Data relates to the year 2000 (instead of 1999).

3.3 Technical information on chapter 3

The totals given in tables 3.2.3.1-3.2.3.13 do not always match the totals indicated in tables 3.2.4.1-3.2.4.13. As a rule, only differences of up to 10% were accepted.

Technical comments

1) What is recorded?
Conviction statistics usually contain decisions taken by the courts, or, as is the case in a minority of countries, by public prosecutors where defendants have accepted their guilt (e.g. German "Strafbefehl"). This type of decision comes close to the "guilty plea" in the American system. Such decisions are counted as convictions and are thus included in the conviction tables. This was the case in Denmark, Finland, Germany, Norway, Russia, Sweden, Switzerland and Turkey. No country considers sanctions imposed by the police or an administrative authority as convictions, at least not in connection with the categories of offences dealt with in the conviction tables. The numbers recorded in the conviction tables often differ from the totals in the sanction tables. Although these differences cannot be fully explained, they usually reflect the different sources and therefore statistical rules used to collect each set of data.

2) Differences between chapters 1 and 3 with regard to offence definitions
The offence definitions, which underlie chapter 1, reflect the definitions that are used in national police statistics. They are usually inspired by a criminological point of view, i.e. they are based on concepts which come close to the everyday life experience of police officers and the public, such as "burglary", "armed robbery", or "motor vehicle theft".

As regards *convictions,* the offence definitions used by the various countries obviously depend on their respective legal traditions and criminal codes. For this reason, "burglary" or "motor vehicle" theft may be punishable as "theft" in many countries, and thus appear in the conviction statistics under the heading "theft", only because "burglary" or "motor vehicle theft" do not exist as specific legal concepts. Along the same lines, "assault leading to death" may, depending on the offender's intent, be counted as "assault" rather than as "homicide" (unlike the definition in chapter 1).

For these specific reasons (i.e. the non-existence of certain legal concepts in certain countries), several countries were not in a position to provide figures for all the tables/items in chapter 3.

The following comments highlight specific differences between the *legal definitions* used in chapter 3 and those used in police statistics (chapter 1).

Albania: Rape includes sexual intercourse with minors even without force.
Denmark: Robbery does not include muggings ("bag-snatching") which are considered as theft. The figures also reflect acquittals.
Estonia: In table 3.2.4.5 robbery does not include theft with minor violence or minor threats. In table 3.2.4.6 figures do not reflect the temporary use of a motor vehicle without authorisation.
France: The definition of assault is broader than the one used in chapter 1.
Greece: Figures given in table 3.2.3.9 (Theft of motor vehicle) relate to the illegal "use" of a car (i.e. without the intent to keep) contrary to police statistics in chapter 1.
Germany: The figures given for burglary refer to aggravated "theft". Armed robbery includes other forms of dangerous robbery, such as gang robbery.
Portugal: Mugging ("bag-snatching") is not in all cases considered as robbery.
Switzerland: Robbery does not include mugging ("bag-snatching").
The figures given in tables 3.2.2 (number of minors) are known since 1999 only. As minors were not included in the conviction statistics for the proceeding years, they are not included in the totals either, in order to keep tables 3.2.1 consistent. In addition, minors are not included in table 3.2.2.1 and 3.2.2.2.
UK: England & Wales: Drug offences include simple possession, cultivation and transportation of drugs, which are excluded from the police statistics.

3.3.1 Data recording methods in connection with tables 3.2.1 and 3.2.2

Table 3.3.1.1: Description of data recording methods for Tables 3.2.1 and 3.2.2

Question	Do the offence definitions used in this table differ from those in the "definitions" section?	Are there written rules regulating the way in which the data shown in this table are collected?	At what stage of the process does the data refer to?	How is a person who is convicted of more than one offence of the same type counted?	How is a person counted who is dealt with for more than one offence in the same year?
Possible answers	1: Yes 2: No	1: Yes 2: No	1: Before appeal 2: After appeal	1= As one person 2=As two or more people 3 = Other	1: As one person 2: As two or more people 3: Other
	CT32AA00	CT32B00	CT32C00	CT32E00	CT32F00
Albania	2	1	2	1	3
Armenia	2	1	2	1	1
Austria	1	1	2	1	2
Belgium	1	1	2	3	3
Bulgaria	2	1	2	1	1
Croatia	2	1	2	2	2
Cyprus	2	1	1	1	2
Czech Republic	2	1	2	3	3
Denmark	2	2	1	1	2
Estonia	2	1	2	1	2
Finland	1	1	1	1	2
France	1	1	2	1	2
Georgia	2	1	2	1	1
Germany	1	1	2	1	2
Greece	1	1	2	-4	2
Hungary	2	1	1	1	-4
Iceland		-2	-2	-2	-2
Ireland	2	1	2	2	2
Italy	2	2	2	1	2
Latvia	1	1	2	1	2
Lithuania	2	2	1	3	2
Luxembourg	...	-2	-2	-2	-2
Malta	...	-2	-2	-2	-2
Moldova	2	1	2	1	-2
Netherlands	2	1	1	1	2
Norway	2	1	2	1	2
Poland	1	1	2	1	2
Portugal	1	1	1	2	2
Romania	1	2	2	1	2
Russia	2	1	-2	-2	-2
Slovakia	1	1	2	1	1
Slovenia	2	1	2	1	1
Spain	2	1	1	1	2
Sweden	2	1	1	1	2
Switzerland	1	1	2	1	2
Turkey	...	-2	-2	-2	-2
Ukraine	2	1	2	1	2
UK: England & Wales	2	1	1	1	2
UK: Northern Ireland	2	1	1	1	2
UK: Scotland	2	1	1	1	2

Description of data recording methods for Tables 3.2.1 and 3.2.2

	Are there written rules regulating the way in which the data shown in this table are recorded?	At what stage of the process does the data refer to?
	1=Yes 2=No	1=Before appeals 2=After appeals
	CT32BOO	CT32C00
Albania	1	2
Armenia	1	2
Austria	1	2
Belgium	1	2
Bulgaria	1	2
Croatia	1	2
Cyprus	1	1
Czech Republic	1	2
Denmark	2	1
Estonia	1	2
Finland	1	1
France	1	2
Georgia	1	2
Germany	1	2
Greece	1	2
Hungary	1	1
Iceland	-2	-2
Ireland	1	2
Italy	2	2
Latvia	1	2
Lithuania	2	1
Luxembourg	-2	-2
Malta	-2	-2
Moldova	1	2
Netherlands	1	1
Norway	1	2
Poland	1	2
Portugal	1	1
Romania	2	2
Russia	1	-2
Slovakia	1	2
Slovenia	1	2
Spain	1	1
Sweden	1	1
Switzerland	1	2
Turkey	-2	-2
Ukraine	1	2
UK: England & Wales	1	1
UK: Northern Ireland	1	1
UK: Scotland	1	1

3.3.2 Age brackets and definition of aliens used in tables 3.2.2.2 and 3.2.2.3

Age brackets used in table 3.2.2.2
All countries count minors as persons who are not yet 18 years old. The only exception is Austria, which included 18 year old (less than 19).

The lower age limit varies widely among countries as far as criminal responsibility is concerned. Persons below the age of criminal responsibility will not be convicted and therefore not counted in conviction statistics (whatever "civil" or administrative treatment or sanction they will actually receive). This was not necessarily the case for police statistics where persons below the age of criminal responsibility were sometimes included (for details see table 1.3.2.2). For the offences considered here, the following age limits were indicated.

Table 3.3.1.2: Minimum age for consideration in conviction statistics 1999

Albania	14
Armenia	14
Austria	14
Belgium	16
Bulgaria	14
Croatia	14
Cyprus	7
Czech Republic	15
Denmark	15
Estonia	13
Finland	15
France	7
Germany	14
Greece	7
Hungary	14
Ireland	14
Italy	15
Latvia	14
Lithuania	14
Moldova	14
Netherlands	12
Norway	15
Poland	15
Portugal	16
Romania	14
Slovakia	15
Slovenia	14
Spain	16
Sweden	15
Switzerland	7
Ukraine	14
UK: England & Wales	10
UK: Northern Ireland	10
UK: Scotland	8

Notes for table 3.3.1.2
Poland: Minimum age is 17 years old apart from particular cases of very serious crimes where minors of 15 and 16 years of age are convicted according to the Criminal Code.

Definition of aliens: See paragraph 1.3.2.

3.4 Sources of the data used in chapter 3

Sources of the data

Albania	Ministry of Justice, Department of Statistics.
Armenia	Ministry of Justice.
Austria	Statistics Austria. Annual Conviction Statistics 1995-1999; Government Report on Security 2000.
Belgium	Données statistiques en matières de condamnations, suspensions, internements – (Forthcoming publication).
Bulgaria	Based on data taken from the publication "Offenses and sentenced persons", issued by the National Statistical Institute. "Demographic and Social Policy" Direction – "Social Activities" Department.
Croatia	State Bureau of Statistics – Department of Judicial and Administrative Statistics: Internal documentation (unpublished – only selected data are published).
Cyprus	"Criminal Statistics" for each year. Statistical Service.
Czech Republic	Statistical Sourcebook of Criminality. Ministry of Justice (2001).
Denmark	Statistics Denmark.
Estonia	Statistical Yearbook of Estonia, 1996-1997. Ministry of Justice (unpublished)
Finland	Yearbook of Justice Statistics, relevant year/Statistics Finland.
France	Ministère de la Justice, SDSED, annual judicial statistics.
Germany	Statistisches Bundesamt (Hrsg.): Strafverfolgungsstatistik 1995-2000. Wiesbaden 1996–2001.
Greece	National Statistical Service of Greece.
Hungary	Ministry of Justice.
Ireland	Annual Reports of An Garda Síochána.
Italy	Istat – National Institute of Statistics.
Latvia	Ministry of Justice – Department of Courts – Section of Courts Statistics (unpublished).
Lithuania	Ministry of Justice – Court Department – Section of Informatics and Statistics.
Moldova	Ministère de la Justice.
Netherlands	Ministry of Justice (WODC) and Central Bureau of Statistics (Not published).
Norway	Statistics Norway, Division for Social Welfare Statistics.
Poland	Ministry of Justice, Department of Statistics.
Portugal	Legal Policy and Planning Office, Ministry of Justice.

Romania	Ministry of Justice, Directorate of Organisation, Human Resources and Judiciary Statistics.
Russia	General Prosecutor Office.
Slovakia	Ministry of Justice of the Slovak Republic.
Slovenia	Statistical office of the Republic of Slovenia. Based on data taken from "Results of Surveys": Crime. Annual publication.
Spain	INE – Instituto Nacional de Estadística. Estadísticas Judiciales de España. Madrid: INE, published annually, Table 35.
Sweden	Official Swedish Criminal Statistics publish by the National Crime Prevention Council.
Switzerland	Office fédéral de la statistique (unpublished).
Ukraine	State committee of statistics of Ukraine; Statistical yearbook of Ukraine for 2000.
UK: England & Wales	Home Office, Research. Development and Statistics Directorate. Criminal Statistics. Annual publication.
UK: Northern Ireland	Northern Ireland Office Statistics and Research Branch.
UK: Scotland	The Scottish Executive Justice Statistics Unit.

4 Correctional statistics

4.1 General comments

4.1.1 Introduction

1. This chapter presents data on detention rates and persons serving non-custodial sanctions and measures administered by the correctional authorities. It also briefly reviews the information available on recidivism.

2. The content of this chapter has been revised considerably compared with the European Sourcebook 1999 and no longer includes data on the number and the capacity of penal institutions and expenditure but now has comprehensive data describing the stock and flow of the execution of custodial and non-custodial sentences.

3. *The "stock" and "flow" perspective.*
Generally speaking, data on custodial and non-custodial sanctions can be described from two perspectives, which generate different, but equally important results. The first perspective concerns "How many persons are there on a given day?" ("stock"). The second perspective concerns "How many people have been admitted during the course of the year?" ("flow").

4. The following data were requested:
Prison statistics
- How many people are there in the prisons ("stock", including pre-trial detention and divided into sub-categories: women, minors, and aliens)?
- How many people are admitted to the prisons ("flow", including pre-trial detention and divided into sub-categories: women, minors, and aliens)?
- What kind of offences have the convicted prisoners committed ("stock", excluding pre-trial detention, but divided into sub-categories: all offences, traffic offences, intentional homicide, completed intentional homicide, assault, rape, robbery, total theft, theft of a motor vehicle, burglary, domestic burglary, total drug offences, drug trafficking)?

Supervision statistics
- How many persons are there under the *supervision* or care of an agent of the correctional services ("stock", divided into sub-categories: suspended sentence, probation, parole or conditional release)?
- How many persons are admitted to the *supervision* or care of an agent of the correctional services ("flow", divided into sub-categories: suspended sentence, probation, parole or conditional release)?
- How many persons are doing *community service*[1] ("stock", divided into sub-categories: community services as an independent non-custodial

---

1 *Community service* = A saction involving designated work outside prison.

sentence, as part of the execution of a non-custodial or suspended sanction, and as part of the execution of an unsuspended custodial sanction)?
- How many persons are admitted to *community service* ("flow", divided into sub-categories: community services as an independent non-custodial sentence, as part of the execution of a non-custodial or suspended sanction, and as part of the execution of an unsuspended custodial sanction)?
- How many persons are there under *electronic surveillance* ("stock", divided into sub-categories: electronic monitoring as an independent sanction, as part of the execution of a non-custodial or suspended sanction, and as part of the execution of an unsuspended custodial sanction)?
- How many persons are admitted to *electronic surveillance* ("flow", divided into sub-categories: electronic monitoring as an independent sanction, as part of the execution of a non-custodial or suspended sanction, and as part of the execution of an unsuspended custodial sanction)?

5. Almost all countries reported data on prison populations ("stock" data) including the different sub-categories. However, only a few countries provided data on yearly admissions. Also, only a few countries provided data on the prison population by type of offence. In general, the data on the execution of non-custodial sentences is less complete across the countries compared with the data on prison statistics.

6. Data describing the prison populations "stock" ("how many prisoners there are" overall in accordance with the data published in the European Sourcebook 1999 and the data published by the SPACE project (*Annual Penal Statistics of the Council of Europe*). The majority of deviations lie in an acceptable margin of +/- 10%. However, data describing prison population's "flow" ("how many prisoners are yearly admitted?") do not show such a good correspondence with the SPACE data. This is not surprising since it is technically more difficult to measure "flow" data than it is to measure "stock" data.

4.1.2 Results

7. Between 1995 and 2000, prison populations in European countries only show moderate changes. The median prison rate in Europe is about 100 prisoners per 100 000 population and the rate has been rather stable (1995 deviates because of missing data). Substantive increases have been reported by Albania and Slovenia, and a substantive decrease has been reported by UK: Northern Ireland.

8. There are considerable differences between the countries as regards the absolute size of the prison population: in 2000, the prison rates range from a low 38 to a high 726 per 100 000. The countries' relative positions have changed only slightly between 1995 and 2000.

9. In accordance with other research, there is no strong correlation between overall reported crime rates and prison rates. High overall crime rates do not necessarily induce high prison rates and vice versa. Neither do high prison rates necessarily induce low overall crime rates and vice versa.

10. Typically, around one-quarter of the prison population consists of pre-trial detainees. This proportion has been stable during the years 1995-2000.

11. The average proportion of females in European prisons is low (4%) and varies very little between the countries.

12. As regards aliens, the percentage varies considerably between the countries, reflecting diverse factors such as geographical location, economic and social development, or immigration policies. Also, definitions vary widely between countries. However, there is no general trend of an increasing proportion of alien prisoners in European prisons.

13. Minors (i.e. persons under the age of 18) do not usually enter the prison system and they only account for 2% of the prison population in Europe.

14. Between 1995 and 2000, the number of prisoners admitted to European prisons ("flow") has increased. On average, the time spent in prison (pre-trial detention included) can be estimated at about five months and is slightly decreasing (SPACE I).

15. In 1999, prisoners ("stock") have been imprisoned for violence (homicide, assault, rape, and robbery) in 30-35% of the cases, for theft in 20-25%, and for drug offences in about 10% of the cases.

4.1.3 Supervision

16. Data on different forms of supervision is less comprehensive compared with data on prison populations. Only 15 countries provided some sort of data. About 100 persons per 100 000 population are under some form of supervision in those countries ("stock" median) and no real change has occurred between 1995 and 2000. About one out of four was paroled or released early from prison; the rest has been sentenced to different forms of supervision in consequence of a non-custodial sentence.

17. Thirteen countries give some information on parole, probation, and supervision from a "flow" perspective. Roughly speaking, the typical length of a period of supervision can be estimated to one and a half years.

18. Data on community service are provided by 13 countries and on electronic monitoring by only 5 countries (Belgium, UK: England & Wales, UK: Scotland, Sweden and Switzerland: no tables provided).

4.1.4 Recidivism

19. Due to many technical and methodological problems, data on recidivism were not collected. However, a brief account of some of the main methodological issues and some common features in the results from available reconviction studies are presented here.

20. Only a few countries measure reconviction rates (e.g. UK: England & Wales, Netherlands and Sweden). Some do this by defining the concept of a recidivist within their Penal Code and simply count the persons that reoffend whilst other countries rely on research studies to estimate reconviction rates of offenders. Some countries have built up large databases of offender histories, which enable reconviction rates and criminal careers to be studied on a regular basis.

21. However, there is little standardisation between countries on the methodology used. In general, results are dependent, among other things, on
- how large the studied sample or population is,
- the characteristics of the offenders (are all offenders chosen or only special sub-groups according to gender, age, prior conviction, type of offence, type of sanction etc.),
- the length of the follow-up period,
- the definition of the event, which constitutes "reconviction"/"recidivism" (e.g. all offences or only special offences/sanctions meet the criterion of reconviction).

22. Indeed, by choosing different offender characteristics, follow-up periods and reconviction criteria, it is possible to synthetically increase or decrease recidivism rates. Therefore, care should be taken in interpreting reconviction rates, even when considering a single country and special care should be taken when comparing rates across countries. Neither should it be forgotten that reconviction rates are, in fact, "rates of recapture", therefore, recidivism rates may depend on the efficiency of the different criminal justice systems.

23. Although reconviction rates vary considerably in their magnitude between the countries, there are some common features in the results, namely
- past criminal history is the most important predictor of reconviction rates, with the highest rates being for offenders with the longest criminal history,
- male reconviction rates are higher than those for females; however, this is mostly explained by differences in their criminal history and age,
- younger persons tend to have higher reconviction rates than older persons,

- reconviction rates are higher for the first year after the initial conviction/release,
- there is no simple relationship between the seriousness of the offence and reconviction,
- there is also no simple relationship between the first conviction and the subsequent offences,
- there is, no simple relationship between the type of sentence and the reconviction rate,
- there is, a growing body of evidence that recidivism rates can be 10 or more percentage points lower for those offenders who complete drug treatment or cognitive behavioural programmes.[2]

---

[2] Doris L MacKenzie, "Criminal Justice and Crime Prevention", http://www.preventingcrime.org/report/index.htm

4.2 Tables

Table 4.2.1.1: Prison population per 100 000 population: STOCK – Total

	1995 R41ST95	1996 R41ST96	1997 R41ST97	1998 R41ST98	1999 R41ST99	2000 R41ST00	% change 1995-2000
Albania	36	39	...	...	...	65	80
Armenia	...	203	213	215	212	225	...
Austria	84	88	91	91	89	86	3
Belgium	73	81	84	81	83	87	18
Bulgaria	109	133	147	147	137	121	11
Croatia	75	70	120	121	95	100	33
Cyprus	28	32	35	30	33	38	37
Czech Republic	189	202	209	214	224	210	11
Denmark	67	62	66	65	69	64	-4
Estonia	297	287	318	331	304	329	11
Finland	59	58	54	50	50	52	-12
France	89	89	88	86	85	77	-13
Georgia	...	194	195	204	169	173	...
Germany	83	87	90	97	98	97	17
Greece	56	52	52	68	71	76	36
Hungary	121	124	131	141	149	153	27
Ireland	56	...	66	71	73	76	35
Italy	83	85	88	86	92	...	...
Latvia	...	...	...	...	...	...	...
Lithuania	362	333	373	396	397	263	-27
Luxembourg	...	...	...	...	...	...	...
Malta	...	50	66	67	59	66	...
Moldova	211	227	220	227	230	220	5
Netherlands	73	83	83	83	85	84	16
Norway	60	60	58	56	57	57	-5
Poland	171	148	149	153	142	169	-1
Portugal	124	142	144	146	128	127	3
Romania	205	193	196	228	229	222	8
Russia	627	688	714	687	692	726	16
Slovakia	149	152	142	128	128	132	-11
Slovenia	34	32	40	41	49	59	74
Spain	119	111	109	112	114	113	-5
Sweden	70	67	59	60	61	63	-10
Switzerland	79	76	75	78	80	79	0
Turkey	...	...	...	...	...	...	...
Ukraine	...	...	...	...	...	...	...
UK: England & Wales	98	106	118	125	123	124	26
UK: Northern Ireland	110	102	101	93	76	66	-40
UK: Scotland	...	115	119	118	116	112	...
Mean	129	134	138	140	138	139	
Median	84	95	101	97	95	98	
Minimum	28	32	4	13	22	38	
Maximum	627	688	714	687	692	726	

Table 4.2.1.2: Prison population: % of Pre-trial detainees in the total STOCK

	1995 P41SP95	1996 P41SP96	1997 P41SP97	1998 P41SP98	1999 P41SP99	2000 P41SP00	% change 1995-2000
Albania	...	...	...	...	...	50	...
Armenia	...	...	...	...	...	...	...
Austria	25	22	23	23	22	22	-11
Belgium	45	43	41	37	39	42	-8
Bulgaria	31	37	33	24	21	16	-47
Croatia	38	29	16	18	21	21	-45
Cyprus	16	7	16	14	18	8	-49
Czech Republic	41	38	36	32	30	28	-32
Denmark	23	26	27	27	27	27	17
Estonia	...	...	29	31	30	35	...
Finland	11	10	11	11	14	14	35
France	40	41	40	39	36	34	-14
Georgia	...	...	...	...	...	...	...
Germany	30	28	28	25	23	23	-23
Greece	31	32	31	35	33	28	-11
Hungary	26	27	27	27	27	25	-3
Ireland	...	...	...	...	...	...	...
Italy	76	78	80	81	83	...	...
Latvia	...	...	...	...	...	...	...
Lithuania	22	18	19	17	15	20	-9
Luxembourg	...	...	...	...	...	...	...
Malta	...	50	66	65	31	31	...
Moldova	19	19	33	30	30	33	70
Netherlands	28	28	31	33	33	35	25
Norway	19	22	23	23	24	23	19
Poland	27	25	25	24	24	29	6
Portugal	38	35	30	29	32	30	-20
Romania	23	25	23	13	10	11	-51
Russia	...	...	...	...	...	...	...
Slovakia	25	23	22	23	27	27	5
Slovenia	29	25	26	26	26	27	-8
Spain	24	24	26	25	23	21	-12
Sweden	19	19	22	24	24	24	25
Switzerland	30	30	34	34	35	32	6
Turkey	...	...	...	...	...	...	...
Ukraine	...	...	...	...	...	...	...
UK: England & Wales	16	15	14	13	12	11	-29
UK: Northern Ireland	18	20	22	25	30	29	62
UK: Scotland	...	15	14	15	15	12	...
Mean	28	28	29	28	27	26	
Median	26	25	26	25	26	27	
Minimum	11	7	11	11	10	8	
Maximum	76	78	80	81	83	50	

Table 4.2.1.3: Prison population: % of Females in the total STOCK

	1995 P41SW95	1996 P41SW96	1997 P41SW97	1998 P41SW98	1999 P41SW99	2000 P41SW00	% change 1995-2000
Albania	3	2	6	4	3	2	-23
Armenia	...	3	3	3	2	2	...
Austria	5	6	6	6	6	...	...
Belgium	5	5	4	4	4	5	-11
Bulgaria	3	3	3	3	4	3	-2
Croatia	2	2	1	2	2	3	10
Cyprus	3	6	3	1	5	4	11
Czech Republic	3	4	4	4	4	4	29
Denmark	...	...	...	...	...	...	...
Estonia	...	1	1	2	2	2	...
Finland	4	5	5	5	5	5	25
France	4	4	4	4	4	4	-9
Georgia	...	2	2	2	2	2	...
Germany	4	4	4	4	4	4	9
Greece	3	4	4	4	4	5	34
Hungary	5	6	6	6	6	6	26
Ireland	2	0	2	3	3	3	56
Italy	4	4	4	4	4	...	...
Latvia	...	...	...	...	...	...	...
Lithuania	5	4	5	5	5	3	-38
Luxembourg	...	...	...	...	...	...	...
Malta	...	5	4	3	2	5	...
Moldova	...	...	3	4	4	4	...
Netherlands	5	5	6	7	7	8	41
Norway	3	4	4	4	4	4	23
Poland	2	2	3	2	2	2	3
Portugal	8	9	10	8	10	9	14
Romania	3	4	4	4	4	4	13
Russia	...	...	...	...	...	...	...
Slovakia	3	3	4	4	4	4	4
Slovenia	4	4	4	3	2	4	-5
Spain	9	9	9	9	9	8	-13
Sweden	4	4	4	4	4	4	-1
Switzerland	6	6	6	7	4	7	5
Turkey	...	...	...	...	...	...	...
Ukraine	...	...	...	...	...	...	...
UK: England & Wales	4	4	4	5	5	5	32
UK: Northern Ireland	2	2	2	2	2	2	8
UK: Scotland	...	3	3	3	4	3	...
Mean	4	4	4	4	4	4	
Median	4	4	4	4	4	4	
Minimum	2	0	1	1	2	2	
Maximum	9	9	10	9	10	9	

Table 4.2.1.4: Prison population: % of Aliens in the total STOCK

	1995 P41SA95	1996 P41SA96	1997 P41SA97	1998 P41SA98	1999 P41SA99	2000 P41SA00	% change 1995-2000
Albania	...	...	...	...	...	0	...
Armenia	...	...	...	...	...	...	...
Austria	25	25	25	27	26	...	...
Belgium	40	40	39	38	39	42	3
Bulgaria	1	1	1	0	2	1	93
Croatia	5	5	3	4	5	4	-16
Cyprus	41	52	35	27	28	39	-3
Czech Republic	16	18	15	14	13	12	-27
Denmark	...	...	...	...	...	...	...
Estonia	...	...	...	...	...	...	...
Finland	2	3	5	5	5	6	161
France	30	28	26	25	23	22	-26
Georgia	...	1	1	1	1	1	...
Germany	19	19	20	20	20	20	9
Greece	...	36	39	45	46	48	...
Hungary	5	5	5	4	5	5	9
Ireland	...	...	...	...	...	...	...
Italy	17	19	21	24	27	...	...
Latvia	...	...	...	...	...	...	...
Lithuania	1	1	1	1	1	1	131
Luxembourg	...	...	...	...	...	...	...
Malta	...	...	...	...	30	32	...
Moldova	...	...	...	...	...	...	...
Netherlands	...	...	...	...	...	56	...
Norway	8	7	7	7	7	6	-24
Poland	2	2	2	2	2	2	-1
Portugal	11	12	11	11	11	12	11
Romania	1	1	1	1	1	1	-35
Russia	...	...	...	...	...	...	...
Slovakia	...	2	2	2	2	3	...
Slovenia	12	22	14	16	16	17	41
Spain	15	16	17	18	17	20	28
Sweden	20	21	20	20	20	22	5
Switzerland	58	58	61	62	66	65	12
Turkey	...	...	...	...	...	...	...
Ukraine	...	...	...	...	...	...	...
UK: England & Wales	9	8	8	8	8	9	8
UK: Northern Ireland	0	1	1	1	0	1	98
UK: Scotland	...	2	2	2	3	2	...
Mean	15	16	15	15	16	17	
Median	11	10	10	9	11	9	
Minimum	0	1	1	0	0	0	
Maximum	58	58	61	62	66	65	

Table 4.2.1.5: Prison population: % of Minors in the total STOCK

	1995 P41SM95	1996 P41SM96	1997 P41SM97	1998 P41SM98	1999 P41SM99	2000 P41SM00	% change 1995-2000
Albania	1	0	0	3	2	4	249
Armenia	...	1	1	1	1	1	...
Austria	3	2	3	3	3	...	...
Belgium	0	0	0	0	0	0	***
Bulgaria	2	2	1	1	1	1	-34
Croatia	4	4	2	2	2	2	-42
Cyprus	0	0	0	0	0	0	***
Czech Republic	4	3	2	2	2	1	-64
Denmark	...	...	...	...	...	...	...
Estonia	...	...	...	...	...	...	...
Finland	0	0	0	0	0	0	***
France	1	1	1	1	1	1	12
Georgia	...	1	1	1	0	0	...
Germany	2	2	2	2	2	2	10
Greece	5	4	7	8	8	7	39
Hungary	4	4	37	3	3	3	-33
Ireland	...	...	...	...	...	...	...
Italy	1	1	1	1	1	...	...
Latvia	...	...	...	...	...	...	...
Lithuania	4	4	4	3	3	2	-45
Luxembourg	...	...	...	...	...	...	...
Malta	...	...	...	...	3	3	...
Moldova	...	...	2	2	2	3	...
Netherlands	8	8	9	10	11	12	54
Norway	0	0	0	0	0	0	***
Poland	...	...	...	...	...	...	...
Portugal	5	6	6	5	5	6	26
Romania	6	6	6	5	4	3	-48
Russia	...	...	...	...	...	...	...
Slovakia	...	...	...	...	...	...	...
Slovenia	1	2	2	2	1	1	-43
Spain	2	2	2	3	2	2	-21
Sweden	0	0	0	0	0	0	***
Switzerland	...	...	...	...	...	...	...
Turkey	...	...	...	...	...	...	...
Ukraine	...	...	...	...	...	...	...
UK: England & Wales	3	4	4	4	4	4	14
UK: Northern Ireland	...	...	...	...	...	...	...
UK: Scotland	...	4	4	3	4	3	...
Mean	3	2	4	3	2	2	
Median	2	2	2	2	2	2	
Minimum	0	0	0	0	0	0	
Maximum	8	8	37	10	11	12	

Comments on tables 4.2.1.1 to 4.2.1.5

Albania: 1. The data for 1995 refers to 1 October 1995.
For the years 1995-1999 the data refers to convicted persons only. Data on pre-trial detainees are missing.
For the year 2000, pre-trial detainees are included.
Regarding aliens, data for convicted prisoners are missing. Thus, the data refers to pre-trial detainees only.
Austria: Data on prison population (stock) refers to 30 November or 1 December of the respective year; except for the data for 2000, which relates to 1 June.
Data on aliens refers to 1 September.
Croatia: The data refers to 31 December 1999.
Czech Republic:
Female – minors excluded; pre-trial detainees and convicted females included.
Aliens – includes pre-trial detainees and convicted persons, both male and female and minors.
Minors – both male and female (persons 15-18 years old).
Estonia: Data at 1 January.
Regarding females figures, *convicted* females only included (excluding pre-trial detainees).
France: Statistical domain: metropolitan France
Refers to figures on 1 October.
Germany: Data refers to 31 March.
Tables do not include persons committed to a psychiatric hospital or an institution for drug withdrawal treatment.
Figures on aliens refers to convicted prisoners and those on remand pending deportation only. Regarding pre-trial detainees, a breakdown by nationality is not possible.
Greece: For the year 1996, the stock refers to 1 December instead of 1 September.
Hungary: For 1995 and 1996, at 31 December; for 1997-2000 at 1 September.
Ireland: 1996 data is at 2 September; all other years at 1 September.
Lithuania: Figures refer to 31 December. Figures may be affected by amnesties in some years.
Netherlands: The stock data refers to 30 September.
The data for *females* and *aliens* are estimates. The concept of alien is according to country of birth.
Poland: Data as of 31 August. Number of total prison population consists of pre-trial detainees, sentenced persons and sentenced by misdemeanour board.
Minors convicted according to Penal Code are included but those treated under the Act of Juvenile Treatment are excluded.
Romania: A significant decrease of the number of pre-trial prisoners can be noticed as a consequence of a change in reporting the activity of the prosecutors' offices, regarding the ordering of the pre-trial detention.
Prisoners who are convicted in first instance but not finally convicted are not included in pre-trial detainees.
Slovenia: Stock Aliens 1999 refers to 1 January 2000.
Spain: Pre-trial detainees: annual average.
Females: annual average.
Aliens: data at 31 December.
Minors: data at 31 December
Sweden: Data refers to 1 October. Data on pre-trial detainees refers to yearly average.
UK: England & Wales: Data at 30 June.
UK: Northern Ireland: Data is average prison population for the year.
UK: Scotland: Data at 30 June. Minors are defined as all those under 18.

Table 4.2.2.1: Prison population per 100 000 population: FLOW – Total

	1995 R42FT95	1996 R42FT96	1997 R42FT97	1998 R42FT98	1999 R42FT99	2000 R42FT00	% change 1995-2000
Albania	...	...	...	...	...	...	...
Armenia	...	...	...	...	...	...	...
Austria	227	215	211	216	205	...	...
Belgium	162	159	150	137	141	143	-12
Bulgaria	71	80	87	113	91	81	15
Croatia	168	160	311	477	441	407	142
Cyprus	120	161	142	163	212	218	82
Czech Republic	230	242	255	265	276	256	11
Denmark	681	651	625	596	574	...	...
Estonia	...	493	551	650	617	581	...
Finland	152	129	121	113	113	127	-16
France	141	136	129	123	123	113	-20
Georgia	...	...	...	...	...	...	...
Germany	795	818	847	897	899	...	...
Greece	...	...	...	...	...	...	...
Hungary	278	306	312	311	286	302	8
Ireland	275	285	311	305	289	306	11
Italy	168	163	159	160	156	...	...
Latvia	...	...	...	...	...	...	...
Lithuania	388	474	396	384	392	346	-11
Luxembourg	...	...	...	...	...	...	...
Malta	175	174	177	179	132	79	-55
Moldova	...	268	243	414	601	618	...
Netherlands	...	...	...	...	...	...	...
Norway	249	237	241	234	...	...	...
Poland	218	197	205	208	192	232	7
Portugal	89	85	78	67	62	59	-34
Romania	204	191	199	196	172	159	-22
Russia	...	...	...	...	...	...	...
Slovakia	185	170	151	132	139	138	-26
Slovenia	115	164	166	227	284	297	158
Spain	141	115	123	119	105	104	-26
Sweden	155	137	103	107	105	103	-33
Switzerland	...	...	...	...	...	...	...
Turkey	...	...	...	...	...	...	...
Ukraine	...	...	...	...	...	...	...
UK: England & Wales	242	232	240	252	257	246	2
UK: Northern Ireland	317	341	340	343	349	318	0
UK: Scotland	...	722	737	722	694	631	...
Mean	238	268	272	290	293	255	
Median	185	194	208	221	212	232	
Minimum	71	80	78	67	62	59	
Maximum	795	818	847	897	899	631	

Table 4.2.2.2: Prison population: % of Pre-trial detainees in the total FLOW

	1995 P42FP95	1996 P42FP96	1997 P42FP97	1998 P42FP98	1999 P42FP99	2000 P42FP00	% change 1995-2000
Albania	...	...	...	...	...	...	...
Armenia	...	...	...	...	...	...	...
Austria	51	52	54	52	54	...	...
Belgium	61	65	68	64	64	67	9
Bulgaria	70	75	71	44	44	35	-51
Croatia	57	57	23	16	20	23	-60
Cyprus	22	25	29	33	28	30	37
Czech Republic	51	50	50	50	50	48	-5
Denmark	66	73	72	71	69	...	...
Estonia	...	...	...	...	...	...	...
Finland	20	25	26	26	27	25	25
France	81	82	80	77	75	78	-3
Georgia	...	...	...	...	...	...	...
Germany	18	18	17	16	15	...	...
Greece	...	...	...	...	...	...	...
Hungary	30	29	26	27	29	31	3
Ireland	...	...	...	...	...	...	...
Italy	79	78	84	85	90	...	...
Latvia	...	...	...	...	...	...	...
Lithuania	56	44	57	56	57	60	7
Luxembourg	...	...	...	...	...	...	...
Malta	62	66	64	52	50	77	23
Moldova	...	40	52	46	77	80	...
Netherlands	...	...	...	...	...	...	...
Norway	29	30	31	31	...	...	...
Poland	...	...	...	...	...	...	...
Portugal	86	82	78	79	86	86	0
Romania	...	...	...	...	...	...	...
Russia	...	...	...	...	...	...	...
Slovakia	39	33	35	39	42	39	-1
Slovenia	38	25	25	22	16	18	-53
Spain	...	...	...	...	...	65	...
Sweden	...	...	...	...	...	...	...
Switzerland	...	...	...	...	...	...	...
Turkey	...	...	...	...	...	...	...
Ukraine	...	...	...	...	...	...	...
UK: England & Wales	44	49	49	49	48	42	-4
UK: Northern Ireland	39	42	40	41	44	42	8
UK: Scotland	...	40	39	40	42	42	...
Mean	50	49	49	46	49	49	
Median	51	46	50	45	48	42	
Minimum	18	18	17	16	15	18	
Maximum	86	82	84	85	90	86	

Table 4.2.2.3: Prison population: % of Females in the total FLOW

	1995 P42FW95	1996 P42FW96	1997 P42FW97	1998 P42FW98	1999 P42FW99	2000 P42FW00	% change 1995-2000
Albania	...	...	...	...	...	...	...
Armenia	...	...	...	...	...	...	...
Austria	7	8	8	7	8	...	...
Belgium	8	8	7	7	7	7	-18
Bulgaria	3	2	4	3	3	3	-19
Croatia	3	3	3	2	3	3	-7
Cyprus	4	6	5	5	9	7	70
Czech Republic	...	...	...	...	...	...	...
Denmark	8	7	7	7	7	...	...
Estonia	...	2	2	3	4	4	...
Finland	4	5	5	5	6	11	160
France	5	5	5	5	5	5	-14
Georgia	...	...	...	...	...	...	...
Germany	5	4	5	5	5	...	...
Greece	...	...	...	...	...	...	...
Hungary	...	...	...	...	...	...	...
Ireland	...	...	...	...	...	...	...
Italy	8	8	8	8	8	...	...
Latvia	...	...	...	...	...	...	...
Lithuania	3	2	3	3	3	2	-29
Luxembourg	...	...	...	...	...	...	...
Malta	8	9	6	5	4	5	-40
Moldova	...	...	...	...	...	...	...
Netherlands	...	...	...	...	...	...	...
Norway	6	7	8	8	...	...	...
Poland	...	...	...	...	...	...	...
Portugal	10	10	10	8	9	10	-1
Romania	...	...	...	...	...	...	...
Russia	...	...	...	...	...	...	...
Slovakia	...	...	...	...	...	...	...
Slovenia	7	4	6	5	4	5	-30
Spain	10	10	10	11	9	8	-16
Sweden	5	5	5	6	6	6	9
Switzerland	...	...	...	...	...	...	...
Turkey	...	...	...	...	...	...	...
Ukraine	...	...	...	...	...	...	...
UK: England & Wales	6	6	7	8	8	8	40
UK: Northern Ireland	3	4	4	4	4	5	55
UK: Scotland	...	...	6	7	7	7	...
Mean	6	6	6	6	6	6	
Median	6	6	6	5	6	5	
Minimum	3	2	2	2	3	2	
Maximum	10	10	10	11	9	11	

Table 4.2.2.4: Prison population: % of Aliens in the total FLOW

	1995 P42FA95	1996 P42FA96	1997 P42FA97	1998 P42FA98	1999 P42FA99	2000 P42FA00	% change 1995-2000
Albania	...	...	...	...	...	...	...
Armenia	...	...	...	...	...	...	...
Austria	...	...	...	...	...	...	...
Belgium	46	42	40	39	40	44	-5
Bulgaria	3	2	2	2	2	3	-4
Croatia	7	8	9	9	10	15	110
Cyprus	38	42	31	28	38	41	8
Czech Republic	...	...	...	...	...	...	...
Denmark	...	...	...	...	...	...	...
Estonia	...	...	...	...	...	...	...
Finland	...	...	...	...	...	...	...
France	30	29	27	24	23	23	-21
Georgia	...	...	...	...	...	...	...
Germany	...	...	...	...	...	...	...
Greece	...	...	...	...	...	...	...
Hungary	...	...	...	...	...	...	...
Ireland	...	...	...	...	...	...	...
Italy	26	27	29	32	33	...	...
Latvia	...	...	...	...	...	...	...
Lithuania	...	...	...	...	...	...	...
Luxembourg	...	...	...	...	...	...	...
Malta	22	22	26	21	19	34	56
Moldova	...	...	...	...	...	...	...
Netherlands	...	...	...	...	...	...	...
Norway	...	...	...	...	...	...	...
Poland	...	...	...	...	...	...	...
Portugal	...	...	...	...	...	...	...
Romania	...	...	...	...	...	...	...
Russia	...	...	...	...	...	...	...
Slovakia	...	...	...	...	...	...	...
Slovenia	6	3	3	2	1	3	-56
Spain	...	...	...	...	...	...	...
Sweden	19	20	21	22	23	25	33
Switzerland	...	...	...	...	...	...	...
Turkey	...	...	...	...	...	...	...
Ukraine	...	...	...	...	...	...	...
UK: England & Wales	...	...	...	...	88	10	...
UK: Northern Ireland	1	0	1	1	1	1	22
UK: Scotland	...	...	1	1	1	1	...
Mean	20	20	17	17	23	18	
Median	20	21	21	21	21	15	
Minimum	1	0	1	1	1	1	
Maximum	46	42	40	39	88	44	

Table 4.2.2.5: Prison population: % of Minors in the total FLOW

	1995 P42FM95	1996 P42FM96	1997 P42FM97	1998 P42FM98	1999 P42FM99	2000 P42FM00	% change 1995-2000
Albania	...	...	...	...	...	...	...
Armenia	...	...	...	...	...	...	...
Austria	4	5	5	5	5	...	...
Belgium	3	2	2	3	3	4	25
Bulgaria	3	3	3	2	3	2	-36
Croatia	1	1	1	1	1	1	-46
Cyprus	0	0	0	0	0	0	***
Czech Republic	...	...	...	...	...	...	...
Denmark	0	0	0	0	0	...	...
Estonia	...	...	...	...	...	...	...
Finland	6	7	5	5	4	5	-13
France	4	4	5	6	6	6	65
Georgia	...	...	...	...	...	...	...
Germany	...	...	...	...	...	...	...
Greece	...	...	...	...	...	...	...
Hungary	...	...	...	...	...	...	...
Ireland	...	...	...	...	...	...	...
Italy	3	4	4	4	2	...	...
Latvia	...	...	...	...	...	...	...
Lithuania	3	2	3	2	2	1	-50
Luxembourg	...	...	...	...	...	...	...
Malta	2	2	2	3	4	3	75
Moldova	...	...	...	...	...	...	...
Netherlands	...	...	...	...	...	...	...
Norway	0	1	1	1	...	...	...
Poland	...	...	...	...	...	...	...
Portugal	11	9	9	9	10	10	-3
Romania	...	...	...	...	...	...	...
Russia	...	...	...	...	...	...	...
Slovakia	...	...	...	...	...	...	...
Slovenia	0	0	0	0	0	0	***
Spain	12	9	8	7	7	7	-38
Sweden	0	0	0	0	0	0	***
Switzerland	...	...	...	...	...	...	...
Turkey	...	...	...	...	...	...	...
Ukraine	...	...	...	...	...	...	...
UK: England & Wales	8	10	10	9	9	9	11
UK: Northern Ireland	...	...	...	...	...	...	...
UK: Scotland	...	...	7	7	7	5	...
Mean	4	3	4	4	4	4	
Median	3	2	3	3	3	3	
Minimum	0	0	0	0	0	0	
Maximum	12	10	10	9	10	10	

Comments on tables 4.2.2.1 and 4.2.2.5
Croatia: The data refers to 31 December 1999.
Estonia: Data: at 1 January.
Convicted women only (excluding pre-trial detainees).
Including all entries and departures (e.g. if a person arrives and leaves during the given period, he/she is calculated twice).
France: Statistical domain: metropolitan France.
Germany: Persons committed to a psychiatric hospital or an institution for drug withdrawal treatment not included.
Hungary: Data at 31 December.
Ireland: 1996 data is at 2 September; all other years at 1 September.
Lithuania: The flow period covers from 1 January until 1 January of the following year.
Figures may be affected by amnesties in some years.
Netherlands: The data for females and aliens are estimates.
Poland: Number of total prison population consists of pre-trial detainees, sentenced persons and sentenced by misdemeanour board.
Minors convicted according to Penal Code are included but those treated under the Act of Juvenile Treatment are excluded.
Romania: A significant decrease of the number of pre-trial prisoners can be noticed as a consequence of a change in reporting the activity of the prosecutors' offices, regarding the ordering of the pre-trial detention.
Prisoners who are convicted in first instance but not finally convicted are not included in pre-trial detainees.
Sweden: Pre-trial detainees are excluded.
UK: England & Wales: Aliens have been taken to mean non-UK nationals.
UK: Scotland: Data is as at 30 June.
Minors are defined as all those under 18.

Table 4.2.3.1: Convicted prison population by offence. Total per 100 000 population

	Criminal offences: Total	Traffic offences	Intentional homicide: Total	Intentional homicide Completed	Assault	Rape	Robbery	Theft: Total	Theft: Theft of a motor vehicle	Theft: Burglary: Total	Theft: Burglary: Domestic Burglary	Drug offences: Total	Drug offences: Drug trafficking
	R43CT99	R43TTT99	R43HOT99	R43HCT99	R43AST99	R43RAT99	R43ROT99	R43THT99	R43TVT99	R43BUT99	R43BDT99	R43DRT99	R43DTT99
Albania	22.4	...	11.8	...	0.7	0.6	5.4	1.7	...	...	...	0.4	...
Armenia	...	...	...	...	...	...	...	...	...	...	...	...	...
Austria	...	...	...	...	...	...	...	...	...	...	...	...	...
Belgium	...	...	...	...	...	...	...	...	...	...	...	...	...
Bulgaria	107.9	1.7	15.4	13.4		5.2	13.3	44.4	...	...	...	...	...
Croatia	54.8	3.7	16.1	10.0	1.4	3.7	5.8	16.3	0.3	6.3	...	10.6	4.1
Cyprus	26.9	1.3	2.8	0.0	0.5	0.7	0.8	8.0	0.0	1.3	1.3	4.2	1.9
Czech Republic	296.1	...	11.4	...	11.4	4.5	24.4	69.4	...	...	...	7.5	1.5
Denmark	...	...	...	...	...	...	...	...	...	...	...	...	...
Estonia	...	...	36.9	...	19.6	9.3	24.5	53.1	...	...	...	...	...
Finland	45.8	6.0	9.4	...	6.0	1.0	3.8	7.1	...	...	...	7.0	...
France	54.9	...	5.7	...	4.9	11.5	...	14.2	...	...	...	8.5	...
Georgia	171.6	...	21.2	...	4.5	1.8	4.0	31.9	6.1	...	...	19.1	5.2
Germany	74.0	5.7	5.3	...	5.7	3.0	9.3	16.8	...	6.3	...	10.7	5.7
Greece	...	...	...	...	...	...	...	...	...	...	...	...	...
Hungary	105.2	...	14.8	...	7.7	4.7	23.1	33.3	...	...	...	1.0	...
Ireland	...	...	...	...	...	...	...	...	...	...	...	...	...
Italy	...	...	...	...	...	...	...	...	...	...	...	...	...
Latvia	...	...	...	...	...	...	...	...	...	...	...	...	...
Lithuania	336.1	...	42.7	...	8.8	15.3	59.4	140.0	...	...	...	6.9	...
Luxembourg	...	...	...	...	...	...	...	...	...	...	...	...	...

Correctional statistics

	Criminal offences: Total	Traffic offences	Intentional homicide: Total	Intentional homicide Completed	Assault	Rape	Robbery	Theft: Total	Theft: Theft of a motor vehicle	Theft: Burglary: Total	Theft: Burglary: Domestic Burglary	Drug offences: Total	Drug offences: Drug trafficking
	R43TCT99	R43TTT99	R43HOT99	R43HCT99	R43AST99	R43RAT99	R43ROT99	R43THT99	R43TVT99	R43BUT99	R43BDT99	R43DRT99	R43DTT99
Malta	40.6	...	5.7	...	0.8	1.3	0.5	12.6	...	0.0	...	17.2	...
Moldova	159.2	...	31.1	...	9.7	10.1	25.7	51.0	...	3.8	...	...	...
Netherlands	84.6	0.8	...	...	...	...	...	...	...	...	...	13.9	...
Norway	31.4	1.5	1.6	1.5	...	0.6	1.4	8.1	0.8	6.4	...	8.4	8.3
Poland	145.9	...	12.1	...	...	4.9	32.8	...	...	39.2	...	...	...
Portugal	87.3	...	...	9.4	2.4	3.1	11.1	17.1	...	...	...	38.5	35.9
Romania	180.1	2.0	28.3	...	0.9	6.8	18.4	106.8	...	...	...	0.5	...
Russia	692.1	...	...	...	...	...	...	...	...	...	...	...	...
Slovakia	...	...	...	...	...	...	...	...	...	...	...	...	...
Slovenia	29.9	...	5.0	...	1.6	2.8	4.0	5.6	...	...	...	2.7	...
Spain	...	...	...	...	...	...	...	...	...	...	...	...	...
Sweden	46.4	...	...	...	11.1	2.3	3.6	7.9	...	...	...	11.2	...
Switzerland	52.7	9.1	3.7	2.6	2.3	1.4	3.0	10.1	...	...	...	18.9	9.5
Turkey	...	...	...	...	...	...	...	...	...	...	...	...	...
Ukraine	...	...	...	...	...	...	...	...	...	...	...	...	...
UK: England & Wales	107.7	6.2	6.4	6.3	1.2	5.0	12.5	27.5	1.9	18.4	...	16.5	4.5
UK: Northern Ireland	51.3	2.4	8.7	...	4.6	3.6	5.8	5.8	0.9	3.1	...	3.6	...
UK: Scotland	109.4	...	16.2	13.7	19.5	2.8	14.1	23.2	3.0	9.5	...	15.4	14.8
Mean	125	4	14	7	6	4	13	31	2	9	1	11	9
Median	85	2	12	8	5	3	9	17	1	6	1	9	5
Minimum	22	1	2	0	1	1	1	2	0	0	1	0	2
Maximum	692	9	43	14	20	15	59	140	6	39	1	39	36

Table 4.2.3.2: Convicted prison population percentage of Females, by offence

	Criminal offences: Total	Traffic offences	Intentional homicide: Total	Intentional homicide Completed	Assault	Rape	Robbery	Theft: Total	Theft: Theft of a motor vehicle	Theft: Burglary: Total	Theft: Burglary: Domestic Burglary	Drug offences: Total	Drug offences: Drug trafficking
	P43TCW99	P43TTW99	P43HOW99	P43HCW99	P43ASW99	P43RAW99	P43ROW99	P43THW99	P43TVW99	P43BUW99	P43BDW99	P43DRW99	P43DTW99
Albania	...	...	...	...	...	...	...	...	...	...	...	...	...
Armenia	...	...	...	...	...	...	...	...	...	...	...	...	...
Austria	...	...	...	...	...	...	...	...	...	...	...	...	...
Belgium	...	...	...	...	...	...	...	...	...	...	...	...	...
Bulgaria	2.9	2.3	4.1	4.3	...	0.0	3.0	2.5	...	...	...	...	...
Croatia	7.0	1.3	4.4	3.5	3.4	1.3	4.5	3.0	0.0	3.3	...	8.4	9.1
Cyprus	4.4	0.0	0.0	0.0	0.0	0.0	0.0	0.0	0.0	0.0	0.0	6.3	14.3
Czech Republic	3.0	...	6.1	...	2.9	0.2	2.7	3.5	...	...	...	6.0	7.5
Denmark	...	...	...	...	...	...	...	...	...	...	...	...	...
Estonia	...	...	5.5	...	1.1	...	4.2	2.6	...	...	...	5.0	...
Finland	4.1	1.9	8.0	...	2.0	...	3.1	1.1	...	...	...	3.2	...
France	3.2	...	6.0	...	4.3	1.7	2.5	2.4	...	...	...	3.6	6.5
Georgia	1.6	...	1.0	...	4.9	0.0	2.2	1.7	...	...	...	5.1	5.6
Germany	3.9	1.3	4.6	...	2.3	0.4	2.2	4.9	...	1.0	...	...	...
Greece	...	...	...	...	...	...	...	...	...	...	...	...	...
Hungary	...	...	...	...	...	...	...	...	...	...	...	...	...
Ireland	...	...	...	...	...	...	...	...	...	...	...	...	...
Italy	...	...	...	...	...	...	...	...	...	...	...	...	...
Latvia	...	...	...	...	...	...	...	...	...	...	...	...	...
Lithuania	4.6	...	7.8	...	7.2	0.4	2.7	4.4	...	...	...	3.6	...
Luxembourg	...	...	...	...	...	...	...	...	...	...	...	...	...

Correctional statistics

	Criminal offences: Total	Traffic offences	Intentional homicide: Total	Intentional homicide: Completed	Assault	Rape	Robbery	Theft: Total	Theft: Theft of a motor vehicle	Theft: Burglary: Total	Theft: Burglary: Domestic Burglary	Drug offences: Total	Drug offences: Drug trafficking
	P43TCW99	P43TTW99	P43HOW99	P43HCW99	P43ASW99	P43RAW99	P43ROW99	P43THW99	P43TVW99	P43BUW99	P43BDW99	P43DRW99	P43DTW99
Malta	3.2	...	0.0	...	0.0	...	...	2.0	...	...	...	4.5	...
Moldova	3.9	...	5.9	...	0.7	0.2	3.5	4.7	...	10.6	...	...	...
Netherlands	7.4	...	...	...	...	...	...	...	...	...	...	...	...
Norway	5.9	6.1	4.2	4.6	...	...	1.6	4.2	11.1	2.1	...	8.8	8.9
Poland	2.3	...	8.0	...	...	0.2	2.0	...	...	0.7	...	...	...
Portugal	8.9	...	...	4.9	8.8	0.0	1.6	2.0	...	...	...	16.0	16.9
Romania	...	...	...	...	...	...	...	...	...	...	...	...	...
Russia	...	...	...	...	...	...	...	...	...	...	...	...	...
Slovakia	...	...	...	...	...	...	...	...	...	...	...	...	...
Slovenia	...	...	...	...	...	...	...	...	...	...	...	...	...
Spain	...	...	...	...	...	...	...	...	...	...	...	...	...
Sweden	...	...	...	...	...	...	...	...	...	...	...	6.7	7.3
Switzerland	6.5	1.7	3.4	3.2	2.4	1.0	2.3	4.0	...	...	...	...	...
Turkey	...	...	...	...	...	...	...	...	...	...	...	...	...
Ukraine	...	...	...	...	...	...	...	...	...	...	...	...	...
UK: England & Wales	4.9	0.9	3.6	3.7	7.2	0.2	2.5	4.9	0.2	1.7	...	10.8	21.1
UK: Northern Ireland	1.1	0.0	1.4	...	0.0	0.0	0.0	2.1	0.0	0.0	...	3.4	...
UK: Scotland	3.8	...	3.0	2.5	2.5	0.0	2.2	5.1	0.0	0.6	...	6.7	5.9
Mean	4	2	4	3	3	0	2	3	2	2	0	7	10
Median	4	1	4	4	2	0	2	3	0	1	0	6	8
Minimum	1	0	0	0	0	0	0	0	0	0	0	3	6
Maximum	9	6	8	5	9	2	4	5	11	11	0	16	21

Table 4.2.3.3: Convicted prison population percentage of Minors, by offence

	Criminal offences: Total	Traffic offences	Intentional homicide: Total	Intentional homicide: Completed	Assault	Rape	Robbery	Theft: Total	Theft: Theft of a motor vehicle	Theft: Burglary: Total	Theft: Burglary: Domestic Burglary	Drug offences: Total	Drug offences: Drug trafficking
	P43TCM99	P43TTM99	P43HOM99	P43HCM99	P43ASM99	P43RAM99	P43ROM99	P43THM99	P43TVM99	P43BUM99	P43BDM99	P43DRM99	P43DTM99
Albania	...	...	...	...	...	...	...	...	...	...	...	...	...
Armenia	...	...	...	...	...	...	...	...	...	...	...	...	...
Austria	...	...	...	...	...	...	...	...	...	...	...	...	...
Belgium	...	...	...	...	...	...	...	...	...	...	...	...	...
Bulgaria	0.7	0.0	0.0	0.0	...	0.2	1.1	1.3	...	...	...	...	...
Croatia	4.5	0.0	2.0	2.3	3.4	1.9	3.2	7.1	7.1	3.0	...	0.2	0.0
Cyprus	0.0	0.0	0.0	0.0	0.0	0.0	0.0	0.0	0.0	0.0	0.0	0.0	0.0
Czech Republic	0.7	...	1.3	...	0.7	0.9	1.9	0.7	...	...	...	0.9	1.9
Denmark	...	...	...	...	...	...	...	...	...	...	...	...	...
Estonia	...	...	...	...	...	...	...	...	...	...	...	...	...
Finland	3.0	2.6	1.4	...	1.0	3.9	5.2	4.9	...	...	...	3.9	...
France	...	...	...	...	...	...	...	...	...	...	...	...	...
Georgia	0.2	...	0.3	...	0.4	3.4	2.0	0.4	0.7	...	...	0.1	...
Germany	1.5	0.2	0.6	...	3.2	0.9	3.5	2.4	...	3.5	...	0.4	0.1
Greece	...	...	...	...	...	...	...	...	...	...	...	...	...
Hungary	...	...	...	...	...	...	...	...	...	...	...	...	...
Ireland	...	...	...	...	...	...	...	...	...	...	...	...	...
Italy	...	...	...	...	...	...	...	...	...	...	...	...	...
Latvia	...	...	...	...	...	...	...	...	...	...	...	...	...
Lithuania	1.6	...	0.3	...	0.9	1.3	2.5	1.8	...	...	...	0.4	...
Luxembourg	...	...	...	...	...	...	...	...	...	...	...	...	...

Correctional statistics

	Criminal offences: Total	Traffic offences	Intentional homicide: Total	Intentional homicide: Completed	Assault	Rape	Robbery	Theft: Total	Theft: Theft of a motor vehicle	Theft: Burglary: Total	Theft: Burglary: Domestic Burglary	Drug offences: Total	Drug offences: Drug trafficking
	P43TCM99	P43TTM99	P43HOM99	P43HCM99	P43ASM99	P43RAM99	P43ROM99	P43THM99	P43TVM99	P43BUM99	P43BDM99	P43DRM99	P43DTM99
Malta	1.9	..	..	..	..	..	..	2.0	..	..	..	3.0	..
Moldova	1.2	..	1.0	..	0.7	3.4	2.2	1.2	..	0.6	..	..	..
Netherlands	11.2	..	..	..	..	..	..	..	..	..	..	..	..
Norway	0.2	..	..	..	..	..	..	..	..	..	..	..	..
Poland	..	..	..	..	..	..	..	..	..	..	..	..	..
Portugal	2.8	..	..	1.8	1.3	3.2	6.4	3.7	..	..	..	1.7	1.8
Romania	..	..	..	..	..	..	..	..	..	..	..	..	..
Russia	..	..	..	..	..	..	..	..	..	..	..	..	..
Slovakia	..	..	..	..	..	..	..	..	..	..	..	..	..
Slovenia	..	..	..	..	..	..	..	..	..	..	..	..	..
Spain	..	..	..	..	..	..	..	..	..	..	..	..	..
Sweden	..	..	..	..	..	..	..	..	..	..	..	..	..
Switzerland	..	..	..	..	..	..	..	..	..	..	..	..	..
Turkey	..	..	..	..	..	..	..	..	..	..	..	..	..
Ukraine	..	..	..	..	..	..	..	..	..	..	..	..	..
UK: England & Wales	3.5	6.1	0.3	0.3	4.7	1.3	6.8	5.8	15.6	5.0	..	0.6	0.0
UK: Northern Ireland	..	..	..	..	..	..	..	..	..	..	..	..	..
UK: Scotland	3.9	..	1.8	1.4	5.5	0.7	2.6	8	14.6	7.5	..	0.5	0.5
Mean	2	1	1	1	2	2	3	3	8	3	0	1	1
Median	2	0	1	1	1	1	3	2	7	3	0	0	0
Minimum	0	0	0	0	0	0	0	0	0	0	0	0	0
Maximum	11	6	2	2	6	4	7	8	16	7	0	4	2

Table 4.2.3.4: Convicted prison population percentage of Aliens, by offence

	Criminal offences: Total	Traffic offences	Intentional homicide: Total	Intentional homicide Completed	Assault	Rape	Robbery	Theft: Total	Theft: Theft of a motor vehicle	Theft: Burglary: Total	Theft: Burglary: Domestic Burglary	Drug offences: Total	Drug offences: Drug trafficking
	P43TCA99	P43TTA99	P43HOA99	P43HCA99	P43ASA99	P43RAA99	P43ROA99	P43THA99	P43TVA99	P43BUA99	P43BDA99	P43DRA99	P43DTA99
Albania	...	...	...	...	...	...	...	...	...	...	...	...	...
Armenia	...	...	...	...	...	...	...	...	...	...	...	...	...
Austria	...	...	...	...	...	...	...	...	...	...	...	...	...
Belgium	...	...	...	...	...	...	...	...	...	...	...	...	...
Bulgaria	0.7	0.0	0.7	0.7	...	0.0	1.1	0.3	...	...	...	...	...
Croatia	10.7	3.2	1.2	0.9	1.7	2.6	1.6	9.0	0.0	5.9	...	5.3	6.8
Cyprus	22.2	0.0	23.8	0.0	75.0	0.0	50.0	5.0	0.0	30	30.0	46.9	71.4
Czech Republic	...	...	...	...	...	...	...	...	...	...	...	...	...
Denmark	...	...	...	...	...	...	...	...	...	...	...	...	...
Estonia	...	...	...	...	...	...	...	...	...	...	...	...	...
Finland	3.3	1.0	2.3	...	1.0	3.9	2.6	1.4	...	...	...	11.9	...
France	...	...	...	...	...	...	...	...	...	...	...	...	...
Georgia	1.0	...	1.3	...	4.0	2.2	3.4	0.7	...	...	...	1.1	3.0
Germany	23.4	...	...	...	...	...	...	...	...	...	...	...	...
Greece	...	...	...	...	...	...	...	...	...	...	...	...	...
Hungary	...	...	...	...	...	...	...	...	...	...	...	...	...
Ireland	...	...	...	...	...	...	...	...	...	...	...	...	...
Italy	...	...	...	...	...	...	...	...	...	...	...	...	...
Latvia	...	...	...	...	...	...	...	...	...	...	...	...	...
Lithuania	1.2	...	...	...	...	...	...	...	...	...	...	...	...
Luxembourg	...	...	...	...	...	...	...	...	...	...	...	...	...

Correctional statistics

	Criminal offences: Total	Traffic offences	Intentional homicide: Total	Intentional homicide: Completed	Assault	Rape	Robbery	Theft: Total	Theft: Theft of a motor vehicle	Theft: Burglary: Total	Theft: Burglary: Domestic Burglary	Drug offences: Total	Drug offences: Drug trafficking
	P43TCA99	P43TTA99	P43HOA99	P43HCA99	P43ASA99	P43RAA99	P43ROA99	P43THA99	P43TVA99	P43BUA99	P43BDA99	P43DRA99	P43DTA99
Malta	18.4	..	22.7	..	..	20.0	..	2.0	..	..	..	28.4	..
Moldova	..	..	..	..	..	..	..	..	..	..	..	..	..
Netherlands	..	..	..	..	..	..	..	..	..	..	..	..	..
Norway	..	..	..	..	..	..	..	..	..	..	..	..	..
Poland	..	..	..	..	..	..	..	..	..	..	..	..	..
Portugal	..	..	..	..	..	..	..	..	..	..	..	..	..
Romania	..	..	..	..	..	..	..	..	..	..	..	..	..
Russia	..	..	..	..	..	..	..	..	..	..	..	..	..
Slovakia	..	..	..	..	..	..	..	..	..	..	..	..	..
Slovenia	..	..	..	..	..	..	..	..	..	..	..	..	..
Spain	..	..	..	..	..	..	..	..	..	..	..	..	..
Sweden	..	..	..	..	..	..	..	..	..	..	..	..	..
Switzerland	61.9	40.6	59.2	53.2	50.3	49.0	56.0	47.2	..	..	..	65.5	88.2
Turkey	..	..	..	..	..	..	..	..	..	..	..	..	..
Ukraine	..	..	..	..	..	..	..	..	..	..	..	..	47.4
UK: England & Wales	..	..	..	..	..	..	..	..	..	..	..	..	..
UK: Northern Ireland	..	..	1.5	1.5	1.5	2.1	1	1.1	0.6	0.8	..	3.0	3.0
UK: Scotland	2.1	..											
Mean	14	9	14	11	22	10	17	8	0	12	30	23	37
Median	7	1	2	1	3	2	3	2	0	6	30	12	27
Minimum	1	0	1	0	1	0	1	0	0	1	30	1	3
Maximum	62	41	59	53	75	49	56	47	1	30	30	65	88

Comments on tables 4.2.3.1 to 4.2.3.4

Croatia: The data refers to 31 December 1999.

Czech Republic: The data is at 31 December 2000 and shows the number of offences committed by convicted persons, i.e. the counting unit is not a person but an offence.

Estonia: Data refers to 1 January 2000.

"Robbery" includes §141 only (stealing from a person with force or threat of force that endangered life or health). "Unconcealed theft" (§140 – stealing from a person with the use of threat or minor violence) is excluded.

"Theft/Total" includes §139 ("Concealed theft", incl. theft of a motor vehicle) and §140 ("Unconcealed theft").

Finland: "Minors" in Table 4.2.3.3 are persons below 21 years of age, i.e. ages 15-20. The figure for "traffic offences" stands for drink driving, other serious traffic offences are not reported separately. The figure for "rape" also comprises other sexual offences. However, these cases are mostly rapes.

France: Data for metropolitan France

The nomenclature for the offences used in prison statistics is less detailed than that for convictions.
Homicide = attempted and completed homicide, excluding assault leading to death;
Assault = assault and bodily injury and assault against children;
Rape = rape and sexual offences;
Theft (total) = aggravated theft (including robbery) and simple theft;
Drugs = misuse of controlled drugs (traffic and use);

Germany: Convicted prison population by offence on 31 March 2000.

Tables do not include persons committed to a psychiatric hospital or an institution for withdrawal [drug] treatment.

Data refers to 31 March 2000.

Intentional homicide: The definition given in the definitions section could not be met here as Assault leading to death could not be included.

Assault: The definition given in the definitions section could not be met here: Assault leading to death had to be included.

Rape: The definition of rape changed in 1998; for details see definitions section. Moreover, the figures given include sexual assault as well as some other forms of sexual offences.

Drug trafficking: The definition of drug trafficking given in the definitions section cannot be met exactly as far as correctional statistics are concerned. Therefore, figures reported here are slightly higher than they would have been if the definition could be met.

Lithuania: Numbers of prison population are at 31 December.

The figures of assault include only intentional grave body injury or infection (Art. 111 of Penal Code).

Malta: Total includes 10 "other cases" of which 1 woman and 3 aliens.

Netherlands: The figures refer not only to the convicted prisoners but also to the pre-trial detainees.

The reference date is 30 September.

The data for Traffic offences and Drug offences are rough estimates.

Norway: Criminal Offences, of which: Traffic offences (defined as criminal): Total number of traffic misdemeanours.

Assault and theft of which Domestic burglary: Included in total, but figures are not available at this level.

Robbery: Including all kinds of blackmail and robbery (impossible to select certain categories).

Data refers to 1 January 1998.

The "total" includes the following types of sanctions: "Sentence to imprisonment", "Security detention" and "Serving sentence in default of paying a fine" (*excluding* custody).
Poland: Convicted prison population by offence:
Data at 31 December and also include pre-trial detainees.
"Intentional homicide" excludes infanticide, euthanasia and assault leading to death.
"Rape" excludes sexual intercourse with a minor without force and other forms of sexual assault.
"Robbery" excludes theft immediately followed by violence.
"Burglary" – numbers contain (following the Polish Penal Code) all thefts by entering and breaking from buildings, other premises, theft from cars, etc. = thefts by burglary. In 1995-1998 numbers also contain thefts under aggravating circumstances (Art. 208 Penal Code of 1969).
Sweden: The definitions of "Assault" and "Rape" deviate from the standard definitions.
Assault = all violent offences (excluding robbery).
Rape = all sexual offences.
UK: England & Wales: Data at 30 June 1999.
"Traffic Offences" taken to mean "Taking and Driving Away", "In charge or Driving while under the influence of Drink or Drugs" and "Other Motoring Offences".
"Intentional Homicide" is taken to mean murder and includes all prisoners who have been tried and convicted of murder. "Completed" is taken to mean prisoners who have been convicted as well as sentenced (as murder attracts a mandatory life sentence in England & Wales).
"Aggravated Theft" has been included under "Aggravated Burglary".
The total under "Theft" includes the offences recorded as "Theft" and "Burglary".
"Theft of a Motor Vehicle" has been taken to mean "Taking and Driving Away".
"Drug Trafficking" has been taken to mean "Unlawful Import/Export".
UK: Northern Ireland: Aliens are not considered to be sentenced prisoners as they are held under the Immigration Act. Age of offender is at time of sentence.
Robbery includes hi-jacking.
UK: Scotland: Data is as at 30 June 1999.
Minors are defined as all those under 18.

Table 4.2.4.1: Persons under the supervision or care of an agent of the correctional services per 100 000 population: STOCK – Total

	1995 R44ST95	1996 R44ST96	1997 R44ST97	1998 R44ST98	1999 R44ST99	2000 R44ST00	% change 1995-2000
Albania	...	...	...	...	...	...	...
Armenia	...	...	...	...	...	...	...
Austria	71.7	75.7	80.0	77.1	75.1	75.8	6
Belgium	...	...	...	...	...	...	...
Bulgaria	...	...	...	...	...	...	...
Croatia	...	...	...	...	...	...	...
Cyprus	8.3	7.7	8.1	11.6	10.2	8.4	1
Czech Republic	...	...	...	...	...	...	...
Denmark	102.2	100.0	104.5	107.9	112.0	138.0	35
Estonia	...	...	...	143.9	353.7	444.0	...
Finland	63.5	61.8	57.7	55.8	51.7	52.6	-17
France	191.4	192.4	212.5	225.2	232.2	240.1	25
Georgia	...	...	...	...	...	...	...
Germany	200.4	209.5	213.0	...	...	...	...
Greece	...	...	...	...	...	...	...
Hungary	37.3	39.9	45.0	49.1	51.4	52.1	39
Ireland	...	...	...	...	...	...	...
Italy	...	...	...	...	...	...	...
Latvia	...	...	...	...	...	...	...
Lithuania	353.5	382.0	385.8	447.7	457.0	386.4	9
Luxembourg	...	...	...	...	...	...	...
Malta	...	...	...	...	...	...	...
Moldova	...	...	...	...	...	...	...
Netherlands	...	...	...	...	...	...	...
Norway	16.7	19.7	34.6	35.8	38.1	39.6	137
Poland	351.5	393.1	400.8	402.3	460.9	516.3	47
Portugal	35.6	35.2	38.9	42.1	42.0	48.5	36
Romania	...	...	...	...	...	...	...
Russia	...	...	...	...	...	...	...
Slovakia	...	...	...	...	...	...	...
Slovenia	...	...	...	...	...	...	...
Spain	...	...	...	...	...	...	...
Sweden	142.6	137.5	128.9	126.1	128.6	129.7	-9
Switzerland	...	...	...	...	64.4	64.2	...
Turkey	...	...	...	...	...	...	...
Ukraine	...	...	...	...	...	...	...
UK: England & Wales	141.9	139.7	141.3	149.7	165.2	172.0	21
UK: Northern Ireland	...	...	...	...	...	...	...
UK: Scotland	...	...	...	...	...	...	...
Mean	132	138	142	144	160	169	
Median	102	100	105	108	94	103	
Minimum	8	8	8	12	10	8	
Maximum	354	393	401	448	461	516	

Table 4.2.4.2: Persons under the supervision or care of an agent of the correctional services: % of Suspended sentence (with supervision) in the total STOCK

	1995 P44SS95	1996 P44SS96	1997 P44SS97	1998 P44SS98	1999 P44SS99	2000 P44SS00	% change 1995-2000
Albania	...	...	...	...	...	...	...
Armenia	...	...	...	...	...	...	...
Austria	55.6	56.5	58.0	61.0	63.3	64.3	16
Belgium	...	...	...	...	...	...	...
Bulgaria	...	...	...	...	...	...	...
Croatia	...	...	...	...	...	...	...
Cyprus	...	...	...	...	...	...	...
Czech Republic	...	...	...	...	...	...	...
Denmark	27.5	26.7	27.7	26.4	25.7	20.7	-25
Estonia	...	...	...	...	...	...	...
Finland	64.2	63.3	60.8	58.5	56.3	54.7	-15
France	77.2	75.5	75.9	77.3	78.1	78.0	1
Georgia	...	...	...	...	...	...	...
Germany	63.1	63.4	63.8	...	...	...	...
Greece	...	...	...	...	...	...	...
Hungary	43.8	49.0	61.5	61.8	62.1	52.8	21
Ireland	...	...	...	...	...	...	...
Italy	...	...	...	...	...	...	...
Latvia	...	...	...	...	...	...	...
Lithuania	80.9	75.9	79.6	82.4	82.0	81.0	0
Luxembourg	...	...	...	...	...	...	...
Malta	...	...	...	...	...	...	...
Moldova	...	...	...	...	...	...	...
Netherlands	...	...	...	...	...	...	...
Norway	45.5	39.5	62.8	65.4	64.7	62.0	36
Poland	75.4	75.8	80.0	83.1	84.3	83.9	11
Portugal	21.3	25.2	20.8	25.5	21.1	20.0	-6
Romania	...	...	...	...	...	...	...
Russia	...	...	...	...	...	...	...
Slovakia	...	...	...	...	...	...	...
Slovenia	...	...	...	...	...	...	...
Spain	...	...	...	...	...	...	...
Sweden	...	...	...	...	1.4	2.9	...
Switzerland	...	...	...	...	...	...	...
Turkey	...	...	...	...	...	...	...
Ukraine	...	...	...	...	...	...	...
UK: England & Wales	0.7	0.7	0.8	1.0	0.9	0.9	30
UK: Northern Ireland	...	...	...	...	...	...	...
UK: Scotland	...	...	...	...	...	...	...
Mean	50	50	54	54	49	47	
Median	56	57	61	61	62	55	
Minimum	1	1	1	1	1	1	
Maximum	81	76	80	83	84	84	

Table 4.2.4.3: Persons under the supervision or care of an agent of the correctional services: % of Probation in the total STOCK

	1995 P44SP95	1996 P44SP96	1997 P44SP97	1998 P44SP98	1999 P44SP99	2000 P44SP00	% change 1995-2000
Albania	...	...	...	...	...	...	...
Armenia	...	...	...	...	...	...	...
Austria	24.9	25.9	24.7	19.7	18.2	17.4	-30
Belgium	...	...	...	...	...	...	...
Bulgaria	...	...	...	...	...	...	...
Croatia	...	...	...	...	...	...	...
Cyprus	100.0	100.0	100.0	100.0	100.0	100.0	0
Czech Republic	...	...	...	...	...	...	...
Denmark	...	...	...	...	...	...	...
Estonia	...	...	...	81.1	92.6	94.2	...
Finland	...	...	...	...	...	...	...
France	...	...	...	...	...	...	...
Georgia	...	...	...	...	...	...	...
Germany	2.2	2.2	2.4	...	...	...	...
Greece	...	...	...	...	...	...	...
Hungary	23.3	18.0	13.6	12.5	9.8	10.8	-54
Ireland	...	...	...	...	...	...	...
Italy	...	...	...	...	...	...	...
Latvia	...	...	...	...	...	...	...
Lithuania	...	...	...	...	...	...	...
Luxembourg	...	...	...	...	...	...	...
Malta	...	...	...	...	...	...	...
Moldova	...	...	...	...	...	...	...
Netherlands	...	...	...	...	...	...	...
Norway	...	...	...	...	...	...	...
Poland	...	...	...	...	...	...	...
Portugal	4.1	3.2	9.7	7.9	14.3	15.5	280
Romania	...	...	...	...	...	...	...
Russia	...	...	...	...	...	...	...
Slovakia	...	...	...	...	...	...	...
Slovenia	...	...	...	...	...	...	...
Spain	...	...	...	...	...	...	...
Sweden	66.5	65.4	63.9	64.0	61.6	60.3	-9
Switzerland	...	...	...	...	...	...	...
Turkey	...	...	...	...	...	...	...
Ukraine	...	...	...	...	...	...	...
UK: England & Wales	73.8	73.9	73.3	72.3	70.3	67.4	-9
UK: Northern Ireland	...	...	...	...	...	...	...
UK: Scotland	...	...	...	...	...	...	...
Mean	42	41	41	51	52	52	
Median	25	26	25	64	62	60	
Minimum	2	2	2	8	10	11	
Maximum	100	100	100	100	100	100	

Table 4.2.4.4: Persons under the supervision or care of an agent of the correctional services: % of Parole or conditional release (with supervision) in the total STOCK

	1995 P44SC95	1996 P44SC96	1997 P44SC97	1998 P44SC98	1999 P44SC99	2000 P44SC00	% change 1995-2000
Albania	...	...	...	...	...	...	...
Armenia	...	...	...	...	...	...	...
Austria	19.6	17.5	17.3	19.3	18.5	18.3	-6
Belgium	...	...	...	...	...	...	...
Bulgaria	...	...	...	...	...	...	...
Croatia	...	...	...	...	...	...	...
Cyprus	...	...	...	...	...	...	...
Czech Republic	...	...	...	...	...	...	...
Denmark	23.1	20.9	19.5	19.6	18.9	15.0	-35
Estonia	...	...	...	18.9	7.4	5.8	...
Finland	35.8	36.7	39.2	41.5	43.7	45.3	27
France	4.4	4.4	4.2	3.5	3.3	3.3	-25
Georgia	...	...	...	...	...	...	...
Germany	34.8	34.4	33.8	...	...	...	...
Greece	...	...	...	...	...	...	...
Hungary	30.8	29.2	24.9	25.5	28.1	36.4	18
Ireland	...	...	...	...	...	...	...
Italy	...	...	...	...	...	...	...
Latvia	...	...	...	...	...	...	...
Lithuania	18.8	24.1	20.4	17.6	18.0	19.0	1
Luxembourg	...	...	...	...	...	...	...
Malta	...	...	...	...	...	...	...
Moldova	...	...	...	...	...	...	...
Netherlands	...	...	...	...	...	...	...
Norway	54.5	60.5	37.2	34.6	35.3	38.0	-30
Poland	24.6	24.2	20.0	16.9	15.7	16.1	-35
Portugal	74.6	71.6	69.5	66.6	64.6	64.5	-14
Romania	...	...	...	...	...	...	...
Russia	...	...	...	...	...	...	...
Slovakia	...	...	...	...	...	...	...
Slovenia	...	...	...	...	...	...	...
Spain	...	...	...	...	...	...	...
Sweden	33.5	34.6	36.1	36.0	37.0	36.8	10
Switzerland	...	...	...	...	...	...	...
Turkey	...	...	...	...	...	...	...
Ukraine	...	...	...	...	...	...	...
UK: England & Wales	25.5	25.4	25.7	26.8	28.9	31.8	24
UK: Northern Ireland	...	...	...	...	...	...	...
UK: Scotland	...	...	...	...	...	...	...
Mean	32	32	29	27	27	28	
Median	28	27	25	23	23	25	
Minimum	4	4	4	4	3	3	
Maximum	75	72	69	67	65	64	

Comments on tables 4.2.4.1 to 4.2.4.4
Austria: Supervision (connected with suspended sentence) in any case is carried out by probation officers.
"Probation" (not based on sentence) includes: voluntary probation; "provisional" probation before conviction, suggested by the examining magistrate; supervision by probation officer accepted as prerequisite for diversion according to drug law, juvenile court law and penal procedure law (after 1999).
"Total" figures include all the Austrian provinces; with regard to Styria figures on suspended sentence, probation and conditional release before 1999 are only based on estimates.
Figures for 1995/1996 differ from those reported for European Sourcebook 1999 as data on Styria was not included in the old questionnaire.
Cyprus: Probation is undertaken only in cases of suspended sentence (with supervision).
Estonia: Correctional service (supervision) was introduced in 1998; therefore data for 1998 include the period: 1 May–31 December 1998.
Finland: Suspended sentence (with supervision).
Parole or conditional release (with supervision).
Probation (does not exist).
France: Data covers metropolitan and overseas territories.
The totals in table 4.2.4.1 comprise the total convicted that correspond to the definitions explained in paragraph 4.1.4. It includes in particular the convicted that serve community service under the responsibility and supervision of probation services (figure of table 4.2.6.1 further down). For this reason the total of table 4.2.4.1 is not the sum of figure from tables 4.2.4.2 to 4.2.4.4.
The counting unit is the measures (sanctions imposed in the community). A person can be given more than one measure/sanction. The process to distinguish between types of measures "under care" is as follows. The number of persons serving their sentence in the community are known but also include the persons that have not been convicted (judiciary pre-trial monitoring), namely on 1 January 1995: 102 254, 1996: 105 222, 1997: 117 061, 1998: 122 959, 1999: 131 367, 2000: 135 020.
Germany: Stock data refers to 31 December.
Data refers to the former West Germany only; data for East Berlin are included. No data available for Hamburg.
No data available for 1998-2000.
Probation: All cases in which a juvenile court made use of section 27 Act on Juvenile Courts are counted.
Lithuania: Figures are at the end of the year – e.g. the data for 2000 are at 1 January 2001. Available numbers on 1 September are provided in the brackets.
Suspended sentence (with supervision) refers to suspension under certain conditions after conviction (Art. 47^1 of Penal Code) – see Comments on Table 3.2.1
Conditional release (with supervision) refers to early conditional release from the imprisonment institution under certain conditions (Art. 54^2).
Probation will be introduced with the new Penal Code on 1 January in 2003.
Norway: There is no "probation" but two other forms of supervision exist:
a) Security sentence which normally is served initially in prison followed by a period of supervision, with the possibility of recall. (May also be served entirely in the community).
   Stock 1 September 2000: 127   Flow 1 September 2000: 36
b) Waiver of prosecution. The prosecuting authority may elect not to prefer an indictment on condition that the offender accepts a period of supervision.
   Stock 1 September 2000: 4   Flow 1 September 2000: 1

Poland: Stock data at 31 December.

Suspended sentence – with supervision by court probation officer.

Conditional release – with supervision by court probation officer. Conditional release is granted by the sanctions enforcement court.

Supervision by a court probation officer is mandatory as far as recidivists, young offenders, and those released from serving life sentence are concerned.

Romania: The Penal legislation does not regulate suspended sentence or parole.

Conditional release does not involve the supervision of the released prisoners.

The number of the prisoners conditionally released was 26 556 in 1995; 27 694 in 1996; 26 939 in 1997; 23 646 in 1998; 29 819 in 1999 and 28 864 in 2000.

Sweden: Data refers to 1 October not 1 September.

Switzerland: The total Stock refers to persons who have obligations imposed on them. Probation does not exist in Switzerland.

UK: England & Wales: The data are figures on 31 December of the preceding year.

Each person is counted only once in the total even if they were subject to several types of supervision at the year-end.

Combination orders, introduced in October 1992 are partly Probation Orders and partly Community Service Orders. These are included in "Other Non-Custodial Sentences".

UK: Scotland: Data relates to financial years (i.e. 1999 = 1 April 1999 to 31 March 2000). Stock data are not available.

Suspended sentence = not applicable.

Parole figures include those released on parole or life licence but exclude prisoners released on licence (not parole) at two thirds point of sentence who are also subject to supervision (source: Parole Board Scotland).

Table 4.2.5.1: Persons under the supervision or care of an agent of the correctional services per 100 000 population: FLOW – Total

	1995 R44FT95	1996 R44FT96	1997 R44FT97	1998 R44FT98	1999 R44FT99	2000 R44FT00	% change 1995-2000
Albania	...	...	...	...	...	...	...
Armenia	...	...	...	...	...	...	...
Austria	32.3	39.5	39.4	35.0	30.7	29.5	-9
Belgium	...	...	...	...	...	...	...
Bulgaria	...	...	...	...	...	...	...
Croatia	...	...	...	...	...	...	...
Cyprus	3.0	3.8	3.6	6.0	3.8	3.0	1
Czech Republic	...	...	...	...	...	...	...
Denmark	...	...	...	...	...	...	...
Estonia	...	...	...	13.3	96.7	92.6	...
Finland	108.4	102.7	99.2	97.0	92.5	95.3	-12
France	...	...	...	...	...	...	...
Georgia	...	...	...	...	...	...	...
Germany	65.9	70.1	73.3	...	...	...	...
Greece	...	...	...	...	...	...	...
Hungary	...	...	...	...	...	...	...
Ireland	...	...	...	...	...	...	...
Italy	20.7	23.8	24.5	27.3	22.5	...	...
Latvia	...	...	...	...	...	...	...
Lithuania	308.9	305.5	318.7	375.0	366.5	315.1	2
Luxembourg	...	...	...	...	...	...	...
Malta	...	...	...	...	...	...	...
Moldova	...	...	...	...	...	...	...
Netherlands	...	...	...	...	...	...	...
Norway	34.9	43.4	49.3	49.2	52.1	55.7	60
Poland	...	...	...	...	...	...	...
Portugal	21.6	19.1	25.7	26.0	27.5	26.6	23
Romania	...	...	...	...	...	...	...
Russia	...	...	...	...	...	...	...
Slovakia	...	...	...	...	...	...	...
Slovenia	...	...	...	...	...	...	...
Spain	...	...	...	...	...	...	...
Sweden	144.3	134.8	126.7	131.8	135.7	131.5	-9
Switzerland	...	...	...	...	28.1	29.9	...
Turkey	...	...	...	...	...	...	...
Ukraine	...	...	...	...	...	...	...
UK: England & Wales	165.4	172.7	182.1	195.1	197.8	186.4	13
UK: Northern Ireland	...	...	...	...	...	...	...
UK: Scotland	...	108.4	112.8	122.2	120.3	...	...
Mean	91	93	96	98	98	97	
Median	50	70	73	49	72	74	
Minimum	3	4	4	6	4	3	
Maximum	309	306	319	375	367	315	

Table 4.2.5.2: Persons under the supervision or care of an agent of the correctional services: % of Suspended sentence (with supervision) in the total FLOW

	1995 P45FS95	1996 P45FS96	1997 P45FS97	1998 P45FS98	1999 P45FS99	2000 P45FS00	% change 1995-2000
Albania	...	...	...	...	...	...	...
Armenia	...	...	...	...	...	...	...
Austria	41.9	43.4	48.4	56.5	50.6	59.6	42
Belgium	...	...	...	...	...	...	...
Bulgaria	...	...	...	...	...	...	...
Croatia	...	...	...	...	...	...	...
Cyprus	...	...	...	...	...	...	...
Czech Republic	...	...	...	...	...	...	...
Denmark	...	...	...	...	...	...	...
Estonia	...	...	...	...	...	...	...
Finland	61.3	61.8	60.8	57.1	54.3	55.2	-10
France	...	...	...	...	...	...	...
Georgia	...	...	...	...	...	...	...
Germany	...	...	...	...	...	...	...
Greece	...	...	...	...	...	...	...
Hungary	...	...	...	...	...	...	...
Ireland	...	...	...	...	...	...	...
Italy	...	...	...	...	...	...	...
Latvia	...	...	...	...	...	...	...
Lithuania	75.9	63.9	74.0	76.6	76.0	69.6	-8
Luxembourg	...	...	...	...	...	...	...
Malta	...	...	...	...	...	...	...
Moldova	...	...	...	...	...	...	...
Netherlands	...	...	...	...	...	...	...
Norway	43.3	43.5	44.7	45.3	44.5	42.5	-2
Poland	...	...	...	...	...	...	...
Portugal	24.6	27.3	15.0	20.7	17.7	17.0	-31
Romania	...	...	...	...	...	...	...
Russia	...	...	...	...	...	...	...
Slovakia	...	...	...	...	...	...	...
Slovenia	...	...	...	...	...	...	...
Spain	...	...	...	...	...	...	...
Sweden	...	...	...	...	...	...	...
Switzerland	...	...	...	...	10.8	13.7	...
Turkey	...	...	...	...	...	...	...
Ukraine	...	...	...	...	...	...	...
UK: England & Wales	0.5	0.6	0.6	0.5	0.5	0.5	9
UK: Northern Ireland	...	...	...	...	...	...	...
UK: Scotland	...	...	...	...	...	...	...
Mean	41	40	41	43	36	37	
Median	43	43	47	51	45	43	
Minimum	0	1	1	0	0	1	
Maximum	76	64	74	77	76	70	

Table 4.2.5.3: Persons under the supervision or care of an agent of the correctional services: % of Probation in the total FLOW

	1995 P45FP95	1996 P45FP96	1997 P45FP97	1998 P45FP98	1999 P45FP99	2000 P45FP00	% change 1995-2000
Albania	...	...	...	...	...	...	...
Armenia	...	...	...	...	...	...	...
Austria	42.9	41.0	33.6	25.7	33.3	22.6	-47
Belgium	...	...	...	...	...	...	...
Bulgaria	...	...	...	...	...	...	...
Croatia	...	...	...	...	...	...	...
Cyprus	100.0	100.0	100.0	100.0	100.0	100.0	0
Czech Republic	...	...	...	...	...	...	...
Denmark	...	...	...	...	...	...	...
Estonia	...	...	...	100.0	90.6	96.3	...
Finland	...	...	...	...	...	...	...
France	...	...	...	...	...	...	...
Georgia	...	...	...	...	...	...	...
Germany	...	...	...	...	...	...	...
Greece	...	...	...	...	...	...	...
Hungary	...	...	...	...	...	...	...
Ireland	...	...	...	...	...	...	...
Italy	...	...	...	...	...	...	...
Latvia	...	...	...	...	...	...	...
Lithuania	...	...	...	...	...	...	...
Luxembourg	...	...	...	...	...	...	...
Malta	...	...	...	...	...	...	...
Moldova	...	...	...	...	...	...	...
Netherlands	...	...	...	...	...	...	...
Norway	...	...	...	...	...	...	...
Poland	...	...	...	...	...	...	...
Portugal	3.4	1.8	13.3	12.0	12.7	13.1	286
Romania	...	...	...	...	...	...	...
Russia	...	...	...	...	...	...	...
Slovakia	...	...	...	...	...	...	...
Slovenia	...	...	...	...	...	...	...
Spain	...	...	...	...	...	...	...
Sweden	57.6	55.4	55.7	55.9	55.3	55.2	-4
Switzerland	...	...	...	...	...	...	...
Turkey	...	...	...	...	...	...	...
Ukraine	...	...	...	...	...	...	...
UK: England & Wales	56.3	54.6	54.2	54.3	53.8	54.7	-3
UK: Northern Ireland	...	...	...	...	...	...	...
UK: Scotland	...	96.1	95.9	95.3	94.4	...	...
Mean	52	58	59	63	63	57	
Median	56	55	55	56	55	55	
Minimum	3	2	13	12	13	13	
Maximum	100	100	100	100	100	100	

Table 4.2.5.4: Persons under the supervision or care of an agent of the correctional services: % of Parole or conditional release (with supervision) in the total **FLOW**

	1995 P45FC95	1996 P45FC96	1997 P45FC97	1998 P45FC98	1999 P45FC99	2000 P45FC00	% change 1995-2000
Albania	...	...	...	...	...	...	...
Armenia	...	...	...	...	...	...	...
Austria	15.2	15.6	18.0	17.8	16.1	17.9	18
Belgium	...	...	...	...	...	...	...
Bulgaria	...	...	...	...	...	...	...
Croatia	...	...	...	...	...	...	...
Cyprus	...	...	...	...	...	...	...
Czech Republic	...	...	...	...	...	...	...
Denmark	...	...	...	...	...	...	...
Estonia	...	...	...	...	9.4	3.7	...
Finland	38.7	38.2	39.2	42.9	45.7	44.8	16
France	...	...	...	...	...	...	...
Georgia	...	...	...	...	...	...	...
Germany	...	...	...	...	...	...	...
Greece	...	...	...	...	...	...	...
Hungary	...	...	...	...	...	...	...
Ireland	...	...	...	...	...	...	...
Italy	...	...	...	...	...	...	...
Latvia	...	...	...	...	...	...	...
Lithuania	24.1	36.1	26.0	23.4	24.0	30.4	26
Luxembourg	...	...	...	...	...	...	...
Malta	...	...	...	...	...	...	...
Moldova	...	...	...	...	...	...	...
Netherlands	...	...	...	...	...	...	...
Norway	56.7	56.5	55.3	54.7	55.5	57.5	1
Poland	...	...	...	...	...	...	...
Portugal	72.1	70.9	71.7	67.3	69.5	69.9	-3
Romania	...	...	...	...	...	...	...
Russia	...	...	...	...	...	...	...
Slovakia	...	...	...	...	...	...	...
Slovenia	...	...	...	...	...	...	...
Spain	...	...	...	...	...	...	...
Sweden	42.4	44.6	44.3	44.1	44.7	44.8	6
Switzerland	...	...	...	...	89.2	86.3	...
Turkey	...	...	...	...	...	...	...
Ukraine	...	...	...	...	...	...	...
UK: England & Wales	43.4	44.8	45.2	45.1	45.6	44.9	4
UK: Northern Ireland	...	...	...	...	...	...	...
UK: Scotland	...	3.9	4.1	4.7	5.6	...	...
Mean	42	39	38	38	41	44	
Median	42	41	42	43	45	45	
Minimum	15	4	4	5	6	4	
Maximum	72	71	72	67	89	86	

Comments on tables 4.2.5.1 to 4.2.5.4

Austria: Supervision (connected with suspended sentence) in any case is carried out by probation officers.

"Probation" (not based on sentence) includes: voluntary probation; "provisional" probation before conviction, suggested by the examining magistrate; supervision by probation officer accepted as prerequisite for diversion according to drug law, juvenile court law and penal procedure law (after 1999).

"Total" figures include all the Austrian provinces; with regard to Styria figures on suspended sentence, probation and conditional release before 1999 are only based on estimates.

Figures for 1995/1996 differ from those reported for European Sourcebook 1999 as data on Styria was not included in the old questionnaire.

Cyprus: Probation is undertaken only in cases of suspended sentence (with supervision).

Estonia: Correctional service (supervision) was introduced in 1998; therefore data for 1998 include the period: 1 May–31 December 1998.

Finland: Suspended sentence (with supervision).
Parole or conditional release (with supervision).
Probation (does not exist).

Germany: Data refers to the former West Germany only; data for East Berlin are included.
No data available for Hamburg.
No data available for 1998-2000.
Flow data refers to cases in which the supervision ended in the respective year.
With regard to flow data, it is impossible to differentiate between suspended sentences and conditional releases. "Total" figures include all the given categories.
Probation: All cases in which a juvenile court made use of section 27 Act on Juvenile Courts are counted.

Italy: Data refers to 31 December.

Lithuania: Numbers are at the end of the year – e.g. the data for 2000 are at 1 January 2001. Available figures on 1 September are provided in the brackets.
Suspended sentence (with supervision) refers to suspension under certain conditions after conviction (Art. 47[1] of Penal Code) – see Comments on Table 3.2.1
Conditional release (with supervision) refers to early conditional release from the imprisonment institution under certain conditions (Art. 54[2]).
The Flow period covers from 1 January until 1 January of the next year.
Probation will be introduced with the new Penal Code on 1 January 2003.

Malta: Persons who receive a suspended sentence, put on probation, parole (not applicable) do not remain under the responsibility of the Correctional Facility.

Norway: There is no "probation" but two other forms of supervision exist:
a) Security sentence which normally is served initially in prison followed by a period of supervision, with the possibility of recall. (May also be served entirely in the community).
   Stock 1 September 2000: 127   Flow   1 September 2000: 36
b) Waiver of prosecution. The prosecuting authority may elect not to prefer an indictment on condition that the offender accepts a period of supervision.
   Stock 1 September 2000: 4   Flow   1 September 2000: 1

Poland: Suspended sentence – with supervision by court probation officer.
Conditional release – with supervision by court probation officer. Conditional release is granted by the sanctions enforcement court.
Supervision by a court probation officer is mandatory as far as recidivists, young offenders, and those released from serving life sentence are concerned.

Romania: The Penal legislation does not regulate suspended sentence or parole.

Conditional release does not involve the supervision of the released prisoners.
The number of the prisoners conditionally released was 26 556 in 1995; 27 694 in 1996; 26 939 in 1997; 23 646 in 1998; 29 819 in 1999 and 28 864 in 2000.
Sweden: Data refers to 1 October.
Switzerland: Probation does not exist in Switzerland.
UK: England & Wales: The data are figures on 31 December of the preceding year.
Each person is counted only once in the total even if they were subject to several types of supervision at the year-end.
Combination orders, introduced in October 1992 are partly Probation Orders and partly Community Service Orders. These are included in "Other Non-Custodial Sentences".
UK: Scotland: Data relates to financial years (i.e. 1999 = 1 April 1999 to 31 March 2000).
Suspended sentence = not applicable.
Parole figures include those released on parole or life licence but exclude prisoners released on licence (not parole) at two thirds point of sentence who are also subject to supervision (source: Parole Board Scotland).

Table 4.2.6.1: Community service per 100 000 population: STOCK – Total

	1995 R46ST95	1996 R46ST96	1997 R46ST97	1998 R46ST98	1999 R46ST99	2000 R46ST00	% change 1995-2000
Albania	...	...	...	...	...	...	...
Armenia	...	...	...	...	...	...	...
Austria	...	...	...	...	...	...	...
Belgium	...	...	...	...	...	...	...
Bulgaria	...	...	...	...	...	...	...
Croatia	...	...	...	0.0	0.0	0.0	...
Cyprus	...	...	...	...	...	...	...
Czech Republic	...	...	...	...	...	...	...
Denmark	8.6	10.3	10.9	13.1	1.6	39.8	363
Estonia	...	...	...	...	...	...	...
Finland	13.6	18.6	20.8	23.5	24.9	23.1	70
France	31.9	35.1	38.1	39.6	39.7	41.2	29
Georgia	...	...	...	...	...	...	...
Germany	...	...	...	...	...	...	...
Greece	...	...	...	...	...	...	...
Hungary	3.0	6.4	11.2	18.0	18.3	31.4	946
Ireland	...	...	...	...	...	...	...
Italy	...	...	...	...	...	...	...
Latvia	...	...	...	...	...	...	...
Lithuania	...	...	...	...	...	...	...
Luxembourg	...	...	...	...	...	...	...
Malta	...	...	...	...	...	...	...
Moldova	...	...	...	...	...	...	...
Netherlands	...	...	...	...	...	...	...
Norway	7.6	7.8	7.6	7.6	7.8	7.3	-3
Poland	...	...	...	...	...	...	...
Portugal	0.8	1.1	1.2	1.4	1.1	1.8	109
Romania	...	...	...	...	...	...	...
Russia	...	...	...	...	...	...	...
Slovakia	...	...	...	...	...	...	...
Slovenia	...	...	...	...	...	...	...
Spain	...	...	...	...	...	...	...
Sweden	...	...	...	...	...	...	...
Switzerland	...	...	...	...	...	...	...
Turkey	...	...	...	...	...	...	...
Ukraine	...	...	...	...	...	...	...
UK: England & Wales	71.1	66.7	62.2	64.1	72.5	86.6	22
UK: Northern Ireland	...	...	...	...	...	...	...
UK: Scotland	...	...	...	...	...	...	...
Mean	20	21	22	21	21	29	
Median	9	10	11	16	13	27	
Minimum	1	1	1	0	0	0	
Maximum	71	67	62	64	73	87	

Table 4.2.7.1: Community service: FLOW per 100 000 population – Total

	1995 R47FT95	1996 R47FT96	1997 R47FT97	1998 R47FT98	1999 R47FT99	2000 R47FT00	% change 1995-2000
Albania	...	...	...	...	...	...	...
Armenia	...	...	...	...	...	...	...
Austria	...	...	...	...	...	7.7	...
Belgium	...	...	...	...	...	...	...
Bulgaria	...	...	...	...	...	...	...
Croatia	...	...	...	0.0	0.0	0.0	...
Cyprus	...	...	...	...	...	...	...
Czech Republic	...	...	15.5	17.3	31.3	69.0	...
Denmark	9.9	11.5	12.9	14.5	18.2	44.0	346
Estonia	...	...	...	...	...	...	...
Finland	53.0	66.1	71.8	78.7	74.7	70.5	33
France	...	...	...	...	...	...	...
Georgia	...	...	...	...	...	...	...
Germany	...	...	...	...	...	...	...
Greece	...	...	...	...	...	...	...
Hungary	8.3	12.4	16.6	18.2	24.4	28.5	242
Ireland	...	...	...	...	...	...	...
Italy	...	...	...	...	...	...	...
Latvia	...	...	...	...	...	...	...
Lithuania	...	...	...	...	...	...	...
Luxembourg	...	...	...	...	...	...	...
Malta	...	...	...	...	...	...	...
Moldova	...	...	...	...	...	...	...
Netherlands	...	...	...	...	...	...	...
Norway	17.9	16.7	15.3	14.4	13.5	13.1	-27
Poland	18.4	27.0	27.8	33.7	39.6	37.5	104
Portugal	0.7	1.2	1.7	1.7	1.7	2.7	274
Romania	...	...	...	...	...	...	...
Russia	...	...	...	...	...	...	...
Slovakia	...	...	...	...	...	...	...
Slovenia	...	...	...	...	...	...	...
Spain	...	...	...	...	...	...	...
Sweden	7.6	7.8	7.2	7.7	11.4	16.0	110
Switzerland	11.8	13.0	27.1	34.5	40.5	43.2	266
Turkey	...	...	...	...	...	...	...
Ukraine	...	...	...	...	...	...	...
UK: England & Wales	94.8	89.3	91.7	96.0	97.6	99.1	5
UK: Northern Ireland	...	...	...	...	...	...	...
UK: Scotland	...	145.0	138.7	134.1	120.9	...	...
Mean	25	39	39	38	39	36	
Median	12	15	17	18	28	33	
Minimum	1	1	2	0	0	0	
Maximum	95	145	139	134	121	99	

Comments on tables 4.2.6.1 and 4.2.7.1

Austria: Up to 1999 no official data available, "Gemeinnützige Leistung" (community service order) being of rather limited significance, restricted to juvenile criminal law. From 2000 on, due to the diversion package, significance can be supposed to increase.
Figure relates to "offers" from the side of prosecutors and magistrates, but not to accomplished community service.

Hungary: Community service is a principal punishment. Only supplementary punishments may be inflicted with another principal punishment (if the other legal conditions of their application exist). If the convict does not voluntarily satisfy his work obligation, this punishment shall be substituted with imprisonment. The figures include these substituted sentences; they are served in prison and counted as community services.

Norway: Figures for 1995-1999 are averages of 4 quarterly reports.

UK: England & Wales: Figures at 31 December previous year.

UK: Scotland: Data relates to financial years (i.e. 1999 = 1 April 1999 to 31 March 2000) and include Probation Orders with a Requirement of Unpaid Work.
Community Service figures prior to 1996-1997 are not available.

4.3 Sources of the data in chapter 4

Albania	General Directory of the Prisons
Tirana, Albania, unpublished
Armenia	Ministry of Justice. Austria Ministry of Justice. Annual report on corrections, 1995-1999; Government Report on Security 2000. Annual Government Report on Security; VBSA (Verein für Bewährungshilfe und Soziale Arbeit) Annual Report.
Government Report on Security
Belgium	– Activity reports Direction générale des Etablissements pénitentiaires 1997, 1998 et 1999 (publication fin 2001).
– Administration des Etablissements pénitentiaires 1995 et 1996.
– Penal statistics sent to the Institut National de Statistique, see www.stabel.fgov.be
– Evaluation reports of Service de travail social du Ministère de la justice, 1995 à 1998.
– Activity reports of the Service des Maisons de Justice du Ministère de la Justice, 1999 et 2000 (forthcoming).
Ministère de la Justice – Direction générale des Etablissements pénitentiaires – Centre National de Surveillance électronique.
Croatia	Ministry of Justice, Administration and Local Self-Governance, unpublished data collected specially for the purpose of this survey.
Cyprus	Annual Reports of the Ministry of Labour and Social Insurance, Republic of Cyprus, years 1995–2000.
Czech Republic	Yearbook of Prison Service of the Czech Republic. Published.
Yearbook of Prison Service of the Czech Republic.
Suspended sentence – Statistical Sourcebook of Criminality.
Ministry of Justice. Published
Conditional release – Yearbook of Prison Service.
Statistical Sourcebook of Criminality. Ministry of Justice. Published.

Denmark	Stock data: Prison and Probation Service
	Flow data: "Kriminalstatistikken", Statistics Denmark
	"Rapport om Ungdomskriminalitet", Justitsministeriet (Ministry of Justice)
	"Kriminalforsorgens Statistik", Direktoratet for Kriminalforsorgen.
Estonia	Ministry of Justice – statistics on prison population – not published.
	Ministry of Justice – Probation statistics (www.just.ee)
Finland	Prison administration
France	Ministère de la Justice, direction de l'Administration pénitentiaire, Annuaire statistique de la Justice.
Germany	Statistisches Bundesamt (Hrsg.) Internal statistics of the Federal Ministry of Justice, unpublished.
Greece	Ministry of Justice. Unpublished data.
Hungary	National Prison Administration.
	Ministry of Justice
Ireland	Department of Justice, Equality & Law Reform.
Italy	National Institute of Statistics-Istat
Lithuania	Ministry of Justice – Prison Department.
Moldova	Département des institutions pénitentiaires, Ministère de la Justice.
Netherlands	Ministry of Justice (WODC) and Central Bureau of Statistics. Not published.
Norway	Statistics Norway, Division for Social Welfare Statistics.
	Manual reports until 1999. From 2000 all reports IT-generated (system name: KOMPIS/KIF).
Poland	Central Prison Authority, Department of Statistics.
	Ministry of Justice, Department of Statistics.
Portugal	Prison Services, Ministry of Justice.
Romania	Ministry of Justice – General Directorate of Penitentiaries – Department of Detention Security and Penitentiary Regime.
Slovenia	Ministry of Justice – Directorate of Prison Administration: National Register of Prisoners
	Annual Reports (1995-2000) of Prison Administration.
	Ministry of Justice – Directorate of Prison Administration: National Register of Prisoners.
	Annual Reports (1999) of Prison Administration.
Sweden	Official statistics published by the National Prison Authority
Switzerland	Office fédéral de la statistique.
UK: England & Wales	Prison Statistics England and Wales. Annual publication
	INMATE Information System
	Probation Statistics England and Wales 1999. Annual publication.
	Research, Development & Statistics Department, Home Office
	Data supplied by Electronic Monitoring contractors.
UK: Northern Ireland	NIO Research & Statistical Bulletin 7/2001: "The Northern Ireland Prison Population in 2000".
	NIO Statistical Prisoner Database.
UK: Scotland	Scottish Prison Service.
	Scottish Executive "Criminal Justice Social Work Statistics, 2000"
	Parole Board for Scotland.

5 Survey data

5.1 General comments

5.1.1 Introduction

1. Important information on the level of crime and offending behaviour for certain forms of crime can also be obtained from surveys, in which a sample of the population is asked about their experiences. Several types of surveys exist. The so-called *victimisation surveys* which are based on interviews of a representative cross-section of the general population are well known. Specific surveys have also been conducted with a view to ascertaining to what extent businesses and other organisations have become "victims" of crime.[1] A rather different approach underlies *surveys of self-reported delinquency*, where the respondents – mostly juveniles – are asked to provide information on their own criminal or deviant behaviour.[2]

2. Such surveys have been carried out, over the last 25 years, in a number of Member States of the Council of Europe, mostly by universities and national or local authorities. However, as the scope, offence definitions, interview techniques, sampling methods etc. of these surveys differ widely, reliable international comparisons are as difficult to achieve.

3. There is one source, though, which can be used as a sufficiently reliable basis for international comparisons. It is the International Crime Victims Survey (ICVS) which, up until now, has been carried out four times, in 1989, 1992, 1996 and 2000 (cf. van Kesteren, Mayhew & Nieuwbeerta, 2000). In this survey, standardised questionnaires and data collection methods have been used with a view to obtaining comparable results for the participating countries. In this chapter, a selection of the main results will be presented.[3]

5.1.2 International Crime Victim Survey: methodology

4. The ICVS is a project in which governmental and academic organisations co-operate. The questionnaire and methodology were originally designed by a small working group (van Dijk, Mayhew, Killias 1990). A reformed working group

---

[1] The International Business Crime Survey (Dijk, J.J.M. van & G.J. Terlouw, An international perspective of the business community as victims of fraud and crime, In: *Security Journal* 7 (1996), pp. 157-167.
[2] The International Self-Report of Delinquency Study (Junger-Tas, J., G.J. Terlouw & M.W. Klein (ed.), *Delinquent Behavior among young people in the western world; first results of the international self-report delinquency study,* Den Haag, 1994, RDC/Ministry of Justice) covered only a very limited number of European countries, and are, therefore, not included in this Sourcebook.
[3] For more results see also (Nieuwbeerta, P. (ed), 'Crime victimisation in comparative perspective') with 25 studies based on the ICVS data.

reviewed both the questionnaire and the methodology used after each 'sweep' of the survey taking into account the practical experience gathered.

5. A great number of countries all over the world participated in (one or more) sweeps of the survey. The methods for collecting data used by the different countries varied to some extent. Basically, Computer Assisted Telephone Interviewing was used to approach a random sample of at least 1 000 individuals in each country. In countries where telephone ownership was not widespread, face-to-face interviews were conducted. In a number of countries, smaller samples of the population were interviewed (sometimes drawn from certain parts of the country only), mainly for financial and practical reasons. In several countries only individuals from the capital or another major urban area were included in the sample; in some cases, this sample was complemented by an additional sample from one or more rural areas.

6. In the tables the 'geographical' reference point is made clear by presenting three columns for each offence. The figures indicated in the first column ("national") are representative at national level. The figures in the second column ("urban") are representative of all urban areas (if figures are given in the first column), or one major urban area only (if no figures are given in the first column). The figure in the third column ("rural") are representative of all rural areas (if figures are given in the first column), or one small rural area only (if no figures are given in the first column). Note that the breakdown between "urban" and "rural" is based on information provided by the respondents (see technical information).

5.1.3 International Crime Victim Survey: results

7. Tables 5.2.1, 5.2.2 and 5.2.3 present some results on victimisation rates of the survey. The figures represent the average victimisation rates over the three last sweeps of the survey. They were computed by summing up the yearly victimisation rates for each of the sweeps and for a given country, and then dividing the sum by the number of sweeps (for details, see the technical information). This procedure was used to ensure a high level of comparability, in particular, in relation to countries which did not participate in each of the three sweeps. Under each of the data tables, the relevant part of the screening question i.e. the question about victimisation in the last year is given (for complete wording, see technical information).

8. The tables show that in many countries victimisation rates differ considerably between urban and rural areas. Overall, they are higher in urban than in rural areas, but not in all countries and not for all offences. In general, countries differ much less with regard to victimisation rates than in relation to police data, which suggests that the latter reflect not only the actual volume of crime but also differences in recording and reporting crime.

9. Table 5.2.4 gives the percentage of the number of offences that is reported to the police of which a person was victim. In general, Eastern European countries (e.g. Albania, Georgia) tend to have lower reporting percentages than Western European countries (e.g. UK: Scotland, the Netherlands). Between offences, it is noteworthy that property crime is reported more often than violent crime.

10. When someone was victim of a certain crime, he or she was also asked how they felt about the seriousness of the crime. There were three possible answers: "Very serious", "Fairly serious" and "Not very serious". The results were recalculated into a scale from 1 to 9 and presented in table 5.2.5. On average, car theft was considered by victims as the most serious crime. However, in many Western European countries, sexual assault was considered the most serious crime.

5.2 Tables

Table 5.2.1: Persons victimised once or more during the last year by assault and sexual assault (% of surveyed population, yearly rate averaged over 3 sweeps: 1992, 1996 and 2000)

	Assault and threat			Sexual assault (women only)		
	national	urban	rural	national	urban	rural
Albania		3.2	2.3		2.4	0.0
Armenia						
Austria	1.9	2.5	1.6	1.7	2.7	1.3
Belgium	2.4	3.0	2.5	0.7	0.7	0.7
Bulgaria		3.4			0.5	
Croatia		2.3			0.8	
Cyprus						
Czech Republic		3.1			1.3	
Denmark	2.7	3.7	2.4	0.5	0.7	0.3
Estonia	5.4	7.5	4.1	1.3	2.3	0.8
Finland	4.3	5.5	3.9	1.8	2.2	1.7
France	4.5	5.3	4.3	0.8	1.9	0.6
Georgia	1.7	2.7	2.1	1.0	1.4	0.7
Germany						
Greece						
Hungary		0.9			0.5	
Iceland						
Ireland						
Italy	0.8	1.3	0.6	0.9	1.2	0.8
Latvia		3.5	1.8		0.5	1.0
Lithuania	3.0	1.8	2.3	0.6	1.4	0.2
Luxembourg						
Malta	3.1	2.9	3.3	0.2	0.3	0.0
Moldova						
Netherlands	3.8	5.6	3.3	1.1	2.6	0.8
Norway						
Poland	3.4	4.4	2.9	1.0	1.8	0.6
Portugal	0.9	0.7	1.0	0.3	0.3	0.5
Romania		3.8	3.3		0.8	4.4
Russia		4.6			1.7	
Slovakia	3.6	1.4	3.7	0.4	0.2	0.4
Slovenia	4.4	5.2	3.7	1.7	2.1	1.1
Spain (Catalonia only)		1.7	1.3		0.5	0.5
Sweden	3.8	4.5	3.6	1.5	2.6	1.2
Switzerland	2.6	2.2	2.5	1.4	1.8	1.2
Turkey						
Ukraine		3.3			1.4	
UK: England and Wales	5.0	6.4	4.8	0.8	1.7	0.6
UK: Northern Ireland	2.0	3.6	1.5	0.4	0.5	0.4
UK: Scotland	4.9	5.9	4.4	0.4	0.2	0.4
Mean	3.2	3.5	2.8	0.9	1.3	0.8
Median	3.3	3.4	2.7	0.9	1.4	0.7
Min	0.8	0.7	0.6	0.2	0.2	0.0
Max	5.4	7.5	4.8	1.8	2.7	4.4

Table 5.2.2: Households victimised once or more during the last year by burglary, theft of car and theft from a car (% of surveyed population, yearly rate averaged over 3 sweeps: 1992, 1996 and 2000)

	Burglary			Theft of car			Theft from a car		
	national	urban	rural	national	urban	rural	national	urban	rural
Albania		3.3	3.7		0.8	0.0		5.0	3.7
Armenia									
Austria	0.8	0.2	1.0	0.1	0.0	0.2	1.4	1.8	1.2
Belgium	2.2	2.6	1.9	0.9	0.7	0.9	3.7	6.1	3.4
Bulgaria		5.2			1.2			9.8	
Croatia		1.3			0.7			2.7	
Cyprus									
Czech Republic		6.9			2.9			12.4	
Denmark	2.5	2.7	2.5	0.9	0.7	1.0	3.2	3.7	3.0
Estonia	4.5	6.1	3.5	1.0	1.5	0.8	7.5	12.1	5.1
Finland	0.5	0.4	0.6	0.5	0.7	0.5	2.9	3.7	2.6
France	1.6	1.5	1.7	1.4	2.3	1.2	6.4	9.2	6.0
Georgia	3.3	3.5	3.7	2.2	1.1	2.1	5.3	8.1	1.9
Germany									
Greece									
Hungary		2.9			2.0			7.0	
Iceland									
Ireland									
Italy	2.4	2.9	2.2	2.6	3.3	2.4	6.9	8.7	6.2
Latvia		2.3	2.5		1.3	1.8		5.6	1.3
Lithuania	4.5	5.2	3.7	0.7	1.2	0.2	6.8	8.6	3.7
Luxembourg									
Malta	0.9	0.6	1.3	1.0	1.3	0.7	7.1	8.7	5.3
Moldova									
Netherlands	2.2	2.5	2.2	0.4	0.7	0.3	5.2	6.7	4.7
Norway									
Poland	2.1	2.7	1.9	0.7	1.1	0.5	4.9	7.7	3.7
Portugal	1.4	1.3	1.4	0.8	0.7	0.7	4.3	4.0	4.7
Romania		1.2	3.3		0.2	0.0		6.1	2.2
Russia		2.2			1.0			7.3	
Slovakia	3.4	7.6	3.1	1.0	1.0	1.0	3.8	9.4	3.7
Slovenia	2.4	3.9	1.3	0.3	0.6	0.2	5.7	8.3	3.7
Spain (Catalonia only)		0.5	1.1		0.4	0.5		4.4	5.3
Sweden	1.6	2.8	1.3	1.3	1.8	1.2	4.7	6.6	4.1
Switzerland	1.5	2.7	1.1	0.3	0.2	0.2	2.1	2.5	1.9
Turkey									
Ukraine		2.7			0.8			3.6	
UK: England and Wales	3.0	4.8	2.6	2.8	3.6	2.5	7.4	9.2	6.9
UK: Northern Ireland	1.5	2.3	1.2	1.4	2.8	0.8	2.3	2.7	2.2
UK: Scotland	1.5	2.3	1.2	1.2	1.3	1.1	5.4	7.5	5.1

Table 5.2.3: Persons victimised once or more during the last year of robbery, pickpocketing and personal theft (% of surveyed population, yearly rate averaged over 3 sweeps: 1992, 1996 and 2000)

	Robbery			Pickpocketing			Other personal theft		
	national	urban	rural	national	urban	rural	national	urban	rural
Albania		2.1	2.3		8.2	7.0		2.7	1.0
Armenia									
Austria	0.2	0.2	0.2	2.9	5.9	1.8	2.1	3.0	1.6
Belgium	1.0	1.6	0.8	1.8	1.6	1.8	1.9	2.4	2.0
Bulgaria		2.0			8.5			2.0	
Croatia		0.8			2.3			1.2	
Cyprus									
Czech Republic		0.7			5.6			2.9	
Denmark	0.6	0.6	0.6	2.1	4.6	1.1	2.2	3.7	1.6
Estonia	2.9	5.0	1.9	3.3	5.1	2.2	3.3	4.2	2.7
Finland	0.7	1.1	0.6	1.6	2.4	1.4	1.9	2.7	1.6
France	1.0	2.0	0.9	2.0	3.9	1.4	2.2	3.3	1.8
Georgia	1.9	2.6	1.4	4.3	8.5	3.0	1.2	3.3	0.9
Germany									
Greece									
Hungary		1.2			5.5			1.9	
Iceland									
Ireland									
Italy	1.3	2.7	0.8	2.3	3.8	1.7	1.4	1.8	1.3
Latvia		3.0	1.0		9.0	8.2		3.4	3.9
Lithuania	2.0	2.4	1.9	6.4	6.9	4.8	2.3	2.5	3.1
Luxembourg									
Malta	0.3	0.2	0.4	1.2	1.0	1.3	1.9	1.7	2.3
Moldova									
Netherlands	0.8	1.5	0.6	2.3	3.3	1.9	3.2	3.9	3.0
Norway									
Poland	1.8	2.5	1.5	5.1	8.1	3.7	1.6	2.1	1.3
Portugal	1.1	2.0	0.8	1.4	2.9	1.2	0.7	1.1	0.8
Romania		0.9	0.0		10.1	2.5		2.7	0.8
Russia		3.2			8.7			2.4	
Slovakia	1.6	0.6	1.6	3.3	6.9	3.2	2.6	4.5	2.4
Slovenia	1.2	1.7	0.8	1.5	2.4	0.9	2.5	3.3	1.8
Spain (Catalonia only)		1.1	0.8		2.4	1.8		1.3	1.6
Sweden	0.5	0.6	0.4	1.3	2.5	0.9	4.2	6.0	3.6
Switzerland	0.8	1.4	0.6	1.3	2.0	1.1	2.0	1.6	2.1
Turkey									
Ukraine		3.8			17.0			2.8	
UK: England and Wales	1.1	1.9	1.0	1.6	2.3	1.4	3.1	3.4	3.0
UK: Northern Ireland	0.4	1.1	0.2	0.5	0.5	0.5	1.7	2.8	1.4
UK: Scotland	0.7	1.3	0.6	1.4	1.8	1.3	3.2	3.8	3.2

Table 5.2.4: Percentage reported to the police related to the last incident per offence type (averaged over 3 sweeps: 1992, 1996 and 2000)

	Assault and threat	Sexual assault (women only)	Burglary	Theft of car	Theft from a car	Robbery	Pick-pocketing	Other personal theft
Albania*	20	17	42	71	20	18	8	11
Armenia								
Austria	22	5	79	100	79	61	57	46
Belgium	33	20	91	95	73	50	70	45
Bulgaria*	21	14	69	89	33	41	19	23
Croatia*	28	21	68	96	62	46	43	42
Cyprus								
Czech Republic*	30	25	70	95	64	45	39	41
Denmark	30	26	88	98	75	73	64	40
Estonia	23	12	60	86	40	38	26	33
Finland	26	12	72	97	67	44	39	42
France	32	28	76	94	62	44	49	41
Georgia	19	19	49	54	22	28	5	18
Germany								
Greece								
Hungary*	18	35	79	90	58	46	25	35
Iceland								
Ireland								
Italy	24	12	66	95	40	42	41	48
Latvia*	21	17	72	90	35	32	13	21
Lithuania	25	37	58	86	46	44	19	28
Luxembourg								
Malta	37	88	77	97	56	27	47	31
Moldova								
Netherlands	42	33	89	92	74	64	65	46
Norway								
Poland	30	23	57	92	47	37	21	28
Portugal	33	24	59	76	41	40	46	16
Romania*	25	16	79	81	53	32	21	13
Russia*	24	12	65	85	29	25	16	19
Slovakia*	35	33	74	99	67	43	51	27
Slovenia	37	11	64	94	62	41	37	35
Spain (Catalonia only)								
Sweden	32	18	69	96	74	76	66	45
Switzerland	33	16	88	88	74	45	42	34
Turkey								
Ukraine*	21	9	58	86	31	32	11	22
UK: England and Wales	40	36	93	93	70	55	51	48
UK: Northern Ireland	56	58	86	95	61	83	38	34
UK: Scotland	43	68	94	94	71	50	55	52

* Based on city surveys only.

Table 5.2.5: Seriousness of crimes as perceived by the victims (averaged over 3 sweeps: 1992, 1996 and 2000)

	Assault and threat	Sexual assault (women only)	Burglary	Theft of car	Theft from a car	Robbery	Pick-pocketing	Other personal theft
Albania*	5.6	5.4	6.1	8.3	3.6	5.4	4.5	4.0
Armenia								
Austria	4.7	6.1	6.0	5.3	3.5	5.9	4.4	3.2
Belgium	4.5	6.3	5.9	6.3	3.3	4.8	4.5	4.2
Bulgaria*	5.9	7.3	6.6	8.6	4.3	5.9	5.3	4.7
Croatia*	5.6	6.8	4.9	6.9	3.9	6.3	5.6	5.5
Cyprus								
Czech Republic*	5.0	6.0	4.2	6.6	3.5	5.7	4.9	4.9
Denmark	4.7	7.2	4.9	4.0	2.3	4.9	3.5	2.8
Estonia	4.6	6.3	5.0	7.1	3.5	4.7	4.0	4.2
Finland	4.5	5.2	5.5	5.5	3.0	5.3	4.2	3.8
France	5.1	6.4	5.1	6.3	3.1	5.3	4.3	4.1
Georgia	5.6	6.7	7.0	7.7	4.8	6.1	3.9	4.7
Germany								
Greece								
Hungary*	4.4	3.0	5.2	7.4	4.1	4.1	4.8	4.4
Iceland								
Ireland								
Italy	6.7	7.9	6.8	6.8	4.4	7.7	5.7	5.3
Latvia*	4.9	5.6	6.5	7.9	4.0	5.3	4.8	4.9
Lithuania	4.3	6.6	5.1	7.3	3.8	5.7	4.3	3.5
Luxembourg								
Malta	5.4	8.5	7.2	7.5	4.2	6.0	5.3	4.4
Moldova								
Netherlands	5.2	7.2	5.8	5.8	3.2	5.3	5.1	3.7
Norway								
Poland	4.8	6.5	5.3	8.1	3.6	5.1	5.1	4.6
Portugal	6.1	7.1	6.6	6.0	3.6	5.0	5.4	4.2
Romania*	5.8	6.8	7.6	8.7	5.3	6.8	5.8	4.9
Russia*	4.3	5.7	5.7	7.2	3.2	3.9	3.9	3.9
Slovakia*	6.5	8.4	6.6	8.3	5.9	7.6	7.2	6.7
Slovenia	6.1	7.2	5.8	8.1	4.7	6.2	5.6	5.2
Spain (Catalonia only)								
Sweden	5.0	6.5	5.5	6.0	3.4	6.6	5.2	4.1
Switzerland	4.0	5.0	5.5	6.0	3.4	3.9	4.0	3.2
Turkey								
Ukraine*	4.2	5.8	5.3	6.3	3.3	4.4	4.1	3.4
UK: England and Wales	5.5	7.1	6.8	6.3	3.5	6.1	5.0	4.5
UK: Northern Ireland	6.8	7.7	7.1	7.7	3.8	7.8	5.2	4.6
UK: Scotland	5.1	7.4	6.4	6.1	3.0	5.8	4.4	4.1
Median	5.2	6.5	5.9	6.9	3.7	5.6	4.8	4.4
Median	5.1	6.6	5.9	7.0	3.6	5.6	4.8	4.3
Minimum	4.0	3.0	4.2	4.0	2.3	3.9	3.5	2.8
Maximum	6.8	8.5	7.6	8.7	5.9	7.8	7.2	6.7

* Based on city surveys only.

Notes for table 5.2.1
Relevant part of questions (for exact wording see technical information):
Assault and threat: "have you been personally attacked or threatened?"
Sexual assault: "has anyone grabbed, touched or assaulted you for sexual reasons in a really offensive way?"

Notes for table 5.2.2
Relevant part of questions (for exact wording see technical information):
Burglary: "did anyone actually get into your house or flat without permission, and steal or try to steal something? (...) not including thefts from garages, sheds or lock-ups?"
Theft of car: "have you or have other members of your household had any of their cars/vans/trucks stolen?"
Theft from a car: "have you or have other members of your household been the victim of a theft of a car radio, or something else which was left in your car, or theft of a part of the car?"

Notes for table 5.2.3
Relevant part of questions (for exact wording see technical information):
Robbery: "Has anyone stolen something from you by using force or threatening you, or did anybody try to steal from you by using force or threatening force?"
Other personal theft: "Apart from theft involving force (...) have you personally been the victim of thefts?"
Pickpocketing: "Was it a case of pickpocketing?"

5.3 Technical information

5.3.1 Introduction

In this section, detailed information is given on the calculation of average victimisation rates, the wording of the questionnaire, the sample sizes and the confidence levels.

5.3.2 Calculation of average victimisation rates and of seriousness of crimes

The figures in tables 5.2.1, 5.2.2 and 5.2.3 are average victimisation rates over the three sweeps of the survey. They were calculated as follows. In each of the sweeps, the respondents were asked if they had been the victim of a certain type of crime over the last five years. If they answered positively, they were asked the exact date of the incident. Only if the victimisation had actually occurred in the year under consideration (the year before the survey), was it taken into account when calculating the victimisation rate number of victims per 100 respondents for that year. The average victimisation rate over the 3 sweeps was computed by summing up the yearly victimisation rates for each of the sweeps, in which a country participated; this sum was subsequently divided by the number of sweeps.

The figures in table 5.2.5 were computed as the averages of a three point scale: 1 = Not very serious, 5 = Fairly serious, 9 = Very serious. This gives a figure on a 1 – 9 scale.

5.3.3 Wording of the questionnaire

In the victimisation surveys, the questions were worded as follows:

Theft of car: "Over the past five years have you or other members of your household had any of their cars/vans/trucks stolen? Please take your time to think about it".
Theft of car, follow up question: "First of all, you mentioned the theft of a car. When did this happen? Was this … (this year/last year/before then/don't know/can't remember)"
Note: the event was counted in the annual victimisation rate only if the victim replied "last year" to the follow up question.

Theft from a car: "Apart from this, over the past five years have you or members of your household been the victim of a theft of a car radio, or something else which was left in your car, or theft of a part of the car, such as a car mirror or wheel?"
Theft from a car, follow up question: "The theft from your car that you mentioned, when did this happen? Was it … (this year/last year/before then/don't know/can't remember)"
Note: the event was counted in the annual victimisation rate only if the victim replied "last year" to the follow up question.

Burglary: "Over the past five years, did anyone actually get into your house or flat without permission, and steal or try to steal something? I am not including here thefts from garages, sheds or lock-ups."
Burglary, follow up question: "You said a burglar got into your home without permission in the last five years. When did this happen? Was it …(this year/last year/before then/don't know/can't remember)"
Note: the event was counted in the annual victimisation rate only if the victim replied "last year" to the follow up question.

Robbery: "Next I want to ask you some questions about what may have happened to you personally. Things that you have mentioned already or which happened to other members of your household must not be mentioned now."
"Over the past five years has anyone stolen something from you by using force or threatening you, or did anybody try to steal something from you by using force or threatening force?"
Robbery, follow up question: "The theft involving force that you mentioned, when did this happen? Was it …(this year/last year/before then/don't know/can't remember)"

Note: the event was counted in the annual victimisation rate for robbery only if the victim replied "last year" to the follow-up question.

Other personal theft: "Apart from theft involving force there are many other types of theft of personal property, such as pickpocketing or theft of a purse, wallet, clothing, jewellery, sports equipment. This can happen at one's work, at school, in a pub, on public transport, on the beach, or in the street. Over the past five years have you personally been the victim of any of these thefts?"
Other personal theft, follow up question: "The theft of personal property that you mentioned, when did this happen? Was it …(this year/last year/before then/don't know/can't remember)"
Note: the event was counted in the annual victimisation rate for other personal theft only if the victim replied "last year" to the follow up question.
Pickpocketing, follow up question: "(The last time) were you holding or carrying what was stolen (e.g., was it a case of pickpocketing?)"
"I would like now to ask you some questions about crimes of violence of which you personally may have been the victim."
Note: the event was counted in the annual victimisation rate for pickpocketing only if the victim replied "last year" to the first follow up question and "yes" to the second one.

Sexual assault: "First, a rather personal question. People sometimes grab, touch or assault others for sexual reasons in a really offensive way. This can happen either at home, or elsewhere, for instance in a pub, the street, at school, on public transport, in cinemas, on the beach, or at one's workplace. Over the past five years has anyone done this to you? Please take your time to think about it."
Sexual assault, follow up question 1: "You mentioned that you had been a victim of sexual offence. Could I ask you about this. When did this happen? Was it … (this year/last year/before then/don't know/can't remember)."
Sexual assault, follow up question 2: "Would you describe the incident as a rape (forced intercourse), an attempted rape, an indecent assault or as just behaviour which you found offensive."
Note: This question was put to female respondents only. The event was counted in the annual victimisation rate for sexual assault only if the victim replied "last year" to the first follow up question and "rape" or "attempted rape" or "indecent assault" to the second one.

Other assault and threat: "Apart from the incidents just covered, have you over the past five years been personally attacked or threatened by someone in a way that really frightened you, either at home or elsewhere, such as in a pub, in the street, at school, on public transport, on the beach, or at your workplace?"
Other assault and threat, follow up question: "The attack or threat that you mentioned, when did this happen? Was it…(this year/last year/before then/don't know/can't remember)"

Note: the event was counted in the annual victimisation rate only if the victim replied "last year" to the follow up question.
Additional follow up questions for all types of offences:
"The last time this happened, did you or anybody else report it to the police (yes/no/don't know)."

"Taking every thing into account, how serious was the incident for you or your household. Was it (very serious/fairly serious/not very serious)?"
(NB: the words 'or your household' were only added for the offences Burglary, Theft of a car and Theft from a car).

5.3.4 Sampling and confidence levels

In table 5.3.1, the sample sizes for each of the sweeps are indicated for the European countries which participated in at least one of the surveys. In this connection, special attention should be paid to the column sub-headings (national, urban, rural). In a number of countries smaller samples of the population were interviewed (sometimes drawn from parts of the country only), and this was mainly for financial and practical reasons; in some cases this sample was complemented by a sample from one or more rural areas.

The breakdown into urban and rural areas is based on the information the respondents provided themselves on the number of inhabitants in their respective communities. A community was considered to be urban, if the number of inhabitants was said to be 100 000 or more. Only in those cases where a sample size is indicated in the column 'national', the sample is actually representative of the total population of a given country. In all other cases, the samples only represent part of the total population that lives in one or more large cities and one or more rural areas.

In table 5.3.2 confidence levels (d) are given. These depend on the sample size (n) and on the percentage observed (p). The meaning is that there is a 90% probability, for instance, that the true value lies between p-d and p+d.

Table 5.3.1: Sample size in individual countries – sweeps of: 1992, 1996 and 2000 (number of valid cases)

	1992			1996			2000		
	national	urban	rural	national	urban	rural	national	urban	rural
Albania					983	217		1498	
Armenia									
Austria				1507	433	1074			
Belgium	1485	242	1243				2501		
Bulgaria*					1076			1505	
Croatia*					994			3043	
Cyprus									
Czech Republic*	1262	237	1025	1801	717	1084		1511	
Denmark							3007		
Estonia*	1000	457	543	1173	364	809	1700		
Finland	1655	420	1235	3830	977	2853	1782		
France				1003	199	804	1000		
Georgia	1395			1137				1000	
Germany									
Greece									
Hungary					756				
Iceland									
Ireland									
Italy	2024	550	1474						
Latvia				1411	1011	400		1002	
Lithuania*				1176	656	520			
Luxembourg									
Malta*				1000	543	456			
Moldova									
Netherlands	2000	409	1591	2008	434	1574	2000		
Norway									
Poland	2033	666	1376	3483	1073	2410	5276		
Portugal							2000		
Romania				1091	1000	91		1506	
Russia		1002			1018			1500	
Slovakia*	508	21	487		1105				
Slovenia*		1000		2053	1107	946	3886		
Spain*									
Sweden	1707	327	1380	1000	234	766	2001		
Switzerland				1000	110	890	4234		
Turkey									
Ukraine*					1000			1509	
UK: England and Wales	2001	496	1505	2171	559	1612	1947		
UK: Northern Ireland				1042	262	780	1511		
UK: Scotland				2194	353	1841	2055		

* See notes on table 5.3.1

Table 5.3.2: 90% confidence levels

Sample size	Percentage observed										
	2/98	5/95	10/90	15/85	20/80	25/75	30/70	35/65	40/60	45/55	50/50
25	4.6	7.2	9.9	11.8	13.2	15.2	15.1	15.7	16.1	16.4	16.5
50	3.3	5.1	7.0	8.3	9.3	10.7	10.7	11.1	11.4	11.6	11.6
100	2.3	3.6	4.9	5.9	6.6	7.6	7.5	7.9	8.1	8.2	8.2
200	1.6	2.5	3.5	4.2	4.7	5.4	5.3	5.6	5.7	5.8	5.8
300	1.3	2.1	2.9	3.4	3.8	4.4	4.4	4.5	4.7	4.7	4.8
400	1.2	1.8	2.5	2.9	3.3	3.8	3.8	3.9	4.0	4.1	4.1
500	1.0	1.6	2.2	2.6	2.9	3.4	3.4	3.5	3.6	3.7	3.7
600	0.9	1.5	2.0	2.4	2.7	3.1	3.1	3.2	3.3	3.3	3.4
700	0.9	1.4	1.9	2.2	2.5	2.9	2.9	3.0	3.0	3.1	3.1
800	0.8	1.3	1.7	2.1	2.3	2.7	2.7	2.8	2.9	2.9	2.9
900	0.8	1.2	1.6	2.0	2.2	2.5	2.5	2.6	2.7	2.7	2.7
1000	0.7	1.1	1.6	1.9	2.1	2.4	2.4	2.5	2.5	2.6	2.6
1200	0.7	1.0	1.4	1.7	1.9	2.2	2.2	2.3	2.3	2.4	2.4
1400	0.6	1.0	1.3	1.6	1.8	2.0	2.0	2.1	2.2	2.2	2.2
1600	0.6	0.9	1.2	1.5	1.6	1.9	1.9	2.0	2.0	2.0	2.1
1800	0.5	0.8	1.2	1.4	1.6	1.8	1.8	1.9	1.9	1.9	1.9
2000	0.5	0.8	1.1	1.3	1.5	1.7	1.7	1.8	1.8	1.8	1.8
3000	0.4	0.7	0.9	1.1	1.2	1.4	1.4	1.4	1.5	1.5	1.5
4000	0.4	0.6	0.8	0.9	1.0	1.2	1.2	1.2	1.3	1.3	1.3
6000	0.3	0.5	0.6	0.8	0.8	1.0	1.0	1.0	1.0	1.1	1.1

Example:
In a survey of 1 000 respondents, 20% said 'yes' to a certain question. The entry in the above table at row n=1 000 and column 20% (column 20/80), shows d to be 2.1%. This means that there is a 90% chance that the true population value lies between 17.9% and 22.1% (20 ± 2.1%, at a confidence level of 90%).

Notes on table 5.3.1
Rural sample sizes for 2000 are missing from the table due to technical reasons.
Bulgaria, Croatia, Lithuania, Malta, Slovakia, Slovenia and Ukraine: The second sweep was carried out in 1997.
Estonia: The second sweep was carried out in 1995.
Slovenia: The third sweep was carried out in 2001.
Czech Republic and Slovakia: The results from the 1992 survey for Czechoslovakia were separated into information for the Czech Republic and the Slovak Republic. This was based on information collected on the place of residence of each respondent.
Spain: The survey was held in Catalonia only.

5.4 Sources of data in chapter 5

Dijk, J.J.M. van, P. Mayhew & M. Killias
Experiences of Crime across the World; Key Findings of the 1989 International Crime Survey
Deventer, 1990, Kluwer (2nd ed. 1991)

Kesteren, J. van, P. Mayhew & P. Nieuwbeerta
Criminal Victimisation in Seventeen Industrialised Countries; Key findings from the 2000 International Crime Victims Survey
Den Haag, 2000, Wetenschappelijk Onderzoek- en Documentatiecentrum

Nieuwbeerta, P.
Crime victimization in comparative perspective
Den Haag, 2002, Boom Juridische uitgevers.

Zvekic, U. & A. Alvazzi del Frate
The International Crime (Victim) Survey in the developing world, In: Scherpenzeel, R. (ed.), *Computerization in the management of the criminal Justice System; proceedings of the Workshop and the Symposion on Computerization of Criminal Justice Information at the Ninth United Nations Congress on the Prevention of Crime and the Treatment of Offenders; Cairo, Egypt, 29 April – 8 May 1995*, 1996
HEUNI/Ministry of Justice of The Netherlands

Appendix I
Offence definitions

The offence definitions given hereafter are operational, not legal definitions ("standard" definitions). They were devised so as to allow national correspondents to provide the necessary data for their countries and to specify the scope of the statistical (and legal) definitions underlying their (police and conviction) statistics. Where the legal concept used differed from the standard definition – which occurred in particular in connection with conviction statistics – this is indicated in the technical comments (see 3.3).

Conviction statistics are indeed more bound to legal concepts than police statistics. This explains why variation in definitions is higher in chapter 3 than in chapter 1. For the offence definitions that follow, we shall first look at those used in chapter 1 and specify, wherever appropriate, eventual deviations from the pragmatic standard definition in chapter 3.

The table below shows which countries were able to meet the standard definitions in *all* respects:

Table 1: Standard definitions met by country and criminal offence

	Total criminal offences	Intentional homicide	Assault	Rape	Robbery	Theft	Theft of a motor vehicle	Burglary	Domestic burglary	Drug offences: Total	Drug offences: Drug trafficking
Albania	YES	YES	YES		YES	YES	YES			YES	YES
Armenia	YES		YES		YES		YES	YES	YES		YES
Austria	YES		YES	YES	YES	YES	YES			YES	YES
Belgium			YES		YES	YES	YES	YES		YES	YES
Bulgaria			YES		YES	YES	YES		YES		YES
Croatia	YES	YES	YES	YES	YES	YES	YES		YES	YES	YES
Cyprus		YES						YES		YES	YES
Czech Republic			YES								YES
Denmark							YES	YES		YES	YES
Estonia	YES			YES	YES	YES				YES	YES
Finland	YES	YES			YES	YES				YES	YES
France		YES	YES	YES	YES	YES		YES		YES	YES
Georgia	YES				YES	YES				YES	YES
Germany		YES	YES	YES	YES	YES	YES	YES	YES	YES	YES
Greece	YES		YES		YES	YES	YES			YES	YES
Hungary	YES		YES				YES	YES	YES	YES	YES
Ireland	YES				YES	YES	YES	YES			YES
Italy	YES		YES			YES			YES		YES
Latvia					YES	YES	YES				YES
Lithuania	YES	YES	YES					YES		YES	YES
Luxembourg		YES	YES	YES	YES	YES	YES		YES	YES	YES
Malta					YES	YES	YES			YES	YES
Moldova	YES		YES		YES	YES	YES				YES
Netherlands	YES	YES			YES	YES					YES
Norway										YES	YES

	Total criminal offences	Intentional homicide	Assault	Rape	Robbery	Theft	Theft of a motor vehicle	Burglary	Domestic burglary	Drug offences: Total	Drug offences: Drug trafficking
Poland	YES	YES	YES							YES	YES
Portugal		YES			YES	YES	YES	YES	YES		YES
Romania	YES		YES		YES	YES	YES			YES	YES
Russia	YES		YES		YES	YES					YES
Slovakia	YES		YES					YES		YES	YES
Slovenia	YES		YES		YES	YES	YES		YES		YES
Spain	YES	YES	YES		YES				YES		YES
Sweden		YES				YES				YES	YES
Switzerland	YES		YES	YES	YES		YES		YES	YES	YES
Turkey	YES	YES		YES		YES	YES		YES	YES	YES
Ukraine					YES			YES	YES	YES	YES
UK: England & Wales		YES			YES			YES	YES	YES	YES
UK: Northern Ireland	YES	YES	YES		YES	YES	YES		YES	YES	YES
UK: Scotland	YES					YES	YES		YES	YES	YES

More specifically:

A) Total criminal offences
According to the standard definition, this category should include all offences defined as criminal by any law, including traffic offences (mostly dangerous and drink driving). "Criminal" offences in this pragmatic sense include acts, which are normally processed by the public prosecutor or a judge, whereas offences processed directly by the police, such as minor traffic offences and certain breaches of public order, are not included.

Among the 39 countries that provided data for this chapter, the following countries did *not include* traffic offences at all:
– Belgium
– Denmark
– France
– Germany
– Malta
– UK: England & Wales.

In Luxembourg, traffic offences are included only before 2000.

In the following countries, *all* (i.e. even minor) traffic offences were *included*:
– Bulgaria
– Cyprus
– Portugal
– Sweden
– Ukraine.

In the following countries, *public order* offences are *included*:
- Bulgaria
- the Czech Republic
- Latvia
- Luxembourg
- Norway
- Portugal
- Sweden.

B) *Intentional homicide*
According to the standard definition, intentional homicide means *intentional killing of a person.* Where possible, the figures *include:*
- assault leading to death
- euthanasia
- infanticide

but *exclude* assistance with suicide.

This means that the providers of the data [= national correspondents] were requested to ensure that "their" figures included, where available from their national statistics, "assault leading to death", "euthanasia", etc.

The following countries were not able to meet the standard definition and *excluded* assault leading to death:
- Armenia
- Belgium
- the Czech Republic
- Denmark
- Estonia
- Greece
- Hungary
- Latvia
- Malta
- Moldova
- the Netherlands
- Norway
- Romania
- Russia
- Slovenia.

The following countries *excluded* cases of euthanasia:
- Estonia
- Georgia
- Greece
- Ireland

- Italy
- Latvia
- Malta
- Russia
- Slovenia.

Infanticide is *included* in homicide in all countries with the exception of
- the Czech Republic
- Greece
- Norway
- Romania.

Assistance with suicide is *included* only in
- Austria
- Bulgaria
- Latvia
- Norway
- Slovakia
- Switzerland
- Ukraine
- UK: Scotland.

C) Assault
According to the standard definition, assault means *inflicting bodily injury on another person with intent*. Where possible, the figures *exclude*:
- assault leading to death
- threats
- acts just causing pain
- slapping/punching
- sexual assault.

The following countries were not able to meet the standard definition in all respects and include in their assault statistics

a) assault leading to death
This list includes the same countries that *exclude* assault leading to death from their homicide statistics (see above A). In addition, the following countries *include* this kind of situation in their statistics of assault:
- Georgia
- Ukraine.

The Netherlands also *exclude* assault leading to death from their statistics on assault.

b) threats
are generally excluded, except in
- Finland
- Georgia
- Latvia
- Malta
- the Netherlands
- UK: England & Wales.

c) acts just causing pain
are *included* in
- Cyprus
- Denmark
- Estonia
- Finland
- Georgia
- Ireland
- Latvia
- Malta
- the Netherlands
- Portugal
- Sweden
- Turkey
- Ukraine
- UK: England & Wales
- UK: Scotland.

d) sexual assault
is *included* in the statistics only in
- Georgia
- Ireland
- Malta
- Norway
- Ukraine.

D) Rape
According to the standard definition, rape means *sexual intercourse with a person against her/his will (per vaginam or other)*. Where possible, the figures *include*:
other than vaginal penetration (e.g. buggery)
- violent intra-marital intercourse
- sexual intercourse without force with a helpless person
- sexual intercourse with force with a minor
- incestual sexual intercourse with or without force with a minor

but *exclude:*
- sexual intercourse with a minor without force
- other forms of sexual assault.

Users of the Sourcebook should be aware that the definition of rape has been subject to change in many countries since 1996. In general, the scope of this offence has been widened, especially in connection with intra-marital intercourse and with respect to minors. These legal changes seem to have affected only moderately the rates reported in the tables.

Countries that were not able to meet the standard definition in all respects are listed in the following table:

a) acts other than vaginal penetration
is *excluded* in statistics on rape in
- Armenia
- Latvia
- Romania
- Russia
- Ukraine
- UK: Northern Ireland
- UK: Scotland.

b) violent intra-marital intercourse
is *excluded* in the rape statistics only in
- Greece
- Romania
- Russia
- Ukraine
- UK: Northern Ireland.

c) sexual intercourse without force with a helpless person
is included everywhere except in the following countries:
- Denmark
- Greece
- the Netherlands
- Norway
- Sweden
- UK: Scotland.

d) sexual intercourse with force with a minor
is *excluded* only in Bulgaria.

e) incestual sexual intercourse with or without force with a minor
is *excluded* in
- Bulgaria
- Denmark
- Finland
- Hungary
- the Netherlands
- Poland
- Russia
- Slovakia
- Ukraine
- UK: England & Wales.

f) sexual intercourse with a minor without force
is excluded everywhere, except in:
- Albania
- Belgium
- Cyprus
- Georgia
- Italy
- Lithuania
- Malta
- Moldova
- Portugal
- Romania
- Slovenia
- Spain.

g) other forms of sexual assault
are excluded from rape statistics everywhere except in:
- the Czech Republic
- Georgia
- Ireland
- Italy
- Lithuania
- Malta
- Portugal
- Romania.

E) Robbery
According to the standard definition, *robbery* means *stealing from a person with force or threat of force.* Where possible, the figures *include:*
- muggings (bag-snatching)
- theft with violence

but *exclude:*
- pickpocketing
- extortion
- blackmail.

Figures for all countries exclude extortion and blackmail, except in Cyprus. Figures exclude pick-pocketing everywhere except in Turkey.

It should be noted that legal definitions of robbery often exclude mugging (or bag-snatching) where the offender takes the object away without directly hurting or threatening the victim. However, police statistics do not differentiate to the same degree between the two situations for obvious practical reasons (the exact circumstances being often unknown at this stage). Therefore, the concept of robbery, as used in chapter 1, is somewhat wider than in chapter 3 (in connection with conviction statistics).

Countries which were not able to meet the standard definition in all respects in chapter 1 are listed here:

a) Countries *excluding* muggings
- the Czech Republic
- Denmark
- Italy
- Lithuania
- Norway
- Poland
- Slovakia
- Sweden.

b) Countries *excluding* theft with violence
- the Czech Republic
- Denmark
- Hungary
- Italy
- Norway
- UK: Scotland.

F) **Theft**
According to the standard definition, *theft* means *depriving a person/organisation of property without force with the intent to keep it.* Where possible, the figures *include:*
- burglary
- theft of motor vehicles
- theft of other items
- theft of small value

but *exclude:*
- embezzlement (including theft by employees)
- receiving/handling of stolen goods.

Countries that were not able to meet the standard definition in all respects are listed here:

a) The following countries replied *not having included* burglary in their total theft *counts:*
- Armenia
- Cyprus
- Norway.

b) Theft of motor vehicles is included in theft statistics of all countries with the exception of Denmark.

c) Theft of other items is *included* in the counts of all countries.

d) Theft of small values is usually *not included* in the statistics of
- the Czech Republic
- Hungary
- Lithuania
- Poland
- Slovakia
- Spain
- Switzerland
- Ukraine.

e) Embezzlement is *excluded* in all countries.

f) Receiving/handling stolen property is *included* in theft counts only in UK: England & Wales.

G) *Theft of a motor vehicle*
According to the standard definition, figures on *theft of a motor vehicle* should, where possible, *include joyriding*, but *exclude theft of motorboats* and *handling/receiving stolen vehicles.*

a) The following countries *excluded* joyriding:
- Cyprus
- the Czech Republic
- Estonia
- the Netherlands
- Poland

- Russia
- Slovakia.

Users of the Sourcebook should be aware that figures on convictions (in chapter 3) for "motor vehicle theft" often include joyriding only. The reason is that the traditional concept of theft (as it had shaped continental as well as anglo-saxon legislations) implied that the object was taken away by the thief *with the intent to keep it*. Wherever that intent is not present, as typically in the case of joyriding, the act is not punishable, at least not as theft. Therefore, most legislators have made it a special offence to steal a motor vehicle for temporary use only. Convictions for this kind of temporary use are recorded in conviction statistics by most countries, whereas "real" theft of a car (where the intent was to keep it permanently) are included in counts of convictions for (common) theft. In police statistics (chapter 1), this differentiation may not apply, because police officers usually will not know the intent of the "thief" when they discover that a motor vehicle has been taken away.

b) Theft of motorboats is *included* in:
- Cyprus
- Finland
- France
- Georgia
- Italy
- Lithuania
- Norway
- Spain
- Sweden
- Ukraine
- UK: England & Wales.

c) Receiving/handling stolen property is *included* in motor vehicle theft counts in:
- Cyprus
- Georgia
- Ukraine.

H) Burglary

According to the standard definition, *burglary* is gaining access to a closed part of a building or other premises by use of force with the intent to steal goods. Figures on *burglary* should, where possible, include *theft from a factory, shop or office, from a military establishment, or by using false keys*; they should exclude, however, *theft from a car, from a container, from a vending machine, from a parking meter* and *from a fenced meadow/compound*.

a) Theft (burglary) from a *factory, shop, or office*
All countries include such incidences in burglary counts, except Italy, Luxembourg, and Norway.

b) Theft (burglary) from a *military establishment*
Such incidences are *excluded* from burglary statistics in Georgia, Italy, Luxembourg and Norway.

c) Theft (burglary) by gaining entrance *with false keys*
Only Georgia, Norway, Switzerland and UK: Scotland *exclude* such incidences from burglary counts.

d) Theft *from a car*
is excluded, in line with the standard definition, from burglary counts in a majority of countries. Only the following countries *include* such incidences in burglary counts:
- Albania
- Austria
- Bulgaria
- the Czech Republic
- Estonia
- Greece
- Latvia
- Malta
- Moldova
- the Netherlands
- Poland
- Romania
- Russia
- Slovenia
- Turkey.

e) Theft *from a container*
is excluded from burglary counts, except in the following countries where it is *included*:
- Albania
- Austria
- Croatia
- the Czech Republic
- Estonia
- Finland
- Georgia
- Greece
- Latvia
- Malta

- Moldova
- the Netherlands
- Poland
- Romania
- Russia
- Slovenia
- Spain
- Sweden
- Switzerland
- Turkey
- UK: Northern Ireland.

f) Theft from a *vending machine*
is included in the same countries as in those who include "burglary" from a container. There are only five countries that, in line with the standard definition, *exclude* theft from a vending machine (but include burglary counts incidences of theft from a container):
- Croatia
- Georgia
- Moldova
- Turkey
- UK: Northern Ireland.

g) Theft from a *parking meter*
is treated everywhere in the same way (i.e. included or excluded) as theft from a vending machine. The only exception is Malta where theft from a parking meter is excluded, in line with the standard definition, whereas theft from a vending machine is included.

h) Theft from a *fenced meadow or compound*
is treated everywhere in the same way (i.e. included or excluded) as theft from a vending machine. The only exceptions are
- Latvia
- Slovenia
- Sweden
- Switzerland

where such incidences are excluded, whereas theft from a vending machine is included. The opposite example is Moldova where theft from vending machines is excluded, but theft from a fenced meadow included.

Readers should be aware that, throughout the continent, burglary is not usually a special offence. In line with traditional concepts of theft in European law, burglary usually constitutes an aggravated form of theft. Therefore, many countries have provided data on aggravated theft in chapter 3, categories in conviction statistics closely following legal definitions. However, conviction statistics include, in the category of "aggravated theft", often other forms of more serious theft along with burglary. "Burglary" counts given in chapter 3 should, therefore, be regarded with some caution.

I) Domestic Burglary

According to the standard definition, *domestic burglary* is gaining access to private premises by use of force with the intent to steal goods. Figures on *domestic burglary* should, where possible, include *theft from an attic or from a basement (in multiple dwellings) as well as theft from a secondary residence (even if unoccupied)*. They should *exclude*, however, *theft from a factory, shop or an office, as well as theft from a detached garage, barn or stable, or from a fenced meadow/compound*. In chapter 3, fewer than 3 countries were able to provide data on convictions for domestic burglary and are not included in the conviction statistics for this reason.

a) Contrary to the standard definition, incidences of theft *from an attic or a basement* were *excluded* from counts of domestic burglary in the following countries:
   - Austria
   - Estonia
   - Finland
   - France
   - Lithuania
   - Norway
   - Russia
   - Sweden.

b) Contrary to the standard definition, incidences of theft *from a secondary residence* were *excluded* from counts of domestic burglary in the following countries:
   - Denmark
   - Estonia
   - Ireland
   - Norway
   - Poland
   - Slovakia
   - Sweden.

c) Contrary to the standard definition, incidences of theft *from a factory, shop or an office* were *included* in counts of domestic burglary in the following countries:
   - Albania
   - Cyprus
   - the Czech Republic

- Georgia
- Latvia
- Malta
- Moldova
- the Netherlands
- Romania.

d) Contrary to the standard definition, incidences of theft from a *detached garage, shed, barn or stable* were *included* in counts of domestic burglary in the following countries:
- Austria
- Belgium
- the Czech Republic
- Georgia
- Greece
- Latvia
- Malta
- Moldova
- the Netherlands
- Romania.

e) Contrary to the standard definition, incidences of theft from a *fenced meadow or compound* were *included* in counts of domestic burglary in the following countries:
- Albania
- Belgium
- the Czech Republic
- Malta
- Moldova
- the Netherlands
- Romania.

J) Drug Offences (Total)

Drug offences are largely uniform through international conventions. According to the standard definition used here, the category of *drug offences* should, where possible, include *possession, cultivation, producton, sale, supplying, transportation, importation, exportation and financing of drug operations*; drug trafficking should *include*, where possible, *such acts as far as they are not in connection with personal use.*

a) Possession of illicit drugs is included in counts of total drug offences in all countries. However, *possession of small quantities (in connection with personal use)* is not an offence or (as in the Netherlands) systematically not prosecuted and, thus, *not included* in the counts of

- the Czech Republic
- Italy
- the Netherlands
- Russia
- Slovenia
- Spain.

In these countries, the figures given in Table 1.2.1.14 will include proportionately more offences of trafficking compared to countries where drug users are often subject to arrest or prosecution. In some countries, possession of drugs has become punishable (or rather, included in total counts) during the period under consideration. This has been the case in Hungary (since 1999), Poland (since 2000) and UK: England & Wales (since 1999). Interestingly, these changes seem to have only moderately affected trends in total drug offences.

b) Cultivation, production, sale, and *supplying* of drugs is covered in drug offences counts in all countries without exception.

c) Transportation of drugs is included in counts of total drug offences in all countries with the exception of Ireland.

d) Importation of drugs is included in counts of total drug offences in all countries except in
- Bulgaria
- Moldova
- Sweden.

e) Exportation of drugs is included in counts of total drug offences in all countries except in
- Bulgaria
- Ireland
- Moldova.

f) Financing of drug operations is included in the counts of total drug offences of all countries with the exception of
- Armenia
- Bulgaria
- Ireland
- Latvia
- Moldova
- Portugal
- Slovenia.

K) Drug Trafficking

Drug trafficking should *include*, where possible, *drug offences (as defined under J) which are not in connection with personal use.* All countries included here have laws making it an offence to commit any such acts (as defined under J). The only relevant differentiation is that some countries do not make it an offence, or reserve milder sanctions, for acts (especially possession) committed by drug users. Some other countries make "serious trafficking" (involving usually large quantities, or large profits) an aggravated offence. With these reservations, the legislation is rather uniform throughout Europe, given the central role of international conventions in this domain. Given the difficulty of distinguishing aggravated and other forms of trafficking, this differentiation (made in the first edition) has been omitted in the present edition.

Appendix II
Population Figures (in millions)

Country	1995	1996	1997	1998	1999	2000
Albania	3.24	3.28	3.32	3.37	3.44	3.49
Armenia	3.41	3.39	3.38	3.37	3.35	3.34
Austria	8.04	8.06	8.07	8.09	8.11	8.13
Belgium	10.14	10.16	10.18	10.20	10.22	10.24
Bulgaria	8.27	8.18	8.08	7.98	7.89	7.80
Croatia	4.46	4.37	4.32	4.26	4.25	4.28
Cyprus	0.73	0.74	0.74	0.75	0.75	0.76
Czech Republic	10.33	10.31	10.30	10.29	10.28	10.27
Denmark	5.23	5.26	5.28	5.30	5.32	5.34
Estonia	1.48	1.47	1.46	1.45	1.44	1.43
Finland	5.11	5.12	5.14	5.15	5.16	5.17
France	57.84	58.03	58.21	58.40	58.62	58.89
Georgia	5.29	5.22	5.15	5.10	5.06	5.02
Germany	81.82	82.01	82.06	82.04	82.16	82.26
Greece	10.49	10.51	10.53	10.56	10.58	10.60
Hungary	10.30	10.27	10.24	10.21	10.17	10.14
Ireland	3.61	3.63	3.67	3.71	3.75	3.80
Italy	57.26	57.34	57.43	57.51	57.58	57.63
Latvia	2.52	2.50	2.47	2.45	2.43	2.40
Lithuania	3.67	3.66	3.65	3.64	3.63	3.62
Luxembourg	0.41	0.42	0.42	0.43	0.43	0.44
Malta	0.38	0.38	0.38	0.39	0.39	0.39
Moldova	4.46	4.45	4.44	4.44	4.43	4.43
Netherlands	15.46	15.53	15.61	15.70	15.80	15.89
Norway	4.36	4.38	4.41	4.43	4.46	4.48
Poland	38.60	38.63	38.66	38.66	38.66	38.65
Portugal	9.97	9.98	9.99	10.01	10.03	10.05
Romania	22.69	22.63	22.56	22.51	22.46	22.41
Russia	148.11	147.76	147.36	146.96	146.52	146.00
Slovakia	5.36	5.37	5.38	5.39	5.40	5.41
Slovenia	1.91	1.91	1.92	1.92	1.92	1.93
Spain	39.75	39.81	39.86	39.91	39.95	40.00
Sweden	8.83	8.86	8.86	8.87	8.87	8.87
Switzerland	7.17	7.20	7.21	7.23	7.24	7.26
Turkey	61.19	62.13	63.05	63.95	64.82	65.67
Ukraine	51.32	50.88	50.42	49.99	49.57	49.15
UK: England & Wales	51.88	52.06	52.23	52.39	52.54	52.67
UK: Northern Ireland	1.61	1.61	1.62	1.62	1.63	1.63
UK: Scotland	5.13	5.15	5.16	5.18	5.19	5.21

1) Total mid-year population.
2) Source: U.S. Bureau of the Census. International Data Base (available online: consulted on 8 August, 2002).
3) In order to make this table easier to read, we have included only two decimals; but we used the original figures with all the decimals to compute the rates presented throughout this work.